T0304261

Alfred Marshall's Mission

Alfred Marshall was anxious to do good. Intended by an Evangelical father for the vocation of clergyman, the author of the path-breaking *Principles of Economics* remained to the end of his days a great preacher deeply committed to raising the tone of life. First published in 1990, *Alfred Marshall's Mission* explains how this most moral of political economists sought to blend the downward sloping utility function of Jevons and Menger with the organic evolutionism of Darwin and Spencer, how this celebrated theorist of social alongside economic growth sought to combine the mathematical marginalism of Cournot, Thunen and Edgeworth with the ethical uplift of Green, Jowett and Toynbee. The conclusion is that perhaps Marshall was, after all, too anxious to do good. Far more economists, however, have not been anxious enough; and that in itself gives this study of Marshall's life and times a present day relevance which would, no doubt, have appealed strongly to the shy Cambridge professor who is its subject.

Alfred Marshall's Mission

David Reisman

Routledge
Taylor & Francis Group

First published in 1990
by The Macmillan Press Ltd

This edition first published in 2011 by Routledge
2 Park Square, Milton Park, Abingdon, Oxon, OX14 4RN

Simultaneously published in the USA and Canada
by Routledge
270 Madison Avenue, New York, NY 10016

Routledge is an imprint of the Taylor & Francis Group, an informa business

Publisher's Note
The publisher has gone to great lengths to ensure the quality of this reprint but
points out that some imperfections in the original copies may be apparent.

Disclaimer
The publisher has made every effort to trace copyright holders and welcomes
correspondence from those they have been unable to contact.

A Library of Congress record exists under ISBN: 0312044917

ISBN 13: 978-0-415-61969-1 (set)
ISBN 13: 978-0-415-66850-7 (hbk)
ISBN 13: 978-0-203-813928-1 (ebk)

ALFRED MARSHALL'S MISSION

David Reisman

MACMILLAN

First published 1990

Published by
THE MACMILLAN PRESS LTD
Houndmills, Basingstoke, Hampshire RG21 2XS
and London
Companies and representatives
throughout the world

Printed and bound in Great Britain by
WBC Ltd, Bristol and Maesteg

British Library Cataloguing in Publication Data
Reisman, David
Alfred Marshall's mission.
1. Economics. Marshall, Alfred, 1842–1924
I. Title
330'.092'4
ISBN 0–333–52416–0

Contents

1 Introduction

Keynes said that Marshall was 'too anxious to do good'.[1] It is never very easy to say precisely how much good each of us ought to be anxious to do, and one also suspects that it is on balance better to be *too anxious* to do good than *not anxious enough*; but the point remains that Marshall was an earnest, conscientious and purposive social philosopher who regarded economic science as never more than the 'servant' of that 'mistress' which must be ethics.[2] As Jacob Viner puts it: 'There have been few of us who have made conscience be our guide as to subjects of investigation and methods of analysis as steadily and as consistently as did Marshall.'[3] Of course Marshall was the master-maker of tools, whose *Principles of Economics* are to this day, to a greater extent than is true of the insights of any other single theoretician of the past, the foundations of our own. Yet no one understands Marshall who understands only consumer's surplus and elasticity of demand, diminishing marginal utility and increasing real cost, the normal value and the equilibrium price, or who loses sight even for a moment of what Keynes so accurately diagnosed as 'the conflict . . . between an intellect, which was hard, dry, critical, as unsentimental as you could find . . . [and] emotions and aspirations, generally unspoken, of quite a different type. When his intellect chased diagrams and Foreign Trade and Money, there was an evangelical moraliser of an imp somewhere inside him that was so ill-advised as to disapprove. Near the end of his life, when the intellect grew dimmer and the preaching imp could rise nearer to the surface to protest against its lifelong servitude, he once said: ' "If I had to live my life over again I should have devoted it to psychology. Economics has too little to do with ideals." '[4] Too little perhaps, but that much more nonetheless because of the contribution of a secular missionary who, endowed with the double nature of the scientific investigator who is simultaneously a member of 'the tribe of sages and pastors',[5] preferred ultimately to give the preeminence to that side of his divided personality which made him issue the following warning to academic introverts deplorably unaware of social duties:

1

'We are not at liberty to play chess games, or exercise ourselves upon subtleties that lead nowhere. It is well for the young to enjoy the mere pleasure of action, physical or intellectual. But the time presses; the responsibility on us is heavy.'[6] It comes in the circumstances as no great surprise to learn that his nephew, the economist Claude Guillebaud, was able to recall in 1970 that Marshall was a serious man of great personal integrity, deeply concerned with the social significance of his discipline as well as with the abstract technical formulations with which, by an irony of intellectual history, his name is for all time inextricably linked: 'He disapproved profoundly if he thought he saw any indication of my having wider interests in life than the only one by which he himself was activated – the furtherance of economics as a branch of knowledge to be used in the service of mankind.'[7] Sanctimonious, self-righteous and even intolerant though Marshall's call to arms may well appear, it is a useful antidote to the approach of those contemporary economists who never stray from the knot garden of the conventional wisdom, sedulously refined and elegantly presented, to contemplate the wider ramifications of their important subject or the ties of ethical responsibility that bind the cells willy-nilly to the organism of which they are a part. If Marshall was *too anxious* to do good, then it would also be true to say that such contemporary economists are *not anxious enough*; and that there is no better place for them to turn for intellectual regeneration and spiritual uplift than to the work of an economic moralist who thought big and whose anthropocentric, holistic, multidisciplinary and quintessentially dynamic analysis of the capitalist market economy, developed while anxious to do good, constitutes one of the most stimulating contributions to the literature which treats of the great issues.

Alfred Marshall was a missionary for economics as a science and for the economic evolution with which it is symbiotically linked; and it is with his mission that we shall be concerned in this study in intellectual biography. Our account will be divided into six central sections headed, respectively, Childhood and Cambridge, Cambridge and Bristol, Oxford and Cambridge, Economics and *Principles*, The Evolution of the *Principles*, and Beyond the *Principles*. No conclusion is reached as to precisely how much good each of us ought to be anxious to do. What does emerge, however, is that little can be said about Alfred Marshall's life and times which does not bear in some way upon the sense of purpose and notion of service that are the twin keys to the complex personality of this most *social* of social economists.

2 Childhood and Cambridge

Alfred Marshall was born at Clapham on 26 July 1842. His father was a cashier in the Bank of England, with the result that Alfred enjoyed a City connection and an exposure to monetary economics at an early age. William Marshall was also somewhat of a despot in his own home (Alfred's writings abound in weasel-words such as 'nearly', 'generally', 'probably', 'perhaps', 'on the whole'; his economics is noteworthy for its qualifications and assumptions; and a psychological explanation for such evasiveness might be the subconscious desire of the oversensitive spirit to avoid confrontation) and a strict Evangelical Christian (a man who, destining his son for a career in the ministry, compelled him to study useful subjects such as Hebrew – often, as was the case with Mill, late into the night – and forbade Alfred not only the self-indulgence of board games but 'the fascinating paths of mathematics' as well: 'His father hated the sight of a mathematical book.').[1] It must have required a great deal of courage for Alfred, at the end of his secondary education at the Merchant Taylors' School (where he was 'small and pale, badly dressed, looked overworked and was called "tallow candles" by his fellows')[2] to turn down a classics scholarship to St John's College, Oxford, in order to study mathematics (supported by a loan from an uncle) at St John's College, Cambridge. He emerged in 1865 with First Class Honours in that subject, Second Wrangler to J. W. Strutt (later Lord Rayleigh, Professor of Experimental Physics and Nobel Laureate, 1904).

His plan was to proceed with the study of molecular physics, but first Marshall took a one-year temporary teaching post at Clifton College in order to repay his uncle, before returning to Cambridge to do some tutoring for the Mathematical Tripos. It was at that time (in 1867) that he joined the Grote Club, a group of young intellectuals who met (like the more famous Apostles) to discuss fundamental issues, including the speculations of philosophy and theology. Marshall later wrote as follows about the impact that those discussions had on him:

For a year or two Sidgwick, Mozley, Clifford, Moulton, and myself were the active members, and we all attended regularly. Clifford and Moulton had at that time read but little philosophy; so they kept quiet for the first half-hour of the discussion; and listened eagerly to what others, and especially Sidgwick, said. Then they let their tongues loose, and the pace was tremendous. If I might have verbatim reports of a dozen of the best conversations I have heard, I should choose two or three from among those evenings in which Sidgwick and Clifford were the chief speakers.[3]

Henry Sidgwick (1838–1900), later to become (in 1883) Knights-bridge Professor of Moral Philosophy in Cambridge and author of seminal works such as *Methods of Ethics* (1874) and *Principles of Political Economy* (1883), was in those very Grote Club days experiencing the severe personal crisis that was inevitably his lot, given the strong desire of that most scrupulous of thinkers to remain 'honest in the sight of all men':

> It is surely a great good that one's moral position should be one that simple-minded people can understand. I happen to care very little what men in general think of me individually: but I care very much about what they think of human nature. I dread doing anything to support the plausible suspicion that men in general, even those who profess lofty aspirations, are secretly swayed by material interests.[4]

As early as 1861, Sidgwick had been expressing his doubts about the Anglican communion in correspondence with his friends Browning (to whom he wrote of his fear of 'perjury': 'I see that there is a great gulf between my views and the views once held by those who framed the Articles')[5] and Dakyns (to whom he confided the great problem he felt he faced 'of reconciling my religious instinct with my growing conviction that both individual and social morality ought to be placed on an inductive basis')[6] but had nonetheless, in 1863, subscribed to the 39 Articles of the Faith at the time of his appointment to a Fellowship at Trinity. It obviously mattered greatly to him that no one should think he had subscribed merely for personal gain while believing only 'laxly' in the doctrines he espoused; and thus it happened in 1869 that the punctilious philosopher felt he had no choice but to resign his Fellowship (without, incidentally, leaving the Church) in order, as he put it, 'to free myself from dogmatic obligations'.[7] Sidgwick's courageous action figured prominently in

the arguments mustered by academic liberals in their attempts (ultimately successful in June 1871) to secure the abolition of religious
tests, and was in addition widely seen as living proof of an instance
where a highminded man had opted to translate his convictions into
practice. Besides that, Sidgwick himself was held in such esteem in
Cambridge that in a sense he was compelled by his reputation to
practice what he preached: as one don later put it, 'though we kept
our own fellowships without believing more than he did, we should
have felt that Henry Sidgwick had fallen short if he had not re-
nounced his'.[8] His courage, his crisis of faith, his intellectual integrity, his search for an ethical system linked more to society than to
Scripture – all of this clearly made a deep impact upon the young
Alfred Marshall, who was later to describe the Sidgwick of the Grote
Club days as his 'spiritual father and mother':[9] 'He was more to me
than all the rest of the University'.[10] Purposiveness was bound to
speak to purposiveness. And the young mathematician was facing a
crisis of his own.

Intended by his father for the vocation of the clergyman, while an
undergraduate still a young man of deep religious conviction, Marshall
by the time he met Sidgwick was himself having serious doubts about
the wisdom of ordination and questioning the desirability of the
theological straitjacket that inhibits all questioning: 'His zeal directed
itself at times towards the field of Foreign Missions. A missionary he
remained all his life, but after a quick struggle religious beliefs
dropped away, and he became, for the rest of his life . . . an agnostic.'[11] Even the saintly Sidgwick never made so radical a move. Yet
Marshall, in turning his back on the faith of his father, never became
militantly anti-religious or sought to replace the Church of God with
the Church of Science. Rather the opposite, in fact: 'He sympathised
with Christian morals and Christian ideals and Christian incentives. . . . At the end of his life he said "Religion seems to have
given me an attitude", and that, though he had give up Theology, he
believed more and more in Religion.'[12] Partly, one suspects, this is
because he saw religion as a spiritual corrective to the greedy materialism of competitive capitalism. Thus he wrote in 1881 that 'religion
has this quality: that it belongs to all men alike; and the joys of
religion are the highest joys of which men are capable. The poor man
who is religious is far happier than the rich man who is not. (I use the
word religion in its widest sense, of all that elevates the soul of man
towards God.)'[13] An advocate of 'fellow-feeling with men far off and
near'[14] and of a society of gentlemen characterised by equality of

respect, Marshall could not but reverence religion – and the Christian religion in particular – precisely because of its stress on equality of humanity irrespective of temporal status. Thus, in one of his few direct references to Christianity, Marshall, speaking of 'the Teutonic races that peopled Western Europe', says: 'They always had a reverence for men as men, and this reverence was promoted by the Christian religion, and fostered by the popular character of the mediaeval church. They did not deliberately treat it as a matter of indifference whether those who did hard work for them lived debased lives. They never got thoroughly to despise the worker or his work; so they have not become frivolous, apathetic or selfish; and their civilisation seems likely to endure.'[15] The concept of Christian charity must in addition have had a great appeal to the theorist of profit-seeking who was also the advocate of 'deliberate unselfishness' such as 'never existed before the modern age':[16] 'Our age', Marshall noted in 1907, 'has reversed the old rules that the poor paid a larger percentage of their income in rates and taxes than the well-to-do',[17] and this increased altruism (the product of increased affluence) is not only a good thing in its own right but fully functional as well. Thus Marshall writes as follows in his celebrated *Principles* (the passage occurs midway between marginal utility and marginal cost but for all the notice it has attracted might well be from a footnote in Petander's *De nationalekonomiska åskådningarna i Sverige 1718–1765* of 1912) about the great importance for adaptation to environment of 'deliberate, and therefore moral, self-sacrifice': 'The struggle for existence causes in the long run those races of men to survive in which the individual is most willing to sacrifice himself for the benefit of those around him; and which are consequently the best adapted collectively to make use of their environment.'[18] Marshall in those early Grote Club days may have lost his religious faith, but it is more than clear that he never lost the ethical orientation of the Evangelical Christianity which had dominated his formative years. As Mary Paley states, referring specifically to the lectures which she heard him deliver when she was his student in the early 1870s: 'He said much about right and wrong expenditure, especially of time. He was a great preacher.'[19] Indeed he was.

From 1868 to 1877, Marshall held a special lectureship in Moral Sciences at St John's College, where he taught logic and other branches of philosophy and was also shunted as a new boy, as if guided by an Invisible Hand, on to what the older boys appear to have regarded as the rather dull line of political economy. Looking back in later life, he reflected that it was hardly a case of love at first sight:

> Psychology seemed to hold out good promise of constructive and progressive studies of human nature and its possibilities: and I thought it might best meet my wants. . . . I taught economics because Pearson did not wish it but repelled with indignation the suggestion that I was an economist. 'I am a philosopher straying in a foreign land: I will go home soon.'[20]

Marshall's background in psychology inevitably broadened his horizons beyond the narrowly mechanistic hedonism of the Benthamite pleasure–pain principle as developed, say, by Jevons (whose *Theory of Political Economy* he reviewed in this period, in 1872, in *The Academy*): Marshall saw that the utilitarian calculus was excessively simplistic in its conceptualisation of motivation – and excessively static in a period when, due not least to the debates surrounding Darwin's *Origin of Species* (1859) and *Descent of Man* (1871), evolutionary advance and adaptive upgrading were in the air (progress and betterment, in other words, and not merely the kaleidoscopic aggressiveness of the *bellum omnium contra omnes* that is suggested by the Social Darwinian catch-phrase of 'survival of the fittest'). Marshall also learned enough of recent advances in ethnography and anthropology to appreciate that, different societies having different *mores*, the generalisations of the Benthamites might be no more than an invalid inference predicated on 'the tacit supposition that the world was made up of city men'[21] when the truth is that 'man is himself largely formed by his surroundings'[22] and therefore changes with them: historical relativism too was in the air and even the would-be Ricardian deductivist could hardly afford to neglect the growing body of empirical evidence on the mutability of human experience.

Marshall, meanwhile, was reading widely in speculative philosophy and coming increasingly under the spell of authors such as Kant ('my guide. . . . . . the only man I ever worshipped')[23] and Hegel (whose *Philosophy of History*, with its account of continuous but gradual change, must have reinforced the intellectual foundations which he had acquired from the Darwinians and the biological teleologists: it was a book, incidentally, which, according to Keynes's account, he 'a few weeks before his death dwelt especially on').[24] Marshall learned German in order to read works such as the *Critique of Pure Reason* in the original language, and acquired in that way not merely a deeper understanding of the concept of duty (a notion to which he returned frequently in his writings throughout his life) but also an unintended appreciation of the contribution of historical economists such as List and Roscher, together with an unplanned exposure to the economic institutions of a country where the landed interest monopolised power in a strong and less-than-democratic state and where a protective tariff generated monopolies and cartels in a manner that revealed the highly competitive British markets to be neither eternal nor universal. Marshall was in Berlin during the Franco-Prussian War, kept in touch with Germany, and made himself in 1914 the strong opponent of national hatred and jingoistic defamation that accompanied the outbreak of the First World War. Writing in *The Times* in August of that year, he made clear that he had no time for 'lurid tales' of civilians being shot in cold blood and other fictions employed by demagogues to whip up unthinking detestation of the Germans: 'As a people I believe them to be exceptionally conscientious and upright, sensitive to the calls of duty, tender in their family affections, true and trusty in friendship. Therefore they are strong and to be feared, but not to be vilified.'[25] Marshall left no doubt in that correspondence that one of the reasons behind his call for fair play was the simple fact that he himself was among those who 'know and love Germany'[26] and that his comparative perspective had been acquired at first hand and was buttressed by sentiment.

Marshall had been attracted to the categorical imperative because it seemed to him a valuable counterweight to the immorality of individualistic utilitarianism; but he soon found to his regret that 'I could not get further' and that 'beyond seemed misty and social problems came imperceptibly to the front. Are the opportunities of real life to be confined to a few?'[27] Thus it was that Marshall drifted from metaphysics into the social sciences, in order to learn something about the actualisation of moral philosophy on earth. As he later reported it, the position in that early St John's period had been this:

> I had come into economics out of ethics, intending to stay there only a short while; and to go back, as soon as I was in a position to speak with my enemies in the gate, that is, with those men of affairs who dashed cold water on my youthful schemes for regenerating the world by saying 'Ah', you would not talk in that way, if you knew anything about business, or even Political Economy.[28]

It was hardly the intrinsic interest of the subject that made him turn his mind from mental science to social science: 'My zeal for economics would never have got me out of bed at five o'clock in the morning, to make my own coffee and work for three hours before breakfast and pupils in mathematics: but philosophy did that.'[29] Philosophy had the intrinsic interest but in the end proved strangely unsatisfying to a lapsed evangelical with a sense of mission who had in any case already been pushed by his College to teach a subject which at the beginning of his appointment in moral sciences he had seen as 'not the most interesting member of the group to me then':[30] 'It has been said that everyone – everyone of the academic tone that is – must have an attack of philosophy as you have an attack of the measles – my attack was a very bad one. Then I thought I should get on better if I read some economics first.'[31] Philosophy had the intrinsic interest, so did psychology, but it was for all that political economy that in the last analysis won out on grounds of social relevance and usefulness to the community as a whole. As Marshall recalled in 1900 in a letter to James Ward:

I always said till about 1871 that my home was in Mental Science. Gradually, however, the increasing urgency of economic studies as a means towards human well-being grew upon me. About 1871–2, I told myself the time had come at which I must decide whether to give my life to psychology or economics. I spent a year in doubt: always preferring psychology for the pleasures of the chase; but economics grew and grew in practical urgency, not so much in relation to the growth of wealth as to the quality of life; and I settled down to it.[32]

Thus did Marshall, anxious to do good, progress from mind to matter, from Kant's *Critique* to Mill's *Principles*, in an attempt to act the secular missionary and render a humanitarian service. In Noel Annan's words: 'Alfred Marshall did not abandon the moral sciences for economics by accident; economics became for him the study which bore most obviously on moral problems.'[33] It is in that sense true with respect to intellectual primacy as it is true with respect to temporal development that, as Keynes says of Marshall (the observation would apply at least as well in the case of Adam Smith), 'it was only through Ethics that he first reached Economics'.[34] It was, of course, only through religion that he first reached ethics, and the threads all came together in that crucial passage in the *Principles* where Marshall seeks to legitimate his discipline by saying that it is 'on the one side a study of wealth', but on the other, *and more important* side, a part of the study of man. For man's character has been moulded by his every-day work, and the material resources which he thereby procures, more than by any other influence unless it be that of his religious ideals; and the two great forming agencies of the world's history have been the religious and the economic.[35]

Marshall the agnostic evidently had no option but to become Marshall the economist if he was indeed to make a practical contribution to the upgrading of man's character and the ongoing improvement of the quality of life.

And to the alleviation of absolute deprivation; for Marshall, like Jevons (both in London and in Sydney), was deeply shocked by the 'social cesspools' which were the slums, by overcrowding and overwork, by ill-health and alcoholism caused by a desire to forget. Marshall used to tell how, about the time he had begun to study economics, he saw in a shopwindow a painting of a down-and-out which he bought 'for a few shillings':

> I set it up above the chimney-piece in my room in college and thenceforward called it my patron saint, and devoted myself to trying how to fit men like that for heaven. Meanwhile I got a good deal interested in the semi-mathematical side of pure Economics, and was afraid of becoming a mere thinker. But a glance at my patron saint seemed to call me back to the right path.[36]

In 1893 he was able to confirm just how high the relief of distress had been on his personal agenda as an economist: 'I have devoted myself for the last twenty-five years to the problem of poverty, and. . . . very little of my work has been devoted to any inquiry which does not bear on that.'[37] It is worth noting, of course, that Marshall himself knew of poverty only through books, Blue Books and walks in working-class districts; and that his inexperience of destitution and degradation at first hand conferred upon his mission the distinctive stamp of middle-class paternalism. Rita McWilliams-Tullberg comments as follows on Marshall's academic detachment:

> There is no indication that he himself ever went hungry from shortage of funds, nor did he have the close contact with poverty experienced by a later generation of Cambridge students through their settlement work. . . . There is no evidence that he ever really appreciated the insecurity and narrowness of financial margins which plagued the poor of his day, and which so often swamped the

virtues of thrift, diligence, and the accumulation of knowledge –
and above all, 'duty' – which Marshall liked to preach. Without any
extravagances himself, it must have been hard for him to understand the minor extravagances of the poor.[38]

Terence Hutchison is even more critical, suggesting that Marshall
was far better at preaching about poverty than at finding practical
solutions: 'It seems, therefore, in some ways rather strange for
Keynes (and especially Keynes) to have complained that "Marshall
was too anxious to do good". It is not very apparent that the good
was very extensive that Marshall was too anxious to do. Certainly
Marshall, like some of the classical economists, was prone to moralizing or preaching. But moralizing and preaching are not so much
oneself doing good or even necessarily being "anxious" *oneself to do
good*. They rather consists in *urging other people to be good*.'[39] Which
is, one is compelled to add, more the contribution of the ordained
clergyman or the moral philosopher that Marshall had early on
decided not to become than that of the professional economist that
Marshall, anxious to do good, had opted to be.

There is much in the observations of both McWilliams-Tullberg
and Hutchison, but they must also be seen in perspective. Of course
Marshall was capable of advocating the harsh regime of the workhouse for drunkards and other irresponsibles who were themselves
the architects of their own misery ('They are the very people whom I
want to deter more still. I want the workhouse discipline to be made
rather more severe for them.').[40] Of course Marshall revealed genuine class-bias in the nature of the advice he gave to the Poor Law
Guardians on matters such as the cross-examination of witnesses
('They should be much more careful with regard to the working
men's evidence than with regard to the evidence of educated
people').[41] Yet at least Marshall made it his business to acquaint
himself with the facts at a time when more complacent Victorians
simply took it for granted that virtually all of their fellow-countrymen
were comfortably situated on the moving staircase of economic
growth that raised per capita national income by a third in the
decades that separated the Great Exhibition from the *Economics of
Industry*; and declared without hesitation that a man who is destitute
of material wealth 'cannot be, if we may say so, what God intended
him to be'[42] at a time when so many less reluctant adherents of
Samuel Smiles' gospel of self-help were all too content simply to
brand the losers with the stigma of failure. Particularly influential in

Marshall's formative years was the Spencerian defence of ruthless competition, appealing both to public-school aggressiveness (by providing a veneer of *ought-to-be* to the would-be winner's maxim of 'might is right') and to the self-righteous intolerance of puritanism (by lending a logic to the imminence of conflict that is captured by the phrase 'fight the good fight'). Spencer had written with grim acceptance that the 'purifying process' by which the lower animals kill off the sickly, the aged, the incapable, the non-functional, was also to be found in human societies, and that such natural selection was in itself a sound reason for *laissez-faire*:

> The poverty of the incapable, the distresses that come upon the imprudent, the starvation of the idle, and those shoulderings aside of the weak by the strong, which leave so many 'in shallows and in miseries', are the decrees of a large, far-seeing benevolence. . . . Harsh fatalities are seen to be full of the highest beneficence – the same beneficence which brings to early graves the children of diseased parents, and singles out the low-spirited, the intemperate, and the debilitated as the victims of an epidemic.[43]

Influenced though he inevitably was by Spencer, Marshall's compassion makes a striking contrast: 'The absence of fresh air, of repose, and of healthy play for children lowers the tone of life; and all the more when work is long and food scarce. Wealth which is now almost wasted may be used so as to secure the benefits of *rus in urbe, urbs in rure*; with full opportunity for wholesome energetic life, physical, mental and moral.'[44] McWilliams-Tullberg is quite right to identify, in declarations such as the following, the unintended arrogance of the outsider who, an undergraduate out of term, takes it into his head to visit the slums as he might visit the zoo. 'I visited the poorest quarters of several cities and walked through one street after another, looking at the faces of the poorest people. Next, I resolved to make as thorough a study as I could of Political Economy.'[45] Seen against the background of his own times, however, Marshall's attitude to the poor appears much less arrogant and much more caring: Pigou says that 'a vivid sense of the paradox of poverty' and 'a strong stream of human sympathy' together constituted 'the feeling that moved his life',[46] and that in itself must have been of greater comfort to the members of the *residuum* (accompanied though it undoubtedly was by tests of intellectual and moral worth and a distinction between the deserving and the underserving poor) than was the indifference and the acceptance of so many of Marshall's contemporaries.

Nor does Marshall confine himself to empty words of sympathy: an economist whose diagnosis is that 'the poverty of the poor is the chief cause of that weakness and inefficiency which are the causes of their poverty'[47] and who then comes up with ideas concerning the ways in which the society can break the vicious circle of deprivation, cannot reasonably be accused of substituting 'moralizing and preaching' for action, however much one might personally wish to see a different mix in his proposals as between Welfare State and Welfare Society. With respect to State intervention, Marshall advocated public spending on education (hardly a very radical recommendation in the shadow of Forster's Education Act of 1871), both because of a *national* need to keep up with competitors such as Germany and because the presence of externalities meant market failure and private-sector under-provision (given the fact, simply put, that 'no individual reaps the full gains derived from educating a child').[48] He advocated regulatory controls to limit entry to the overcrowded slums ('When a steamer is full, admission should be refused to any more, even though they themselves are willing to take the risk of being drowned')[49] and called for State support to collective amenities such as public parks and a public health inspectorate so as to ensure that no child at least should be crippled in character by the curse of an underprivileged background: 'I should *like* an expenditure comparable with that required for the South African war to be devoted to the removal of this source of degradation for a good many years to come.'[50] He was in favour of the safety-net of the Poor Law, flirted (inconclusively) with the idea of a minimum-wage law, and defended the progressive income tax not only with the economic argument of equalisation of subjective sacrifice but with the ethical argument as well that the *haves* by virtue of their good fortune have a positive obligation to assist the *have-nots*: 'I myself certainly think, that the rich ought to be taxed much more heavily than they are, in order to provide for their poorer brethren the material means for a healthy physical and mental development.'[51] In all of these ways Marshall showed himself to be far more open to State intervention of a practical nature than Hutchison's reference to 'moralizing and preaching' would seem to suggest. It is easy enough to point to policy-measures which Marshall ignores (the Social Services Department, the negative income tax, the National Health Service), let alone to those such as the council estate which he cites only to dismiss: 'Municipal housing seems to me scarcely ever right and generally very wrong.'[52] Naturally he could have gone further than he did. What is impressive is how far he actually went down the Welfare State road. Besides which, of course, Marshall was a strong advocate of a mixed welfare environment, and believed with unquestionable sincerity that Welfare State would increasingly be complemented by Welfare Society as economic growth continued to uplift character and inculcate generosity: the Poor Law Guardians would thus increasingly benefit from the voluntary services of the Charity Organisation Societies, the minimum wage would be paid without legal compulsion by increasingly chivalrous employers ('The character that fits them to take the lead in the arts of production is likely also to make them take a generous interest in the wellbeing of those who work for them'),[53] the relocation of the London poor to cottages with gardens in new towns would increasingly be peformed by *ad hoc* committees of enthusiastic philanthropists, and in these and other ways material and moral advance in the *private* sector would increasingly come to play a role alongside that of the State with respect to the relief of poverty. A little economic growth is clearly a powerful thing; and for that reason the compassionate economist whose sympathies are engaged should devote his attentions to the acceleration of advance as well as to the redress of abuse.

Marshall issued a warning to market-minded liberals about 'the mirage which is caused by the fact that the comfort of a few rich men sometimes has a higher bidding power in the market than more urgent needs of many poor'.[54] His anxieties concerning the optimality of the outcome that is brought about by the unfettered forces of supply and demand are closely paralleled by those of the eminent social democrat, R. H. Tawney, whose distinction between 'utilities' and 'futilities' reposes upon the observation that, 'while the effective demand of the mass of men is only too small, there is a small class which wears several men's clothes, eats several men's dinners, occupies several families' houses, and lives several men's lives'.[55] One would in the circumstances have expected that social democrat to have seen in the Victorian eclectic who undertook to promote redistribution from rich to poor 'by every means in my power that were legitimate' ('and I would not be specially scrupulous in interpreting that word')[56] an intellectual forebear and an important ally. One would have been mistaken, for all that Tawney appears to have detected in the 'body of occasionally useful truisms'[57] that were employed by orthodox economists when they 'exchanged apples for nuts in the best manner of Marshall'[58] was amorality of intent (and 'no amount of cleverness will get figs off thistles'),[59] irrelevance of purpose (as where, speaking of the industrial system, Tawney declared that analysis orientated towards efficiency is 'the shallowest of claptrap': 'What is at issue is not whether it is efficient, but whether it is just'),[60] and unalloyed 'twaddle': 'There is no such thing as a science of economics, nor ever will be. It is just cant, and Marshall's talk as to the need for social problems to be studied by "the same order of mind which tests the stability of a battleship in bad weather" is twaddle.'[61] If, however, the LSE professor failed to see in the critic of 'those rights of property which lead to extreme inequalities of wealth'[62] a forebear and an ally, then neither, it must be said, did the first director of his institution, who wrote as follows to Sidney Webb on 22 September 1898:

> You may be gratified to know, if you don't know it already, that in Germany you and Mrs Webb are held in the highest estimation of all English writers on economics. Marshall is nowhere. His book is not considered intrinsically important; and even amongst those who might be expected to agree with him his ideas are not considered original.[63]

Hewins seems to have been all but totally unaware of the reforming zeal of a secular missionary who wrote to him in the following words only two years later: 'I am more in accord with some Fabian opinions than are many academic economists.'[64]

Nor was Beatrice Webb any more perceptive in her approach to the contribution of one of the few economists ever to have ranked activities above wants: 'Unused economic faculty rapidly deteriorates into the intermittent state – and efficient economic desire, if satisfied without the obligation to produce, quickly becomes parasitic – a conclusion which I had failed to reach from the abstract economics of Ricardo and Marshall.'[65] Beatrice Webb's attitude to the views of a social theorist who, anxious to do good, wrote so extensively about the proper relationship between the mixed welfare environment and the relief of poverty is one-sided, to say the least. What is even more surprising, however, is the fact that she did not see in the prophet and the moralist who repeatedly stated that he wished wages to 'increase at the expense of the incomes of the well-to-do classes as fast as possible without causing the latter to strike permanently'[66] a troubled spirit clearly suffering from the guilt and the *malaise* which she captured in the phrase 'a new consciousness of sin among men of intellect and men of property'[67] and which she explained in greater detail as follows:

> When I say the consciousness of sin, I do not mean the conscious-
> ness of personal sin. . . . The consciousness of sin was a collective
> or class consciousness; a growing uneasiness, amounting to convic-
> tion, that the industrial organisation, which had yielded rent,
> interest and profits on a stupendous scale, had failed to provide a
> decent livelihood and tolerable conditions for a majority of the
> inhabitants of Great Britain.[68]

Marshall's emphasis on service alongside self, on obligation alongside
statification, on moral conduct even without the supernatural sanction ('The fallen children of the Evangelicals kept up the old
standards',[69] as Noel Annan wisely observes), on Welfare State and
Welfare Society – all of this would seem to suggest that Marshall was
very far from being an abstract thinker and little else, as the then
Miss Potter believed him to be. No less distinguished a theorist of
welfare capitalism than J. K. Galbraith reports a sense of relief
among younger economists when planning descended upon the
United States in 1940 and at last 'we were able to escape the stern
Marshallian market principles to do what the approach of war made
essential',[70] and he returns the following verdict on the overall value
of Marshall's economics: 'Marshall taught and greatly systematized
the subject, and his huge textbook excluded the undiligent and
unworthy; but no really great innovation, either in ideas or policy,
bears his name.'[71] Virtually the only theorist on the middle ground to
have drawn any real nourishment from Alfred Marshall's contribution to social policy seems to have been his namesake, T. H.
Marshall,[72] who correctly identified in the earlier Marshall's idealisa-
tion of the one-status society in which 'by occupation at least, every
man is a gentleman',[73] that very craving for an integrated community
and a common culture which was later to inspire the architects of the
modern British Welfare State to press for universalistic wards, un-
streamed comprehensives and the flat-rate pension. T. H. Marshall
recognised the spark of social democracy in the work of an author
who seems to have opted to pay for a quiet life in the coin of
deliberate obfuscation and multilateral conciliation. R. H. Tawney
and W. A. S. Hewins, Miss Potter and Professor Galbraith, did not.
It is one of the greatest ironies surrounding Alfred Marshall's mission
that by no means everyone saw what it was.

Alfred Marshall between 1868 and 1877 – between the ages of 26
and 35 – made an intellectual journey from mathematics to ethics,
from ethics to psychology and from psychology to economics in

search of the instrument that would deliver across-the-board betterment to all Englishmen, rich and poor. He also, in that period, made
another journey of a more traditional kind. In 1875 Marshall received
a bequest of £250 (a large sum of money to a bachelor Fellow living,
apparently without any particular envy of contemporaries able to
supplement their stipends from private incomes, on £300 a year); and
he used the money to travel for four months (June to September
inclusive) in North America. He covered a vast amount of ground,
visiting towns such as New York, San Francisco, Albany, Springfield,
Boston, Lowell, Providence, Norwich, Rochester, Niagara, Toronto,
Hamilton, Cleveland, Chicago, Omaha, St Louis, Indianapolis, Cin-
cinnatti, Columbus, Pittsburgh, Philadelphia, together with a number of rural communities (including some of the communistic
settlements of the Shakers, the Pentacostalists and the Oneida Per-
fectionists). At Yale he met Francis Amasa Walker and William
Graham Summer, in Boston Dean Howells, Ralph Waldo Emerson
and (probably) Samuel Bowles, and in Philadelphia Henry Carey,
then 83 years of age. The eminent protectionist made a deep impression upon the young free-trader from a country which almost
thirty years earlier had unilaterally melted its tariffs into comparative
advantage only to find its competitors depressingly unprepared to do
likewise: years later the free trader was still referring in lectures,
books and evidence to Royal Commissions to the stimulating discussion he had had with the protectionist, and not least to 'Mr Carey's
splendid anger, as he exclaimed that foreign commerce had made
even the railways of America run from east to west, rather than from
north to south'.[74] The impact of Carey's arguments was in a sense to
be expected, given that Marshall had set himself the task while in
America of studying 'the problems of national industry and international trade from the American point of view' and had made up his
mind not to make up his mind in advance: 'I was quite prepared to
learn, not indeed that the American system was applicable to England,
but that it might contain ideas capable of adaptation to English
conditions.'[75] The impact of Carey and other protectionists was
undeniable, but so too was the spectacle of greedy interest-groups
passing specious evidence to shortsighted politicians in an attempt to
twist the public interest to their own advantage: it was this econ-
omics-of-politics argument, as well as the more conventional line of
reasoning that focuses on the international division of labour, that
ultimately led Marshall to the conclusion that 'a Protective policy in
fact was a very different thing from a Protective policy as painted by

sanguine economists, such as Carey and some of his followers, who assumed that all other people would be as upright as they knew themselves to be, and as clear-sighted as they believed themselves to be'.[76] Marshall's lifelong commitment to free trade is particularly striking in the light of the factory-visits which he conducted while in America: he saw economies of scale at work at production-line level, came away impressed by the spirit of initiative, free enterprise and individualism of the Americans, anticipated that the United States would soon become a major world economic power, but never yielded nonetheless to the temptation to propose that the workshop of the world be shielded by a tariff-wall from the aggressive competition of the nascent nation.

Marshall's impressions of America were reported, upon his return, in a paper entitled 'Some Features of American Industry' which he read on 17 November 1875 to the Cambridge Moral Science Club. Naturally enough, he commented favourably on the economic advance he had seen in the New World; but he also expressed reservations in the field of ethics (reservations similar to those of de Tocqueville in the 1830s) associated with the fact that the American was too self-reliant to join in the valuable support system represented by the corporate constraint of all over each in the modern cooperative or trades union, too mobile always to care for a good reputation and the esteem and trust of those around him. Money, Marshall informed the Moral Science Club,

> is a more portable commodity than a high moral reputation. The doctrine that honesty is the best policy is at a disadvantage when it submits itself to the judgement of a man whose associates would continually be changing even were he stationary; who knows that if he makes money but loses his reputation, he can pack up his money and make it help him to earn a new reputation amid new surroundings; but that if he starts by building up a good reputation it is not unlikely that he may want to migrate into a new career in which but little of his reputation will follow him. It cannot, I think, be denied that a short-sighted man is thus exposed to great temptations in America.[77]

3 Cambridge and Bristol

In 1877 Alfred Marshall married Mary Paley (1850–1944), a former student who had taken over from him the task of lecturing in political economy to the twenty women students at the Old Hall, Newnham. In her case it appears to have been an attack of love at first sight: 'I then thought I had never seen such an attractive face with its delicate outline and brilliant eyes.'[1] What he felt is less well documented but, since marriage meant the loss of his Fellowship, one must assume that he knew what he was doing. They remained happily married for 47 years; and in that time, in Keynes's words, 'his dependence upon her devotion was complete. Her life was given to him and to his work with a degree of unselfishness and understanding that makes it difficult for friends and old pupils to think of them separately or to withhold from her shining gifts of character a big share in what his intellect accomplished.'[2] They had no children.

Mary Paley was the great-granddaughter of William Paley, Archbishop of Carlisle and author of the *Principles of Moral and Political Philosophy* (1785): the book reminded the reader of the extent to which the Benthamite pleasure–pain principle had been anticipated by the Christian utilitarianism implicit in the familiar juxtaposition of Heaven and Hell and was an important influence on the Philosophic Radicals of the early nineteenth century. Her father was a Yorkshireman and a country rector, 'an evangelical clergyman of the straitest Simeonite sect'[3] who burnt her dolls, saying that she and her sister were making them into idols. Dickens was forbidden reading, although not Shakespeare, *Gulliver's Travels*, the *Arabian Nights*, the *Iliad*, the *Odyssey* and Scott ('I suppose that there is a religious tone in Scott which is absent in Dickens',[4] she mused in later life). Her childhood was permeated by religion: apart from her home background, the community was intensely Christian, many of the local children even being 'named after Old Testament worthies such as Amos, Ezekiel, Obadiah, Keziah. . . . After a long search for a biblical name of a dog, it was called "Moreover"'.[5] Her father was a man of strict moral principles: 'If he met the hounds he would do his

best to mislead them and if he attended the races it was to stand at the
entrance and distribute tracts on the evil of betting.'[6] In spite of his
seriousness and the strength of his beliefs, however, he could also be
'the loving playmate of his children',[7] a man who enjoyed reading
aloud to them, encouraging them to practice their French and German
at table, sharing with them his enthusiastic interest in recent developments in fields such as electricity and photography: he was clearly a
man who was able without difficulty to reconcile his fundamentalist
convictions (with respect, say, to the Flood) with a commitment to
scientific advance. It was no doubt because of his commitment to
learning as an end in its own right that he was apparently 'proud and
pleased'[8] (despite the fact that it was 'in those days an outrageous
proceeding')[9] when his independent-minded daughter elected in 1871
to live with Miss Clough at 74 Regent Street, Cambridge (later the
Glengarry Hotel), to attend lectures on the subjects in the Moral
Sciences Tripos (these were regarded as suitable for girls, as the list
contained philosophy and political economy but neither mathematics
nor classics), and to take the degree-examination (but not the degree:
Cambridge degrees were not yet open to women) in 1874. She was
one of the first two 'industrious virgins' of that nucleus that later
became Newnham College to have done so. One of her lecturers was
Henry Sidgwick who, having made a negative move in 1869 by
resigning his Trinity Fellowship, subsequently wanted to take a
positive step (in this case, by helping to further the education of
women) and whom Mary later recalled as follows: 'He used to
frighten us by tipping his chair back and then just recovering in time.
He liked to use his fingers when lecturing, he would make neat tapers
out of bits of paper, and we used to lay out a variety of things for him
to play with, red tape being a chief favourite.'[10] Another was Alfred
Marshall, who gave her her first-ever lecture on political economy
and whom she remembered as being 'rather nervous . . . very earnest and with shining eyes'.[11]

Mary Paley had come to Cambridge for general cultivation and to
escape from boredom at home after her sister had married and her
own engagement had been broken off. The idea of the examination
had come later. While in Cambridge, however, she came to see that
she was changing and that it would not be easy to go home again:
'Mill's Inductive Logic and *Ecce Homo* and Herbert Spencer and the
general tone of thought gradually undermined my old beliefs. I never
talked on these subjects with my father but we both knew that the old
harmony between us had melted away.'[12] She, like Alfred, experi-

enced in Cambridge a crisis of faith and therewith an estrangement from the strict Christianity of her father and her childhood. It was in the circumstances rather fortunate that an opportunity presented itself for her to remain in the University town rather than returning to the Rectory at Ufford near Stamford: she was, in 1875, approached by Henry Sidgwick (who had himself taken and furnished the house in Regent Street, and whose wife was to succeed Miss Clough) to teach the Newnham women. She became in that way the first woman lecturer on economics in Cambridge. W. S. Jevons had been the external examiner for her own economics papers in 1874 (Marshall and Jevons met for the first time on the occasion of Jevons' visit to Cambridge in that year). Returning for further examinations in 1875 (the year in which another of Marshall's most distinguished students, John Neville Keynes, took his First), Jevons encountered Mary, then a lecturer, once again, and reported in a letter that she 'pleased me very much'.[13] She was 25 and clearly a young woman of potential and promise.

Alongside her Newnham teaching Mary also began work on an elementary economics textbook intended for use by Cambridge University Extension lectures: the text even then, and despite the marginalist incursions of the early 1870s, remained Mill's *Principles* (with Smith, Ricardo, Cairnes – and, incidentally, Jevons – as supplements), and there was a demand for something new. After she became engaged to Alfred in 1876, he gradually took it over, and when *The Economics of Industry* appeared in 1879, it was clearly not her first book (and thus not even her last) but rather his: 'It was published in our joint names in 1879. Alfred insisted on this, though as time went on I realised that it had to be really his book, the latter half being almost entirely his and containing the germs of much that appeared later in the *Principles*.'[14] A second edition (with minor alterations) appeared in 1881, the book was reprinted ten times in all, and a remarkable total of 15 000 copies were sold. Marshall, its success notwithstanding, was never satisfied with it: his working copy of 1885, now in the Library at Newnham College, is so heavily cut and critically annotated that it is no surprise he abandoned plans for a third edition and indeed allowed the book to go out of print altogether in 1889. As Mary explains: 'He never liked the little book for it offended against his belief that "every dogma that is short and simple is false", and he said about it "you can't afford to tell the truth for half-a-crown"'.[15] In a letter to Seligman in 1900 Marshall recalled with obvious regret that he had, two decades earlier, been involved in 'a hollow *Economics of Industry* in which truth was economized for the benefit of feeble minds'[16] ('forcibly simplified for working class readers',[17] he explained elsewhere with uncharacteristic frankness); while in a letter to Colson dating from 1908 or 1909 he begins by blaming the failure on his wife ('I married; found myself committed to writing a cheap popular book') and then says that the book was a project 'which was necessarily superficial, and which I loathed'.[18] Marshall, it would appear, was not only over-sensitive to the opinions of others but also over-critical of himself – and of the economics textbook *per se*: 'The task of combining simplicity with thoroughness is more difficult in this than in almost any other subject. Several scores of books have been written in the hope of doing this; but they have perished quickly.'[19] The central doctrines of economics, Marshall consistently maintained, are not simple and cannot be made so. His scholarly reluctance to simplify is easy enough to grasp; but then, Marshall was something more than simply a scholar, namely a shrewd expositor whose textbooks, simplify though they may, have the essential merit of opening doors to a difficult discipline to which many otherwise would have been denied *entrée*. Seldom if ever was there a greater need for the systematisation of the economics textbook than in the rapidly changing intellectual climate of the 1870s; and Foxwell is entirely right to pay tribute to the 'modest little treatise on the *Economics of Industry*' which, published 'at a critical time', was 'extremely useful in reconstructing the science which had been so rudely assaulted'.[20] Besides that, the novelty of some of the arguments presented in the 'modest little treatise' should not be neglected: particularly where it attacks earlier authors such as Mill for over-emphasising cost of production and later authors such as Jevons for over-emphasising subjective satisfaction, the book of 230 pages is strikingly similar in its unique line of argumentation to its more celebrated successor of 754 pages for which it was in many respects a trial run. One of the few commentators who saw through the synthesisation to the novelty hidden in the oblique mode of presentation was none other than the eminent historical economist T. E. Cliffe Leslie (1827–82), then Professor of Jurisprudence and Political Economy at Queens College, Belfast, who, writing in *The Academy* of 8 November 1879, was moved to declare: 'The book before us makes greater changes in economic method and doctrine, compared with previous text-books, than might be perceived at first sight, for they are made without sufficient warning to call the student's attention.'[21] But that too was part of Alfred Marshall's mission, to generate new knowledge while teaching old, and to run the one into the other without any indication as to when the beaten track had petered out, leaving the guide no choice but to blaze his own trail.

And there is more. Not only did Cliffe Leslie identify a studious avoidance of controversy on the part of the authors of the *Economics of Industry* such as caused them to mute their own trumpet, he also said he was able to detect in the Marshalls' book an antipathy to abstract theory and an awareness of situational contingency which he must himself have found exceptionally congenial to his own relativistic and concrete approach to social science problems: 'One characteristic merit of Mr. and Mrs. Marshall's work is that they do not make use of provisional doctrines or generalizations . . . as premises from which trains of deduction can be made, but as starting points for the investigation of actual phenomena, and the ascertainment of the presence and operation of their actual causes and conditions.'[22] He gives the example of the law of value; and points out, with evident approbation, that 'the authors distinguish emphatically between what they call normal values, or those which would result from the undisturbed action of competition, and market values, or those actually resulting from the existing constitution and usages of the industrial world'.[23] Cliffe Leslie goes so far as to state that the authors of the *Economics of Industry* were so aware of the essential dynamism in economic phenomena as to share his view that the normals and the equilibria of the long-run (a 'lax and unscientific phrase')[24] are first approximations and nothing more – with, naturally enough, the obvious implication for the prediction that prices in competitive conditions ultimately gravitate to costs:

> Industrial liberty, and the eager pursuit of gain, produce an economic world, the vastness, variety, complexity, incessant change, speculation, and potent influence of chance in which are absolutely incompatible with the knowledge and nice calculation of relative profits, upon which the theory rests that the prices of commodities are regulated in the long run by their cost of production.[25]

While some readers will no doubt wish to assert that Leslie's stress upon the Marshalls' attitude to deviations, irregularities, uncertainty and chance tells us more about Leslie than it does about the Marshalls, there is no question that the kaleidoscope of perpetual upheaval is indeed an element in the *Economics of Industry* and that Leslie can hardly be faulted for confusing its presence with its significance at a time when so many readers of the Marshalls' book found in it nothing but eternal verities and comparative statics. Cliffe Leslie was perceptive – and he was not alone in welcoming the Marshalls' book as a defence of humanity against dogmatism. Arnold Toynbee in particular was much impressed by the 'admirable little treatise' and strongly recommended it to any student of the social sciences who wanted to read common sense in place of depersonalised vagaries dressed up as natural laws:

> He would find the proper distinction made between political economy as a theoretical science, and political economy as a practical science; he would find the relations of political economy to social science explained; and, above all, he would observe with pleasure that abstract political economy, the laws of which are true only under certain assumptions, used not to blind men to the facts of the industrial world, but to throw light upon them in all the confusion and entanglement of actual experience.[26]

There is in truth far more about abstractions and laws in the *Economics of Industry* than Toynbee seems to appreciate, but the realism and the search for relevance which Toynbee praises so highly are without any doubt there as well – central, indeed, almost by definition to the real-world mission of an economist who was anxious to do good.

The success of that mission was advanced in no small measure by marriage in 1877 to a woman

> without whose understanding and devotion his work would not have fulfilled its fruitfulness. . . . For the next forty years her life was wholly merged in his. This was not a partnership of the Webb kind, as it might have become if the temperaments on both sides had been entirely different. In spite of his early sympathies and what he was gaining all the time from his wife's discernment of mind, Marshall came increasingly to the conclusion that there was nothing useful to be made of women's intellects. . . . Yet it was an intellectual partnership just the same, based on profound dependence on the one side (he could not live a day without her), and, on the other, deep devotion and admiration, which was increased and not impaired by extreme discernment. Nothing escaped her clear, penetrating and truthful eye. She faced everything in order that he, sometimes, need not. . . . Neither in Alfred's lifetime nor afterwards did she ever ask, or expect, anything for herself. It was

always in the forefront of her thought that she must not be a trouble to anyone.[27]

She protected her husband from interruption and agitation, made sure he had enough rest, and took charge of the household finances: 'Alfred never wanted to trouble about money so, though we had a joint banking account, I drew the money for our everyday expenses and he seldom wrote a cheque.'[28] Her selfless devotion to Alfred and to Alfred's work is a perfect illustration of the conception of marriage which Alfred had formally propounded as her lecturer in the early years of 1871–4, when she reports him as having declared: 'The ideal of married life is often said to be that husband and wife should live for each other. If this means that they should live only for each other's gratification, it seems to me intensely immoral. Man and wife should live, not for each other but with each other for some end.'[29] The precise nature of their relationship would appear to be, moreover, a perfect illustration of the ideal which Professor Marshall held up to Miss Potter in 1889 when, concluding with the professor's statement that 'if you compete with us we shan't marry you', Miss Potter later recorded the essence of the professor's observations as follows:

Interesting talk with Professor Marshall, first at dinner with the Creightons, and afterwards at lunch at his own house. It opened with chaff about men and women: he holding that woman was a subordinate being, and that, if she ceased to be subordinate, there would be no object for a man to marry. That marriage was a sacrifice of masculine freedom, and would only be tolerated by male creatures so long as it meant the devotion, body and soul, of the female to the male. Hence the woman must not develop her faculties in any way unpleasant to the man: that strength, courage, independence were not attractive in women; that rivalry in men's pursuits was positively unpleasant. Hence masculine strength and masculine ability in women must be firmly trampled on and boycotted by men. *Contrast* was the essence of the matrimonial relation: feminine weakness contrasted with masculine strength: masculine egotism with feminine self-devotion.[30]

Contrast is evidently the key to a healthy relationship between male and female:

If women attempt to equal men and be independent of their guidance and control, the strong woman will be ignored and the weak woman simply starved. It is not likely that men will go on marrying if they are to have competitors for wives. *Contrast* is the only basis of marriage, and if that is destroyed we shall not think it worth our while to shackle ourselves in life with a companion whom we must support and must consider.[31]

Marshall, one learns with no great surprise, was no great fan of the Suffragettes and similar manifestations of what he regarded as 'a selfish desire among women to resemble men' such as tends, most regrettably, to 'destroy that balance and mutual supplementary adaptation of masculine and feminine character, which enabled a man to secure rest and repose by marriage; though he might probably have been worried beyond endurance by the lifelong incessant companionship of another man.'[32] A man with such conceptions and ideals is not, of course, every woman's cup of tea. Mary Paley was, however, an exceptional woman.

Following her marriage in 1877, Mary's own research effectively came to an end, but she did continue to maintain her academic interests by lecturing in economics at Bristol (the University later conferred upon her an honorary D. Litt. – the only degree she ever was awarded) and (after the Marshalls returned to Cambridge) at Newnham. Besides that, she would appear not only to have protected Alfred from disturbance and helped him to conserve his energies (physical and mental) but also to have acted as an informal sounding-board on matters of economic significance. As Marshall says in a fragment dating from 1923: 'My wife has counselled and aided at every stage of my every outpouring: and given the best part of her life to aiding me by counsel in all matters large and small at every stage.'[33] What went on at home is one thing, but public performance is quite another – and on public performance Maynard Keynes (through his father a long-serving courtier at Balliol Croft and himself all of 41 at the time of the great man's death) was absolutely clear: 'She never, to the best of my recollection, discoursed on an economic topic with a visitor, or even took part in the everlasting economic talks of Balliol Croft. For the serious discussion she would leave the dining-room to the men or the visitor would go upstairs to the study, and the most ignorant Miss could not have pretended less than she to academic attainment.'[34] Marshall, evidently convinced that even academic women were not good at generalising or at thinking big, advised the future Lady Passfield to confine her ambitions to the study of female labour: 'To sum up with perfect frankness: if you devote yourself to the study of your own sex as an industrial factor, your name will be a household word two hundred years hence: if you write a history of co-operation it will be superseded and ignored in a year or two.'[35] What is surprising is that Marshall did not advise his own well-educated wife to go at least as far, but rather encouraged her to be satisfied with simple economic tasks such as the compilation of the index (not a very good one) for the original edition of his *Principles*. Though he believed that the woman's mind is genuinely inferior to that of the man, the very fact that he had lectured to women students (including Mary Paley) shows that he did not then believe them to be totally incapable of grasping the fundamentals of political economy, and it must therefore remain a mystery why he did not invite the former bluestocking to go full-time in the collection of material and the conducting of simple inquiries on his behalf. The mystery is that much greater when one remembers that the Alfred Marshall of the 1870s was not the Alfred Marshall of the 1890s: his articles in the labour journal *The Bee-Hive* in 1874 contain the statement that it is 'iniquitous'[36] for women to be excluded from the medical profession, while a letter to his mother, Rebecca Marshall, written from North America in July 1875, betrays more than a little enthusiasm for the fact that the women in that continent (whom he found 'independent, without being unwomanly') enjoyed 'thorough freedom in the management of their own concerns.'[37]

Marshall also wrote in 1875 of the kind of woman he hoped one day to marry, and made clear that cooking and cleaning were not enough: 'I do not care for naivety alone: any more than I like sugar alone: but when mingled with enterprise it is very delicious; of course it would not take the place of strong diet: for steady support I would have the strength that has been formed by daring and success.'[38] Two years later Marshall married the woman he had been waiting for – and promptly informed her that her place was in the home. If Alfred's sudden conversion to the *mores* of his father is surprising, however, then the unquestioning acceptance by Mary that her own career was over is no less so. H. M. Robertson met her when, cataloguing his books and papers for posterity and making the notes posthumously published as *What I Remember* (the *what* is, predictably enough, virtually synonymous with a particular *whom*), she had progressed from 'cossetting Alfred' to cossetting his memory. He found her self-denying service less than easy to understand:

I confess it was a little surprising to reflect on how this obviously mentally alert and spiritually young and lively old person, who clearly enjoyed the company of the young, could for so long have abandoned, as to speak, her own personality as a scholar and teacher in her own right, to become part nurse, part amanuensis, part subordinate research assistant, merely 'devilling' material for someone else to use, for a man who from all accounts, for all his genius, had become something of a valetudinarian, something of a recluse, something of an eccentric and, indeed, something of a domestic tyrant.[39]

Alfred Marshall's strong opposition in 1896 to the granting of Cambridge degrees to women must have come as a particular wrench to her; 'but Mary Marshall had been brought up to know, and also to respect and accept what men of "strict principles" were like. This was not the first time that her dolls (whom she was in risk of making into idols) had been burnt by one whom she loved.'[40] She loved him and pampered him and put up with his ways, and, whatever the reasons, this much is clear: if Alfred Marshall's mission was economics, then Mary Paley Marshall's mission was Alfred.

Marriage in 1877 meant the loss of his Cambridge Fellowship as Cambridge Fellows (the restriction was only lifted in 1882) were then forced to make a choice between the cloister and the hearth which none other than Henry Sidgwick, while still single, was able to defend in the following words:

It always seems to me rather a noble thing for a person of great natural elevation not to marry, except under peculiar circumstances. If other human relations develop in us an equal flow of love and energy (the primary and paramount branch of self-culture), there is no doubt that the greater freedom of celibacy, the higher self-denial of its work, the time it leaves for useful but unlucrative pursuits, the material means it places at our disposal for the advantage of our fellow-creatures ought to have great weight in the balance – in a densely-populated country the last especially, and in a commercial age the last but one.[41]

Rothblatt, looking at the experience of the post-1882 period, comments as follows on the anticipated contradiction between marital and college interests: 'It has been suggested that the removal of celibacy restrictions weakened college life, that marriage made fellows even more aloof from undergraduates, but there is no evidence that this was actually the case.'[42] Be that as it may, the fact is that the Cambridge of the pre-1882 period had much of the character of a monastery where the right to hold an academic appointment carried with it the duty to respect the communal ideal. Marshall in the circumstances was in 1877 compelled to find another job. He was 35 years of age and had published next to nothing: a defence of Mill on value in the *Fortnightly Review* (1876), an essay on 'The Future of the Working Classes' which had been accepted by his college magazine, the *Eagle* (1874), a note on monopoly which appeared in the *Proceedings of the Cambridge Philosophical Society* (1873), and the review of the *Theory of Political Economy* in *The Academy* (1872) of which Jevons wrote in 1874 to J. D'Aulnis that 'there was indeed a review in the *Academy* of 1st April 1872, but though more fair than that of the *Saturday Review*, it contained no criticism worthy of your notice'.[43] In giving up a Cambridge Fellowship in order to get married, Alfred Marshall was undeniably taking a great risk with his academic career: he could all too easily have disappeared into a minor boys' public school and never been heard of again. Marshall could not have known that he would land on his feet – as, indeed, he always did in an academic career in which the right things always seemed to happen for him, as if guided by an Invisible Hand, at just the right time.

Thus it happened in 1877 that marriage and loss of the Fellowship were rapidly succeeded by Marshall's being appointed Professor of Political Economy and first Principal of University College, Bristol. One of his referees was Henry Sidgwick, who referred in particular to the importance and originality of Marshall's work in progress on the theory of trade, foreign and domestic. The other was Jevons, whose open testimonial, sent to Cambridge from Hampstead and forwarded thence to Bristol, is full of praise for Marshall's unpublished work on trade (it will, Jevons says, 'place you among the most original writers on the science') and for Marshall's academic contribution in general:

There can be no doubt that the College is be congratulated on counting you among the candidates, but as you have many intimate friends who will speak of your remarkable fitness for the Principalship I will restrict myself to saying that in appointing you to the Professorship, they will add to their staff of Professors one of the most able and experienced teachers of Political Economy in England. . . . I consider it superfluous to say more, for I cannot imagine that there is likely to be any other candidate comparable to you in fitness for the joint posts for which you are going to apply.[44]

Jevons was, of course, ideally placed to assess the calibre and potential of the man of 35 who had published next to nothing: as external examiner at Cambridge, he had come in contact with Marshall the thinker and expositor at one remove, by examining the students that Marshall had taught. Even allowing for the exceptional ability of some of Marshall's early pupils (H. S. Foxwell, J. N. Keynes, J. S. Nicholson, H. H. Cunynghame, for example, to say nothing of Mary Paley), Jevons was perceptive enough to recognise the signs of exceptional merit in their much-unpublished teacher: already in October 1875 he was writing from his eyrie at 36 Parsonage Road, Withington, to propose Marshall as a substitute for him in London in the transitional years between Jevons' appointment to the Professorship at University College and his actual departure from Owens, Manchester.[45] It was clearly personality and promise, not publications, that most impressed Sidgwick and Jevons when they so enthusiastically sponsored Marshall for the Bristol posts. And they were not alone: 'When he was a candidate for the post Jowett asked him for a week's end to Balliol; but though they walked and talked together nearly the whole of the Sunday, the subject of University College was never alluded to. They talked about architecture, about Herbert Spencer, about theology at Cambridge, and many other things, and it was only when Marshall was leaving that Jowett said, "I don't know how this election may turn out, but at any rate I am glad to have made your acquaintance." This was the beginning of an intimate friendship with the Marshalls.'[46]

The University College at Bristol had been set up in 1876 by Balliol and New College, Oxford, to widen access to higher education. Its foundation is an early instance of the 'teach and preach' position which was coming increasingly to dominate the social thinking of the Oxford Idealists, and which was within a decade to find its full flowering in the Oxford Extension Movement of which Kadish has written as follows:

> The missionary zeal was a special feature of the Oxford Extension. . . . Lecturers did not join the Movement for the mere purpose of pointing out to the working class the way to material progress – indeed it is difficult to imagine the direct material benefits derived from lectures in English literature or Italian art. The objective was moral improvement; and whenever material progress was discussed it was but the means for the same ojective.[47]

The Movement was to have a great appeal to Oxford's young economists in the 1880s, offering them 'the chance to teach political economy and economic history as well as offering the challenge of realizing Toynbee's impassioned promise to England's working class. Through the Extension young Oxford idealists could dedicate themselves to the education and betterment of the working classes on a grander and more ambitious scale than through the co-operative classes or Toynbee Hall.'[48] The moral crusade, the ethical imperative, that were to constitute the impetus for the Extension in the 1880s, were the very focus that had led to the foundation of the College in the 1870s; and that is why its new Principal, a man of commitment, ethics and purpose despite the fact that Cambridge (far more so than Oxford) tended to stress the detached pursuit of knowledge for its own sake, must have found in the non-rational *Geist* that preached equality of opportunity through adult education a much-valued ally in the struggle for social reform. Nor is it likely that the sensitive and astute Jowett had failed to notice that the self-effacing and much-unpublished newly-wed with whom he walked and talked for nearly the whole of an October Sunday in 1877 was, indeed, in Pigou's words, 'for all of us who knew him, a shining example of single-eyed devotion to an unselfish aim':[49] as the Master wrote to Mary in summary of the first decade of intimate friendship, 'I think that you and Alfred make as near an approach to the Early Christians as is possible in the 19th Century.'[50] Jowett knew an Early Christian when he saw one. He also knew that nothing short of an Early Christian would do for the University College.

Much of the teaching in Bristol was in the evening, in an attempt to provide a service for professionals, businessmen and the working classes (although it must also be reported that the last-mentioned group appears to have been singularly under-represented). A significant number of both day and evening students were women, many of them combining part-time study with family commitments. One of Marshall's principal objections in later years to the higher education of women was to be that the training of women leads to the employment of women at temptingly high rates of pay – 'a great gain in so far as it tends to develop their faculties; but an injury in so far as it tempts them to neglect their duty of building up a true home, and of investing their efforts in the personal capital of their children's character and abilities'.[51] Given the lifelong concern of this secular missionary with the upgrading and betterment of human character, Marshall's expressed fears about the decay of family life simply cannot be laughed off as indicative of nothing more substantial than the subconscious desire of a childless Victorian himself to enjoy the

full-time attentions of an acknowledged subordinate who was prepared to look after him: no one who believes in the value of a good
home will find entirely unacceptable Marshall's statement that 'the
elevation of the ideals of life . . . is due on the one side to political
and economic causes, and on the other to personal and religious
influences; among which the influence of the mother in early childhood is supreme',[52] however much the sympathetic critic would wish
to incorporate the influence of the father as well. Marshall in the
1870s was strongly in favour of education for women: before coming
to Bristol he had written that 'our progress would be accelerated if we
would unwrap the swaddling clothes in which artificial customs have
enfolded woman's mind and would give her free scope womanfully to
discharge her duties to the world',[53] while in later years he went so far
as to state that he had been attracted to the new institution 'chiefly by
the fact that it was the first College in England to open its doors freely
to women'.[54] Marshall in the 1870s was also concerned about the
survival of family life. The part-time principle at the new University
College seems to have been central in assuaging his anxieties as to the
fact that a woman receiving higher education was also a woman who
was not at home with her family. Thus, writing to the *Western Daily
Press* on 25 January 1887 Marshall declared: 'It has always seemed to
me that those women who are able to get all the highest education
they want without leaving their homes, and breaking themselves
away from the associations of domestic life are singularly fortunate.
And I have often pointed with happy pride to the splendid classes of
women at Bristol.'[55]

Marshall saw the new University College as providing an education
which would at one and the same time be intellectually challenging,
vocationally useful and morally uplifting. Intellectually challenging,
as in the case of mathematics, which 'should give the mind strength':

> It is the special work of mathematics to give the power of reasoning
> correctly and of knowing when a thing is proved. There is not, and
> as far as we can see there cannot ever be, a study which can do this
> work nearly as well as mathematics can. So that, even if we looked
> only at its use in nourishing a man's mental vigour, we might say
> that mathematics is to the mind what bread is to the body, the staff
> of life.[56]

Vocationally useful, as in the case of mechanics and physics, which
should lead the trained practitioner to 'do his work better and help
England to hold her own against foreign competitors': 'The engineer

or the builder who knows exactly where there is the greatest strain in each beam or girder of a bridge or a building need not use nearly as much material as he would have to use without any such knowledge.'[57] Morally uplifting, as in the case of political economy, which should enlighten the shortsighted egotist as to the real incidence of the 'grave evils' which he mistakenly thinks he is 'inflicting on others' and on others alone:

> Political economy will help us rightly to apply the motive force of duty, but the will to do one's duty must come from some other source. Still political economy will doubtless show, in many cases, that selfish action is also foolish and suicidal. And on the whole it does show, in almost every case, that when a man adopts action which injures others, he injures himself more than he thinks he does.[58]

Marshall in the Bristol period saw political economy as morally uplifting for the further reason that it was uniquely well-placed to accelerate the evolutionary process whereby activities waxed in importance as wants waned:

> To convince a man that his work is sordid when it is not sordid is to do him a deadly injury. The belief that it is sordid will cramp him, and go a long way towards making him sordid. But if there is room in his business for vigorous and creative intellect, adapting means to ends, devising new means and new ends and you can convince him of this, you will do him a great service. All his force and the energy that is within him will be drawn out towards his work, and he will become strong by doing hard things. . . . He will aim at excellence for the sake of excellence; he will take an artistic pride in the things that he makes and sells.[59]

Besides which, Marshall in the Bristol period made clear, political economy is morally uplifting precisely because its concern with allocation in order to secure growth imposes upon it the task of decomposing revealed preferences into those ('necessaries') which are productive of further expansion in the wealth of nations and those ('luxuries') which gratify the consumer but make no lasting contribution to the society as a whole: 'A man's "necessaries" in the economic sense I take to be those things the want of which would be likely to diminish the efficiency of his work by a value greater than their own cost.'[60] Marshall's distinction in the *Pall Mall Gazette* of 1 December 1883 between that consumption which contributes towards social

progress and that consumption which does not, antedates by almost a
quarter of a century the following distinction in the *Economic Journal* of 1907 – which, however, is in its economic content almost
exactly the same:

> Anyone who bears heavy responsibilities, and uses his brain much,
> needs larger house-room, more quiet, lighter and more digestible
> food, and perhaps more change of scene and other comforts than
> will suffice for maintaining the efficiency of unskilled work, and
> even of artisan work; and, from the higher social point of view, it
> would be bad economy that such a man should cut his expenditure
> down below these 'necessaries for efficiency' for his responsible
> work.[61]

Marshall's emphasis in his Bristol lectures of 1877 on 'excellence for
the sake of excellence', similarly, antedates the celebrated discussion
in the *Principles* of the fisherman who, 'even when no one is looking
and he is not in a hurry, delights in handling his craft well' in a society
in which increasing affluence brings with it an increasing premium on
the 'exercise and development of activities', in which even leisure 'is
used less and less as an opportunity for mere stagnation; and there is
a growing desire for those amusements, such as athletic games and
travelling, which develop activities rather than indulge any sensuous
craving'.[62] Marshall's explication in Bristol of the functionality of the
categorical imperative, finally, both looks backward to the lessons he
gave to the liberated ladies of Newnham (on smuggling, for example:
'It is a crime of a very grave nature. It is as much worse than ordinary
stealing as getting drunk in church is than getting drunk in the streets,
for it is an offence against the religious feeling towards the state')[63]
and forward to the lessons he was to give to his nation as a whole in
his *magnum opus* (on truthtelling, say: 'Modern methods of trade
imply habits of trustfulness on the one side and a power of resisting
temptation to dishonesty on the other, which do not exist among a
backward people').[64] With respect to the categorisation of consumables, the primacy of activities, and the importance of self-policing
ought-to-bes, in short, the views which Marshall expressed at the
University College, Bristol, were for all intents and purposes those
which he would continue to express throughout the whole of his long
life. Be that as it may, it was the mix between the intellectually
challenging, the vocationally useful and the morally uplifting which
the new Principal and Professor most wanted to get right when he
contemplated and discussed the syllabus that would be most appropriate for the new University College.

The College was a new one and had to be publicised; and as Marshall wrote to Hewins in 1899, 'my duties as advertiser in chief were specially onerous [and] . . . nearly killed me'.[65] There was so little in the way of back-up staff that the Principal himself (although appointed as an academic, widely respected in Cambridge) was at one point involved in helping students to find accommodation. Marshall was, at Bristol, burdened with so much routine administration that his academic work suffered. So did his health, partly due to overwork and nervous strain, partly due to a kidney stone – to such an extent, indeed, that Sidgwick secured his permission to publish for private circulation two long chapters from an unfinished manuscript on trade on which Marshall had worked from time to time in the years between 1869 and 1877. The chapters appeared in 1879 as *The Pure Theory of Foreign Trade* and *The Pure Theory of Domestic Values*, respectively. Sidgwick could hardly have anticipated that his friend, then seriously ill, would still be recycling their content over 40 years later in Appendix J to *Money Credit and Commerce*; for the fact is that he, like many others, believed that Marshall's goose was cooked. Edwin Cannan describes seeing Marshall in Bristol at this time: 'He was then about thirty-seven, but looked to me very old and ill. I was told he had one foot in the grave, and quite believed it.'[66] Marshall himself seems to have entertained a similar view, as he recalled almost three decades later: 'I became very ill, and expected not to be able to write anything considerable. . . . I expected to depart this life. But I slowly recovered.'[67]

Marshall slowly recovered in health. Not, however, in confidence: 'He remained for the rest of his life somewhat hypochondriachal and inclined to consider himself on the verge of invalidism. He proved, in fact, to have considerable constitutional strength under apparent weakness, and he remained in harness as a writer up to a very advanced age. But his nervous equilibrium was easily upset by unusual exertion or excitement or by controversy and difference of opinion; his power of continuous concentration on difficult mental work was inferior to his wishes; and he became dependent on a routine of life adapted even to his whims and fancies.'[68] The serious illness of the late 1870s brought with it the frightening feeling that he was 'unlikely to be able to do any more hard work'.[69] The fear that the number of years left to him for academic work was strictly limited thereafter became something of an obsession with him. His personal correspondence amply demonstrates his concern with his own frailty. In 1901, for example: 'The work is very long; and my life is ebbing away.'[70] And again, also in that year: 'Now that I am getting to feel the deadening hand of age press heavily on me, I am looking more and more towards a future when I shall be silent except in so far as some faint echoes of my voice may be mingled in among the sounds of progress in which some of my old pupils are leaders.'[71] Or in 1910: 'I shall not live to serve up to table one half of the dishes which I have partly cooked.'[72] Or in 1914: 'I am able to work only for a very short time without a break: and my long promised book goes very slowly. I am quite well: but feeble. So I generally avoid letters and conversation.'[73] Or in 1915: 'I am in excellent health: wholly free from illness of any sort. But the smallest excitement sets up blood-pressure and cripples me for the rest of the half day. And I may not even write quietly for much more than an hour on end; and, still less, talk.'[74] One is bound to reflect that a man fond of declaring that 'my power of work is waning',[75] capable of excusing a delay in completion of a manuscript of at least 15 years by pleading 'weak health and constitutional unfitness for rapid work',[76] apt to describe himself as a 'worn-out old pedagogue',[77] is likely to prove a great trial to his friends and associates.

Becasue of the breakdown in his health Marshall resigned the Principalship in 1881 (but not the Professorship). His successor was William Ramsay. Ramsay, clearly not much impressed, described him privately as 'an ascetic man, all mind and no body. He hesitates in his speech and weighs things carefully.'[78] Freed from the yoke, Marshall spent the year 1881–2 (he was then 39) recuperating in the warm climate of Florence, Venice and Palermo, the Italian winter being financed by letting the house in Clifton, Bristol, and using part of savings made while he was Principal. This was a happy time: 'His powers were at the height of their fertility. There was no controversy, no lectures, no tiresome colleagues, none of the minor irritations to his over-sensitive spirit which Mary was to spend so much of her life soothing away.'[79] Mary sketched, shopped and looked after the invalid; Alfred, denied tobacco because of his kidney problem and the shortlived substitute of knitting and sewing because of his nerves, gradually resumed his scholarly labours; and it was in that year (most notably in the five months which the couple spent at the Oliva Hotel, Palermo) that work began in earnest on the *Principles*. Mrs Marshall reports: 'Book III on Demand was largely thought out and written on the roof at Palermo Nov. 1881–Feb. 1882.'[80] Keynes says: 'Mrs Marshall tells me that he hit on the notion of elasticity, as he sat on the roof at Palermo shaded by the bath-cover in 1881, and was highly delighted with it.'[81] It was precisely the health problems of the 1870s and the enforced sabbatical to which they led which stimulated the coming to fruition of some of Marshall's most penetrating insights; and for that reason Marshall's repeated description of himself as 'a man who has lost ten of the best years of his life – from 37 to 47 – through illness',[82] a man who 'between 1877 and 1887' had 'rather lost ground in his studies than conquered fresh',[83] should be taken, one suspects, with more than a small pinch of salt. However one might wish to describe those years of ill-health and subsequent recovery, it is very hard indeed to accept Marshall's own verdict – a 'barren decade'.[84] There can be few economists who would not jump at the chance of experiencing a barrenness of such exceptional and lasting fertility.

4 Oxford and Cambridge

Marshall returned to Bristol in 1882. It was, coincidentally, the very year in which Jevons was drowned while only in his forty-seventh summer. His premature death means that there is loss as well as hope to be detected in Foxwell's declaration to Walras in the last week of that year, that 'the ablest of our living Economists is Professor Alfred Marshall, University College, Bristol'.[1] Foxwell in 1884 once again expressed his admiration for 'Mr. Alfred Marshall, beyond doubt the most competent of living writers to judge of the value of Mr. Jevons' work on all its sides';[2] while in 1887, speaking of the rising standard of economic instruction in England in the sixteen years that had elapsed since the *Theory of Political Economy*, he said that 'among living writers there is no one who has done so much to bring about this advance as Professor Alfred Marshall'.[3] There is loss as well as hope to be detected in Foxwell's repeated use of the word 'living'. Things might have been different had Jevons lived. As it was, however, the loss of Jevons inevitably consolidated the hope that was associated with Marshall. Foxwell saw clearly what Marshall was worth. So did Jowett.

Benjamin Jowett (1817–93) was Master of Balliol and as such a Governor of the University College. He used to stay with the Marshalls when visiting Bristol. According to Mary, he enjoyed Alfred's company and held him in high esteem: 'He enjoyed discussing economic questions with Alfred and would bring out his little notebook and would take down a remark that specially interested him. He once told me that Alfred's talk was the best he knew. At another time he said: "Alfred is the most disinterested man I have ever known".'[4]

Jowett's principal subject was not economics, and when occasionally he taught it he seems not to have been entirely comfortable with its more abstruse technicalities (Sir Henry Studdy Theobald, a former student, recalled how once 'when someone asked him what was the relation between supply and demand he replied in his gentle staccato voice, "Well, you know, the world is a very large place."'[5]).

What Jowett did bring to economics was an inquiring mind which was simply not prepared to settle for the circus tricks of high theory such as are embodied in abstract formulations incorporating mathematical symbols: 'I do not object to their application to Political Economy', the Master wrote to Marshall in 1884, 'provided they are not regarded as a new method of discovery, but only as a mode of expressing a few truths or facts which is convenient or natural to the few whose minds easily absorb such symbols. Political Economy is human and concrete and should always be set forth in the best literary form: the language of symbols may be relegated to notes and appendices.'[6] Jowett, furthermore, a translator and an interpreter of Plato, consistently ranked right conduct above buying cheap and selling dear, and consistently expected other students of economic problems to share his concern with moral values: 'I should like to see a political economy beginning with the idea not how to gain the greatest wealth, but how to make the noblest race of men.'[7] Marshall in later years had occasion to write as follows of Jowett the moral economist:

> He took a great interest in political economy, especially on the social side . . . and he more than once preached on the right use of wealth. His teaching on the subject was admirably adapted to guide and stimulate: it was full of shrewd common-sense, and pithy hints as to details; and, at the same time, brought home to his hearers the responsibility under which money is spent, and led them towards high ideals in its use. . . . His sincerity was infectious. He knew how to get hold of what was best in men, and to make them good citizens. . . . A very great number of those who are forming public opinion to-day, or discharging high duties for the State, have learnt from personal contact with him, that money, though a good servant, is a bad master, and that private advantage is but poor exchange for the sense of having worked faithfully for one's country.[8]

Jowett practised what he preached: he paid for the son of his charwoman to do a degree at Cambridge, he sat up reading the Bible to a friend suffering from insomnia, he gave money to Ashley to have a holiday abroad, and he clearly intended that these kindnesses should be returned not to him personally but in the form of similar kindnesses shown to others in need. Balliol in the 1880s acquired a considerable reputation for high moral tone. One of the reasons for that reputation was the personality and impact of Benjamin Jowett, of whom Mary Marshall writes: 'I believe a secret of his influence was that he always seemed to take for granted that one was acting from the best motives, which made one ashamed of acting from any other. "Many a many by being thought better than himself has become better", said the Master.'[9]

Even when they had lost their faith in God, the lapsed Evangelicals of mid-Victorian England retained, in Noel Annan's words, a strong belief in 'right conduct, in the same ethical standards, in the supreme importance of the individual's relation to the Good.'[10] Annan's instance is Leslie Stephen, ordained Anglican clergyman turned 'militant agnostic', who himself declared in later life that 'I now believe in nothing . . . but I do not the less believe in morality' and about whom Annan observes as follows: 'The power of religion over the very minds which denied it is nowhere more subtly instanced than in Stephen's evolutionary ethics.'[11] Christianity for Stephen was dissolved into morality, and even into a science-based morality that derived the legitimacy of the laws from the strict imperatives of functionalism, organicism and adaptation to environment. The similarity with Jowett could not be clearer, that both men maintained that it was not the selfish self but rather the wider community that the individual was honour-bound to serve. The difference lies in the fact that Jowett was a committed Christian anxious to establish the Kingdom of God within each man on Earth and whose religious beliefs Geoffrey Faber has described as follows:

> The main conditions of human life have been willed by God; the institutions which men have contrived for their better living together, shaped by these conditions, have at least the value of a tried human solution to a divinely appointed problem. To turn your back upon the things of this world is not, on this view, a mark of true religion. It is better to do your duty in that state of life unto which it shall please God to call you . . . Jowett was the last man to prevent ability from finding its proper level. But to the doctrine that religion requires every man to do his job as well as it can possibly be done he gave his absolute assent.[12]

Alfred Marshall sharing so strongly this inner-worldly asceticism and this devotion to duty, it is no surprise that morality and mission should have been among the characteristics that caused the cautious agnostic and the committed Christian to recognise in the other a kindred spirit.

There were further similarities. A lifelong fascination with Plato's great interdisciplinary synthesis of economics and politics, for example: as Keynes reports, speaking of Marshall, 'one day in his eighty-second year he said that he was going to look at Plato's *Republic*, for he would like to try and write about the kind of Republic that Plato would wish for, had he lived now.'[13] Or, again, a belief in the abstract economic theory that had been developed by Ricardo, albeit fleshed out with the empirical evidence of which socially-contingent policy-proposals are made. Then there was a concern with evolution, both in the sense of Darwin (as in the case of Marshall contemplating the greatest uncertainty of old age: 'His greatest difficulty, he said, about believing in a future life was that he did not know at what stage of existence it could begin')[14] and in the sense of Hegel (as in the case of Jowett approaching the influential German when young and impressionable and subsequently exposing the Grail to his own disciples, including T. H. Green: Jowett 'said himself . . . that he had received a greater stimulus from Hegel than from anyone').[15] Temperamentally too, Marshall and Jowett had much in common. Shy, reclusive men, both with painful memories of an unhappy childhood, both victimised and lonely when at school (the Professor of Political Economy had been called Tallow Candles, the Master nicknamed Melchizadec), both moderately eccentric in later life (Jowett in particular seems to have been all too aware just how much his high-pitched voice, aversion to physical intimacy and conspicuous celibacy made him a figure of fun in a College which had for him, especially after the death of his sister, the important status of a surrogate family), both capable of displaying a redoubtable strength of character such as is not always to be encountered in persons of self-acknowledged frailty and vulnerability, the Professor and the Master obviously felt comfortable in each other's company. And thus did Marshall's years in Bristol come to an end. In 1883 Dr Jowett invited Marshall to become a Fellow of Balliol. The new statutes opening the doors to married Fellows at Oxbridge having just come into force, Marshall could equally well have returned to Cambridge. But, as he wrote to J. N. Keynes, 'after all Oxford is a rich and nearly empty field in economic work – we are sure we are right in making our choice'.[16] It probably did not escape Marshall's notice that the Drummond Professor of Political Economy, Bonamy Price (1807–88), was then a very old man, although apparently in good health.

The vacancy had arisen due to the unexpected death, at the young age of 30, of Arnold Toynbee, whom Herbert Foxwell quite correctly calls a 'unique figure among English economists': 'Sensitive, intensely sympathetic, altruistic almost to asceticism, his intellectual being seemed to rest, like a thin transparent crust, upon a deep suppressed sea of emotions.'[17] Jowett himself says as much – high praise indeed from the head of a crusading college where moral tone was not *obiter dictum* but *de rigueur*: 'The secret of his influence . . . was his transparent sincerity. No one could find in him any trace of vanity or ambition. Whether he received money or not, if he could only supply his moderate wants, was a matter of indifference to him. He was equally indifferent to the opinion of others, and probably never in his life said anything for the sake of being appreciated. He seemed incapable of entertaining a personal dislike to any one, and it may be doubted whether he ever had an enemy.'[18] Marshall describes him as the 'ideal modern representative of the medieval saint',[19] Ashley as a 'sensitive and overwrought scholar who lived a saintly life'[20] – and Koot, more cautiously, as a young man with a reputation for saintliness that must inevitably have owed something 'to his brief life, unsoiled by the compromises of maturity'.[21] Jowett tactfully observes of 'distinguished young men generally' how frequently 'it must be admitted that their best thoughts partake of the nature of dreams, which cannot be realised in the daylight of experience'.[22] Whether or not he regarded Toynbee as a case in point is not entirely clear. What is not in dispute, however, is his own personal admiration for the saintly youth who wrote, 'Every morning I read my Bible and the *Imitation*. I try daily to be good and unselfish; I am not very successful, but I do try'[23] and of whose mission on earth Alon Kadish has written as follows: 'Toynbee is representative of a confused and deeply troubled generation of Victorian middle-class, intellectual liberals. . . . With the help of T. H. Green and R. L. Nettleship he had emerged from an adolescent spiritual crisis with a strong sense of mission aimed at the realization of a moral, Christian commonwealth. With the Church's dogma, which he found unpalatable, safety separated from faith, and with faith expressed, and thereby defined, by duty and service, Toynbee approached the problems of modern industrial society with the confidence of a missionary.'[24]

Chief among those problems, in Toynbee's view, was that of poverty. As Jowett puts it: 'The "imitation of Christ" was to him the essence of Christianity; the life of Christ needed no other witness. His labours among the poor were constantly sustained by the conviction that some better thing was reserved both for them and for us; he saw them as they were in the presence of God; he thought of them as the heirs of immortality.'[25] His father, a surgeon, an FRS and a philanthropist, had been active with Edwin Chadwick and other social reformers in sanitation schemes and improved housing for the disadvantaged; and had sought to guide his own personal conduct not so much by Mill on individual rights as by Mazzini on *The Duties of Man*. Arnold's voluntary involvement in municipal politics and the Charity Organisation Societies in that sense only carried on the family tradition of self-sacrifice and community service (as opposed to the self-seeking self-interest of the utilitarians and the economists around him). Behind his work as a Poor Law guardian, in the University Extension Movement, in the friendly societies, would appear, moreover, to have been more than a modicum of the sense of guilt that too was the patrimony of a sensitive child born into the privilege of Savile Row affluence – a sense of guilt nowhere betrayed more vividly than in the following *mea culpa* proclaimed to a working-class audience in the very evening of his life:

> We – the middle-classes, I mean, not merely the very rich – we have neglected you; instead of justice we have offered you charity. . . . You have to forgive us, for we have wronged you; we have sinned against you grievously – not knowingly always, but still we have sinned, and let us confess it; but if you will forgive us – nay, whether you will forgive us or not – we will serve you, we will devote our lives to your service. . . . We will do this, and only ask you to remember one thing in return. We will ask you to remember this – that we work for you in the hope and trust that if you get material civilisation, if you get a better life, if you have opened up to you the possibility of a better life, you will really lead a better life.[26]

What the working-class audience made of this is less clear than is the undoubted sincerity of the speaker, together with his own personal sense of guilt.

The problem of poverty is the central concern of Toynbee's principal scholarly work, the *Lectures on the Industrial Revolution in England* (published posthumously, in 1884). Writing as an economic historian, Toynbee's conclusion was that the impact of the upheavals of the eighteenth century had been catastrophic for the working classes. The reason for the pauperisation was not mechanisation, he argued, but rather the replacement of human ties and shared traditions by 'brute struggle' and the cash nexus: 'The essence of the Industrial Revolution is the substitution of competition for the mediaeval regulations which had previously controlled the production and distribution of wealth.'[27] The Industrial Revolution, Toynbee seems to be saying, was not so much a revolution in technology and instrumentality as a revolution in market institutions and business practices. It was, more specifically, nothing other than freedom to compete that fostered the degradation and the immiseration of those dark days by removing the bulwarks of the traditional order that had previously prevented the weak from being trampled underfoot by the strong. Fortunately, Toynbee argued, those dark days of unfettered *laissez-faire* now belong to the past, and mankind has come increasingly to recognise that 'the whole meaning of civilisation is interference with this brute struggle': 'Competition, we have now learnt, is neither good nor evil in itself; it is a force which has to be studied and controlled; it may be compared to a stream whose strength and direction have to be observed, that embankments may be thrown up within which it may do its work harmlessly and beneficially.'[28] It is precisely the lesson of the Industrial Revolution that the 'competitive impulse' unguided by the man-made embankments and channels of 'wise regulation' can and will produce social abominations that a more enlightened citizenry will rightly refuse to tolerate: 'The effects of the Industrial Revolution prove that free competition may produce wealth without producing wellbeing. We all know the horrors that ensued in England before it was restrained by legislation and combination.'[29] Legislation and combination – the former captured by Alfred Marshall's own declaration 'So I cry "*Laissez-faire*:– let the state be up and doing"',[30] the latter by Marshall's vivid description of modern unionism as 'the greatest of England's glories',[31] and both, to Marshall as to Toynbee, important correctives to the 'ordeal of economic freedom' that scarred the unprepared Britain of the late eighteenth century: then 'free competition, or rather, freedom of industry and enterprise, was set loose to run, like a huge untrained monster, its wayward course. The abuse of their new power by able but uncultured business men led to evils on every side; it unfitted mothers for their duties, it weighed down children with overwork and disease; and in many places it degraded the race.'[32] Marshall may well have criticised Toynbee the scientist for providing heat when what was required was light – 'His intellect, fresh and vigorous as it was, was not the chief part of him: the leading controlling strain of his character was emotional'[33] – but it simply cannot be denied that he shared far more of Toynbee's passion with respect to the transitional excrescences of the Industrial Revolution than he would have wanted to admit. Together, of course, with a healthy respect for the pragmatism of Toynbee's twin correctives of legislation (the State) and combination (corporatist self-help).

With respect to legislation, Toynbee was a historian who had read Sir Henry Maine on *Ancient Law* and had drawn a surprising conclusion with respect to the British evidence on the stages of development: 'The real course of development has been first from status to contract, then from contract to a new kind of status determined by the law – or, in other words, from unregulated to regulated competition.'[34] Economic freedom, Toynbee took great care to stress, remains the *sine qua non* for rapid economic growth that is itself the key to rapidly rising wages: 'On the moral side, our political institutions, being favourable to liberty, have developed individual energy and industry in a degree unknown in any other country.'[35] At the international level as well as at the domestic, moreover, since 'foreign competition would prevent a knot of capitalists from ever obtaining full control of the market' – a lesson, Toynbee believed, which had sadly been lost on the tariff-minded Americans, with the entirely predictable consequences for living standards: 'Protection . . . diminishes real wages by enhancing the cost of many articles in common use, such as cutlery. It is owing to protection also that capitalists are able to obtain exceptionally high profits at the expense of the workmen. By combining and forming rings they can govern the market, and not only control prices but dictate the rate of wages.'[36] International freedom of trade had been the 'most prominent'[37] of the causes of national affluence since 1846, Toynbee believed, domestic freedom another; but these competitive forces had only so successfully worked their wonders because of the simultaneous recognition that 'the economic interest of the individual is certainly not always identical with that of the community' and therewith the introduction of State controls over the 'hundred and one devices of modern trade by which a man may grow rich at the expense of his neighbours'.[38] Where a trade is carried on with borrowed capital, for example, 'it may be a clever man's interest to sell as large a quantity of goods as possible in a few years and then throw up his business',[39] and in such a case, where the producer is more interested in a quick profit than in the defence of an old-established reputation, it is 'wise regulation' and not market freedom that must constitute the primary bulwark against fraud and adulteration, the exploitation of unequal information (necessitating public sector curbs on jerrybuilding) and the abuses born of unequal power (the case for State paternalism with respect to factory conditions and the provision of Boards of Conciliation). To say that Toynbee could have gone much further in his proposals for man-made law in preference to the natural order is to state the obvious. What is striking is just how important a role he assigned to legislation at a time when so many of his contemporaries denied that the competitive order was likely significantly to turn malign.

With respect to combination, Toynbee took as his point of departure Adam Smith's eulogy of beneficent outcomes founded upon equal rights and stressed the extent to which economic realities had made a nonsense of Smith's power-free theories: 'Liberty was to him the gospel of salvation; he could not imagine that it might become the means of destruction – that legal liberty, where there was no real economic independence, might turn to the disadvantage of the workman.'[40] Yet it is precisely the case that the economic strength of the employer is normally greater than is that of the employee; and had Smith only appreciated that fact, 'he would have discovered that what he sought to establish was the *free competition of equal industrial units*, that what he was in fact helping to establish was the *free competition of unequal industrial units*'.[41] Smith's error, Toynbee argued, was a simple one: he sought to abolish existing combinations (those of employers) when what was really needed was the countervailing power of new associations (those of employees). Such associations, fortunately, have indeed developed, and they have done great good: 'Trade-Unions . . . have done much to avert social and industrial disorder, and have taught workmen, by organisation and self-help, to rely upon themselves.'[42] They act as provident societies for members who are ill and old; they temper the excessive individualism of the times by setting a non-conflictual example of 'duty and the love of man';[43] and they provide training in small-group democracy such as was bound to appeal to the more secular theorist of stable social institutions that was Alfred Marshall.

Marshall shared with his eminent predecessor at Balliol a belief in unions and intermediate corporations; an advocy of wise regulations that provide appropriate channels for competitive freedom; a fear that competition unregulated was too savage to be tolerable; a concern with the problem of poverty. He also shared with Arnold Toynbee a concern with right and wrong expenditure which reveals, in the work of the one author as in that of the other, an almost total refusal to separate the economic from the ethical, the material from the moral. Thus it is that Marshall, shouldering aside the revealed preferences of sovereign consumers, was quick to weigh in with pertinent questions about the feedback effect of wants on activities: 'Even for the narrower uses of economic studies, it is important to know whether the desires which prevail are such as will help to build up a strong and righteous character.'[44] As with Marshall, so with Toynbee, who never missed an opportunity to marry personal to social religion by preaching that 'morality must be united with economics as a practical science'[45] and who expressed himself as follows on moral and immoral consumables:

> High wages are not an end in themselves. No one wants high wages in order that working men may indulge in mere sensual gratification. We want higher wages in order that an improved material condition, with less anxiety, and less uncertainty as to the future, may enable the working man to enter on a purer and more worthy life.[46]

As, happily, the Invisible Hand of evolutionary uplift powered by sustained economic growth was already having the beneficence to provide:

> Those who have had most experience in manufacturing districts are of opinion that the moral advance, as manifested, for example, in temperance, in orderly behaviour, in personal appearance, in dress, has been very great. . . . In 1855 there were nearly 20 000 persons convicted for drunkenness, in 1880 there were not many more than 11 000.[47]

Alfred Marshall was pleased to render a similar report: 'Doubtless some indulgences are positively harmful; but these are diminishing relatively to the rest. . . . Those drinks which stimulate the mental activities are largely displacing those which merely gratify the senses. The consumption of tea is increasing very fast, while that of alcohol is stationary.'[48] Both the Fellow of Balliol who placed Christian ethics above materialism and his secular successor who ranked morality above *Manchestertum* had therefore this in common, that consumer preferences, adaptational upgrading and the tone of life were in no sense and at no time to be seen as things apart.

Marshall replaced Toynbee at Oxford in 1883, one social missionary relieving another while keeping the nature of the mission surprisingly unaltered. Toynbee was gone, but his distinctive mix of personal altruism, social activism and historical investigation lived on in the work of the young Oxford economists whom he had inspired. It was the second tragic loss experienced by Jowett's Balliol in as many years: T. H. Green (1836–82) had died a year earlier, another Victorian idealist exhausted before his time by the burden of social duties and public service that was the practical concomitant of the notion of positive liberty. T. H. Green, full of missionary zeal, had preached a gospel of active involvement and other-regarding self-sacrifice which ranked good works and social reform above idle faith, passive contemplation and solitary piety. Steeped in the duty-based theories of Kant and Hegel somewhat more than in the utilitarian individualism of Bentham and Mill, Green's social idealism, his stress on community commitment and State intervention, had an exceptional appeal to the detribalised Englishmen of the late-Victorian period who desperately wanted an outlet for conscience and soul and could no longer make do with revelation. As Richter explains, speaking of Green:

> His work had an avowed religious purpose. He sought to replace fundamentalist Evangelicalism by a metaphysical system that would transform Christianity from a historical religion into an undogmatic theology. This would turn the attention of those disciplined in Evangelical families away from the means of personal salvation in the next world to improving the condition of this one. In politics as in theology, the doctrine of citizenship and reform developed by Green can best be understood as a surrogate faith appealing to a transitional generation.[49]

Green's social philosophy stressed self-help and cooperation, morality of intent rather than merely efficacy of outcome, corporate obligation above individual interest. The sheer generosity of its *freedom to* (which it ranked far above the gross amorality of *freedom from*), extending as it did to matters of State, actually rendered it, according to Richter, 'something close to a practical programme for the left wing of the Liberal Party'.[50] Of course the eminent libertarian Albert Dicey was also a Fellow of Jowett's Balliol; and the famous *Lectures Introductory to the Study of the Law of the Constitution* were actually delivered in 1884–5, the very year that Alfred Marshall spent at the College. Of course the *laissez-faire* social Darwinism of Herbert Spencer was then at its zenith – the essays on economic initiative, organic adaptation and the catastrophic errors of wise regulators that were to become *The Man versus the State* actually appeared in the *Contemporary Review* for 1884. But if rules-utilitarianism and anarchy plus the constable were in the air, so too was political pragmatism, both at the level of phenomena (the reform of the civil service, the Common Lodging-Houses Acts, the Contagious Diseases Acts, the Education Act of 1871) and at the level of ideas; and it was coincidentally also in 1884 that Jevons' own last word on State intervention appeared, in his posthumously published *Investigations*. The influential Jevons concluded that it would be foolish to lay down hard and fast rules, and proposed instead to treat every case in detail on its merits: 'Practical action in legislative and in ordinary matters almost always depends upon a balance of a great many advantages and disadvantages.'[51] The minimal State was in the air in the mid-1880s, as too was political pragmatism, and, most important of all, perhaps, for the sensitive in search of their soul, was T. H. Green – who, through his teaching and his writing (including his *Lectures on the Principles of Political Obligation*, published posthumously in 1885) and through his personal example (the demonstration of commitment to local government through service on the Oxford Town Council, to temperance through the establishment of a coffee-shop in that town), was rapidly coming to acquire the status of an intellectual superstar which his subsequent eclipse makes it all the more difficult for the present-day to grasp: 'Between 1880 and 1914', Richter has written, 'few, if any, other philosophers exerted a greater influence upon British thought and public policy than did T. H. Green.'[52] Toynbee Hall was being established and Canon Barnett often came to Oxford (and to Balliol) to enlist public-spirited young men willing to take up their cross among the neglected and the destitute in the squalor of the East End of London – Marshall obliged with a lecture in Autumn 1885 on 'The Pressure of Population on the Means of Subsistence' in which the childless Londoner with a strong belief in the value of good Anglo-Saxon genes appears conspicuously to have abstained from recommending preventive checks to the denizens of the Whitechapel Road.[53] The Charity Organisation Societies had just been founded as an outlet for philanthropic involvement – Mary Paley Marshall became a member in Oxford, as later she did in Cambridge. Even John Ruskin (who was in Oxford at the same time as Marshall, giving drawing lessons and fulminating against the ugliness of cash-nexus industrialism) became caught up in the gospel of personal activity and direct labour – as when he attempted to convert undergraduates from self-regarding sports to community-orientated work by enjoining them to improve, with him, a road through the village of North Hinksey. Ruskin was no great friend of the 'dismal science'. It would be fair to say, however, that the economists whom he accused of being indifferent to 'design' and 'function' (the kind of economists who made themselves the champions of 'illth' rather than wealth simply because there existed for it the effective demand of the greedy pig) were not entirely those who had passed through the purifying

brook of fire of Jowett's Balliol and Green's social religion – not
entirely economists, in other words, like Alfred Marshall.

At Oxford Marshall was spared Toynbee's administrative duties of
Tutor and Senior Bursar to the College (these had never represented
a particularly prestigious contribution for a man of Toynbee's standing, and were rightly deemed inappropriate for Marshall) but continued to lecture on political economy, particularly to probationary
candidates for the Indian Civil Service. Toynbee had taken his
responsibilities very seriously, recognising the impact that his students
were likely to have on the future administration of India. His successor, no less earnest a man, made an effort while at Oxford to learn
something about a part of the world with which he was initially hardly
well-acquainted. Marshall retained a lifelong interest in the subconti-
nent (which, however, he never visited), corresponding with Indian
economists and giving evidence to Royal Commissions when invited
to do so. While at Oxford, Marshall also had the opportunity to mix
extensively on a social basis with intellectuals and politicians of the
stature of Huxley, Matthew Arnold, Goschen, Mundella, Asquith
and Balfour: despite his initial shyness with strangers, Dr Jowett
upon closer acquaintance proved gregarious and fond of parties. And
it was at Oxford, at the Clarendon Hotel on 14 March 1884, that
Marshall became involved in a public debate with the American
radical and Ricardian socialist Henry George, whose *Progress and
Poverty* (appearing in America in 1880 and in Britain a year later)
had already sold 100 000 copies in the United Kingdom alone.
Marshall had given three public lectures in Bristol in February/March
1883 on themes connected with the book, and reports in the local
press indicate that he did not take very seriously the socialist's
hostility to private property in land, deduced though the proposals
for expropriation avowedly were from the insights of the great
Ricardo himself on the functionless surplus and the zero supply-
price:

> Some Socialistic writers have been men of great scientific capacity
> who have understood the economic doctrines which they have
> attacked. Mr. George is not one of these. He is by nature a poet,
> not a scientific thinker. The real value of his work does not lie in his
> treatment of questions that require hard study and clear thought,
> but in the freshness and earnestness of his views of life.[54]

Damning with faint praise (while conspicuously avoiding the central
point about rewards, incentives and productivity) is far easier in a

public lecture, of course, than it is in a direct confrontation. Marshall was fond of saying that he detested controversy. True though this undoubtedly was, his face-to-face exchange with Henry George (and later with Hyndman) in the four terms he spent in the shadow of the dreaming spires proves that he was not incapable of forcefully probing and parrying should the need genuinely arise.

Henry Fawcett (1833–84) had been Professor of Political Economy at Cambridge since 1863. His *Manual of Political Economy* of 1863 was a simplification of Mill's *Principles* – a popularisation which he never found time to follow up with a major original work not least because it cannot be easy for a blind man (let alone a sighted one) to be both Cambridge Professor and Cabinet Minister (as Postmaster-General) at one and the same time. In 1884 he died unexpectedly and Marshall, barely established at Balliol, his furniture barely unpacked after the move from 31 Apsley Road, Bristol, to 46 Woodstock Road, Oxford, was on 13 December of that year elected to the Chair. The choice was an odd one in view of how little he had published (each publication was bound to have attracted more attention, of course, than it would have done in a later period when incremental change in the technical literature was less modest and gradual), but undeniably a good choice in the light of what was to come. As early as 1879 Cliffe Leslie had been making the perceptive observation that Marshall's genius was not to be approximated by the number of his publications: 'Mr. Marshall has been known for several years, though less widely than if his pen had been more active, as one of the most accomplished and learned economists in England.'[55] Foxwell bleated in 1887 (three years *before* the *Principles*) that the new Professor was not to be regarded as just another Fawcett, just another Price: 'Half the economic chairs in the United Kingdom are occupied by his pupils, and the share taken by them in general economic instruction in England is even larger than this.'[56] Admittedly there were not many chairs in economics in any case; but for all that, the early emergence of Marshall as the great father-figure of the economics profession in Britain simply cannot be denied. His reputation as well as his achievement clearly had something to do with his success in 1884. Besides which, there appears to have been only one serious competitor for the chair, namely R. Inglis Palgrave. The Chairman of the Board of Moral Science was none other than Henry Sidgwick, who in that very year is known to have written 'Marshall is an old friend'.[57] Thus did Marshall once more land on his feet: Bristol was there when he needed it, Balliol when he grew tired of Bristol,

Cambridge when it was time to rise to his destiny, and all of this without family connections and inherited wealth. It is easy to see why Marshall in later life could be so open to the notions of self-help, meritocracy, *la carrière ouverte aux talents*, and so hostile to those spokesmen of the poor who blamed the rich and powerful for the misery of the failures: a man who accedes to a Cambridge Chair with little more than brains to recommend him is bound to wonder if it is not after all the poor themselves who are the guilty parties with respect to the crime of poverty.

In leaving Balliol, Marshall was leaving the spiritual home of Toynbee and Green – determined, however, to take back with him cuttings from the great tree of idealism which he hoped would take root and flourish in the more rational climate of the Cambridge colleges. As John Maloney puts it: 'Balliol was in the business of training missionaries, sacred and secular, and a missionary, in Marshall's eyes, was what Cambridge economics needed.'[58] What Cambridge economics did *not* need, on the other hand, was inevitably the excessive emphasis on empirical evidence and historical demonstration which, in Marshall's eyes, had rendered the Oxford economists all but incapable of making theoretical generalisations of practical utility for policy-purposes. His letter to Neville Keynes in 1888 concerning the Drummond Chair left vacant by Price's death (Keynes applied, Thorold Rogers was re-elected to the post he had held during the years 1863–8, and Keynes did not apply again in 1890 when Rogers himself expired) betrays nothing so much as the proselytiser's zeal to ensure that his own personal attempts to convert the anti-analytical heathen should not have been made in vain:

> I want you to consider this. You have, which I have not, the strength to carry through the work singlehanded at Oxford. You *would* be alone there. There is no one else who has given the best part of his life to mastering economic theory. On the other hand teachers of history abound there; there is a plethora of them. Putting aside all personal considerations, that seems to me (and I think it will to others) to be a sufficient ground for believing that you are *the* man wanted.[59]

He had earlier attempted to interest Keynes (without much success) in the Balliol post which he vacated upon his translation to Cambridge: he extolled Keynes's merits to Jowett and was apparently prepared to face the difficult years ahead without the aid of a colleague whom, even before his departure for Bristol, Marshall had come to regard as an ally. Such generosity is not untinged with interest when one reflects just how much Marshall would have liked to have seen the Oxford inductivists exposed to a dose of good solid logic such as Keynes (who had gone up to Cambridge in 1872 to read mathematics before switching to the moral sciences) would have been the ideal candidate to administer. If, of course, Marshall had felt that strongly about the Oxford heretics, he could himself have stayed on at Balliol in anticipation of the Drummond Professorship. Be that as it may, Cambridge beckoned, Marshall was obviously pleased to be going home at last, and he took up, early in 1885, the Chair which he was to occupy continuously until his retirement in 1908.

In Cambridge the Marshalls built a house, Balliol Croft, in Madingley Road, on land belonging to St John's College – the house cost them £1100. Alfred, we are told, 'was anxious to have his study on a higher floor, as he thought that in Cambridge it was well to live as far from the ground as possible'.[60] In summer he was able to sit out in the garden, which he enjoyed. He loved grass and trees but cared little for flowers, and once wrote as follows to Mary about vegetables: 'I have always held that a kitchen garden at its best is more pictur-esque than a flower garden at its best. There is more depth and serenity and unconsciousness.'[61] They had one servant for 43 years – Sarah – who, as Keynes points out, 'belonged to the Plymouth Brethren, the gloomiest sect of a gloomy persuasion'.[62] She appears to have had religious difficulties, culminating in all but annual threats to leave (normally in November – 'that most trying month',[63] as Mary described it). She was, according to Mary, 'troubled by the feeling that she was not being of enough use in the world, but was consoled when she realised that by good cooking she was keeping Alfred in health and was enabling him to write important books.'[64] She too had a mission.

Marshall loved his research and used to come down from his study and say, 'I have had such a happy time, there is no joy to be compared to constructive work.'[65] Another man might have been daunted by the enormity of the task and the sheer finitude of his own energies – two constraints on Alfred Marshall's mission which are admirably picked up by Hewins in the following observations con-cerning the Cambridge Professor: 'He was a slow writer, and said he thought he wrote on an average about seventeen words an hour and often when he had finished one chapter and gone on to the next, the development of the arguments in the new chapter forced him to scrap the former one, so he did not make very rapid progress. His

Principles of Economics is an admirable work, but too full of qualifications. He was attempting to do as an individual what, if it ever is to be done, can only be accomplished by a school of writers working together under a leader.'[66] Marshall was fully aware of these constraints. Oversensitive though he certainly was, what is very much to his credit is the fact that he never allowed despondency or self-doubt significantly to interfere with the deep if quiet enjoyment which he derived from his academic investigations.

Marshall had reclusive tendencies but was, however, hardly a hermit. Working-class leaders, trades-unionists, co-operators were often invited, particularly in the earlier days before 1900, to spend the weekend with him at 6 Madingley Road; and in that way Marshall came personally to know men of the calibre of Ben Tillett, Tom Mann and Thomas Burt. He also appreciated the company of fellow economists, both British (such as Edgeworth) and foreign (such as Pierson and Taussig). Despite his declaration in a letter to Wicksell that 'I *never* go to the British Association',[67] he in fact acted as one of the hosts when the BA came to Cambridge in 1904; and Sarah considered that week – when there were often twelve to dinner at the house – as one of the happiest of her life. When the Marshalls went on holiday (as, for instance, to the South Tyrol, where Alfred enjoyed the opportunity to walk – and to work – in the open air and where he seized the opportunity to meet Böhm-Bawerk and Wieser), they invited poor people from Southwark to use Balliol Croft for their own holidays while the Professor and his wife were abroad. He was not one to dine frequently in Hall or attend College functions, but his regular 'at homes' were another matter: 'I am "at home" for six hours in every week', Marshall wrote in 1894 to E. C. K. Gonner (with L. L. Price one of the two most distinguished candidates he had managed to influence in the year at Balliol), 'to any student who chooses to come to see me. . . . If he is interested in any matter, I pursue it at length, sometimes giving an hour or more to a point which is of no great general interest, but on which his mind happens to be troubled.'[68] Marshall took particular care with the detailed advice he gave to students about books: 'I never recommend the same list to any two. Nor will I give a man any advice at all till I know a good deal about his mind.'[69] Marshall was known to be a private man, but student after student has paid tribute to what A. L. Bowley (who was an undergraduate just after the publication of the *Principles*) has called 'a very remarkable and attractive personality': 'His attitude towards his students . . . was from the beginning of his

Professorship at Cambridge in 1885, one of a friend and adviser as well as that of a teacher. . . . There was never any doubt that outside the lecture room his house was the hospitable focus of all that was significant in Cambridge economics.'[70] Marshall encouraged his students to read widely and lent out his own books, as well as maintaining at his own expense a small lending-library for economics undergraduates in the University. He founded a triennial Essay Prize of the value of £60 to encourage original research and personally paid the stipends of £100 each to two or three young lecturers a year whom the University would not otherwise have been able to employ as teachers of economics. He himself lived on his professional salary – he did no paid examining, consultancy or journalistic work – and Maynard Keynes (who never tired of praising the great man's 'immense disinterestedness and public spirit')[71] said of the author of the bestselling texts that 'he never regarded books as income-producing objects, except by accident'.[72] Marshall, Keynes concluded, had little or no interest in financial success; and, indeed, 'used to say, when Macmillan's annual cheque arrived, that he hardly knew what to do with the money'.[73]

As a teacher, there is no question that Marshall was capable of being inspiring as well as stimulating, driven as he was by his double nature to combine the felt intensity of moral fervour with the highest standards of intellectual integrity in such a way as to produce an effect which Keynes describes as follows: 'The pupil would come away with an extraordinary feeling that he was embarked on the most interesting and important voyage in the world . . . convinced that here was a subject worthy of his life's study.'[74] Marshall's former student, C. J. Hamilton, writing from Patna in *The Servant of India* about a man whom he could not have seen for something like three decades, is particularly vivid on the hypnotic effect which the remarkable duality in his teacher's personality appears to have exercised:

> On the one side he was a recluse, a scientist, concerned with the accumulation of data and the entirely dispassionate tracing of cause and effect to whatever conclusions it might lead. On the other he was a prophet, an evangelist, almost an emotionalist. 'The Joys of Religion', he said, 'are the highest joys of which men are capable.' For him religion was the bettering of the common lot of his fellow-men.[75]

Marshall preached economics as well as taught it, and the result would appear to have been lectures that were, in the words of L. L.

Price, 'vividly alive and wonderfully instructive. One went away each time with something stimulating to think over. It might indeed puzzle or seem hard, but it was hard grit.'[76] William Cunningham himself went to hear Marshall in the early 1870s and found him, in the words of his daughter, 'an admirable teacher, extraordinarily lucid and with a love of paradox that was very stimulating'.[77] The *Oxford Magazine*, reporting on the lectures he delivered in his first term (Michaelmas 1883) at Balliol, said they were 'delivered without the use of notes and with considerable impressiveness of voice and manner' and were well-attended despite being awkwardly scheduled: 'Oxford has gained a very accomplished lecturer as well as a learned economist in Mr. Marshall', the *Magazine* concluded.[78]

Good students such as Benians (who attended his lectures in 1900–1901) were able to appreciate his teaching methods: 'He was certainly a unique teacher. He seemed to grip the mind of his hearer and force it through unaccustomed exercises, with many a violent jolt and breathless chase. He loved to puzzle and perplex you and then suddenly to dazzle you with unexpected light.'[79] Good students found him exciting, but the slow and the lazy must have been terrified by a lecturer who was prone to greeting them at the start of a new session with the reassurance that 'if you have come to me for the knowledge with which to pass the Tripos you will certainly fail. I know more than you and I shall defeat you. You had better go elsewhere.'[80] Marshall knew that his teaching methods were simply not suitable for the second-raters and the curriculum chasers, for 'students whose minds are merely receptive; and who require of their teachers to render plain their path in the systematic study of a text-book; or even to speak an elementary text-book at them if they cannot or will not find the time to read a text-book for themselves. . . . I always warn such students away from my lecture-room.'[81] Marshall was, as Pigou confirms, 'not out to get people through examinations; that sort of thing did not interest him at all'.[82] Of course, the rote-learners were frightened off by the lecturer's apparent lack of notes; by his conspicuous avoidance of systematic coverage in favour of seemingly *extempore* digressions; by Marshall's endearing propensity to talk, 'with complete discontinuity between one lecture and another, on any matter of economic interest that had occurred to him on the way to his class, or that the morning paper had suggested';[83] by Marshall's disarming custom of lecturing for twenty minutes and then announcing to the unquestioning scribblers that 'all I have been saying up to now is perfect nonsense'.[84] Yet it was not the rote-learners that

Marshall most wanted to influence, but rather those students who had come to University precisely because they had wanted to learn to think. As Mary Marshall remembered: 'He said that the reason why he had so many pupils who thought for themselves was that he never cared to present the subject in an orderly and systematic form or to give information.'[85] Students found his style as a lecturer more than a little bit demanding – and that, of course, was his intention:

> There is something to be said for a plan, under which the lecturer prepares beforehand sufficiently to require to use only a few notes as guide-posts: he then thinks the matter out as he goes, and *gets his class to think with him*. If he strays into an unpremeditated illustration or influence; the class, seeing the effort of his mind, and stimulated to work with it, will have their strength brought out more in a few minutes than it would be in an hour in which information is loaded into their minds as goods are loaded into trucks.[86]

The model, here as elsewhere in Marshall's work, is the acquisition of powerful intellectual machinery by means of constructive observation and instinctive sympathy: 'The best way to learn to row is to row behind a man who is already trained. . . . And so the trained teacher should, I think, work his own mind before his pupils', and get theirs to work in swing with his. The graduate picks up the swing quickly.'[87] L. L. Price detects something similar in his style as an author: 'The chief characteristic of Professor Marshall's writing seems to consist in its pregnant conciseness. It will not allow the student, even the junior student, to learn by rote; it compels him throughout to think for himself.'[88] When one reflects how difficult it was for even the best students to find a logical unity in Marshall's lectures – for Keynes in 1906 ('It was impossible to bring away coherent notes'),[89] for Benians five years earlier ('Marshall's style was not popular. . . . He did not impart information, but sought to awaken understanding. One gave up notetaking in despair. . . . I doubt if the originality of Marshall's ideas could ever be vindicated, as that of Adam Smith's has been, from a student's notes')[90] – one is tempted to excuse oneself, accepting Price's parallel, if occasionally one finds his *Principles* as elusive and as baffling as it is stimulating: Marshall was a teacher who sought to lead his class on 'until they had got pretty well into the middle of a real difficulty and then help them to find their way out',[91] but not every reader of the introductory textbook genuinely enjoys being challenged, being shaken out of his rut, in this manner. Besides which, Benians and Keynes had the benefit of conscientiously corrected essays and the opportunity to ask questions. The reader of the *Principles*, on the other hand, is on his own.

Marshall's teaching methods were not to everyone's taste. Nor, it must be said, was his personality; for the fact is that Marshall, and increasingly so as he grew older, was not only modest, polite and tactful but also strange and even eccentric. He had his table-knives electroplated to spare the labour of polishing – but they ceased to cut. He devised a form of boot with elastic webbing over the instep to spare the labour of fastening – but it let in the rain. He designed Balliol Croft in such a way as to provide every room with sunshine – but forgot to include stairs in the plan. He had a great sense of dignity and of his own authority (rightly so: as MacGregor observes, 'he could not help knowing that there was nearly as possible nobody else in the economic leadership'),[92] and thus appears to have accentuated his natural solemnity and even pomposity: rather than being a man of 'playful witticisms', Lionel Robbins concludes, Marshall was a detached ascetic 'whose sense of humour often seems to me to have been somewhere in the neighbourhood of absolute zero.'[93] Beatrice Potter (always a bit frightened by his intelligence and perspicuity) calls him 'the little professor, with bright eyes',[94] but the full account she renders of the man she saw deliver the Presidential Address to the Co-operative Congress of 1889 indicates that she regarded him, somewhat less affectionately, as all but a tourist in the world of reality: 'He looks every inch a professor. A small slight man with a bushy moustache and long hair, nervous movements, sensitive and unhealthy pallid complexion, and preternaturally keen and apprehending eyes, the professor has the youthfulness of physical delicacy. In spite of the intellectuality of his face he seems to lack the human experience of everyday life.'[95]

Even those closest to the 'little professor' seem to have shared Miss Potter's impression of him as a marginal figure. Thus his nephew, Claude Guillebaud, admitted to H. M. Robertson that 'Marshall really was in many ways a very odd and idiosyncratic individual. Keynes is said to have characterised him, as a human being, as "preposterous".'[96] The Keynes in question could have been either. Maynard Keynes (1883–1946), for example, who recalled in print after Marshall's death that the professor 'might sometimes seem tiresome and obstinate'[97] to his Cambridge colleagues, and went somewhat further in a conversation with Sir Roy Harrod: 'A very great man, but I suppose rather a silly one in his private character. . . . He was an utterly absurd person, you know.'[98] Or Neville Keynes (1852–1949), whose diaries abound in statements like 'Marshall's long disquisitions are very tiresome', 'Marshall said a good many silly things', 'I really have not time to be on a Board of which Marshall is a member',[99] and of which Maloney has written as follows:

> No careful reader of Keynes' diaries can fail to conclude that he disliked Marshall as much as Marshall liked him. Irritation with Marshall's behaviour on committees is a constant theme; examples could be quoted almost endlessly. Narrow and egotistical, a dreaded prospect as head of faculty, a dreadful bore, exceedingly irrelevant, 'the most exasperating talker I know', as ridiculous as usual . . . this is no more than a short-list. . . . The Keyneses entertained extensively: the diaries record every guest list for more than thirty years. Not once does Marshall's name appear. . . . In the light of this, Marshall's insistence that Keynes was his principal ally can only be seen as the wishful thinking of an isolated and disappointed man.[100]

Maloney's conclusion is that Marshall succeeded not because of a charming personality but rather despite a talent for generating antagonism and resentment. The important point, however, is that Marshall did succeed. Economics as a profession has had more than its share of eccentrics, and Marshall's standing, like that of Adam Smith, was evidently not much threatened by his strangeness. Wicksell and Veblen were not so fortunate.

5 Economics and *Principles*

Marshall arrived at Cambridge at a time of some crisis in the discipline. *The Times*, on 30 May 1885, was doing no more than stating the obvious when it commented as follows on his Inaugural Lecture, 'The Present Position of Economics': 'Political Economy is on its trial. It is not merely its relation to other branches of science which is under dispute. Its worth, its substance, its vitality are all denied.'[1] Less than a decade had passed since Francis Galton (founder of eugenics and for five years General Secretary of the British Association) had, in 1877, laid before the Council of the BA a paper proposing the abolition of Section F on the grounds that the discipline was simply not capable of prosecuting its inquiries in a scientific spirit: 'The general verdict of scientific men would be that few of the subjects treated fall within the meaning of the word "scientific".'[2] The status of economics was hardly improved by John Kells Ingram's impassioned reply, in his Presidential Address to the Dublin Meeting of the following year, that economics was in fact the science that 'has the most momentous influence of all on human welfare',[3] but admittedly not the narrow and abstract economics of Senior and Ricardo such as had caused sceptical public opinion quite rightly to regard the study of wealth and exchange with 'uneasy distrust'[4] and had brought upon the Section the justified contempt of Galton and other pure scientists whom the proper methodology of Comtean sociology would easily have been able to satisfy: 'If the proper study of mankind is man, the work of the Association, after the extrusion of our Section, would be like the play with the part of the protagonist left out. What appears to be the reasonable suggestion, is that the field of the Section should be enlarged, so as to comprehend the whole of sociology.'[5] What public opinion, together with Francis Galton and other pure scientists, made of this plea for replacing orthodox economics with a unitary social science is not known; but one doubts if Ingram's diagnosis of failure and prescription of interdisciplinarity did much to restore the professional standing of the subject-area at a time of some crisis.

Less multi-disciplinary than Ingram but, like him, committed to the inductivist approach that ranked historical evidence above analytical rigour, and collection of facts above general statements, were Walter Bagehot, William Cunningham and Bonamy Price. All three contributed to the atmosphere of crisis by attacking the timelessness and the universality of the deductivist economics, and by making clear that a wholly different approach to the wealth of nations was being developed by the historical school, British and German. All three in addition made public their belief that Adam Smith's great science had fallen from grace and come to deserve the odium which it had brought upon itself. Thus Walter Bagehot, in his paper 'The Postulates of English Political Economy', paid tribute to the great book of which he was marking the centenary in 1876 ('The life of almost everyone in England – perhaps of everyone – is different and better in consequence of it')[6] but added that, despite its past glories (including 'guiding the finance of Napoleon, who hated ideologues, and who did not love the English'),[7] the once-popular science of political economy was generally perceived in his own times to have run out of steam: 'It lies rather dead in the public mind. Not only does it not excite the same interest as formerly, but there is not exactly the same confidence in it. Younger men either do not study it, or do not feel that it comes home to them, and that it matches with their most living ideas.'[8] Two years later, writing in *Mind* on 'Political Economy as a Moral Science', William Cunningham was equally negative about the influence and standing of the speculations which only a half-century earlier had been the intellectual jewel in the crown of the workshop of the world:

> To those who are interested in Economic Science, few things are more noticeable than the small hold which it has upon the thoughts of our generation. . . . We find a widespread tendency to look upon its teachings with suspicion. . . . The mercantile public are not swayed by it; working-class leaders notoriously disregard it, and foreign statesmen do not pretend to listen to its preachings. Those who regard the teachings of the science as not only true but important truths, cannot ignore the general neglect into which it has fallen.[9]

A loss of ground from which Bonamy Price (whom Maloney describes, not without some justification, as 'an old gentleman who was never quite sure whether economic theory was impossible or merely undesirable')[10] was able, in his *Chapters on Practical Political*

Economy of 1878, to derive a certain grim satisfaction: 'The truths proclaimed by Political Economy are ultimately truisms – processes which have always been known to all the world',[11] Price maintained, and for that reason it was all but inevitable that ordinary people would opt one day to 'arrive at their judgements through their own untrained sagacity, and not through the teaching of authorities who must be taken as guides. It is the authority of economical writers which is declining. . . . Men take a shorter and far clearer path through their own observations than through the tangled jungle of scientific refinements.'[12] Economic laws such as supply and demand being 'mere tendencies', propositions totally without 'absolute and uniform character', the Drummond Professor of Political Economy felt compelled to state that 'to call them scientific principles is nothing but inflated language'[13] and actually to welcome the increasing reliance on common sense which he believed to be a characteristic of his times:

> To be accused of contradicting Political Economy is an argument which now carries less weight than it did formerly. The man to whom it is addressed will probably think that what is quoted to him as a law is probably no law at all. He feels that he can obtain what is important for him to learn in some easier way by the aid of his natural lights.[14]

Such a protestantisation of economic science, Bonamy Price suggested, was a development which even the learned professors of the redundant jargon ought to acknowledge as a genuine step forward. His diagnosis that 'general neglect' is a sign of progress, that scientific treatment of economic issues is doomed by its very nature ultimately to lie 'rather dead in the public mind', honestly meant though it undoubtedly was, can hardly have done much to boost the standing of Political Economy in its hour of need.

Multi-disciplinarians such as Ingram, historical relativists such as Walter Bagehot, William Cunningham and Bonamy Price, all had this in common, that they identified in the years immediately before and immediately following Francis Galton's unprecedented challenge a time of some crisis in the discipline. Deductivists such as Cairnes and Jevons would not have wished to disagree, at odds as they were not merely with the inductivists within the camp and the physical scientists at the gate but with one another at will. Thus Cairnes, aware of the new theories of marginal utility and the subjectivist, demand-based approach to the ratio of exchange that was to be found in

Jevons' book of 1871 ('I have certainly taken every pains to understand it'),[15] continued to champion the traditional classical orthodoxy
that value is an objective entity, resident not in the mind but in the
thing and explicable first and foremost in terms of supply: 'Cost of
production', Cairnes wrote in 1874, 'is undoubtedly the principal and
most important of the conditions on which normal value depends.'[16]
Cairnes can hardly have been very happy with what he must have
seen as Jevons' attempt, in 1871, to stand the true system of economics on its head by means of declarations such as the following:
'Cost of production determines supply; supply determines final degree of utility; final degree of utility determines value.'[17] Nor would
Cairnes, had the author of *Some Leading Principles of Political
Economy Newly Expounded* of 1874 not expired in 1875 at the
relatively young age of 52, have been entirely satisfied with the
celebrated assessment of his most influential theoretical forebear that
was to appear in the Preface to the 1879 edition of the *Theory of
Political Economy*: 'When at length a true system of economics
comes to be established, it will be seen that that able but wrong-
headed man, David Ricardo, shunted the car of economic science on
to a wrong line.'[18] Wish as he might that things were different,
however, Cairnes would have had no choice but to agree with Jevons'
declaration in 1876 that recent theoretical innovations had seriously
shaken up the discipline, to the extent that 'respect for the names of
Ricardo and Mill seems no longer able to preserve unanimity':[19] 'In
short, it comes to this – that one hundred years after the first
publication of the 'Wealth of Nations', we find the state of the science
to be almost chaotic. There is certainly less agreement now about
what political economy is than there was thirty or fifty years ago.'[20]

Jevons was too tactful to point out that it was not merely the
strengths of the demand-based theories that had led to the chaos but
the widely-perceived weaknesses of the classical economics itself.
Foxwell says: 'After the appearance of Mill's *Principles*, English
economists, for a whole generation, were men of one book.'[21] Yet it
is hardly in the best interests of standards and advance for scholars
slavishly to devote themselves to the exegesis of a single great work;
and in that sense it must be true to say that the intensity of the
controversies in the 1870s owed a great deal to the relatively high
degree of complacency and consensus in the two decades that preceded the *Theory*. Besides that, Mill's *Principles* was not in itself a
book that could appeal to all sectors of the community. Unionists, for
example, objected strongly to the manner in which it championed the

wages-fund doctrine, which stated, in its simplest form, that combination stood no real chance of improving pay: 'Wages . . . cannot rise, but by an increase of the aggregate funds employed in hiring labourers, or a diminution in the number of the competitors for hire.'[22] The unions took issue with the economists for espousing a doctrine which had already been proven false by events. They must have been delighted with Mill's own recantation in 1869: his acceptance of W. T. Thornton's criticisms fully 21 years after the first appearance of his book, together with the growing belief that the laws of population and of diminishing returns were similarly open to question, cannot but have played its part in undermining residual confidence in the validity of the classical theories. Neither Ricardo nor Mill could be relied upon, moreover, for an explanation of the depressed conditions (the fall in agricultural prices, for example) that afflicted large segments of the British economy between 1873 and 1896: prosperity lost, in contrast to prosperity gained, appears, in the words of Coats, to have caused many who had previously been willing to accept the conventional wisdom quickly to discover 'in the state of trade ample evidence of the deficiencies of the laws of political economy. Thus the public attitude toward the science cannot be dissociated from the circumstances of the time.'[23] If the depressed conditions of the 1870s caused a fickle public to become disenchanted with the faithful companions of a century's progress, then so too did the – perhaps quite undeserved – reputation of the thinkers from Smith to Mill for opposing even moderate social reform and for championing a radical form of *laissez-faire* which many regarded as outdated and undesirable: protectionists were particularly virulent in blaming what they saw as the free-trade cosmopolitanism of the classical economists for undermining Britain's industrial potential. An *ad hoc* approach to State intervention was in the air, and a Jevons was known to supply what the *Zeitgeist* demanded: 'I do not in the least underestimate the wastefulness of government departments, but I believe that this wastefulness may be far more than counterbalanced in some cases by the economy of public property.'[24] A Smith or a Mill had said the same and said it frequently, but always at times when the late-nineteenth century was out to lunch or otherwise engaged. The classical economics became linked in the popular mind with the minimal State. As the minimal State was increasingly called into question, and not least by the depressed conditions that were the silent witnesses to the great debates of the marginal revolution, so therefore was the fossilised ideology that was generally taken to be that of the classical economists.

Jevons had formulated his *Theory* in terms of the eternal verities of physics (notably gravitation and equilibrium) and most of all of mathematics (as he asserted was implicit in Adam Smith's great work: 'I hold that his reasoning was really mathematical in nature').[25] His confidence in the scientific value of the constant and the mechanistic was not shared by the social biologists and the social Darwinians such as Herbert Spencer (1820–1903), who were at their most influential in the troubled years that separated Jevons' *Theory* from Marshall's *Principles*. Their insistence upon organism (not design), perpetual dynamics (not comparative statics), progressive evolution (not random mutation), general interdependence (not individualistic atomism), inevitably played its own small part towards rendering the period a time of crisis in the discipline of economics. A public increasingly stimulated by the neo-classicals to believe that the science was principally concerned with the allocative choices made consciously and deliberately by rational housewives and self-interested businessmen must have been at a loss to know what to make of the macroeconomic objectivities *as if* in possession of a life of their own that are eloquently encapsulated by Spencer in passages such as the following: 'We cannot cut a mammal in two without causing immediate death. Twisting off the head of a fowl is fatal. . . . If in high societies the effect of mutilation is less; still it is great. Middlesex separated from its surroundings would in a few days have all its social processes stopped by lack of supplies.'[26] Spencer's starting point is growth, and most of all the manner in which the division of labour, both in the individual and the social organism, is productive of a seamless web of mutual support in which everything depends on everything else:

> In both kinds of organisms the vitality increases in proportion as the functions become specialised. . . . Along with advance of organisation, every part, more limited in its office, performs its office better; the means of exchanging benefits become greater; each aids all, and all aid each with increasing efficiency; and the total activity we call life, individual or national, augments.[27]

Thus is organic betterment at one and the same time the result of past differentiation and the cause of future, *as if* guided by an Invisible Hand: 'Under primitive government the repression of individuality is greatest, and . . . it becomes less as we advance.'[28] The model is the 'frequently recurring struggle for existence'[29] which Darwin claimed to have found in Malthus on population pressures and competition for subsistence, which he described as the adaptive force of natural selection, and which his study of animal and vegetable kingdoms led him most emphatically to laud: 'Natural selection . . . is a power incessantly ready for action, and is as immeasurably superior to man's feeble efforts, as the works of Nature are to those of Art.'[30] Darwin supported his defence of the unplanned as against the man-made with the illustration of variation in the quality of pelts: 'It is well known to furriers that animals of the same species have thicker and better fur the more severe the climate is under which they have lived.'[31] The *Origin of Species* is moderately less lucid but in a sense even more revealing on the moderately less familiar topic of the functionality of sterile females in ant-colonies: 'We see so many strange gradations in nature, as is proclaimed by the Canon, "Natura non facit saltum".'[32] *Natura non facit saltum* – Darwin's phrase has a strangely familiar ring. These things happen.

Economists debating Jevons on the last unit of happiness or Walras on the *prix crié au hasard* will no doubt have found it difficult to derive any direct inspiration from Darwin on pelts and ants, Nature and Art – but Herbert Spencer did, making the Darwinian theory of adaptive upgrading the centrepiece of his argument that intervention by politicians and civil servants in the natural flow of social processes is deeply misguided; 'The great political superstition of the past was the divine right of kings. The great political superstition of the present is the divine right of parliaments.'[33] Spencerian economics is about nothing so much as the superiority of the 'industrial' over the 'militant' society – and about the catastrophic fate that awaits that foolish society that seeks to substitute compulsory coordination for the spontaneous rendering of mutual services on a voluntary basis:

> Practical extinction may follow a gradual decay, arising from abolition of the normal relation between merit and benefit, by which alone the vigour of a race can be maintained. And in yet further cases may come conquest by peoples who have not been emasculated by fostering their feebles – peoples before whom the socialistic organization will go down like a house of cards, as did that of the ancient Peruvians before a handful of Spaniards.[34]

The feebles in the Dickensian workhouses or in the slums and the sweatshops depicted in 1883 in the Reverend Mearns' *Bitter Cry of Outcast London* were in one sense regarded by Spencer as the justifiable pathologies of other people's progress. Only in one sense, however, for Spencer was an evolutionary thinker with a strong conviction that 'human beings are cruel to one another, in proportion as their habits are predatory';[35] and that with freedom of trade and increasing affluence inevitably come character-traits such as kindliness, generosity, benevolence and charity such as ensure (perhaps somewhat unexpectedly in a model firmly rooted in the notion of the survival of the fittest) that even the losers will be winners and will be given prizes. Spencer's insistence that self-policing ethical values enjoy a high income-elasticity of demand may be somewhat unexpected but it is also quintessentially Darwinian, since the year that saw the publication of Jevons' *Theory of Political Economy* was also the year in which the *Descent of Man* sought to demonstrate empirically the functionality not merely of the 'love-antics' of various genera of Australian birds and the ornamental feathers of the Indian drongo but (Adam Smith's *Theory of Moral Sentiments* of 1759 is cited approvingly in this connection)[36] of 'patriotism, fidelity, obedience, courage, and sympathy'[37] as well. Even a savage would sacrifice his life rather than betray his fellows, his other-regarding devotion to the common good being precisely what is required if his collectivity is indeed to survive:

> When two tribes of primeval man, living in the same country, came into competition, if the one tribe included (other circumstances being equal) a greater number of courageous, sympathetic, and faithful members, who were always ready to warn each other of danger, to aid and defend each other, this tribe would without doubt succeed best and conquer the other.[38]

If other-regarding traits were required for the survival of the collective whole, then other-regarding traits would be sure to develop within the character-patterns of the approbation-seeking, blame-avoiding individuals who are the discrete cells of the social organism:

> As the reasoning powers and foresight of the members became improved, each man would soon learn from experience that if he aided his fellow-men, he would commonly receive aid in return. From this low motive he might acquire the habit of aiding his fellows; and this habit of performing benevolent actions certainly strengthens the feeling of sympathy.[39]

And thus it was that Darwin and Spencer were able so confidently to predict the evolution of altruism and of honesty; for moral upgrading in their view, far from being incompatible with the survival of the fittest, was in truth the precondition for that survival and for sustained growth as well. Their methodology and their hypotheses, it would be fair to say, were somewhat at variance with those of classicals and neo-classicals alike. By opening yet another front, the social biologists and the social Darwinians inevitably confused the public still further as to what it was, precisely, that the economists were seeking to achieve.

The social biologists and the social Darwinians had a great deal to say about survival of the fittest. So too, calling it the competitive market and freedom of enterprise, did virtually all other schools of economics. Naturally enough, the morality and the modifications were also there, together with the instinctual sympathy and the social virtues which render the economic man not red in tooth and claw but only a dainty shade of pink. Once again, however, when it came to the *caveats* and the qualifications, the sad truth is that the late-nineteenth century was simply not listening. Not listening but also commenting; and saying in particular that the perceived crisis in the discipline was due not merely to internal differences but also to the distorted image of human nature which seemed to be the economists' stock in trade. It was that image, Jevons said, which had caused many in 1876 to take the view 'that the political economists had better be celebrating the obsequies of their science than its jubilee', and which was a principal reason why the subject had never been a popular one: 'I am aware that political economists have always been regarded as cold-blooded beings, devoid of the ordinary feelings of humanity – little better, in fact, than vivisectionists.'[40] The dismal science which, in the celebrated exaggeration of the distinguished satirist, had wished to solve the Malthusian problems of too many people and not enough food by encouraging the poor to eat their children was in that sense, in the 1870s and early 1880s, passing through a period of some crisis in the discipline, not merely because the Spencers did not speak to the Cairneses and Jevons had next to nothing in common with Ingram save for a shared resentment of Galton, but also, quite simply, because it was perceived by many to be a science of illth, not wealth, of the stomach and not the soul. Particularly influential in the attack on the 'Midas-eared Mammonisms'[41] of the learned professors who wished to substitute Greatest Happiness for Greatest Welfare, on the 'ossifiant theory of progress'[42] which relies on interest rather than duty when the truth is that 'no human actions ever were intended by the Maker of men to be guided by balances of expediency, but by balances of justice',[43] were the writings of romantics and moralists such as Carlyle (who proclaimed himself deeply offended by 'the Stygian mud-deluge of Laissez-faire, Supply-and-demand,

Cash-payment the one duty')[44] and Ruskin, whose last word on the economic scientist seems to be that 'the man who does not know when to die, does not know how to live':[45] 'Among the delusions which at different periods have possessed themselves of the minds of large masses of the human race, perhaps the most curious – certainly the least creditable – is the modern *soi-disant* science of political economy. . . . I do not deny the truth of this theory; I simply deny its applicability to the present phase of the world.'[46] Once upon a time, Ruskin said, the world was poor enough genuinely to require the sordid services of the professional economiser of scarce resources. Those times, however, are not our own, and with affluence comes the new imperative of ensuring that things do not leap into the saddle and ride man. That new imperative is clearly not satisfied by the dodo economics handed down from the past which has become inappropriate for the needs of the present:

> The real science of political economy, which has yet to be distinguished from the bastard science, as medicine from witchcraft, and astronomy from astrology, is that which teaches nations to desire and labour for the things that lead to life; and which teaches them to scorn and destroy the things that lead to destruction.[47]

Ruskin's example of the relationship between consumables and lasting satisfaction – a parable concerning the wreck of a ship – is particularly evocative: 'One of the passengers fastened a belt about him with two hundred pounds of gold in it, with which he was found afterwards at the bottom. Now, as he was sinking – had he the gold? or had the gold him?'[48] Ruskin's illustration finds counterpart after counterpart in the work of the no-less high-minded Carlyle, who started from the premise that 'things. . . . are growing disobedient to man'[49] and proceeded thence to the conclusion that 'our successful industry is hitherto unsuccessful'[50] by means of the observation that 'we have sumptuous garnitures for our life, but have forgotten to *live* in the middle of them. It is an enchanted wealth; no man of us can yet touch it.'[51] The good life is not an economic commodity, Carlyle stressed, and he was sharply critical of the learned professors for arousing the unrealistic belief that true wellbeing can be acquired via the cash-nexus. That way, Carlyle said, lies deep unhappiness and the most terrible frustration, pointing to the perversions of plenty which he found all around him in his own affluent society – 'Many men eat finer cookery, drink dearer liquors – with what advantage they can report, and their Doctors can';[52] 'With gold walls, and full barns, no man feels himself safe or satisfied';[53] 'Money is miraculous. What miraculous facilities has it yielded, will it yield us; but also what never-imagined confusions, obscurations has it brought in.'[54] Money-worship, Carlyle said, has led 'almost to total extinction of the moral-sense in large masses of mankind'[55] – an inversion of the Spencerian schema which was a cause of considerable anxiety to Ruskin as well: 'If we once can get a sufficient quantity of honesty in our captains, the organization of labour is easy, and will develop itself without quarrel or difficulty; but if we cannot get honesty in our captains, the organization of labour is for evermore impossible.'[56] Money-worship, Carlyle argued further, leads to a divided society in which the idle rich live shoulder to shoulder with the needy poor and where, 'in the midst of plethoric plenty, the people perish'[57] – an additional indicator of moral decline, and one which not unexpectedly was capable also of provoking the ire of Ruskin: 'Luxury at present can only be enjoyed by the ignorant; the cruellest man living could not sit at his feast, unless he sat blindfolded. . . . Whereas it has long been known and declared that the poor have no right to the property of the rich, I wish it also to be known and declared that the rich have no right to the property of the poor.'[58] Money-worship, Carlyle announced finally, was fundamentally incompatible with the *laborare est orare* that was so central to the social thought of an eminent Victorian who liked to quote from Schiller that *Ernst ist das Leben*: 'All true Work is Religion: and whatsoever Religion is not Work may go and dwell among the Brahmins, Antinomians, Spinning Dervishes, or where it will; with me it shall have no harbour.'[59] As with Carlyle, so with Ruskin, whose North Hinksey improvement scheme was intended to be doubly beneficial to the impressionable undergraduates who took part in it by teaching them the profound satisfaction which practical labour in the service of a beauteous environment could yield. Toynbee was aboard and glad of the opportunity. It is unlikely that many pure inductivists or detached deductivists, classicals or neo-classicals, social biologists or social mechanicals were there as well. They regarded Carlyle and Ruskin as over-emotional utopians who knew nothing of practice. Carlyle and Ruskin regarded them as money-grubbing suppliers and demanders who knew nothing of right and wrong. There was little love lost between the calculative men of markets and the instinctual men of morals, largely because there was little love there to begin with; and thus did yet another locus of dissension contribute in its own way towards the popular perception in the 1870s that the period was indeed one of crisis in the discipline of economics.

Given the divisions and the dissensus, the acknowledged loss of confidence and the perceived state of crisis, it is in a sense surprising just how successfully the dinner went that was held by the Political Economy Club at the Pall Mall Restaurant on 31 May 1876 to celebrate the centenary of the *Wealth of Nations*. Gladstone was in the Chair: with Cobden and Bright he could reasonably claim the lion's share of the credit for having translated Adam Smith's great insights on free trade into economic reforms. The speakers could hardly be expected to have agreed on all questions and in fact they did not: scarcely had one speaker sat down, for example, after identifying as Smith's 'most remarkable achievement' the demonstration that the main truths of political economy are not to be collected *a posteriori* by the statistician but rather derived *a priori* by means of logic proceeding from 'assumptions with regard to what mankind will do in particular circumstances, which assumptions experience has verified and shown to be true',[60] but another speaker was on his feet to declare of Smith that 'of all writers on Political Economy he was the one man who least of all started from hypothetical theories. . . . On the contrary, he always appeals to facts, *i.e.* he framed inductions for the conclusions at which he arrived.'[61] While the latter speaker (Thorold Rogers, who had produced an edition of the *Wealth of Nations* and was closely acquainted with all the references) was arguably more knowledgeable about the great Scotsman's greatest work than was the former (Robert Lowe, a mere Chancellor of the Exchequer), the crucial point is that each was really referring at least as much to his own perception of what it is that economists should do as to the insights of the distinguished pioneer whom the dinner was intended to honour – and that they clearly did not agree.

In the circumstances, therefore, it is remarkable that the evening went as well as it did. Thus Robert Lowe (with, it must be said, a practical politician's conspicuous lack of sensitivity) drew the conclusion that the house of economic science was more or less complete:

At present, so far as my own humble opinion goes, I am not sanguine as to any very large or very startling development of Political Economy. . . . The controversies that we now have in Political Economy, although they offer a capital exercise for the logical faculties, are not of the same thrilling importance as those of earlier days; the great work has been done.[62]

And George Norman (a founder-member of the Club some 55 years earlier – the only survivor of the original team to be present) mentioned the great names of Ricardo, the two Mills, Malthus, Tooke and then reinforced the assessment that had been made by Lowe by proclaiming the old theories not only unvanquished but actually 'unattackable': 'It seems to me that the real doctrines of Political Economy as they were first taught by Adam Smith, and as they were subsequently explained by the persons whose names I have ventured to quote, remain unimpeached; that they have never been successfully attacked; that they are, in fact, unattackable; that they are true now and will be true to all time.'[63] Neither Lowe nor Norman seems to have had any idea of just how divided the discipline of economics had become and was popularly perceived to have become; but *The Times* of 30 May 1885 knew – and Alfred Marshall knew. The opening paragraph of *The Times* on Marshall's Inaugural Lecture contained the memorable phrase 'Political Economy is on its trial'. The opening paragraph of the Lecture itself contained a phrase which is no less memorable: 'Never was there a science more urgently in need of all the work that all her best sons could give her than Economics is now.'[64] What Marshall said was true and all but Lowe and Norman knew that it was true. The divided discipline in a state of crisis was in the circumstances anxious to learn with which camp the much-unpublished new professor of economics would ultimately opt to associate his influence and prestige. Marshall's Inaugural Lecture, 'The Present Position of Economics', gave to practitioners and observers alike the unambiguous statement of intent which they so urgently required.

Comteans, British and Continental, had argued for the absorption of pure economics into the multi-disciplinarity of a generalised sociology. Marshall took the opportunity of his Inaugural Lecture to reveal that he was entirely in sympathy with their aspirations: 'One of the chief debts which we owe to Comte's genius, lies in the clearness and vigour with which he showed how complex social phenomena are, how intricately interwoven with one another, and withal how changeful.'[65] The Lecture even supplies a vivid illustration of its own of the manner in which internalised social norms (via an appeal to the generosity or the sense of duty which form part of a given common culture) in combination with non-ego social sanctions (not excluding the informal power of public opinion) can provide a source of motivation fully as powerful as that of money: 'Sometimes indeed the gratitude, or esteem, or honour which is held out as an inducement to the actions may appear as a new motive: particularly if it can be crystallised in some definite outward manifestation; such as for instance in the right to make use of the letters C. B., or to wear a star or a garter.'[66] Marshall, in short, took the opportunity of his Inaugural Lecture to reveal just how much he was in sympathy with the unified social science of the Comteans – except, of course, for the mundane practicality that 'it does not exist; it shows no signs of coming into existence'; and 'we must do what we can with our present resources' rather than 'waiting idly for it'.[67] That mundane practicality apart, however, the multi-disciplinary ideal itself Marshall pronounced as good; and thus did the Comteans go home happy from Alfred Marshall's Inaugural Lecture.

Inductivists had pressed for an economics rooted firmly in historical experience and statistical evidence, deductivists for an economics proceeding by logic and reason to develop robust theories with predictive power and a comprehensive framework of interpretive hypotheses having the force of social laws. Marshall took the opportunity of his Inaugural Lecture to convey his belief that they were right. The inductivists were right because 'there is wanted wider and more scientific knowledge of facts',[68] and that is why the investigations of the historical school had been so valuable:

> It would be difficult to overrate the importance of the work that has been done by the great leaders of this school in tracing the history of economic habits and institutions. It is one of the chief achievements of our age, and is an addition of the highest value to the wealth of the world. It has done more than almost anything else to broaden our ideas, to increase our knowledge of ourselves, and to help us to understand the central plan, as it were, of the Divine government of the world.[69]

The deductivists were right because 'facts by themselves are silent',[70] and that is why the guidance on selection and grouping of the analysers and the generalisers had been so important: 'In order to be able with any safety to interpret economic facts, whether of the past or present time, we must know what kind of effects to expect from each cause and how these effects are likely to combine with one another.'[71] The deductivists were right and most right of all when they founded their theoretical speculations on the studies of real-world phenomena that had been conducted by the inductivists: 'Such studies have led directly to some broad generalisations that have greatly illumined our path with a broad diffused light, which has made our notions as to the general bearing of economic problems clearer and truer.'[72] The inductivists were right, and most right of all when they employed as their map in the collection of their raw data the carefully-prepared intellectual schemata that had constituted the unique contribution of the deductivists: 'The growth of the science is itself chiefly dependent on the careful study of facts by the aid of this knowledge.'[73] To the deductivists was given the 'chiefly dependent', to the inductivists 'the central plan, as it were, of the Divine government of the world'; and thus did the inductivists and the deductivists alike go home happy from Alfred Marshall's Inaugural Lecture.

Social biologists and social Darwinians had championed the analogy of human society not with a manufactured machine but with a growing organism. Marshall took the opportunity of his Inaugural Lecture to identify himself with 'the biological group of sciences' of which the star, he made clear, was in the ascendant, and to distance himself from any approach to human phenomena which assumes a subject matter that is 'constant and unchanged in all countries and in all ages'.[74] Matter is in motion, said the middle-aged Hegelian with his finger on the pulse of the *Philosophy of History*; evolution is taking its course, said the student of time absolutely continuous who was soon enough to announce that 'the Mecca of the economist lies in economic biology rather than in economic dynamics';[75] distinctive 'stages of development'[76] in human societies are clearly to be identified, said the student of List, only once more in his lifetime to substitute peak after peak for perpetual ascent;[77] and the upshot of this process of mutability without interruption, said the convinced adaptationist with a tendency towards environmental determinism, is the increasingly widespread perception that 'man himself is in a great measure a creature of circumstances and changes with them'.[78] Human nature being a variable and not a constant, Marshall stressed, what is needed is not a unique body of economic dogmas so much as different theories relating to different times and different places. A believer in improvement and betterment, moreover, he took the view that change was not random but progressive; and thus did the social biologists and social Darwinians go home happy from Alfred Marshall's Inaugural Lecture.

Romantics and moralists had called for an anti-economics in which beauty and service would replace injustice and greed. Marshall took the opportunity of his Inaugural Lecture to praise the insights of all anti-economists (not excluding the 'wild rhapsodies' of the socialists, 'men who felt intensely')[79] and to pay tribute to the fact that it was they who had stumbled upon 'hidden springs of human action of which the economists took no account': he clearly felt that he himself had found something of lasting importance in their 'shrewd observations and pregnant suggestions'[80] and reassured them that economists and philosophers were increasingly learning from their work. Marshall went further and tried to communicate to his shrewd and pregnant friends the important intelligence that they in fact harboured a desperately distorted notion of what it was that economists actually thought and did. Of course economists use the *quid pro quo* construct and concern themselves preponderantly with pecuniary incentives – but this interest in money is merely an 'accident': economics is a quasi-psychology that explores the balancing of desire against denial, and it so happens, at least 'in the world in which we live', that 'money, as representing general purchasing power, is so much the best measure of motives that no other can compete with it'.[81] Of course economists are frequently associated with the anti-Statism that some German writers have come to call *Smithianismus* – but even Adam Smith himself 'admitted that self-interest often led the individual trader to act injuriously to the community'; and in any case *laissez-faire* 'was not his chief work'.[82] Of course economists (precisely because of their interest in market-exchanging and the quantification of motivation) are prone to utilise a self-interest axiom – but this axiom must be read not as stating that the economic man is believed to be greedily self-seeking but merely as indicating that the learned professors regard him as an animal in whose nature it is consciously to weigh costs against benefits in such a way as to render his behaviour-patterns essentially predictable: 'Whenever we get a glimpse of the economic man he is not selfish. On the contrary he is generally hard at work saving capital chiefly for the benefit of others. The fact is that the desire to make provision for one's family acts in a very regular way and is eminently capable of being reduced to law: it is prominent in all economic reasoning, because, though unselfish, it is measurable.'[83] Of course economists present themselves as value-free searchers after truth rather than as socially-committed social reformers ('It is true that an economist, like any other citizen, may give his own judgement. . . . But in such cases the counsel bears only the authority of the individual who gives it: he does not speak with the voice of his science')[84] – but a discipline of which a central maxim is happiness, and a popular methodology the subjectivist, will inevitably be led by its own internal logic to favour the relatively deprived ('taking account of the fact that the same sum of money measures a greater pleasure for the poor than for the rich'),[85] and it must be remembered in addition that it is the poverty-stricken who stand most to gain from the universal upgrading through more efficient allocation and more rapid growth to which the dismal science makes so glorious a contribution (reflecting 'the faith, that modern economists have, in the possibility of a vast improvement in the condition of the working classes').[86] Economists, Marshall indicated, were not cynical money-maximisers who wanted nothing so much as to beat the poor with the iron law of wages, but rather men of conscience and soul who were on the side of altruism in the ongoing struggle against oppression; and thus did the romantics and moralists go home happy from Alfred Marshall's Inaugural Lecture.

Neo-classicals such as Jevons had sought to shunt the car of economic science back on to a right line; neo-Ricardians such as Cairnes were in favour of leaving the car shunted precisely where the classical greats had shunted it. Marshall in his *Principles* was later to bring peace and not the sword by proclaiming utility and cost not substitutes but complements: 'We might as reasonably dispute whether it is the upper or the under blade of a pair of scissors that cuts a piece of paper, as whether value is determined by utility or cost of production.'[87] Marshall in his Inaugural Lecture was less concerned with esoteric technicalities such as demand and supply. He took the opportunity of his Inaugural Lecture to express his belief that the Ricardians were deep thinkers who 'did not, however, make their drift obvious'[88] (a point which was later to reappear in the assertion that Ricardo 'knew that demand played an essential part in governing value' but, being a poor communicator prone to taking short-cuts, regrettably confused posterity when he 'passed it lightly over').[89] He indicated further than Jevons too had done good work and would have made an even greater contribution 'if his life had not been cut short'[90] (a point which seems to be crying out for amplification into the conjecture that Jevons, had he lived, would have provided a companion to his utility-based theory of demand in the form of a disutility-based theory of supply – Marshall's failure ever to pursue this speculation is all the more remarkable in view of the fact that there is, arguably, more truth in it than there is in his interpretation of Ricardo on demand). Marshall in 1885 made clear that Ricardo and Jevons were both worthy of attention, but he had nothing further to say about the law of value or the conditions of exchange; and thus did the neo-classicals and the neo-Ricardians go home less happy from Alfred Marshall's Inaugural Lecture than they would have done had their Solomon deigned to address himself to their primary concerns. Marshall could not reasonably be expected, however, in the space of a single Inaugural, to throw a bone to *every* dog. Their bones, moreover, had not been forgotten and were yet to come. The theory of value apart, however, it is to the credit of Marshall's Inaugural Address on 'The Present Position of Economics' that it gave to practitioners and observers alike the unambiguous statement of intent which they, living in a period of some crisis in the discipline, so urgently required.

It also gave them hope and inspiration; for Marshall, becoming a Cambridge professor, had not lost sight of his 'patron saint', the down-and-out, or of the terrible blight of poverty which he had identified long before the results of empirical investigations such as those of Charles Booth in the East End of London *circa* 1889 (published over the years 1889 to 1903) and of Seebohm Rowntree in York in 1899 (published in 1901) had shocked public opinion into a recognition that Disraeli's 'Two Nations' were divided by nutrition and health as well as by accent and Ascot. On the contrary; for Marshall, becoming a Cambridge professor, saw himself as being better placed than ever before to translate generous sentiments into economic and social realities. His Inaugural Lecture concludes with his promise to devote himself to the task:

> It will be my most cherished ambition, my highest endeavour, to do what with my poor ability and my limited strength I may, to increase the numbers of those, whom Cambridge, the great mother of strong men, sends out into the world with cool heads but warm hearts, willing to give some at least of their best powers to grappling with the social suffering around them; resolved not to rest content till they have done what in them lies to discover how far it is possible to open up to all the material means of a refined and noble life.[91]

Such a concern with service to the poor and the degraded is hardly what one would have expected from a learned professor in 1885 (to say nothing of later times); but it is precisely what one would expect from a secular missionary who, defining himself to be an idealist and a crusader in the mould of Wilberforce and Shaftesbury, Florence Nightingale and Dr Livingstone, Gordon of Khartoum and the martyrs who took up the white man's burden, was anxious to do good.

Marshall would not have denied that he was an idealist and a crusader, but he would have wished to add that he was a materialist and an evolutionist as well – that , in short, he was a professional economist, and for that very reason not merely a preacher of the *ought-to-be* but also a builder of an *is* which the preacher in him could contemplate with pride and pleasure. To study allocative efficiency, to promote economic growth, Marshall believed, is by its very nature to turn on the tap of social as well as economic progress; and in that sense every economist, anxious or not, is led *as if* by the Invisible Hand that drafted his job-description to become actively involved in the doing of good. Thus change normally means improvement – in consumer preferences, from alcohol and ostentation to tea and durability; in character-patterns, from inward-looking egotism to honesty, respect for persons, the pursuit of excellence and generosity alongside the deliberateness which modern business life is more widely recognised to breed and form. Change, of course, can have its negative side as well – as where the consumer opts for manipulated fashions in preference to the stabilities of aesthetics; or where the family comes under threat due to increasing opportunities for wives and mothers to take paid employment outside the home; or where speculative gambling fosters deviousness of character and opens the door to credit-cycles emanating psychologically from changes of mood; or where healthy competition either turns cut-throat and zero-sum or, alternatively, is superseded by the price-fixing of the powerful cartel.[92] Marshall never denied that there could arise aberrations on the road to advance. What he did believe, however, is that exceptions are exceptions and the rule is the rule. Looking around him at rising living standards, falling interest-rates, improving education and an overall upgrading of the labour-force from unskilled to skilled, Marshall concluded that 'we never find a more widely diffused comfort alloyed by less suffering than exists in the western world today'[93] and declared himself proud to be an economist.

To be an economist – and not to be a socialist; for, despite an early 'tendency to socialism'[94] which first becomes apparent in his paper of 1873 on 'The Future of the Working Classes' and was evidently much stimulated by his reading of Mill's essays on the subject of socialism in the *Fortnightly Review* for 1879, Marshall by 1885 had become convinced that his mission was linked to gradual upgrading and not to sudden (perhaps violent) upheaval. An important landmark was the paper which he presented to the Industrial Remuneration Conference. The delegates, unimpressed by his plea for patience and his defence of slowly-rising pay proportioned to slowly-rising productivity, apparently found the professor's attitude 'timid' and his proposals 'paltry'. What they missed was the evolutionary dimension and the long-term theory of social progress via free and competitive markets which provides the legitimation for the short-run moderation of demands that the professor so strongly recommended to their attention. Other members of the working classes had less difficulty in seeing in Marshall not a capitalist hack determined to shunt the car of labour on to the wrong line of low pay and exploitation but rather a man of humanity with a sincere commitment to the masses. Thus Edgeworth states that 'Marshall's success in handling the theory of wages was largely due to his sympathy with the wage-earners. . . . I can well believe what I have heard from the Principal of Ruskin College that work-people studying the *Principles of Economics* recognized in the author a sympathetic friend.'[95] Besides which, of course, the 'ultimate goal' which was the pot of gold at the end of the rainbow in the paper which Marshall presented to the Industrial Remuneration Conference of 1885 was in truth one with which many high-minded representatives of labour, even if not the delegates to the Conference itself, must inevitably have wished to identify themselves: 'I hold that the ultimate goal for all endeavour is a state of things in which there shall be no rights but only duties; where everyone shall work for the public weal with all his might, expecting no further reward than that he in common with his neighbours shall have whatever is necessary to enable him to work well, and to lead a refined and intellectual life, brightened by pleasures that have in them no taint of waste or extravagance.'[96] The money-minded delegates to the Conference of 1885 appear not to have shown any real appreciation of the fact that the philosopher in the sense of Kant turned economist in the sense of Smith was propounding to them an economic ideal reminiscent of nothing so much as the socialist principle 'From each according to his ability, to each according to his need'. Whether money-minded businessmen were significantly more alert in recognising in the state of things 'in which there shall be no rights but only duties' a potential threat to themselves is less well-documented. Certainly they would have been quick to spot the danger if only they had been party to the nervous professor's innermost thoughts – thoughts that must be inferred from unpublished observations such as that 'economic rights are economic wrongs justifiable only in order to prevent greater wrong'.[97] Private property, Marshall noted to himself, is the *sine qua non* for risk-taking and experimentation that are the *sine qua non* for economic growth and thence for social progress; and 'if it were not, it would be true that

"Property is theft" and the rich man would deserve only less condem-nation than the society which tolerated his existence'.[98] Such a defence of private property in terms of social function and little else is as unlikely to appeal to that rich man as is yet another unpublished note (one headed 'The future of mankind'), in which Marshall analyses various socialist alternatives and then concludes with emphasis: *'But the time for all this is not yet'*.[99] What is not now is *yet* to come, Marshall seems to be saying; and that is why that rich man is likely to identify in the opponent of socialism (in the man who in 1909 said that he regarded 'the Socialistic movement as not merely a danger, but by far the greatest present danger to human well-being')[100] a natural enemy in the form of an implicit proponent of evolutionary socialism (a man who, also in 1909, made known his continued ranking of social duties above individual rights: 'Morally everyone is a trustee to the public – to the All – for the use of all that he has').[101] The mature Marshall's views on socialism, one is compelled to state, are somewhat less clear than is the fact that the youthful Marshall had a 'tendency to socialism' – a tendency which first becomes apparent in his paper of 1873 on 'The Future of the Working Classes' and which may (or may not) have exhausted itself by the time of the important contribution which Marshall made in 1885 to the proceedings of the Industrial Remuneration Conference.

The paper to the Industrial Remuneration Conference has a further significance in that it contains early references to two of the themes with which Marshall's name was later closely to be identified. The first of these is 'economic chivalry' and the importance of ethical constraint in the decentralised market economy – a topic which was to recur elsewhere, notably in the *Principles* and in the 1907 paper on 'Social Possibilities of Economic Chivalry'. The second was the notion of a tabular standard of value and of indexation as a means of combating crises born of uncertainties and adjustment-lags: as early as 1887, in his 'Remedies for Fluctuations of General Prices', Mar-shall was to return to the subject of nominal and real values, making specific proposals as to how the index was to be calculated, indicating that the provision of this public good, like all others, was properly the responsibility of the State, and stressing that the employment of an index for purposes of contract was to be on a voluntary basis. Meanwhile, in 1886, in his 'Graphic Method of Statistics', Marshall made an attempt to apply the concept of elasticity which had come to him in Palermo. In 1889 he delivered the Presidential Address to the Twenty-first Annual Co-operative Congress (and praised the cooperative mode of corporate self-help for assisting the individual both to get more out of society's scarce resources and to develop his higher nature through integrated action within intermediate collectivities, larger than the family but smaller than the nation). In 1890 he delivered the Presidential Address to Section F of the British Association for Advancement of Science (and praised freedom of trade, domestic and international, for its role in the encouragement of competitive conditions, while simultaneously showing his awareness of the extent to which trusts and cartels were already emerging abroad in consequence of scale-economies). All in all, therefore, Marshall's first five years as a Cambridge professor were good ones for him, pleasant and productive.

They were also the years in which Marshall completed the great neo-classical synthesis which, almost two decades after Jevons' *Theory*, finally filled the perceived gap in the literature that had been left by the intellectual upheavals of the 1870s and 1880s. Few books in the history of economics have had greater influence or represented state-of-the-art thinking for a longer period of time. In the words of F. W. Taussig:

> As with Adam Smith, so with Marshall, the beginner who has been introduced into the subject as currently expounded, and then has been led to explore among the great writers of the past, quite possibly will get an impression similar to that of the youth who read *Hamlet* for the first time: he did not think much of it, because it was so full of quotations.[102]

Marshall himself sensed the importance of his *Principles*: as Sir Frederick Macmillan was later to recall, he 'had little doubt that this book would at once take a leading place in the literature of Economics'.[103] Marshall also sensed that, influential or not, the book would be his *magnum opus*, and said as much in 1887 in a letter to his publishers: 'I am writing a book on "Economics", which will cover about the same ground as Mill's Political Economy. . . . The book will be the central work of my life; and I shall regard it differently from anything I have written or may write.'[104] Because he wanted his book to reach as wide an audience as possible, he specifically requested (an important request in a pre-paperback period) that the publishers set a low price for the volume: 'I should like the price of the octavo edition to be not very high: partly because books on economics are read by many students whose means are small, and who are not taking the subject up for examination, so that they avoid high priced books on it.'[105] Macmillan seem in fact to have reduced their proposed price in deference to Marshall's wishes.

Macmillan wanted to use Marshall's *Principles* as the basis for an experiment in resale price maintenance; and the great advocate of freedom of trade, curiously enough, gave his permission for the restrictive practice to be attempted. It is unlikely that he would have consented to this mode of price-fixing by the producer if he had fully grasped all the details of the scheme in advance. By 1898 he was better informed and confessed that he had made a mistake: 'I cordially approved the net system, for my book, when it was suggested to me. But that was because I misunderstood the proposal. I thought that it aimed at giving the bookseller about 1 sh. or at the outside 1/6 as profit on orders to cash buyers, with of course freedom to charge more on credit accounts.'[106] What it did in fact was to prevent booksellers from offering discounts for settlement in cash. Marshall was deeply embarrassed and wrote as follows to the publishers: 'My opinion that cash payments ought to be encouraged and not discouraged grows. . . . I have the strongest objection to being a party to any imposition, by however indirect a method, of penalties on booksellers on the ground that they sell books for cash at a lower price than for credit.'[107] His embarrassment was magnified by his growing conviction that the imperfection was causing booksellers to obtain an unjustifiably large share in the price of books appealing by their nature to a small, specialist audience:

> As an economist I feel that the progress of the world is seriously impaired by the recent growth of combinations in many trades; whereby prices are adjusted not naturally and in proportion to services rendered, but artificially in proportion to superiority in tactical strength of the contending parties. None are weaker tactically than the writers of grave scientific books: and I think it a great evil that booksellers should be helped to derive a disproportionate share of their profits from the small earnings – often none being left – of men whom the public ought to subsidize rather than select for specially heavy burdens.[108]

The position of the scholarly author is, Marshall believed, a singularly exposed one even at the best of times: 'Those few people who resist the temptation to write rapidly, and who like to do their best slowly, are those whom the public ought to subsidize. But if they are young they are generally meek and little acquainted with business. If they are old they are inclined to be indifferent about money.'[109]

Either way, they ought not to be exposed to the depredations of greedy booksellers such as the net book scheme served to encourage. Marshall was in the circumstances deeply embarrassed by the fact that he had originally given his consent to the experiment. Nor can he have been very pleased by the extension of the restrictive practice to other books in consequence of its financial success in the case of his own.

Marshall had intended that his *Principles* should be in two volumes. Volume II (which never appeared) was to be 'more concrete'[110] than Volume I and was to cover topics such as foreign trade, money and banking, credit and fluctuations, collectivism and taxation, and 'aims for the future':[111] somewhat optimistically, perhaps, in view of his propensity to combine perfectionism with a prolixity which made the professor himself wonder if he was not too 'long-winded' ('My book do grow: Oh! It *do* grow! B. B. Bother it!!',[112] he moaned to Neville Keynes in the course of completing his Volume I), Marshall planned that the second volume should follow the first within the space of two years. Volume I (the numeral was only deleted in the sixth edition of 1910, when the sub-title 'An Introductory Volume' was added) was the more abstract and theoretical of the two volumes: Marshall's lasting contribution to economic science would clearly have been very different if it had been the first volume rather than the second that was abandoned, and students who quarry their principles from Marshall's should therefore keep in mind that they have before them only a part of the syllabus to which the secular missionary had intended that they should be exposed. There is more to Marshall's *Principles*, in other words, than supply and demand, value and distribution, treated analytically. More, in fact, than Marshall himself ever came to write.

Volume I appeared in July 1890. The print-run was 2000 copies. The book was 754 pages in length, cost 12/6, and was clearly 'the work of a man who had been studying and thinking economics for a quarter of a century'.[113] It was an instantaneous success, critical and popular. The *Manchester Guardian* said that it 'will inform and stimulate everyone who reads it' and that 'it has made almost all other accounts of the science antiquated or obsolete'; the *Daily Chronicle* that 'it will serve to restore the shaken credit of political economy, and will probably become for the present generation what Mill's *Principles* was for the last'; the *Saturday Review* that 'this book is, without doubt, among the most important contributions to political science made by English authors within recent times. . . . Mr.

Marshall had vindicated Political Economy from the reproach of being a thing of dry and unreal abstractions'; *The Times* that 'this great treatise on Economic Science bids fair to take for the present generation the place which Mr. Mill's work took for the generation of forty years ago. . . . It is a contribution of capital importance to the higher literature of economic science.' The *Bristol Western Daily Press* loyally paid tribute to 'Professor Marshall, whose wonderful book, "The Principles of Economics" has made him the greatest authority on the subject', while the *Leeds Mercury*, in a similar vein, declared the book to be 'original and even brilliant': 'Professor Marshall's *Principles of Economics* is, in our judgement, without exception, the most valuable and suggestive contribution to political economy which has been made in this country during a considerable term of years.' Such was also the judgement of J. S. Nicholson, writing in *The Scotsman* ('There can be no question that it is the most important and valuable contribution to the general theory of political economy, whether in this country or abroad, since the publication of J. S. Mill's *Principles*') and of F. Y. Edgeworth, writing in *The Academy* ('*Natura non facit saltum*, the motto which Professor Marshall has adopted, is not altogether appropriate to a treatise which advances the position of science as it were by leaps and bounds'). As with Nicholson and Edgeworth, so with *The Journal of Education*, which recognised an important book when it saw one: 'All who interest themselves in Political Economy are aware what a wealth of harmony, what a strictness of argument, what general good sense and sobriety of tone characterize the first volume of the "Principles of Economics".' All in all, therefore, the position was more or less as Schumpeter depicts it , that 'the *Principles* were received with a universal clapping of hands, and the newspapers, which at first were rather cold to the *Wealth*, vied with one another in complimentary full-dress reviews of the *Principles*'.[114]

Particularly perceptive were those reviews which saw what Marshall did not say, that he regarded the abstractions and the theories of his Volume I as no more than the means to some higher end. The review in *The Athenaeum*, for example: 'What perhaps pleases us most in Professor Marshall is that he can retain his clearness of vision, his sharp mathematical accuracy of perception, while sharing to the full the most enthusiastic reformers' sympathy with distress and their desire for a more equitable, or at least a more humane, distribution of the goods of this world.' The review in *The Athenaeum* correctly identified in Marshall's book the seriousness of purpose of the born social reformer. So too did the review in *The Church Times*: 'In the opening pages of this great work we are practically told that Political Economy is the Study of Poverty; or at least that the question *whether Poverty is necessary* gives its highest interest to economics. That the Cambridge Professor, the ablest living of the orthodox English economists, should strike this note at the beginning of his book is significant of much; and especially of the greater hopefulness of modern political economists.' The review in *The Church Times* correctly identified in Marshall on the wealth of nations a wealth of hope with respect to poverty and disadvantage. So too did the later review in *The Christian Commonwealth* which found in Marshall's book a 'gospel of abounding hope' with respect to conduct and character as well: 'It is a great uplift for the mind to turn from the dismal predictions of those politicians who talk so ignorantly about "human nature being what it is" and "the natural laws of economics", and other meaningless phrases of a similar kind, to the extraordinary, inspiring insights of a leading political economist. . . . They help one to see brighter visions and to dream nobler dreams. . . . All who believe in the essential goodness of human nature and in the power of an in-dwelling Spirit, will rejoice and be glad.'

Some reviewers, it is clear, were able to find in Marshall's *Principles* a message of material and moral betterment such as served in some measure to justify self-seeking individualism and the never-ending process of maximisation. Other reviewers saw in it the long-awaited successor to Mill's *Principles*, the much-delayed content that was at last to fill the much-perceived vacuum. The two strands, the *why* and the *how*, the evolutionary and the technical, come together in the enthusiastic review of Marshall's book which appeared in *The Observer*: 'Since Mill's work on political economy was published, we know of none, except, perhaps, Karl Marx's disquisition on *Capital*, which can approach it for fulness of knowledge and rich variety of practical illustration. . . . Not a fact essential to a complete knowledge of economic science escapes his close analysis. There is not one generous aspiration of the age with which he is not in sympathy.' It bears eloquent testimony to the 48-year-old professor's clarity of expression that not all reviews were able to discern the distinguished author's duality of purpose – and that *The Observer* should have known so little about him as to take him for a collectivist: 'Professor Marshall, we believe, is classed as an "economic Socialist", or, as they would say in Germany, "a Socialist of the Chair". His duty, however, in this work has been that of an expositor and a critic. He has thus been careful to betray no sign of partisanship.' What Marshall made of this compliment is not known. What is known is that genuine socialists did not repeat *The Observer's* mistake by regarding the learned professor as one of them. Thus Sidney Webb, on an outing in Epping Forest with Beatrice, mentioned that he was to review the *Principles* for the *Star* and betrayed a reaction which can best be described as lukewarm: 'It is a great book, nothing new – showing the way, not following it. For all that, it is a great book, it will supersede Mill. But it will not make an epoch in Economics. Economics has still to be re-made.'[115] *Justice*, which spoke for the Social Democratic Federation and for the leftist ideas of H. M. Hyndman, was somewhat less moderate: Alfred Marshall, it complained, 'has just said nothing in 750 pages. He declares that Marx was a noodle. Why doesn't he try to prove it?' Not only does Marshall fail to prove that Marx was a noodle, *Justice* percipiently pointed out, but his *critique* of the iron law of wages is simply not supported by the scientific evidence: Professor Marshall, the journal therefore recommended, 'should re-examine the facts before he again attempts to theorise'. Even *Justice*, however, could not in the last analysis prevent itself from interjecting a note of praise for a socially-minded economist who clearly was no friend of the economic man: 'Nevertheless, it is something that Professor Alfred Marshall, improving upon Professor Sidgwick's incomprehensible eclecticism, has begun to examine the problems of society from the point of view of the community at large.' The Marshall of the *Principles* was probably not still (or, alternatively, possibly not yet) a socialist; but even *Justice* evidently found something in his book that evoked a positive response.

Not so *The Nation*, which, virtually alone in this respect, published a virulent condemnation of the work. Its conclusion is totally unambiguous: 'We do not consider this treatise, regarded as a whole. . . . to possess great scientific value.' The reasons for its extreme antipathy are somewhat more difficult to discover, however, as the review is couched in a rhetoric which is in the event stronger on emotion than it is on logic:

> Professor Marshall's book is altogether too big. . . . His book is full of repetitions – careless and unnecessary repetitions. The same similes are repeated at length in almost the same words; the same instances are quoted again and again. . . . It becomes exasperating to the last degree to be told, not once and again, but scores of

times, after a subject has been taken up, that further consideration
of it must be postponed to a later period in the investigation; and
few readers have the patience to go back and gather up these loose
ends when the time comes to weave them in. . . . We cannot
regard this practice otherwise than as indicating a feebleness of
grasp, an inability to bring unity out of diversity, that seriously
impairs the value of the work.

The Nation was apparently more exercised about Marshall's style
than about Marshall's content. Marshall's style was not quite self-
indulgent enough to merit so negative a reaction, but there is no
doubt that it is difficult and that even his admirers found it difficult:
thus even Edgeworth, in his generally enthusiastic account of Marshall's treatise on upgrading through growth ('He deliberates upon
the means to that great end with the cautious sagacity of an economist who has probably made fewer mistakes than any other equally
original writer on the most difficult of the sciences'), felt compelled to
comment, in his review in *The Academy*, not only on the 'painfully
small print' in the Mathematical Appendix and Notes, but also, more
significantly, on Marshall's propensity to treat of the same subject in
different places ('And the student may complain that he is not
sufficiently assisted by the index in bringing together all the remarks
relating to the same topic').[116] J. S. Nicholson, in his review in *The
Scotsman*, eschewed all such criticisms. What he was saying in his
private correspondence about Marshall and his book is, however, a
different matter: 'His history is vague, old-fashioned and excessively
weak; his examples are mainly of the old a priori kind or at best
curious rather than important; the repetition is so great that the plan
must be faulty; and if he is to cover the whole ground of what I
understand by Political Economy he will at the same rate take 6
volumes.'[117] A different matter it may well be, but the fact remains
that Nicholson in public was not Nicholson in private – and that
Nicholson in public undeniably joined his voice to the great chorus of
praise with which British economics welcomed the publication in July
1890 of Marshall's great *Principles*.

The *Principles of Economics* is a unified system. The connecting
link is the functional interdependence between marginal utility (normally diminishing) and marginal sacrifice (normally increasing). The
disparate elements in the single whole include the following: partial
and general equilibrium, internal and external economies, time-
periods and market structures, entrepreneurship and expectations,
substitution and elasticity, consumer's surplus and quasi-rent, *ceteris*

paribus and social progress, perfect knowledge and radical uncertainty, mathematical analysis and historical evidence, the stationary state and perpetual dynamics, representatives and normals, price-formation in free markets and the scope for State intervention, the problem of poverty and the nature of monopoly. Marshall's synthesis is clearly an intensely ambitious one, drawing together so many individual insights and reconciling the perspectives of so many different authors and schools of authors. His greatest intellectual contribution is his search for cohesion and his recognition that the atomistic parts are meaningless save when situated within the context of an integrated whole. It is his greatest intellectual contribution precisely because it so closely parallels at the level of ideas and doctrines the fabric of economic interdependence that is of such fundamental significance at the level of phenomena. Thus Schumpeter has written as follows of the greatest theorist of unification and synthesis:

> Unlike the technicians of today who, so far as the technique of theory is concerned, are as superior to him as he was to A. Smith, he understood the working of the capitalist process. In particular, he understood business, and businessmen better than did most other scientific economists, not excluding those who were businessmen themselves. He sensed the intimate organic necessities of economic life even more intensively than he formulated them, and he spoke therefore as one who has power and not like the scribes – or like the theorists who are nothing but theorists.[118]

The motto of his *Industry and Trade* was *The Many in the one, the one in the many* – a principle of interrelatedness that is none other than one would expect from an economist who regarded theories of isolated individuals making unit choices as no more than a first step down a very long road. The motto of his *Principles of Economics* was *natura non facit saltum* – a principle of organic development (not of manufacture and not of plan) by means of which the evolutionary thinker who at the time of his death was labouring on a manuscript entitled *Progress: its Economic Conditions* was seeking to draw attention not merely to slowness but to wholeness as well. Economists would therefore be ill-advised to search for Ricardo and Jevons in the pages of Marshall's *Principles* without at the same time recognising the heritage of Hegel and Spencer: to do so is to miss the important truth that Marshall was first and foremost a maker of systems, and only secondarily a maker of tools.

Marshall's synthesis is an important intellectual contribution. No less important, however, is the fact that the personality of the book, to an extent that is virtually unique in the history of economics, simply cannot be separated from the personality of the author. To understand the nature of the contribution it is thus necessary to understand the aspirations of the intellectual, and three of those aspirations most of all: to minimise controversy, to maximise clarity and to emphasise continuity. Those three objectives will accordingly form the subject-matter of the three sub-sections which now follow and which complete the argument of this chapter.

(a) **Controversy.** Henry Sidgwick was a quiet scholar who, alarmed by the acrimonious wranglings of the mid-nineteenth century, wrote as follows in 1863: 'This is a disagreeable age to live in; there are so many opinions held about everything, and the advocates of each abuse their opponents so violently that it quite frightens a modest man.'[119] Marshall would have had no great difficulty in sympathising with Sidgwick's fears, for the truth appears to be that he suffered throughout his adult life from an acute anxiety with respect to conflict and confrontation – and to controversy in economics.

Thus he wrote in 1883 to Foxwell in the following terms concerning the opposition he proposed to mount to the ideas of Henry George:

> As a general proposition I maintain that it is more important to establish truth than to confute error; and that controversy should be left to people with sound digestions. . . . I would rather put in one brick just where it should be in the slowly rising economic edifice than plant a hundred brickbats with the utmost dexterity exactly between the eyes of Mr. George.[120]

In 1892 he wrote as follows in defence of his practice of not replying to books and articles critical of his *Principles*:

> In the aggregate they are not very much less bulky than the unwieldy Volume to which they refer: I do not work fast; and if I attempted to reply as I should wish to do, my progress with writing my second Volume, which is now slow, would altogether cease. So any acknowledgements I have been able to make to my critics have been in deeds rather than words.[121]

The Times of 23 November 1903 reprints a letter from Marshall to the Secretary of the Unionist Free Food League in which he enters yet another plea for running away: 'I deeply regret that I am unable to co-operate in the great work which the Unionist Free Food League is doing, for I have ever acted on the principle that academic economists should avoid joining leagues and should belong to no political party, unless, indeed, they give themselves largely to politics.'[122] Writing at about the same time to Pigou on practical political involvement he maintained that he studiously avoided it: 'My own position is that I have no time or aptitude for writing on questions of the day, as such. If I condemned aloud all the words and deeds of, say, Mr. Chamberlain or Mr. Webb, which I do not approve, I should have my hands full.'[123] A year later, writing to Wicksell, he explained that it was not sheer blind panic that made him so reluctant to enter into debate with Böhm-Bawerk concerning the theory of capital but rather the British national interest: 'England is going to the bad, because we English economists have not time and strength enough to deal with the real problems of our age. How could I be right in wasting my time by controversy about such paltry personalities?'[124] Even in correspondence with allies, his reticence to engage in academic debates is striking – as in the following letter to Edgeworth dated 27 April 1909: 'If I made any reply to your gentle criticisms I should be on the inclined plane which leads down to controversy: so my silence under rude blows might be more awkward than it is, if I once broke through my rule to leave controversy to the stronger.'[125] And at the very end of his life, revising *Industry and Trade*, he stated that whatever few corrections he had made had been made 'chiefly on the suggestion of friends': 'I have been under no temptation to controversy, the sterile consumer of time and energy.'[126] The picture which emerges is clear enough – if not from Marshall's own repeated restatement of his fears and anxieties, then from the general assessment which Maloney makes of him: 'Marshall's characteristic mixture of timidity, conscientiousness, anxiety to be liked, priggishness and vanity suggest a highly introverted man who would temperamentally be more interested in resolving his own internal contradictions than the disagreements of his colleagues. This is the real key to Marshall's career.'[127]

Indeed it is; and thence the temptation to see in Marshall's *Principles* the work of a rather vulnerable recluse who, desperate to avoid the psychological traumas which he knew to be the poisoned fruit of economic controversy, opted therefore for the conciliatory and the reconciliatory tone when what really was required was the fist of iron and the cutting edge. The temptation must be resisted. Of course Marshall said there was room in the house of economics both for the inductions of the historical school and the theoretical generalisations of the deductivists; for the final increment of utility of the Jevonians

and the human cost of production of the Ricardians; for the mechanistic equilibration of the pendulum of the price as it gravitates into
rest and the cyclical organicism of the firm of which the rise and fall
so closely parallels that of the trees of the forest. Yet to seek in this
way to broaden the perspectives of the science is not necessarily to be
cowardly or unassertive. Marshall said that the useful economist,
eschewing the futilities of dogmatism, ought to be open to evidence
and analysis, satisfaction of demand and cost of supply, physics and
biology. There cannot be many contemporary economists who would
regard these elements as substitutes rather than complements; or
who would accuse a scholar who sought to combine them of having
the same strength of character as a scholar who defined every animal
to be a pig purely in order to simplify the preparation of his index.
Marshall himself repeatedly rejected the suggestion 'that I try to
"compromise between" or "reconcile" divergent schools of thought.
Such work seems to me trumpery. Truth is the only thing worth
having: not peace. I have never compromised on any doctrine of any
kind.'[128] There being not a single pair of irreconcilables that Marshall
conspicuously forced into reconciliation, the reader must take him at
his word. It is worth pointing out in addition that the public declaration to so many alternative schools of economists that their pet
schemes were not the whole truth but only a part of the truth must
have ruffled more than a few feathers; and that the ruffling of feathers
is hardly what one would have expected from a rather vulnerable
recluse if his pen was genuinely powered above all by fear.

Edgeworth is right to say, however, that 'it is difficult to abstract
the work of Marshall from himself';[129] and there can be no doubt that
an acute anxiety with respect to controversy in economics in the
event constituted an important part of that self. The reconciliatory
orientation of Marshall's *Principles* is probably not a good indicator
of Marshall's adverse reaction to controversy, but the oblique style
and the opaque syntax are quite a different matter. Keynes is particularly good at identifying the ambiguity:

> The lack of emphasis and of strong light and shade, the sedulous
> rubbing away of rough edges and salients and projections, until
> what is most novel can appear as trite, allows the reader to pass too
> easily through. Like a duck leaving water, he can escape from this
> douche of ideas with scarce a wetting. The difficulties are con-
> cealed; the most ticklish problems are solved in footnotes; a
> pregnant and original judgement is dressed up as a platitude.[130]

And thus it is that the desire to reach a wider, non-specialist public (the objective of clarity), together with the wish to acknowledge the great insights of past originators (the objective of continuity), make common cause with a shy man's reluctance to turn the spotlight of publicity upon himself and upon the nature of his innovativeness. The use of the footnotes is a celebrated instance of the manner in which Marshall avoided controversy by concealing his contribution. Keynes again: 'Marshall had a characteristic habit in all his writings of reserving for footnotes what was most novel or important in what he had to say' – to such an extent, in fact, that 'it would almost be better to read the footnotes and appendices of Marshall's big volumes and omit the text, rather than *vice versa*.'[131]

Marshall avoided controversy by concealing his contribution. He also avoided controversy by delaying his response. Thus Keynes observes of Marshall that he suffered from a 'fear of being open to correction by speaking too soon' and says that that fear, reinforced by Marshall's ingrained perfectionism and commitment to high standards, accounts in part for the fact that an investigation commenced in 1867, a manuscript began in 1881, only became a book at the late date of 1890: 'Marshall was too much afraid of being wrong, too thin-skinned towards criticism, too easily upset by controversy even on matters of minor importance. An acute sensitiveness deprived him of magnanimity towards the critic or the adversary.'[132] Had Marshall not been so afraid of being wrong, his great contribution to economic theory might have been made long before 1890 – perhaps as early as 1870 – and he might more universally be regarded as a participant in the marginal revolution rather than in essence its heir.

Marshall avoided controversy, but he was for all that not quite as much a shrinking violet as he would have us believe. A careful reading of his letter to *The Times* of 25 January 1889 turns up not merely a refusal to get involved in day-to-day debates by entering into 'the battle that is now being waged in your columns' but also the intelligence that he had already taken care to put his views on record: 'My opinions on the subject of bimetallism are already published at great length, in the final report of the Commission of Gold and Silver.'[133] Where his views were not on record and he believed the issue to be of importance, he was the last man on earth to look the other way. Witness his letter to *The Times* of 19 August 1910 on the causal association between 'parental intemperance' and 'filial degeneration', where Marshall announced that it was his sense of social responsibility alone that had impelled him to write: 'That is the only cause which induced me to break my almost absolute rule against controversial correspondence.'[134] Witness his letter to *The Times* of 22 August 1914 on the use of popular lectures to stimulate hatred in time of war, where Marshall wrote as follows in spirited defence of fair play and respect for persons: 'Those who know and love Germany, even when revolted at the hectoring militarism which is more common there than here, should insist that we have no cause to scorn them, though we have good cause to fight them.'[135] Marshall must have known that such an appeal, coming so soon after the outbreak of the First World War, would inevitably lead to the name-calling nastiness which he most abhorred; and indeed it did. Thus Mr. T. E. Page, writing from Godalming, was in print only three days later with a message beginning 'To plain folk, who are not professors, but mere men . . .',[136] while a correspondent preferring to go under the name of 'Union Jack' was even more insulting about academics who talk about 'love' and 'friendship' in time of war: 'I yield to none in honouring the great qualities of the German people, or in gratitude for the many splendid services they have rendered us all in every branch of knowledge. But unless I read their character and their history quite amiss, they are too wise and too brave to value the respect and amity of cravens.'[137] Marshall must have known that his letter would unleash precisely such abuse, but that did not prevent him from entering into controversy when he felt that the cause was so just as to leave him no choice but to speak out. His subsequent reply to T. E. Page was characteristically dignified: 'My "professorial" duties have made me endeavour to ascertain at first hand the conditions and points of view of other nations.'[138] The same must be said of his reply to 'Union Jack', where the sensitive professor, clearly irritated, this time counselled his critic to be 'careful of speech': 'The true "craven" is he who vents his courage in the reckless use of offensive adjectives.'[139] *The Times* wisely stopped the correspondence before it came to blows (although there is a curious postscript on 29 December of the following year, when it carries a letter from Marshall complaining that it is the Germans this time who are fomenting hatred by falsely accusing the English of preventing adequate supplies of milk from reaching German children: 'I know that England has not intercepted Germany's external supplies of milk').[140] Marshall did not go looking for a fight. At least as far as T. E. Page and 'Union Jack' were concerned, however, one is compelled to say that, when provoked, he could give as good as he got.

Marshall wrote a number of letters to *The Times* on matters of contemporary interest and was a signatory to the famous manifesto on tariff reform which appeared in that journal in 1903. He was actively involved in controversy within his own university. He regularly rethought passages in the *Principles* in response to the suggestions of his critics, friendly and hostile alike – Cannan on capital,[141] for example, or Nicholson on consumer's surplus,[142] or Cunningham on economic history.[143] It would, in short, be a grave error to conceive of Alfred Marshall as a timid recluse who categorically refused to react to the world outside his study. The fact remains, however, that he did not like controversy; and that the impact of that personal dislike is clearly visible in the personality of his greatest work. It manifests itself through obfuscation and procrastination. There is no reason to think that it manifests itself through moderation and modulation as well.

(b) Clarity. Marshall was a secular missionary who wanted his academic work to have a practical influence. In order for economic ideas to have real-world consequences, he realised, they would have to be accessible to businessmen and to a wider public than that of the economics profession alone. Thence the need for clarity: 'I have promised Macmillan to keep the text of the book (not the *appendices*) in a form as attractive as I can to the practical man',[144] he wrote to a correspondent about the manuscript which later became *Industry and Trade*. What he says of that contribution is equally true of his objectives in the *Principles of Economics*. If economics is to have an impact on events, Marshall reasoned, then a treatise – at least, *his* treatise – could afford, in recognition of the dual market, only to be 'as scientific as is compatible with an attempt to catch the general reader':[145] the professional audience will find the arguments amplified in calculus and geometry in the appendices and the footnotes, Marshall argued, but a liberal use of equations and curves in the text itself (he seldom cites statistics) would weaken his appeal to the men who actually make history, as opposed to those who merely study it. The compromise, he said, was 'unsatisfactory',[146] but less unsatisfactory at least than the alternative of maximising precision by means of complexity and thereby rendering oneself incomprehensible to all but a few: Cambridge, Marshall wrote to Gonner in 1894, 'suffers much from the lack of men who can put important truths in easy language that is attractive to able men who are not specialists'.[147] Refusing to separate his work into journalism and scholarship, Marshall clearly set out to straighten the bent rod by ensuring that even his *magnum opus* should be accessible to the wider public.

Businessmen (if indeed they troubled to open the *Principles* at all) will have welcomed as clarity what pure scholars (none of whom appear to have put this point on record) will have dismissed as oversimplification. The praise of businessmen (if indeed any was forthcoming) will greatly have strengthened the secular missionary in his resolve to bring the practitioners directly into contact with the thinkers – and students and lecturers directly into contact with 'the problems of social and economic life'.[148] Such contact Marshall prided himself on having taken the trouble to seek out. Marshall saw himself as a scrupulous collector of technical and technological details to whom business realities had become all but second nature. Thus Pigou recalled:

> He told me once that, in his early days, he had set himself to master the broad principles of all the mechanical operations performed in factories: that, after a time, when he visited a factory, he was able to guess correctly the wages that different workmen would be getting by watching them for a few moments, and that, when his guess was significantly wrong, there was always some special explanation.[149]

Confronted with the particular, it is characteristic of Marshall's analytical temperament that he sought immediately for the generalisable. The crucial point in the present context remains, however, that the concrete was not sacrificed in his own mind to the abstract but was to serve, rather, as a full partner in his enterprise.

The importance of the concrete is especially apparent in the case of a work of applied economics such as *Industry and Trade*, of which H. S. Jevons rightly has said: 'It is indeed remarkable that the author, who needed the academic seclusion of Cambridge for the writing of so great a work, has yet kept himself so closely in touch with the current of modern events and contemporary opinion.'[150] Marshall would no doubt have wished to argue that, implicit if not explicit, the facts are the foundations of his *Principles* as well. It is tempting to see Marshall as an unworldly bookworm who relied upon his wife to write the cheques and who got himself into a muddle over the intricacies of resale price maintenance; who worried lest his lectures be too full of topical content and who selected as his faithful adjunct an economist whose interest in current affairs outside Cambridge University was so modest that he did not take a daily newspaper

(John Maloney's revelations concerning Neville Keynes's diaries indicate a man, indeed, who was detached to the point of indifference: 'The only indirect reference to the agricultural depression of the 1880s is that his aunt's farm is losing money; the only indirect reference to Lloyd George's fiscal policies concerns his own tax position').[151] History may be tempted to see Marshall as an unworldly bookworm, but that was not in any sense the way that Marshall himself viewed his personality and his attack. Marshall visited factories, served on Royal Commissions, walked with entrepreneurs, trades unionists and co-operators; and, as Pigou explains,

> what he aimed at in all this was to get, as it were, the *direct feel* of the economic world, something more intimate than can be obtained from merely reading descriptions, something that should enable one, with sure instinct, to set things in their true scale of importance. . . . Germans, he said once, when they write, try to say everything that is true: Englishmen everything that is true *and* important. In this he was typically an Englishman.[152]

Marshall, in sum, prided himself on having taken the trouble to hew his nuggets of economic wisdom directly from the inexhaustible mine of economic experience. He sought to learn from businessmen as well as to instruct them – perhaps *in order to* instruct them. But at the end of the day it was to be the Cambridge professor who did the teaching and the rest of the community that did the listening; and for communication to be effective in a difficult subject like economics, Marshall believed, there was simply no alternative but for the communicator to express himself with clarity.

Few things are more lacking in clarity than clarity, however, and few books more lacking in clarity than Marshall's *Principles*. Marshall, writing of Mill's great text, makes an observation which strikes closer to home than Marshall himself appears to have appreciated: 'He wished to compress into it a vast amount of matter; but his style is so easeful as to incite his readers to overmuch rapidity.'[153] Pigou, writing of Alfred Marshall and his book, makes a very similar observation about an author who set himself the objective of being clear: 'The first time one reads the *Principles* one is very apt to think that it is all perfectly obvious. The second time one has glimpses of the fact that one does not understand it at all. . . . One discovers behind the smooth sentences, which hide it like a façade, an engine of polished steel.'[154] Keynes too, reflecting on the seeming platitudes, the occasional asides, the apparent *obiter dicta*, all of which stand a good chance of being essential links in the intellectual chain, issues a warning that 'the way in which Marshall's *Principles of Economics* is written, is more unusual than the casual reader will notice' and encourages the reader to search for 'buried treasure' in the work:

> How often has it not happened even to those who have been brought up on the *Principles*, lighting upon what seems a new problem or a new solution, to go back to it and to find, after all, that the problem and a better solution have always been there, yet quite escaping notice! It needs much study and independent thought on the reader's own part, before he can know the half of what is contained in the concealed crevices of that rounded globe of knowledge, which is Marshall's *Principles of Economics*.[155]

And Pigou, like Keynes convinced of the importance of the insights hidden in Marshall's oblique constructions, records how frequently it befell him as well that he felt he had laboriously made an original discovery but 'then turned to Marshall's *Principles*' – 'and almost invariably in some obscure footnote there was half a clause, inside a parenthesis perhaps, which made it obvious that Marshall had solved this problem long ago but had not thought it worth while to write the answer down.'[156] It is a curious kind of clarity, however, that hides polished steel, buries treasure and does not think it worth while to write the answer down; and there is a very real sense in which it would be true to say that the practical man's gain is the professional economist's loss. Marshall could have made more use of specialist terminology, rigorous demonstration, carefully-formulated definitions, properly explicated assumptions. Had he done so he would have been less accessible to the general public but more accessible, probably, to academic experts who as it is are likely to find his work vague, ambiguous and even evasive to an extent that they would not have expected in a scholarly contribution penned by a Cambridge professor. The view of Dennis Robertson is indicative of that of many, that he is not always entirely certain precisely what point Marshall is making: 'One may rise even from a hundredth reading of Marshall with a certain muzziness in the head.'[157] Clarity to the general public being confusion to the profession, there are some grounds for reasoning that Marshall should have targeted his book at either of the two markets but not at both.

William Smart was perceptive enough to recognise, however, that not all the confusion in the *Principles* could be put down to the pursuit of clarity, and that some at least could only be explained in terms of the ambivalent personality of its author: 'I find', he wrote to Richard T. Ely in 1895, 'there is a great deal more in Marshall than meets the eye – perhaps more than he himself knows – and the time is not wasted in getting thoroughly into his mind. I wish, however, he were not so abominably cautious.'[158] Walter Weisskopf, more recently, has analysed Marshall's book from a psychological perspective and has found just such ambivalence both in its structure and in its content. With respect to its structure, Weisskopf says that the very sequence of Marshall's arguments is indicative of his hesitancy: 'Marshall's organization shows his ambivalence, because it reverts again and again to the same problems, thus betraying his own inner doubts about the validity of his own conclusions.'[159] With respect to its content, Weisskopf detects duality after duality in Marshall's arguments (static equilibrium and dynamic development, for example, or *ceteris paribus* and general interdependence, or the upward-sloping supply curve of labour and the ultimate triumph of activities over consumables, or perfect knowledge and radical uncertainty, or product homogeneity and special demand-curves, or analytical detachment and social commitment, or long-run market stability and long-run increasing returns), and reflects that such apparent contradictions in Marshall's thought are at least superficially reminiscent of the inner conflicts of an indecisive schizophrenic – as where Marshall first praises the pecuniary measurement of mind via the value-free price mechanism and then, almost as if ashamed of what he has said, adds that economic science does not neglect the moral and spiritual side of man's nature despite its concern with the material and the empirical: 'One can feel Marshall's ambivalence from sentence to sentence. As soon as he describes the quantifying monetizing method of economics and the resulting ethical neutrality, he takes it back by re-emphasizing the importance of higher values.'[160] The most pathological explanation of Marshall's reluctance to commit himself would be some deep-seated fear to enter into an intellectual struggle with the internalised voice of a tyrannical father. The most constructive explanation, on the other hand, is the cautious scholar's apperception that 'nearly' and 'almost' are not weasel-words but rather the substance of life: 'My only confident dogma in economics is that every short statement on a broad issue is inherently false',[161] Marshall wrote in defence of complexity, and that is why he was able to complain in 1891 to the young Beatrice Potter about her *Cooperative Movement* that 'on the whole things seem to me less simple than they do to you. Where you say that A is caused by B, I generally think that

C, D, E and F have had at least as much to do with it as A has. . . .
You are constantly saying that there are two alternatives where there
seem to me to be fifty.'[162] Whether the reason for Marshall's ambivalence was fear of his father or fear of oversimplification, however,
the crucial point is that the reader mistakes Marshall's meaning who
neglects the nuances both of structure and of content or tries to find
in the *Principles* a single-valued intelligibility which simply is not
there. Economics is a difficult subject, Marshall was a difficult man,
and it is, all things considered, impossible to read Edgeworth on
Marshall the expositor of his own ideas, without seeing in Edgeworth's comments a double meaning which is hardly likely to have
been intended: 'I hesitate to report Marshall's opinions in words
other than his own. Everyone who has studied his writings. . . . must
be aware how exactly his words were fitted to his thoughts, how
unwilling he was that other words should be substituted.'[163] Marshall's words were fitted to his thoughts, both the style and the
message point up hesitancy as often as they do confidence, and the
conclusion with respect to clarity must inevitably be that it was not
merely because he wanted to reach a general public that Marshall
said a good many things which a professional audience could not but
find profoundly confusing.

Marshall's clarity helps to account for the influence of his *Principles*: 'It flows in a steady, lucid stream', Keynes correctly says, 'with
few passages which stop or perplex the intelligent reader, even
though he know but little economics.'[164] So too, however, do the cut
corners and the loose ends, precisely because confusion about the
exact meaning of the authoritative work stimulated extensive debate
about the theoretical issues raised by the great textbook. As Terence
Hutchison explains it, the position was that, in the case of his caution
as in that of his clarity, Marshall benefited from his habitual good
luck and landed as usual on his feet:

> The immense extent of the Marshallian literature is obviously in
> large part due to the unique standing and importance and the
> wealth of original and fertile ideas in Marshall's work. But this is
> not the only reason. Much of the discussion could hardly have
> continued so long were it not for the variety of interpretations,
> some times conflicting, some times complementary, which can be
> put on Marshall's work at so many points.[165]

Marshall evidently stimulated economists to think as much by his
confusion as by his clarity, and that is why the verdict of Lionel

Robbins on the dominance of the *Principles* – 'This great work . . . long tended to stifle the development of other lines of thought in this country'[166] – cannot seriously be taken at its face value: some lines of thought were undoubtedly stifled (further speculation about the classical distinction between productive and unproductive labour, for example), but other lines of thought were actually encouraged (witness the controversy in the interwar years about the contribution of increasing returns to efficiency and progress on the one hand, concentration and monopolisation on the other, that was the inevitable result of Marshall's failure to spell out in detail the long-term consequences of the forward-falling supply curve). Nor would Lionel Robbins himself have wanted his verdict on the dominance of the *Principles* to be taken too literally. His own recollections of what it meant to read Marshall as a student at the LSE in the 1920s demonstrate just how much innovation could without difficulty be encompassed within the flexible framework of a perspective which had the twin advantages of being clear and being confusing:

> The Cambridge slogan of those days that it was 'all in Marshall', although certainly not based on extensive knowledge of the work of other schools, has considerably more to be said for it than most of the rest of the world was prepared to believe. But Marshall had buried so many of his best thoughts in footnotes and appendices and set forth so much of his fundamental construction by implication rather than by overt statement that it was really not surprising that, in my generation, those of us who were not under the spell should have had to rediscover them of ourselves or should have spent much time pursuing apparently new scents whose falsity he had already realized. Moreover, it was not *all* there. The process of rediscovering did yield genuinely new insights and it was certainly very exhilarating tagging along with the discoverers and thinking out minor contributions.[167]

And thus it happened that the confusion of an author whose objective it was to be clear came to make a contribution all its own to the subsequent development of economic science – a contribution nonetheless real for being largely unintended. Economics, one is reminded yet again, is the story of invisible hands. So, for that matter, is life itself.

(c) Continuity. Marshall sought to minimise controversy and to maximise clarity. He also strove to emphasise continuity, both in the

development of economic phenomena and in the evolution of economic theories. Marshall employed the quintessential gradualism of
the differential calculus, he indicated that time is 'absolutely continuous'[168] (and as with his time-periods, so with his market-structures),
and he issued the following declaration in defence of *natura non facit
saltum*: 'In economics, as in physics, changes are generally continuous. Convulsive changes may indeed occur, but they must be dealt
with separately: and an illustration drawn from a convulsive change
can throw no true light on the processes of normal steady evolution.'[169]
Marshall also applied his 'Principle of Continuity'[170] and his concept
of incrementalism to the steady but slow advance of science itself:
'Nearly all important knowledge has long deep roots stretching
downwards to distant times',[171] he said, and in his own case took
pains to indicate how great was his debt to earlier authors such as
Smith, Ricardo and Mill in whose long shadow he was only too proud
to be privileged to creep along.

Marshall, Stigler observes, was 'probably the most loyal of all the
great economists', but he also suggests that Marshall's 'veneration for
the classical economists'[172] was likely to have been a mixed blessing.
For one thing, Stigler states, Marshall was on occasion prepared to
sacrifice rigour in order to uphold convention, as in his genuinely
idiosyncratic defence of what he accepted were the obsolete theories
of productive labour of the classical school: 'They have a long
history; and it is probably better that they should dwindle gradually
out of use, rather than be suddenly discarded.'[173] Besides that, Stigler
points out, Marshall 'had a pronounced tendency so to phrase his
own doctrines as to minimize the change from the classical tradition',[174]
and yet there is something inherently questionable about concealing
a revolution that one is simultaneously engaged in making. Marshall,
Stigler says, 'was almost incomparably superior to his immediate
predecessors and his early contemporaries in the profundity and
originality of his thought, in his consistency, and in the breadth of his
vision.'[175] Marshall, Stigler implies, should in the circumstances have
been more open about the intellectual innovations he was intro-
ducing, rather than seeking to slip them in under the guise of
continuity. The anxious thinker's fear of controversy, the communicator's concern with perceived clarity, the natural conservative's
commitment to the power of the past, all of these factors help to
account for the Newtonian modesty with which Marshall clothed his
shrewdest and most pregnant insights. As Keynes says concerning
Marshall's work, 'passages imputing error to others are rare', 'claims
to novelty or to originality on the part of the author himself are

altogether absent', and the very 'way in which Marshall introduces Elasticity, without any suggestion that the idea is novel, is remarkable and characteristic'.[176] All of which is well and good, but only so long as the reader either ignores Marshall's personal contribution altogether or follows the example of Stigler and Keynes in treating the great man's hidden curriculum with amused tolerance.

Historically speaking, however, not every reader has been prepared either to ignore or to tolerate. Léon Walras is one who was not:

> Il est pitoyable de voir Marshall, *ce grand éléphant blanc de l'économie politique*, et Edgeworth par. . . . impuissance et jalousie s'évertuer à remettre en honneur la théorie de Ricardo et de Mill sur le prix des produits. Les Autrichiens ont eux le mérite de faire servir leur *Grenznutzen* à éviter cette sottise.[177]

Edwin Cannan on Alfred Marshall is a second:

> He would have done better for himself and for economics if he had given his life to advancing and defending and developing what was fresh and new in his doctrine instead of including it very slowly and awkwardly among a mass of uninteresting attempts to rehabilitate traditional and often obsolete doctrines. . . . He could not bear to say, or even to think, that he had improved anything in the work of the masters, to say nothing of washing it out.[178]

A. W. Coats is a third:

> Alfred Marshall, who exerted a greater influence in his day than any other single economist, was unduly deferential to the great figures of the past, extremely slow to publish his own ideas, and very careful not to exaggerate the novel features of his own writings or those of his contemporaries. There was, in his outlook, much of what he once termed the 'Chinese element', and by constantly impressing on his pupils the conviction that the development of economic ideas was a slow evolutionary process he may have unintentionally inhibited the progress of theoretical speculation.[179]

The message is a clear one, that filial reverence is an expensive luxury, fear of criticism a punitive tax, and that Marshall would have done well, publicly jettisoning the crutches he had inherited from the past, to proceed thence in the bright light of unshaded day to unfold his individual contribution: were that contribution to have been a genuinely revolutionary one, then a hidden curriculum born of intense secretiveness and best approached with a good measure of amused tolerance might actually have impeded the identification of the novelties served up under the name of continuity by a cautious thinker afraid of the radical breach.

Alternatively, of course, one can take Marshall at his word and, playing down the novelty of his personal contribution, seek to situate his principles precisely where he said they belonged, in the mainstream of English classical economics amplified by a proper explanation of the shortcuts made by the wise cost-of-productionists when dealing with a topic as readily accessible to common sense as was that of utility and demand. Marshall's insistence that the classical doctrines had emerged unscathed from the debates of the 1870s and 1880s is not likely to have been shared by many economists in his own times, let alone of subsequent generations. His modesty with respect to his own breaking of new ground is, however, a different matter, and here no less a thinker than Schumpeter has found reasonable grounds for agreement:

> A 'marginalist' treatise published in 1890 – or, for that matter, in 1880 – could have improved and developed existing doctrine (which Marshall certainly did) but it could not have revealed fundamentally new truth. According to what I believe to be the ordinary standards of scientific historiography, such merit as there was in the rediscovery of the marginal utility principle is Jevons'; the system of general equilibrium (including the theory of barter) is Walras'; the principle of substitution and the marginal productivity theory are Thünen's; the demand and the supply curves and the static theory of monopoly are Cournot's (as is the concept, though not the word, price elasticity); the consumers' rent is Dupuit's; the 'diagrammatic method' is also Dupuit's or else Jenkin's.[180]

All of which leads Schumpeter to the conclusion that Marshall did right to gloss over his own path-breaking constructions precisely because these were few and far between, precisely because, 'when inquiring into the nature and importance of Marshall's deviations, *in what purport to be fundamentals*, from the Jevons–Menger–Walras analysis: they are negligible.'[181] *Natura non facit saltum*, Schumpeter would seem to be saying, and neither did Alfred Marshall, who simply unified a wealth of insights drawn from the writings of a number of economists, classical and neo-classical alike, without himself making any significant advance on the stock of knowledge which he inherited. Marshall emphasised continuity and played down the novelty of his own personal contribution. Schumpeter took a similar view of the originality of Marshall's doctrines.

So much so, in fact, that he is able to draw the unexpected conclusion that, through 'inadequate acknowledgement of priority', Marshall actually made the originality of his own contribution seem greater than it was:

> The case of Jevons is the most obvious one. But the case of Walras is worse. Marshall, of all men, mathematically trained as he was, entertaining as he did the highest opinion of the central importance of his own note xxi, cannot have been blind to the greatness as well as the priority of Walras's achievement. Yet Walras's great name occurs in the *Principles* only on three unimportant occasions that have nothing to do with that achievement. . . . The one exception is Thünen. . . . But Cournot received only general recognition and is not referred to where we should have expected specific reference, primarily in the theory of monopoly. . . . In striking contrast to the generosity he lavished on Ricardo and Mill, Marshall was less than generous to all those whose contributions were closely related to his own.[182]

Marshall, Schumpeter says, simply did not make his debts known – 'with the result that the reputation of others has suffered. . . . The reason for this state of opinion is largely Marshall's own fault.'[183] Marshall unjustifiably failed to make the proper acknowledgements, Schumpeter argues, and the curious outcome was to magnify the significance of his own theories, to point *de facto* to rupture while all the time insisting that he was far too humble to point to anything but continuity.

Marshall himself, it would be fair to say, took a somewhat different view of his practice: 'My rule has been to refer in a footnote to anyone whom I know to have said a thing before I have said it in print, even though I may have said it in lectures for many years before I knew that it had ever occurred to him: I just refer, but say nothing about obligations either way.'[184] Marshall evidently saw himself as a man with a strong commitment to intellectual honesty, the kind of man who strives to make himself 'wholly superior to the temptation so to lower the reputation of previous writers that his own may be the more eminent', the kind of man who takes great care not 'so far to pre-occupy his thoughts as to hinder him from perceiving all that these truths have worked in the minds of others'.[185] Lionel

Robbins, attempting to adjudicate between Marshall's generosity and Schumpeter's *critique*, comes down in favour of the former and in opposition to the latter:

> I should not be prepared to contend that Marshall was always an altogether agreeable character. . . . But there is really no evidence at all that he did not handsomely acknowledge the debts of which he was conscious. His references to Cournot and von Thünen probably did more than anything else to revive and spread the reputation of these authors, and his solicitude for the position of Ricardo even comes under rebuke from Schumpeter.[186]

It is evidently Robbins' view that Marshall scrupulously acknowledged his debts and in that way sought to show that his own small contribution was only made while standing on the shoulders of giants. Marshall said that advance in economic science 'is, and must be, one of slow and continuous growth', and he presented his *Principles* as nothing more than a tidying-up exercise in the wake of the unnecessary conflicts of the recent past between those theorists who sought for value in supply and those who sought for value in demand:

> Some of the best work of the present generation has indeed appeared at first sight to be antagonistic to that of earlier writers; but when it has had time to settle down into its proper place, and its rough edges have been worn away, it has been found to involve no real breach of continuity in the development of the science. . . . The present treatise is an attempt to present a modern version of old doctrines with the aid of the new work, and with reference to the new problems, of our own age.[187]

That and no more than that; for the truth is that *natura non facit saltum* and neither, if its author is to be believed, did Marshall's *Principles*. The author is not, however, always and everywhere the best judge of his own contribution; and besides that, both Marshall and his book were far too complicated to permit of any simple conclusion.

6 The Evolution of the *Principles*

Marshall began seriously to study economic theory in 1867 (when he was 23) and turned, naturally, to the as-yet-unchallenged classics of Smith, Ricardo and, of course, John Stuart Mill. As he later recollected:

> I read Mill's *Political Economy* in 1866 or '7, while I was teaching advanced mathematics; and, as I thought much more easily in mathematics at that time than in English, I tried to translate him into mathematics before forming an opinion as to the validity of his work. I found much amiss in his analysis, and especially in two matters. He did not seem to have assimilated the notion of gradual growth by imperceptible increments; and he did not seem to have a sufficient responsibility. . . . for keeping the number of his equations equal to the number of his variables, neither more nor less.[1]

Marshall obviously had reservations about the author of the standard textbook of his youth and complained about the 'lack both of scientific instinct and of careful habits of observation, which deprived Mill's unrivalled faculty of exposition, and his fine spirit of humanity, of much of their power for good, whenever he ventured far beyond Ricardo's track'.[2] Whatever Mill's shortcomings, however, Marshall maintained consistently throughout his life that it was from the English classical economics as presented in Mill's great book that he had derived the basis of his marginalism: 'My main position as to the theory of value and distribution was practically completed in the years 1867 to 1870: when I translated Mill's version of Ricardo's or Smith's doctrines into mathematics; and. . . . when Jevons' book appeared, I knew at once how far I agreed with him and how far I did not.'[3]

Schumpeter is sympathetic to Marshall's account of his own early development:

A man such as Marshall, who was trained in mathematics and physics and to whom the concept of limits and hence the formal part of the marginal principle would be as familiar as would be his breakfast bacon, need only have allowed his mind to play on Mill's loose statements and to work out their exact model (system of equations) in order to arrive at a point where the purely theoretical parts of the *Principles* came in sight.[4]

Howey is somewhat less in sympathy with the tale of the translations: 'This is an old story, often repeated, for which there is no evidence. It is certain that Marshall's equations in his "Mathematical Appendix", the only equations he ever published in any number, do not relate to Mill or Ricardo.'[5] Hewins for his part is content simply to repeat the story as he heard it from Marshall himself: 'He told me once he had started his economic career with the idea of bringing Mill up to date, and interpreting his economics in the light of modern developments.'[6] Hewins makes no mention of value theory in particular, and perhaps that is wise: such manuscripts as survive from the late 1860s and the early 1870s (the detailed 'Essay on Value' most of all)[7] would seem to bear out Marshall's contention that he arrived at the theory of the downward-sloping demand curve in advance of being exposed to Jevons' exposition, but Howey's contention as well, that there is no surviving proof that the famous translations and retranslations of Mill were in fact ever made.

Yet there is more to Mill than shrewd and pregnant hints concerning limits and margins; and even if it was not value theory in particular that Marshall happened in the event to quarry from the subsequent editions of the *Principles of Political Economy* (the first appearing as early as 1848 when Marshall was six years of age, the seventh and last appearing more than two decades later in the same year as Jevons' *Theory*), it cannot be denied that there is a whole body of valuable theory in Mill's book which must have offered the greatest possible stimulus to the mind of an earnest young mathematician who was anxious to do good. Mill on the single price in the single market tempered by the practice of price discrimination, for example: 'Not only are there in every large town, and in almost every trade, cheap shops and dear shops, but the same shop often sells the same article at different prices to different customers.'[8] Or Mill on the adverse income effect that is brought about by price-rises where the good in question is a necessity: 'It is other things rather than food that are diminished in quantity by them, since, those who pay more for food not having so much to expend otherwise, the production of other things contracts itself to the limits of a smaller demand.'[9] Or Mill on economies of scale, diseconomies of scale, cartels, combinations, the capacity of trade unions to do good where they defend the interests of the weak but also harm where they secure for their members in employment a 'partial rise of wages' that is regrettably 'gained at the expense of the remainder of the working class'.[10] Or Mill on well-justified State intervention (perhaps through the taxation of an industry experiencing diminishing returns, perhaps by giving advice and promulgating intelligence, perhaps even by 'offering better education and better instruction to the people, than the greater number of them would spontaneously demand')[11] within the broader context of an individual liberty which is both an end in its own right and the optimal means, via the intelligence that is the free-market price and the initiative-taker's flair for picking winners, for attaining the further goals of allocative efficiency and economic growth: 'Even if a government were superior in intelligence and knowledge to any single individual in the nation, it must be inferior to all the individuals of the nation taken together.'[12] Or Mill on the importance to the economist of evolutionary schemata and an openness to history-to-come: seeing as he did 'the economical condition of mankind as liable to change', Mill recommended to his fellow economists the addition of 'a theory of motion to our theory of equilibrium – the Dynamics of political economy to the Statics.'[13] Or Mill on the sheer ugliness of the market society that is powered by aggressive competitiveness to the detriment of 'mental culture' and common humanity:

> I confess I am not charmed with the ideal of life held out by those who think that the normal state of human beings is that of struggling to get on; that the trampling, crushing, elbowing, and treading on each other's heels, which form the existing type of social life, are the most desirable lot of human kind, or anything but the disagreeable symptoms of one of the phases of industrial progress.[14]

Or Mill on the transcendence of Malthusian over-population by educated *embourgeoisement*, on the need for poor-relief provided on the less-eligibility principle until such a time as a general rise in affluence had caused the *residuum* to wither away, on the considerable benefits that could be derived by the disadvantaged not only from emigration or from peasant proprietorship but from a widespread adoption of the co-operative mode of organisation. Mill's insights on progress and poverty are set out with particular clarity in his chapter 'On the Probable Futurity of the Labouring Classes',[15] Marshall's in his paper on 'The Future of Working Classes'.[16] Marshall in that essay pays tribute to his great and high-minded predecessor, and he does so in a number of other places as well – not least in a letter to Foxwell dated 14 April 1897, where he observes concerning Mill that 'even when I differ from him, he seems to keep my mind in a higher plane of thought than ordinary writers on economics'.[17] Direct influence in the history of ideas can seldom be proven with any degree of certainty. What can be established are resonances and resemblances; and it cannot be denied there are any number of intellectual links between Mill and Marshall on matters as wideranging as price discrimination and co-operatives, the future of the working classes and the future of sustained economic growth. So numerous are these intellectual links that it seems rather unkind to sift through Marshall's books and manuscripts in search of Mill on marginal utility, mathematically defined: even if there is no surviving proof of the famous translations and retranslations, there is abundant proof that Marshall was deeply influenced by Mill and lectured on him at an early stage. The following reflection is taken from the lecture-notes on Mill that Marshall prepared for delivery in Cambridge in the early 1870s: 'When we speak of progress. . . . we do not mean every change that comes with the progress of time, e.g. not the destruction of the arts of Rome by the Goths; or of the Moors and the Mexicans by the Spaniards: at least this is progress backwards.'[18] Marshall chose to lecture on Mill, but on Mill Book IV, clearly, and not on Mill Book I. His choice is a significant one, and one which reminds the reader yet again of just how much there was in Mill quite apart from the theory of value that was capable of firing the imagination of an earnest young mathematician who was anxious to do good.

Mill (1806–73) built on Ricardo (1772–1823); and there can be no question that the abstract deductivist in Marshall had a very great respect indeed for the 'marvellous scientific instincts'[19] of the rigorous logician whose valuable theories, sadly, were 'so expressed as almost to invite misunderstanding'.[20] The distinguished author of the *Principles of Political Economy and Taxation* (of which the first edition appeared in 1817, the third and last in 1821) was not 'wrong-headed',[21] as Jevons said he was, but it is not to be denied that 'he made a mistake in not stating explicitly what he was doing':[22] had the earlier author not been guilty of quite such 'reticence',[23] Marshall argued, there would not have been a need for the perceived innovation in the area of value of the later one, the simple truth being that 'the foundations of the theory as they were left by Ricardo remain intact'.[24] Ricardo, Marshall maintained, 'did not get hold of the right words in which to say it neatly',[25] but was for all that aware not merely of the importance of utility in general but of specifically *marginal* utility in particular: 'By Riches he means total utility, and he seems to be always on the point of stating that value corresponds to the increment of riches which results from that part of the commodity which it is only just worth the while of purchasers to buy.'[26] Nor did Ricardo make the mistake, Marshall argued further, of assuming that incremental utility was constant utility: Ricardo was aware that more means less, as indeed one would be right to expect from an author who had devoted such care to the formulation of a theory of diminishing returns to the factor of land (a proposition which, in the history of economics, was, in Marshall's view, 'the first to be subjected to a rigid analysis of a semi-mathematical character').[27] Whatever Mill's shortcomings in the theory of value, therefore, it would appear that Marshall found more than enough to satisfy his curiosity with respect to subjectivity and demand in the work of the great giant who had blazed the track that was subsequently followed by the unrivalled expositor.

Economists are, as it happens, unlikely ever to reach any real consensus as to what it was, precisely, that the wise but reticent Ricardo was 'always on the point of saying'; and thus it is that Marshall's controversial interpretation of the classical on utility must inevitably become a subject for debate in its own right. Marshall's opponents will, in that debate, point to Ricardo on the gold/air paradox in defence of the proposition that subjective satisfaction is a necessary but not a sufficient condition, in the *Principles of Political Economy and Taxation*, for the establishment of equilibrium market exchange ratios: 'Utility then is not the measure of exchangeable value, although it is absolutely essential to it.'[28] Marshall's opponents will cite Ricardo to the effect that labour-cost is the 'foundation of all value', to the effect that the 'relative quantity of labour' and not perceived pleasure is 'almost exclusively determining the relative value of commodities';[29] and they will emphasise that Ricardo in any case made no distinction between total and marginal utility even when referring specifically to those exceptional values that are exclusively demand-determined. Thus, when speaking of the value of non-reproducible commodities ('some rare statues and pictures, scarce books and coins, wines of a peculiar quality'), Ricardo states simply that the value is 'wholly independent of the quantity of labour originally necessary to produce them, and varies with the varying wealth and inclinations of those who are desirous to possess them':[30]

Ricardo here incorporates desiredness and scrupulously avoids by-gones, Marshall's opponents will conclude, but shows no sign what-soever of being 'on the point' of drawing attention to the unique significance of the final unit. Critics and historians more sympathetic to Marshall's gloss will, however, suggest that the relevant insights are to be found in Ricardo's discussion not of long-run equilibrium but of short-run equilibration, and will insist on reading the prop-osition that price varies continuously with *rareté* into passages such as the following: 'Possessing utility, commodities derive their exchange-able value from two sources: from their scarcity, and from the quantity of labour required to obtain them.'[31] As scarcity is dimin-ished over time, Marshall's supporters will say, so it is Ricardo's conception that price should fall, the relevant schedule being implicit in Ricardo's theory of competitive markets even if never actually made explicit by a poor communicator who was enamoured of 'short cuts':[32] 'The proportion between supply and demand may, indeed, for a time, affect the market value of a commodity, until it is supplied in greater or less abundance, according as the demand may have increased or diminished; but this effect will be only of temporary duration.'[33] As Marshall himself had a theory of prices gravitating over time to long-run normals, one must infer that he read Ricardo on short-run disequilibrium states with some appreciation. Nor is it only in the theory of value that he is likely to have detected the signs of marginalism in the work of an author widely regarded as a doctrinaire cost-of-productionist. A moment's reflection on Ricar-do's theory of the equalisation of profit-rates, for example, must have convinced him that Ricardo was an undeclared incrementalist: it is not, after all, the *total* stock of capital that shifts in response to perceived disparities in returns, but *some part* of it. Most unambigu-ous of all, of course, is the demand-led marginalism of the Ricardian theory of differential rent, to which none other than Jevons himself had paid tribute in 1871: the 'general correctness' of the marginalist constructions, Jevons had stated, 'derives great probability from their close resemblance to the theory of rent, as it has been accepted by English writers for nearly a century'.[34] Shove has written that Mar-shallian economics 'is of the true Ricardian stock, neither a cross-bred nor a sport'.[35] Marshall would have wished most enthusiastically to agree – and would, no doubt, have singled out for particular praise the valuable if oblique contribution that the wise but reticent classical had made to the theory of the margin and of utility.

    Yet there is more to Ricardo than buried margins and concealed utilities; and there is in truth much more in Ricardian economics that

Marshall rejected than can reasonably be encompassed within the confines of Shove's assessment. The wages-fund, the distinction between productive and unproductive labour, the inverse relationship between payment to labour and payment to capital, the dismal relationship between population expansion and the subsistence standard of life, the logical deductions proceeding asociologically from the universalist axiom of economic man, the reliance on comparative statics and equilibrium states to the detriment of permanent dynamics and search without end, the tendency to derive policy-proposals from *a prioris* and simplified hypotheses *as if* guided by an invisible vice – all of these sins of commission on the part of the Ricardian economists were, seen from the perspective of their Marshallian counterparts, positively compounded by their failure scientifically to buttress their assertions with hard evidence, their failure properly to explain the institutional evolution of a nation growing wealthy, their failure to defend the profits of the capitalists and *a fortiori* the rents of the landowners against the charge that if labour alone could create value-added then labour alone was entitled to receive the product. There is evidently a very great deal indeed in Ricardo's *Principles* that Marshall regarded as of eminently dubious validity and chose not to incorporate in his own book. On the other hand, of course, there are the similarities (the guarded adoption of Say's Law and the quantity theory of money, the shared preference for free trade over protection and the limited State over the interfering State, the deep concern with the laws which regulate the distribution of the national product as between the suppliers of the three factor-inputs at different stages of social development): these remind the reader that it was not only because of the poor communicator's implicit commitment to the principle of diminishing marginal utility that the Cambridge professor found in the older economics so much that linked it to the new.

Of no less interest than the differences and the similarities are, however, the analogies and the extensions which demonstrate, most clearly of all, perhaps, just how carefully Marshall had studied Ricardo's work. Thus the quasi-rent that is the reward to a factor fixed in the short run is clearly modelled on the concept of rent payable for the services of an endowment of land that is fixed for all time; while the theory of consumer's surplus is nothing more nor less than the translation into the language of demand-curves of the theory of differential rent as additional units are added to existing. More controversial is Marshall's incorporation of the stationary state (not as a zero-growth, low profit pessimum but merely as an intellectual butterfly-net by means of which to capture the representative firm),[36] of rising rents to land (not because of the premium on agricultural produce but because of urbanisation and concentration),[37] of diminishing returns (where Marshall, after acknowledging the effects of free trade and scientific farming in reversing the Ricardian price-rises, warns gloomily that the world as a whole must expect the Ricardian problem of more means worse to reassert itself in due course)[38] and of real cost (where Marshall, building on Ricardo's notion that all cost is labour-cost, first converts objective units into subjective and then includes additional felt disamenities such as waiting, in such a way as to cause Robbins, with some understatement, to observe: 'It can legitimately be argued, I think, that in this respect Marshall was more Ricardian than Ricardo'[39]).[40] It is, one feels sure, not quasi-rent and consumers' surplus but rather the more imaginative and far-fetched of Marshall's analogies and extensions that Schumpeter had in mind when he expressed his opinion that Marshall's real relationship to Ricardian economics comes dangerously close to something that in less elevated circles would go under the name of name-dropping: 'Marshall's theoretical structure, barring its technical superiority and various developments of detail, is fundamentally the same as that of Jevons, Menger, and especially Walras, but . . . the rooms in this new house are unnecessarily cluttered up with Ricardian heirlooms, which receive emphasis quite out of proportion to their operational importance.'[41] The clutter of heirlooms, perhaps; but it was the clutter of a distinguished thinker anxious to prove that a much-respected authority had not after all shunted the car of economic science on to a wrong line. That attempt in itself is not without significance. It is easy enough for the contemporary observer to dismiss Marshall's frequent protestations of fidelity to the time-tested insights of the classics as reflecting no more than a strong preference for evolution rather than revolution in economic theory, continuity rather than *caesura*. However prominently the superiority of tradition over breach may have figured on Marshall's hidden agenda, it must be remembered that what he himself states is something different, that it was the English classicals such as David Ricardo who pointed him in the right direction.

Mill built on Ricardo, Ricardo on Adam Smith (1723–1790); and the inspiration which Marshall derived from the Enlightenment classics of the *Theory of Moral Sentiments* (1759) and the *Wealth of Nations* (1776) was in truth as least as great as his intellectual debt to the later classicals who penned the *Principles*. What Marshall says of Mill is therefore entirely applicable to himself as well – that he was 'finely jealous for his predecessors: he gave not only to Ricardo, but in opposition to the current of the time, to Adam Smith whatever credit he could.'[42] Whitaker points to Marshall's growing interest in Smithian economics: 'The reverence for Adam Smith grew with Marshall's broadening interest in the applied and historical side of his subject. Ultimately, if he had an exemplar, it was surely Smith.'[43] Marshall himself spoke as follows in 1904 in a conversation with Edwin Cannan: 'I verily believe that everything which later economists have discovered is in Adam Smith.'[44] It was a declaration which he was to make time and time again, and not least in the *Principles* itself, where Marshall says of Smith that, all things considered, 'there is scarcely any economic truth now known of which he did not get some glimpse': 'Though he undoubtedly borrowed much from others, yet the more one compares him with those who went before and those who came after him, the finer does his genius appear, the broader his knowledge and the more well-balanced his judgement.'[45] Much the same could be said of Marshall himself. Like attracts like, in economics as in nature, and Marshall, as Schumpeter observes, was no exception to the rule: 'He is reported to have said: "It's all in A. Smith." There is more in this remark than mere recognition of the fact that today's work necessarily grows out of yesterday's – there is recognition of kinship.'[46]

Thus it was that both authors made their greatest contribution in the field of systemic integration and the unified synthesis. Marshall in his *Principles* having so successfully fitted the disparate pieces into some sort of ordered whole, it is only to be expected that he would have a not-inconsiderable admiration for the work of the first artisan to have dared to think big: 'Since he was the first to write a treatise on wealth in all its chief social respects, he might on this ground alone have a claim to be regarded as the founder of modern economics.'[47] Both authors built ambitious theoretical systems – and built them out of the eclectic's mix of the deductivist's pure logic and the inductivist's empirical data, scrupulously gathered. In building their systems, moreover, both authors, at least in Marshall's personal interpretation of their common methodology, chose to concern themselves with the practical bearings of abstract reasonings[48] and took care to remain 'in constant contact . . . with the actual facts of business life'[49] Thus Marshall said, 'I love to linger in the foundry'[50] and wrote as follows in later life of the way in which he had as a young man determined to acquire trade and technical knowledge at first hand:

> In the years of my apprenticeship to economic studies, between 1867 and 1875, I endeavoured to learn enough of the methods of operation of the greater part of the leading industries of the country, to be able to reconstruct mentally the vital parts of the chief machines used in each. . . . After continuing on this course for some years, I began to ask my guide to allow me to guess the wages. My error did not very often exceed two shillings a week on the one side or the other: but, when it did, I stopped and asked for an explanation.[51]

Marshall maintained that it had consistently been his objective to learn from businessmen as well as to instruct them. He also maintained that the same had been true of Adam Smith – whose work not only encompassed 'all that was best in all his contemporaries' but also demonstrated 'much knowledge of the actual conditions of business', knowledge that could only have been acquired through 'intimate association with Scotch men of business'.[52] Marshall's verdict on Smith and the other classical economists (that they were 'well acquainted with the practical workings of business')[53] will not, one suspects, meet with universal approbation. More important in the present context is, however, the fact that Marshall himself regarded Smith as an abstract reasoner who never lost touch with the real-world realities of the practical business life. Thence the recognition and thence the kinship.

There is a further similarity between Marshall and Smith, and this lies in their common attitude to the eternal trade-off between perfecting and preaching which Schumpeter has encapsulated in the following words:

> Both the *Wealth* and the *Principles* are what they are, partly at least, because they are the result of the work of decades and fully matured, the products of minds that took infinite care, were patient of labor, and indifferent to the lapse of years. This is all the more remarkable because both Smith and Marshall were extremely anxious to preach their wisdom and to influence political practice – yet neither of them allowed himself to be hurried into print before his manuscripts were as perfect as he felt able to make them.[54]

What with Smith at 53 and Marshall at 48 in the year of his *magnum opus*, each author having devoted at least ten years to the researching and refining of his great book, both may more easily be accused of an excess of cautiousness than of prematurely rushing out a tract for the times because of an anxious impatience to do good. That both were anxious to do good is not, however, in question. Both praised the market mode of resource-allocation but not in so doctrinaire a manner as to close the door to pragmatic State intervention in instances where the author even if not his community believed that free enterprise left unguided was likely to fail (the case of the Scotsman on the Navigation Acts and the Usury Laws, the Englishman on the Tabular Standard and the Poor Laws). Both were convinced that the private vice of individual interest was on balance a force for great good in the specific context of economic efficiency, but only where the normal measure of self-seeking was combined with the normal measure of self-restraint in the proportions specified by the unambiguous normative consensus of an ongoing collectivity. As Marshall wrote in an unpublished fragment dating from 1902: 'Adam Smith: "kept his moral sentiments for Sunday", they say. No he did not. But he laid dominant stress on wealth of nations.'[55] Both, indeed, were so strongly committed to the economic optimist's notion that with material advance goes moral betterment, to the historical evolutionist's idea that an opulent society is more likely to be altruistic and cultivated and a savage society more likely to be savage, that neither would have wanted in any case to draw too clear a distinction between the wealth of nations, on the one hand, the ethics of nations on the other: given enough time, both authors argued, both the wealth and the ethics were likely to move in step, the one reinforcing the other and being in its turn reinforced by it.

Both Smith and Marshall sought to bolster their assertions with scientific arguments (as where Smith infers that it is the very conditions of business life themselves that inculcate in the businessman the morally-virtuous and socially-desirable character-traits of 'industry, frugality, and attention',[56] or where Marshall indicates that it is nothing other than rising standards of living born of occupational upgrading and improvements in productivity to which a morally-minded community is first and foremost indebted for the welcome fact that, nowadays, 'the consumption of tea is increasing very fast, while that of alcohol is stationary').[57] Neither denied that the evidence pointed to abominations as well as to advantages (the 'mental mutilation'[58] of the factory operative in the system of extensive division of labour in the case of Smith, for example, or the 'selfish desire' of liberated women more and more to 'resemble men'[59] in an industrial era of higher incomes and greater opportunities in that of Marshall), but both were convinced that the advantages far out-weighed the abominations; and that the wealth of nations was in the circumstances something which a sensitive man with 'the philosophic temper and the broad interests of the great thinkers of past times'[60] could with a clear conscience bring himself to support. Both had reservations about the technocratic nature of instrumental econ-omics, reservations encapsulated in Marshall's recollection that his science had in fact started badly: 'Modern economics had at its origin a certain rudeness and limitation of scope, and a bias towards regarding wealth as an end rather than a means of man's life.'[61] Both were of the opinion, however, that the man capable of wide-ranging 'philosophical thought'[62] was entirely right to make common cause with the man incapable of seeing beyond his own myopic *how to* precisely because of the fact that growth meant betterment and was therefore good. Each had expected as a young spark to spend his life as an ordained clergyman. Each had converted somewhere on the road to Oxbridge to a peculiarly high-minded form of agnosticism which resembles nothing so much as Christian ethics without Chris-tian theology. Each had come to believe that the road to normative reformation leads through economic advance and that the perfecting of economic arguments was not, therefore, antithetical to the preaching of ethical values, but rather the essential precondition for it – and for the success on earth of his own self-appointed mission.

Smith was a great preacher, but he was also a great economist; and the student of the downward-sloping subjective utility curve who stubbornly refuses to follow Marshall in finding the linkage between perceived valuation and market price spelled out in the greatest detail, if in invisible ink, between the lines of Mill's book and Ricardo's, will discover more than enough in the work of the Scottish eclectic to convince himself that the greatest of all the classicals was simultaneously a great neo-classical as well. Thus Smith in the *Wealth of Nations* was perfectly prepared to set to one side the toil and the trouble, the deer and the beaver, at least in the context of the Marshallian market-period that is also the natural habitat of the Walrasian *tâtonnement*, and to focus instead on the marginal adjust-ment that becomes operative whenever there happens to be excess demand for a thing on the part of the would-be consumers: 'Rather than want it altogether, some of them will be willing to give more. . . . Among competitors of equal wealth and luxury the same deficiency will generally occasion a more or less eager competition, according as the acquisition of the commodity happens to be of more or less importance to them.'[63] Men of equal incomes but unequal preferences here drop out of the auction as the price rises, and the existence of an implicit schedule or demand-curve in no way escapes the attention of the businessman – the corn-trader, for example: 'It is his interest to raise the price of his corn as high as the real scarcity of the season requires, and it can never be his interest to raise it higher. By raising the price he discourages the consumption.'[64] Smith was evidently familiar with the notion that, more rigorously formulated, was later to acquire fame as the price elasticity of demand, as is indicated by the following: 'The coal masters and coal proprietors find it more for their interest to sell a great quantity at a price somewhat above the lowest, than a small quantity at the highest.'[65] There is, in short, considerably more in the *Wealth of Nations* about the impact of demand on value than is picked up by committed cost-of-productionists who add up the rent, the pay and the profit that are 'neither more nor less than what is sufficient'[66] if the factors are to be retained in the trade, who freeze the institutional parameters into an eternal *stasis* by means of the closed *sesame* of the implicit *ceteris paribus*, and who take statements such as the following (which concerns the restoration of the long-run equilibrium stationary state) as the essence of Adam Smith's message with respect to the nature of economic processes:

> The natural price, therefore, is, as it were, the central price, to which the prices of all commodities are continually gravitating. Different accidents may sometimes keep them suspended a good deal above it, and sometimes force them down even somewhat below it. But whatever may be the obstacles which hinder them from settling in this centre of repose and continuance, they are constantly tending towards it.[67]

Such a statement hardly brings out the continuous fluctuations in price which result from 'the abundance or scarcity of the commodity in proportion to the need for it': 'If the commodity be scarce, the price is raised, but if the commodity be more than is sufficient to supply the demand, the price falls. Thus it is that diamonds and other precious stones are dear, while iron, which is much more useful, is so many times cheaper.'[68] There is no evidence that Marshall came into contact with that precise passage before 1896, when Edwin Cannan published (under the title of *Lectures on Justice, Police, Revenue and*

Arms) the celebrated notes taken in the 1762–3 session by one of Adam Smith's more assiduous students in the University of Glasgow. What must not be forgotten is just how many similar passages can be found, as we have seen, in the *Wealth of Nations* itself. One would have expected nothing less from a philosopher trained in the natural law tradition of Samuel Pufendorf (whose *De Jure* of 1672 specifies that price depends not only on 'the need of the article' but on degree of availability as well: 'The Scarcity of Money and Buyers proceeding from some particular Cause, meeting with a Glut of Commodities, sinks the Price. As, on the other side, the Plenty of Buyers and Money, or the Scarcity of the Commodity, raises it.')[69] and exposed at an impressionable age to the idiosyncratic utilitarianism of the 'never-to-be-forgotten' Francis Hutcheson (whose *System of Moral Philosophy* of 1755 makes clear that price depends 'on these two jointly, the *demand* on account of some use or other which many desire, and the *difficulty* of acquiring, or cultivating for human use').[70] Marshall, one would hope, had the perspicuity to detect utility and scarcity, demand and desiredness even in the *magnum opus* of his greatest mentor on which he so obviously relied so heavily while developing his own *Principles*. Even if he did not, however, he could hardly have been as unaware in the 1870s and 1880s of the work of Pufendorf, Hutcheson and other early subjectivists as he was of the content of the lectures that Smith had delivered in Glasgow more than a century earlier on the impact of *rareté* on exchange value. Marshall in any case had no need to rely on the later works of Mill and Ricardo for inspiration in the formulation of his theory of demand: the rudiments of the theory were not new but old and many earlier authors had sought to make constructive use of them – including Adam Smith.

Smith's value theory has strands not only of subjectivism but of sociology as well. His openness to the institutional framework and to the nature of cultural interaction is yet another example of the exceptional breadth of his reading and interests. It is also a further similarity between Smith's creative approach to the social sciences and that of Alfred Marshall. Thus both authors were fully aware of the phenomenon that Veblen in 1899 termed 'conspicuous consumption' and about which Adam Smith had written as follows: 'With the greater part of rich people, the chief enjoyment of riches consists in the parade of riches.'[71] The Scottish ascetic was critical to the point of intolerance of that competitive emulation which his English counterpart castigated as 'silly show';[72] and an important reason for the hostility of both economists to the parade of riches was their shared perception that premature discarding means waste of resources. Thus Smith wrote with evident admiration of 'a stock of houses' such as, if 'well built and properly taken care of, may last many centuries', contrasting it with the evanescent non-durability of a 'great wardrobe of fine clothes' such as, he made clear, was properly to be regarded as little more than 'trifling'.[73] Smith's views on discarding and durability constitute one of those curious instances in social philosophy where natural conservatism and growth economics both generate the same recommendations – to Marshall as to Smith, moreover, as is only to be expected from a high-minded author who complained that rapid changes in fashion were 'baneful',[74] indicative of 'fickle habits',[75] and hardly the friend of the made-to-last: 'Increasing wealth is enabling people to buy things of all kinds to suit the fancy, with but a secondary regard to their powers of wearing.'[76] Both Smith and Marshall, in short, demonstrated a sociologist's awareness that consuming is a social as well as an individual activity. As with consuming, needless to say, so with other dimensions of the economic problem. The impact of custom in the determination of wage-differentials is one illustration. The incorporation of social class and the intergenerational transmission of social status is a second. The insistence on self-policing constraints via internalised collective standards is a third. In all of these ways Smith showed that he was able successfully to amplify the perspective of the economist with more than a little of the sociological imagination – and so too did Alfred Marshall.

Marshall had come to the classical economics of Mill, Ricardo and Smith from the idealist metaphysics of Kant and Hegel. His intellectual development in that sense closely resembled that of another secular missionary determined to eradicate the blight of poverty, namely Karl Marx (1815–83). Some English economists were so hostile to Marxian ideas as even to attack Ricardo's *Principles* for having inspired the heresy: thus Foxwell made a note in his own copy of Ricardo's treatise to the effect that it was 'the first edition of this disastrous book which gave us Marxian Socialism and the Class War. Deductive Playthings of this type, completely divorced from realities, make very dangerous literature for the half educated. It is like giving a child a razor to play with.'[77] Marshall (perhaps because he was somewhat more Ricardian) was somewhat more moderate. The first volume of *Capital* was published in 1867 but only became influential in England in the late 1880s, most obviously because it was not translated until 1887, more controversially because of high unemployment throughout the 1873–96 period, the spread of the 'new unionism' among the less-skilled in the 1880s, and the increasing militancy of the labour-force, as is exemplified by the London dockers' strike of 1889 (a dispute manifesting a degree of class conflict that could hardly have been foreseen by Parliament in 1874–5 when it legalised the use of the strike weapon). Marshall read Volume I not in 1887 when it was translated into English, but as early as 1870, and in the original German. Why he did so is not at all clear save insofar as he was at the time interested in all forms of socialism (including Ricardian socialism). Whatever initially drew Marshall to Volume I, what is clear is how much he there found to admire in Marx's use of historical evidence and concern with the practical resolution of present-day problems. As Marshall wrote in 1889 about the author whom more than one modern commentator has been content to dismiss as a derivative deductivist and a minor post-Ricardian: 'I owe much to him. I read his book in 1870, & his extracts from English blue-books – garbled though many of them are – were of great service to me. Now everyone knows about the state of factory labour early in the century; in 1870 very few people had given their attention to it.'[78] Marshall referred to Marx in a lecture in Bristol in 1883, calling him 'the great German Socialistic writer'.[79] Once back at Cambridge, he included a section on Marx in the course he gave in 1886 on 'Socialism and the Functions of Government': passages are cited in German, Marshall evidently expecting much from his undergraduates. Marshall in 1886 was fair to Marx, but also indicated that Marx the abstract theoretician left much to be desired: thus Marshall at one point states the formula for surplus value, says that Marx related it to exploitation, and then comments witheringly that 'as I can't find out what exploitation means, I am not in a position to contradict this'.[80] The labour theory and the surplus recur in the *Principles*, where Marshall expresses his respect for 'Marx's sympathies with suffering'[81] but proceeds nonetheless to accuse the author of Volume I of presenting 'little more than a series of arguments in a circle . . . shrouded by mysterious Hegelian phrases'[82] – and of imputing to the great Ricardo the nonsensical proposition ('it is really as opposed to his explicit statement and the general tenor of his theory of value, as it is to common sense')[83] that capital can be supplied without authentic sacrifice in the form of the labour of waiting: the Marxians and other socialists, Marshall says, 'argued that labour always produces a "surplus" above its wages and the wear-and-tear of capital used in aiding it: and that the wrong done to labour lies in the exploitation of this surplus by others. But this assumption that the whole of this surplus is the produce of labour, already takes for granted what they ultimately profess to prove by it; they make no attempt to prove it; and it is not true.'[84] Marshall clearly had a greater respect for Marx the inductivist than he ever did for Marx the minor post-Ricardian; and this (coupled with his growing disaffection with all forms of socialism) may go some way to explaining why it was that Marshall never troubled to acquaint himself with the high theory and the abstract demonstrations of Volumes II and III. That he continued to believe that Marx ought to be read is, however, absolutely clear, as may be illustrated by a letter to Foxwell dating from 1906: 'I think no one can lecture safely on German Socialism without having studied recent writings, including Marx's *Capital* Vols 2 & 3, and other posthumous works. I have not read them. But whenever I talk to Germans about Socialism, they come to the front. I have looked at them sufficiently to think that they do not save Marx's position. But I should not be willing to lecture on the subject till I have read two or three thousand pages of recent German literature.'[85] Marshall, fond as he was in later life of distinguishing between 'economists' and 'socialists', was never a Marx-baiter or a Marx-hater; and Maloney's conclusion about the marginalists in general – 'Attempts to use neoclassical doctrine explicitly against socialism were rare'[86] – is clearly of relevance in the case of Marshall in particular. Maloney writes as follows about the attitudes of the great neoclassicals in the period from 1885 to 1908: 'There was little conscious inclination among English economists to use marginal analysis actively as a weapon against Marxism. Nor is there any correlation between enthusiasm for marginalism and distaste for Marx.'[87] Marshall was precisely such an enthusiast for marginalism who showed little distaste for Marx. When all is said and done, however, the influence of Chalk Farm on Cambridge cannot be said to have been great. Marshall no doubt respected Marx as a scholarly socialist who had had the common sense to ground his system in the solid analyses of Mill, Ricardo and Smith; but who then proceeded to erect an edifice which was totally inappropriate both for the intellectual foundations and the surrounding realities. Marshall evidently did not think much of the edifice. The debt to Mill, Ricardo and Smith was another matter, however. They were, after all, his mentors as well; and Marshall was not one to point at his origins with his left hand.

Schumpeter, like Pareto every inch the intellectual cosmopolitan, makes much of Marshall's rootedness: 'First and last, Marshall was, and felt himself to be, the great *English* economist of the period.'[88] An Englishman first and last, a prophet of continuity in ideas as in phenomena, the product of a sheltered background, a cultural conservative at heart, Marshall, it might have been expected, would have taken great care to concentrate his reading on the classical works of his distinguished countrymen. Such an expectation would have been incorrect; for the truth is that Marshall was strikingly open to new impressions, surprisingly adventurous with respect to lesser-known authors. Two of those authors in particular – both foreigners and both writing in foreign languages – appear to have exercised an influence on the development of his principles which was so profound as almost to rival that of Mill, Ricardo and Smith for pride of place. One of those authors was Antoine Augustin Cournot (1801–76), of whom Marshall says that 'as a fact my obligations are solely to Cournot':[89] 'Cournot's genius must give a new mental activity to everyone who passes through his hands.'[90] The other was Johann Heinrich von Thünen (1783–1850), for whom Marshall had at least an equal regard: 'I owed much to the mental discipline afforded by Cournot; but the one book which really guided me was written by a landowner, who had very slight knowledge of mathematics, and indeed occasionally talked ·great nonsense in them. It was von Thünen.'[91]

Cournot's *Recherches sur les principes mathématiques de la théorie des richesses* was published in French in 1838 but only translated into English (appearing, however, with an introduction by none other than Irving Fisher) in 1897. The book was not well-known in England at the time when Marshall came into contact with it. Writing later to Clark he said: 'I fancy I read Cournot in 1868.'[92] Writing in 1883 to Walras (and obviously annoyed at Walras' suggestion that he had borrowed the idea of final utility expounded in the *Economics of Industry* of 1879 from Jevons' *Theory of Political Economy* of 1871), he assigned an exceptional importance to the contribution earlier made by Cournot: 'I cannot be said to have accepted Mr. Jevons doctrine of "final utility". For I had taught it publicly in lectures at Cambridge before his book appeared. . . . Following the lead of Cournot I had anticipated all the central points of Jevons' book, and had in many respects gone beyond him.'[93] Marshall, in the preface to the first edition of his *Principles*, was quick to acknowledge the impact upon his marginalism of the economics of the two Continentals, and of Cournot most of all:

> Under the guidance of Cournot, and in a lesser degree of von Thünen, I was led to attach great importance to the fact that our observations of nature, in the moral as in the physical world, relate not so much to aggregate quantities, as to increments of quantities, and that in particular the demand for a thing is a continuous function, of which the 'marginal' increment is, in stable equilibrium, balanced against the corresponding increment of its cost of production.[94]

Continuous functions and marginal increments are the stuff of which Marshall's economics is made. They are also the essence of his debt to Cournot, who formulates his law of demand (without explicit reference to utility) in the following words: 'The variations of the demand will be sensibly proportional to the variations in price as long as these last are small fractions of the original price. Moreover, these variations will be of opposite signs, *i.e.* an increase in price will correspond with a diminution of the demand.'[95] To Cournot as to Marshall, evidently, exchangeable value is a relative magnitude and not an objective absolute – a magnitude, moreover, which can only meaningfully be analysed in the context of the maximising framework and the small change.

Cournot's *Recherches* abound in shrewd and pregnant observations on a number of important issues in economic theory. For one thing, Cournot did away with the classical distinction between productive and unproductive labour: 'Although we make continuous and almost exclusive use of the word *commodity*, it must not be lost sight of . . . that in this work we assimilate to commodities the rendering of services which have for their object the satisfaction of wants or the procuring of enjoyment.'[96] Cournot, again, was aware of the income effect, as in the case of the levying of a tax on a businessman's revenues: 'By reducing the wealth of the producer so taxed, it reduces his means as a consumer and affects the law of demand for other articles.'[97] Cournot, moreover, appreciated the significance of the elasticity of demand (his loosely-formulated illustration loosely resembling the similar example that was loosely formulated by Adam Smith): 'There is no doubt that there might be a book of which it would be easier to sell a thousand copies at sixty francs, than three thousand at twenty francs.'[98] Like Adam Smith, Cournot even sought to explain the steepness or flatness of the downward-sloping demand curve in terms not simply of the individual housewife wondering if she wants a bit more or a bit less but also in the light of the important sociological variable of social class. Thus Cournot, writing of luxuries, inferred a real-world correlation between market instability and social structure: 'Articles of luxury, of which the consumption is reserved to the wealthy classes of society, are generally characterized in the economic system by this property, that slight variations in the demand, or in the competition of purchasers, may cause very considerable variations in price.'[99] Cournot drew a not dissimilar inference in the case of lower-class necessities such as food staples: 'Enormous variations in price correspond to slight variations in the quantities produced, because the poorer classes find themselves compelled to sacrifice all other demands to those for these commodities.'[100]

Cournot, anxious to maximise the elegance of his theoretical presentation, was evidently far more sensitive to real-world complexities such as those associated with social stratification than is many a later theoretical economist; and the social realist in him is bound to have appealed strongly to the young Alfred Marshall, anxious to do good. Thus Cournot the theoretician was quite capable of issuing a quasi-Walrasian call 'for a complete and rigorous solution of the problems relative to some parts of the economic system' (it being, after all, 'indispensable to take the entire system into consideration') and then immediately to defer to Cournot the realist, who gently reminded him that the statistical estimation of general interdependencies, however valuable, was also impossible: 'This would surpass the powers of mathematical analysis and of our practical methods of calculation.'[101] Cournot the realist exercised a similarly dampening influence on the pure theory of monopolistic pricing that was developed by Cournot the theorist: monopoly is only one case among many of impeded competition, the realist said, and it is an essential characteristic of intermediate market structures such as duopoly and what subsequent generations would call oligopoly that they are characterised by radical uncertainty, strategic interaction and conjectural guesstimate to such an extent as to make outcomes indeterminate and theories therefore untidy. Marshall, just such a realist wanting to be just such a theorist, must have sympathised strongly with the dual nature of Cournot's approach: Cournot made clear that he would not allow himself to fall victim to the blinkered vision of abstract demonstration devoid of institutional relevance, and his young English disciple had the wisdom too to keep the demonstration in its proper place of servant to a master, and means to an end. Having decided to become an economist, the last thing Marshall wanted was to remain a mathematician.

Facts are facts, however; and the truth is that the would-be social economist with a sense of mission was in 1868 a trained mathematician and little else. Cournot having come to economics from mathematics as well, it is no surprise that Marshall, recognising a common language even before he had time to identify a kindred spirit, rapidly adopted him as his Charon and his guide. Thus it was that the older Marshall, looking back, pointed to the importance of the bridge-building influence that had been exercised by Cournot's work

> on a young man, accustomed to think in mathematics more readily than in English, and bewildered on his sudden entry into the strange land of economics, where many of the cardinal doctrines seemed to be mathematical propositions overlaid by the complex relations of real life; and at the same time distorted and stunted because the older economists had not recognized the mathematical conceptions that were latent in their own.[102]

If Marshall found the cardinal doctrines to be distorted and stunted because the older economists had failed to make use of the 'terse, compact, precise language of mathematics'[103] as a form of shorthand and a mode of discipline, then the same must be said of Cournot, frustrated beyond endurance by the example of Ricardo, struggling on at 'tiresome length'[104] to express in words or in simple arithmetic propositions which could have been expressed so much more clearly and accurately had Ricardo only employed mathematical symbols: 'Anyone who understands algebraic notation, reads at a glance in an equation results reached arithmetically only with great labour and pains.'[105] Cournot speaks of algebraic notation but what he means and what he employs is nothing less than the differential calculus, where the first derivative is conveniently synonymous with the incremental and the marginal and where functions are normally taken to be continuous. Cournot was hardly the first to express economic generalisations in mathematical language – as witness the work of Giovanni Ceva in 1711, Daniel Bernouilli in 1738, Cesare Beccaria in 1764, William Whewell in 1829, to say nothing of von Thünen – but he did maintain that he was familiar (save by title) with the publications of only one of his predecessors, one Canard by name, whose

Principes de l'Economie Politique of 1801 he was later to shoot down in the following words:

> These pretended principles are so radically at fault, and the application of them is so erroneous, that the approval of a distinguished body of men was unable to preserve the work from oblivion. It is easy to see why essays of this nature should not incline such economists as Say and Ricardo to algebra.[106]

His own essay Cournot obviously intended should be that much better and that much more influential. The symbolic notation did not, of course, appeal to all observers of the human condition (despite the fact that Cournot made clear his intention to 'put aside questions, to which mathematical analysis cannot apply'),[107] and not every reader was entirely *au fait* with the calculus. Cournot's medium undoubtedly impeded the absorption of his message. That it made a deep impact on the thinking of a young mathematician anxious to do good cannot, however, be denied.

Marshall records that in Venice in 1882, very early on in the glorious decade that was to culminate in the *Principles*, he 'began to re-read Cournot and to recast, so as to get somewhere near the final form, the first few chapters'.[108] Naturally he saw in the *Recherches* the sophisticated theory of monopoly which he acknowledged as an influence on his own,[109] just as he recognised in Cournot (and not Walras) the supreme theorist of all determining all: 'He taught that it is necessary to face the difficulty of regarding the various elements of an economic problem – not as determining one another in a chain of causation, A determining B, B determining C, and so on – but as all mutually determining one another.'[110] Nor is there any doubt that he was impressed by the presentation in the *Recherches*, in the words of Walras (in 1889), of 'Cournot's. . . . *supply and demand curves* which a number of English economists, following the lead of Mr. Marshall of Cambridge, are wont to employ.'[111] Yet Marshall, appreciative as he was of Cournot's many insights and mathematical rigour, was also struck by a central *lacuna* in Cournot's account of market capitalism. That *lacuna* had to do with the operation of increasing returns over time, and more specifically with Cournot's failure to explain why economies of size do not always and everywhere lead to widespread monopolisation. As Marshall wrote to Flux in 1898 about the *lacuna* that he had detected in his early years: 'My confidence in Cournot as an *economist* was shaken when I found that his mathematics *re* I. R. led inevitably to things which do not exist and have no near relation to reality. One of the chief purposes of my Wander-jahre among factories, etc., was to discover how Cournot's premises were wrong.'[112]

One result of what Marshall perceived to be Cournot's misleading misapplication of the mathematical method was the development, in the two decades after 1868, of more robust theoretical constructs, including that of the representative firm.[113] Another result was delay: 'His failure contributed to make me hold back most of my diagrams as to value from formal publication for twenty years.'[114] Cournot's *lacuna* in the area of industrial concentration would seem to have been a significant reason for the fact that Marshall chose not to make himself a first-generation marginalist by means of publishing his own theoretical work on value and exchange in the early 1870s. Without the benefit of Cournot's many insights and mathematical rigour, of course, it is disputable whether Marshall would have been able to accomplish that theoretical work in the first place. Much depends, one suspects, on just how much implicit mathematics and closet marginalism Marshall had already managed to discover in the work of the great English classicals before he fell in with Cournot relative to that which he subsequently came to notice as a direct consequence of his being exposed to the *Recherches*. Just how much that was, no prudent observer can state with any degree of certainty. Hazarding a guess, one is tempted to say that it was not very much; and that Marshall learned a great deal indeed from the work of Cournot.

Alongside Cournot, Marshall in the late 1860s ('probably in 1869 or 70',[115] the later date due to the need to acquire sufficient German) came into contact with von Thünen and *Der Isolierte Staat*, of which the first part had appeared in 1826 and the second in 1850. Cournot's influence, Marshall later recollected, was rapidly eclipsed:

> My impression is that I did not derive so much of the substance of my opinions from him as from von Thünen. Cournot was a gymnastic master who directed the form of my thought. Von Thünen was a *bona fide* mathematician, but of less power. . . . He was a careful experimenter and student of facts and with a mind at least as fully developed on the inductive as on the deductive side. . . . I loved von Thünen above all my other masters.[116]

Marshall, looking back on the impact on his ideas of the man whom he called 'the great unrecognized'[117] said that 'my own obligations to him are greater than to any writer excepting only Adam Smith and

Ricardo'.[118] Memory plays tricks, and Marshall seems to have said much the same on different occasions about Cournot. Whatever the order of priority, however, there is no doubting the existence of the influence and the nature of the debt.

The second volume of *Der Isolierte Staat* (the volume which Marshall apparently regarded as the more important of the two)[119] opens with a declaration which Marshall must have found very much to his taste: 'In economics Adam Smith was my mentor.'[120] Smith may have been his mentor, but Ricardo was quite clearly his inspiration when von Thünen chose to concentrate his investigation on the distribution of factor incomes (as opposed to the wealth of nations) and to focus his discussion on the conditions at the extensive margin – at the no-rent frontier, in other words, where land is free and the problem of sharing-out is no more nor less than the allocation of the product as between labour and capital. Few Europeans may actually have visited the no-rent margin in person (although it was, arguably, still to be found in the less-developed areas of continents like North America and Australia), but every good Ricardian had visited it in theory and visited it frequently. Marshall was no exception, and that in itself helps to explain his instinctual responsiveness to von Thünen's mode of attack. As he recalled in 1898:

> The general notion of distribution in the *Economics of Industry* published by my wife and myself in 1879 is the same as in my *Principles*. There are changes: for I was unwilling at that time to write upon distribution at all, because I did not then see my way clearly as to some parts of it. But I had settled the main outlines of the problem to my own satisfaction very early, under the good guidance of von Thünen. And the chapter on distribution in our little book proceeds on his plan of marching off to the margin of cultivation (*Die Grenze*) of his 'Isolated State', where there was lordless (*herrenlos*) land, and to get rid of rent before starting on the general problem of distribution: so that the whole annual produce might be taken as divided between labourer and capitalist.[121]

So great did Marshall in 1898 recall the intellectual influence to have been that it is a genuine mystery why there seems not to be a single reference to the 'good guidance' of the 'great unrecognized' in the whole of the *Economics of Industry* (the book in which, as Stigler states, Marshall 'advanced the marginal productivity theory in England for probably the first time since Longfield and Butt wrote').[122]

Even more curious is Marshall's suggestion in 1900 that he might in fact have settled the main points of his theory of distribution *in advance of* his reading of von Thünen's book:

> I cannot recollect whether I formulated the doctrine 'normal wages' = 'terminal' (I got 'marginal' from von Thünen's *Grenze*) productivity of labour before I read von Thünen or not. I think I did so partially at least; for my acquaintance with economics commenced with reading Mill, while I was still earning my living by teaching Mathematics at Cambridge; and translating his doctrines into differential equations as far as they would go. . . . That was chiefly in 1867–8.[123]

Marshall would appear not entirely to have made up his own mind as to the precise impact on his thinking of von Thünen's book. What is clear, however, is his instinctual responsiveness to von Thünen's mode of attack: Marshall could not but have seen much of his beloved Ricardo in the work of an author whose most prominent concern was distribution and whose point of departure was the no-rent-frontier, and was bound therefore to regard the unknown German landowner with some respect.

Ricardo had deployed his marginalism principally in the context of his theory of differential rent accruing to different plots. Von Thünen generalised that marginalism and used it to explain the payments received by labour and capital as well. In Marshall's words: 'Von Thünen worked out his theory with several curious subtleties, and some perversities but he gave a good lead by suggesting symmetrical relations between labour and capital; the earnings of each being defined by the last profitable application of each at the margin.'[124] Von Thünen was fond of presenting his marginal productivity theory in the form of simple agricultural illustrations – as where he asks at what point a profit-seeking farmer will cease hiring additional peasants to harvest potatoes before he provides the answer that is the essence of his message: 'Unquestionably at that point where the value of the additional product obtained compensates for the work which has been applied.'[125] It was presumably the abundance of the arable and the pastoral in illustrations such as this which led Marshall (in contrast, say, to J. N. Keynes) to categorise von Thünen as an applied economist as well as an economic theoretician, as a man above all else whose '*métier* was that of an agricultural reformer. His abstract economics come in by the way. He was up to his eyes in facts about rye and manure and so on.'[126]

Von Thünen's own estates would clearly have suffered badly if their owner had been a pure deductivist and little else, and it is certainly conceivable that von Thünen had his own personal experience in mind when he wrote as follows on the subject of diminishing marginal physical productivity in agriculture: 'It is in the nature of agriculture – and this is a circumstance that must be stressed – that the additional yield is not in direct proportion to the number of additional laborers, but every additional laborer brings an additional product lower than the preceding.'[127] That there is rye and manure in this account is clear, but so too is there Ricardo: the interpretation of von Thünen as a rustic foreign hayseed rather conceals the fact that the author of *Der Isolierte Staat* had earlier, as a student of economics at Göttingen, come into contact with a wide range of the great books of the discipline, many of them in the original languages. Besides that, von Thünen was quite capable of demonstrating what Marshall called his 'characteristic breadth of view'[128] by opening out his initial simplifications. The following passage, where agriculture is replaced by industry and trade and physical productivity by revenue, is a case in point: 'Every additional capital, additionally invested in an enterprise or trade, brings less revenue than capital previously invested. This phenomenon manifests itself also in practical life, where not a year's work, but money, is the measurement of capital.'[129] Marshall singled out von Thünen's contention that the (marginal) efficiency of capital might reasonably be approximated by remuneration received for particular praise[130] and described as 'well shown'[131] the problems associated with risk-taking in the account rendered of them in the *Isolierte Staat*. The fact that he also said that von Thünen's theory of rent was 'noteworthy',[132] von Thünen's explanation of the linkages between fertility, situation, cost and value the proof of 'brilliant researches',[133] must not therefore be taken as indicative of some belief that the contribution in question was relevant only to the agrarian communities: von Thünen believed his theory of marginal productivity to be of general applicability, and so did Alfred Marshall.

Von Thünen reached the conclusion that 'the value of the labor of the last worker employed is also his wage.'[134] Not his wage alone, moreover, but the wage payable to all existing workers in the same grade as well: 'The wage that the last employed worker receives must be the norm for all workers of the same skill and proficiency because for the same effort there cannot be paid an unequal wage.'[135] That statement is echoed in the *Principles*, where Marshall writes: 'The wages of every class of labour tend to be equal to the net product due to the additional labour of the marginal labourer of that class.'[136] Marshall also writes: 'On the margin of indifference between hand-power and horse-power their prices must be proportionate to their efficiency; and thus the influence of substitution will tend to establish a direct relation between the wages of labour and the price that has to be paid for horse-power.'[137] That statement is echoed in the *Isolierte Staat*, where von Thünen writes: 'The efficiency of capital must be the measure of its compensation; if the work of capital would be cheaper than that of man, the enterpriser would dismiss workers: in the other case, he would increase the number of workers.'[138] Von Thünen also writes: 'I very much fear that the algebraic calculations have exhausted the patience of many of my readers, as it is no secret how irksome and tedious algebraic formulations are, even for some scholars. But the use of mathematics must be permitted wherever the truth cannot be found without it.'[139] That statement is echoed in the *Principles*, where Marshall writes: 'The chief use of pure mathematics in economic questions seems to be in helping a person to write down quickly, shortly and exactly, some of his thoughts for his own use. . . . But when a great many symbols have to be used, they become very laborious to any one but the writer himself.'[140] With respect, in short, to the use of calculus in economics (including, by implication, the *ceteris paribus* assumption), with respect to the concept of marginal substitutability of factor inputs (a step in the direction of continuity and integration and away from the fixed coefficients of the classical wages-fund), with respect to the theory of factor price equalisation (including, by implication, the sub-theory of occupational and geographical mobility), the undeniable similarities between the *Isolierte Staat* and the *Principles* remind the reader most forcibly of the careful study which Alfred Marshall had devoted to the German Ricardian whom informed contemporaries tended to regard as little more than a gifted amateur.

There was one important issue on which von Thünen and Marshall were not in agreement, however, and that was von Thünen's calculation of $w = \sqrt{ap}$ which Marshall called 'his blunder as to the natural wage'.[141] Marshall's early notes on von Thünen's book betray an increasing impatience with the precise demonstration of a proposition which meant so much to von Thünen that he asked for it to be engraved on his tombstone and which meant so little to Alfred Marshall that he was prepared to dismiss it as inherently false: barbed comments abound, such as 'Now von Thünen makes the arbitrary assumption, without apparently knowing it. . .', 'This is the result

which von Thünen *ought* to get but does not', and 'Thus, absolutely
arbitrary as are his original assumptions, he has to make another (of
inferior importance) in order to get his result.'[142] Marshall is equally
dismissive in the *Principles* of the 'quaint result that the natural rate
of wages of labour is the geometric mean between the labourer's
necessaries, and that share of the product which is due to his labour
when aided by capital': that result, he observes, depends entirely
upon the acceptance of initial assumptions 'as to the causes that
determine the accumulation of capital and as to the relations in which
wages stand to the stock of capital', initial assumptions, as it happens,
which upon closer acquaintance reveal themselves to be 'fanciful and
unreal'.[143] Von Thünen and Marshall evidently differed in their
willingness to accept the assumptions which produced the $w = \sqrt{ap}$;
and the reader has a strong temptation to share the latter's reservations in preference to the former's deductions. Von Thünen hardly
enlists the reader's wholehearted sympathy when he insists both that
man is logically prior to capital ('Capital. . . . is the result of human
labor')[144] and that man without capital, at least in colder climates
such as Europe, simply cannot survive ('Capital. . . . must precede
the human being if he is to exist at all').[145] Obviously aware of the
contradiction, von Thünen manages to alienate the reader still
further by his suggestion that perhaps the original capital was not in
fact accumulated in the cold countries but was instead brought in
from warmer countries such as 'Southern India, central Africa or
Peru':[146] 'Europe . . . . belongs to the countries which have been
inhabited only by the immigration of peoples with capital.'[147] Von
Thünen's vision of Peruvians clothing themselves in banana leaves,
dwelling in log huts, and then taking off with the surplus of savings
for a Europe sadly lacking in capital because of the higher cost of
living is not one which will win the enthusiastic support of each and
every reader (many of whom will no doubt complain that a retreat
into some hypothetical prehistory not only opens the door to infinite
regression but simultaneously closes it to any evaluation of $w = \sqrt{ap}$
based on an inspection of the evidence). It did not win the enthusiastic support of Alfred Marshall. Marshall was forced to conclude
that von Thünen's assumptions were far too fragile to bear the weight
of von Thünen's deductions – and that $w = \sqrt{ap}$ could not therefore
be taken as an indisputable formulation of the natural wage.

Von Thünen takes pains to stress that the natural wage is 'the right
one' only in the most literal sense that it is the wage that is 'determined by nature'.[148] Other writers, he says, had concerned themselves with questions of the 'just price' and the morally-correct rate of

remuneration. He himself, he adds, is interested solely in explaining the *what is*, not in postulating some ideal *ought to be*: 'The discussion here is not concerned with almsgiving.'[149] Von Thünen presents himself, in sum, as the detached positive scientist whose study it is to identify the natural wage but not to evaluate it. Yet von Thünen was also a deeply religious man whose *Isolierte Staat* is peppered with references to 'the world spirit',[150] 'Providence itself',[151] 'the great hidden lawgiver . . . God',[152] a committed humanitarian of whom Alfred Marshall himself has written: 'Above all he was an ardent philanthropist.'[153] It is in the very nature of such a man that he should find it impossible simply to pocket the *is* without simultaneously asking himself if that *is* is genuinely to his taste, if that *is* is more likely to be the parent of good outcomes than the source of major catastrophes. Alfred Marshall, like von Thünen an economist with a strong moral sense, repeatedly asked himself to what extent the ethical and the economic were likely to coincide. So, when all is said and done, did von Thünen, whose search for the *is* was in essence that of an intellectual whose boots were covered in rye and manure but whose mind remained free to dream.

Free to dream, and to dream most of all of freedom. Nowadays, von Thünen said, a large sector of the community lives in thrall to want: 'A part of humanity now suffers under the burden of manual work and can hardly enjoy life.'[154] Such impoverishment, he argued, was deeply to be regretted, and that is why he, precisely like Alfred Marshall, rejected the 'socialist fantasies which arise out of their ignorance of the laws of economics'[155] in favour of the potent medicine of upgrading and growth: 'Let the socialists direct their whole attention to making labor more productive; if they succeed in this, they will truly better the condition of the worker.'[156] As a student of Adam Smith, von Thünen was convinced that individual self-interest could and did promote collective welfare – a clear instance where economic mechanisms are the source of good outcomes, as if guided by an Invisible Hand. In his restatement of the *Harmonielehre* von Thünen was if anything even more optimistic than had been his mentor about the complementarity of self-seeking activities: 'Workers and capitalists have a mutual interest in increasing production, that both lose when production declines and that both gain when it increases.'[157] Self-interest leads to economic advance, von Thünen said, and advance to the obviation of need born of scarcity: 'The workers, though striving for physical well-being, are led to freedom and dominion over suffering; that is, to the attainment of a great good.'[158]

Von Thünen had studied his Smith, but he had also studied his Hegel; and the reader must take great care not to ignore the wealth of meaning that von Thünen was fond of packing into deceptively familiar formulations such as the *dictum* that 'what is advantageous for the whole is also advantageous for the individual'.[159] What von Thünen says is precisely what von Thünen means and, contrary to first appearances, that is in the event something more ambitiously totalitarian than the private vices, public virtues argument to which the *dictum* seems obliquely to be paying homage. The private vices, public virtues argument says that if the individual aspires and labours, so in consequence of his striving does his collectivity flourish and prosper. Von Thünen's *dictum* retains the property of complementarity but goes virtually as far as is possible within the framework of market-orientated economics in the direction of inverting the respective significance of the causal and the caused:

> Mankind here appears as a large organic whole; every injury to the individual member of the whole is experienced by the whole, and complete health is impossible for the individual member if the whole is not healthy. The individual is a tiny particle of the spirit of mankind, and as such can participate in freedom only incompletely. The whole human race, organized for unity, can raise itself to unconditional freedom. [160]

The free is the whole, von Thünen seems to be saying – and to be saying it, moreover, even when his chain of reasoning begins in the time-honoured fashion with the isolated cells and not the interdependent organism, as it does in the following:

> Nature and freedom lead to one and the same goal. The workers will, then, for the sake of their own advantage working toward a greater physical well-being, be led to the fulfilment of their freedom. But insofar as the attainment and protection of this freedom is connected with a better rearing of their children, they are, while working for physical well-being, contributing to a higher goal, the enlightenment and intellectual development of the whole human race. In other words, out of that effort for well-being there comes forth, unbeknownst to them, a far greater good.[161]

If each upgrades, in other words, then all are uplifted, then, as if guided by an Invisible Hand, there 'comes forth another good which is not striven for by them, an even higher good: the enlightenment of all humanity'[162] – and this, moreover, even when the philosopher-economist's chain of reasoning begins in the time-honoured fashion with nothing more enlightened than the acting individual's pursuit of his self-interested egotism.

Nor does von Thünen's chain of reasoning always begin in the time-honoured fashion with interest and individualism. Von Thünen was so much the intellectual totalitarian that he was quite prepared in places, dispensing altogether with the doctrine of unintended outcomes, explicitly to couch his theory of social welfare in the language of the parts consciously seeking to serve the whole. One instance of such seeking and serving has to do with the happiness of all insofar as it is the precondition for the happiness of each: 'Only when all deal justly does evil disappear. The happiness of the individual is thus tied to the happiness of all, and therefore the task of life becomes to develop and educate his powers for the enlightenment and happiness of others.'[163] A second instance relates to that 'salvation' in the sense of von Thünen, that 'survival' in the sense of Hobbes, that is the welcome result when no member of the community elects to play the free rider with respect to the public good of a shared moral principle: 'Do that which will attain salvation for you if all others do the same, and willingly make the sacrifice which the principle demands even if others do not follow it themselves.'[164] In the one instance as in the other, it is clear, 'what is advantageous for the whole is also advantageous for the individual'; and to the extent that it is, the age-old antithesis between self-interest and self-sacrifice is thereby transcended. Alfred Marshall, like von Thünen a student of Hegel as well as Smith, a believer in altruism as well as egotism, a sociological holist above all, cannot but have been much impressed by the transcendence of that troublesome antithesis – and by the intellectual alongside the material progress to which he, like von Thünen, believed both *freedom from* and *freedom to* to have so great a contribution to make.

Both Marshall and von Thünen made much of the constructive self-approbation that von Thünen called 'the delight which every man feels after every noble dealing'.[165] Both authors also made much of 'the obligation of the well-to-do toward the proletarians'[166] that von Thünen captured in the following *ought-to-be*: 'The moral obligation rests on him who has become aware of what is right in relation to the laborer to bring these rights to fulfilment insofar as it lies within his power.'[167] Alfred Marshall, convinced that even at the current stage of economic evolution 'there is much nobility to be found in business',[168] insistent furthermore that 'the rich have duties as well as rights in their individual and in their collective capacity',[169] was pleased to be able to report that self-approbation was already coming to reinforce moral obligation not only in society taken as a whole but, and very significantly, at the level of the individual enterprise as well. Marshall cited the examples of occupational training provided by a caring capitalist even to a worker who is likely to move on, remuneration in excess of productivity paid by a compassionate employer to a half-starved operative, in support of his general contention that business-men, at least those who are 'aiming at leading the race', were already acknowledging the extent to which they were, ethically speaking, the servants of their staff: 'The character that fits them to take the lead in the arts of production is likely also to make them take a generous interest in the well-being of those who work for them.'[170] Von Thünen, interestingly enough, consistently argued the opposite case, that it is wrong-headed and dangerous to confuse Christian charity with business economics: 'This is not the way to realize the moral obligation of the rich to relieve the needs of the poor; there must be some other way.'[171] Marginal productivity, von Thünen concluded, is far from constituting *the* meta-principle of justice, but nor should the logic of the exchange paradigm be entirely neglected by misguided philanthropists who in their haste to do good fail to notice the harm that they are causing: high wages mean high costs, high costs drive our customers to foreign competitors, domestic firms lay off staff, the low paid become the no-paid, 'workers would then become completely without bread',[172] and such, all things considered, is hardly an obvious way to acquit 'the obligation of the well-to-do toward the proletarians'.

Von Thünen is not at his best in saying how, precisely, the well-to-do should pay their debts if not through higher costs incurred at enterprise level. His general message, for all that, is one of hope: higher productivity leads to higher wages, 'education capital' being 'invested'[173] upgrades skills, increased savings mean increased mobility into the class of capitalist, a more open and flexible social structure is conductive to the Marshall-like society of gentlemen that von Thünen believed to be a characteristic of life on the landlordless American frontier ('No crude division exists there among the various social orders'),[174] and thus is the natural solution of economic growth demonstrably more efficient than is the manmade alternative in alleviating the severe social blight of poverty. Alfred Marshall was able to assign more of a role to conscious action than was von Thünen but, not unexpectedly, less of a role than he, in common with von Thünen, was able to assign to economic growth. To be an economist was therefore, precisely because of the unbreakable link between wealth and poverty, to be a missionary as well. Those observers who believe Marshall's debt to von Thünen to lie exclusively in the technical development of marginal productivity theory are, it would appear, in danger of neglecting the multiple other influences of the German landowner who was anxious to do good: of course the margin is there, but so too are individual and organism, growth and betterment. These matters are not the less central to Marshall's economics for having been relegated to the status of footnotes in the work of the economists without sense of mission or perception of right and wrong who have sought to follow in his footsteps.

Regarding other early marginalists, Marshall wrote to Seligman in 1896 that 'my obligations are solely to Cournot; not to Fleeming Jenkin or Dupuit'.[175] It does, indeed, appear likely that Marshall did not see Jenkin's *Recess Studies* paper on 'The Graphic Representation of the Laws of Supply and Demand' (1870) before developing his own theory of consumer's surplus – and did not see Jenkin's other contribution ('On the Principles which Regulate the Incidence of Taxes', *Proceedings of the Royal Society of Edinburgh*, 1871–2) until after 1890.[176] He consistently denied that he had borrowed any part of his theory from Jenkin's work: 'I make it a point of honour to acknowledge my obligations – whenever I contract them, and when they are not obvious. I do not attempt to estimate how much I owe to Adam Smith or Ricardo. But I purposely worded my reference to Jenkin so as to imply that I was under no obligation to him.'[177] Jenkin's demand curve was not in any case intended as a utility curve (Jenkin denied that there was any objective measure of essentially subjective variables); and many aspects of his theories would, no doubt, have evoked a strong sense of *déjà lu* on the part of a student of Ricardo on rent who claimed he had developed his own doctrine of quasi-rent as early as 1868[178] and who was insistent that his translation of the classical surplus into the welfare triangle had been performed long before he learned of the existence of Jenkin. As Marshall stated in the Preface to the second (1891) edition of the *Principles* (the acknowledgement was later omitted without explanation): 'The notion of consumers' rent was suggested to the present writer by a study of the mathematical aspects of demand and utility under the influence of Cournot, von Thünen and Bentham.'[179] Marshall mentions Dupuit (*De la mesure d'utilité des travaux publics*, 1844) in his *Principles*, as he does, for that matter, 'the profoundly original and vigorous, if somewhat abstract, reasonings of Gossen'[180]

(*Entwicklung der Gesetze des menschlichen Verkehrs*, 1854): he was probably no more influenced himself by the work of these authors than he was by that of Fleeming Jenkin, but he clearly held it in high esteem. Not enough of their own contemporaries had done so, he reflected sadly (bracketing them with Cournot in this respect); 'their work was forgotten; part of it was done over again, developed and published almost simultaneously by Jevons and by Carl Menger in 1871, and by Walras a little later'.[181] Marshall was always inclined to play down the novelty of the celebrated contributions of the 1870s and to stress instead the extent to which the great English classicals and the most perceptive Continentals had in effect said it all before. In Professor Hutchison's words: 'If . . . there is any significant sense in which Marshall's theory represents a synthesis, it is of Cournot and Thünen with the English classics, and not of the latter with Jevons and the Austrian school.'[182]

Marshall came to marginalism after Jevons' paper, 'Notice of a General Mathematical Theory of Political Economy', was first read to Section F of the British Association in 1862, but before the publication of *The Theory of Political Economy* in 1871. William Stanley Jevons (1835–82) was for all intents and purposes the great British economist of the 1870s. Alfred Marshall was not. Marshall for his own part consistently maintained that he had arrived at his own marginalist theories in advance of the *annus mirabilis* when the unexpected publications of others annoyingly deprived many of his most promising constructs of whatever novelty they would otherwise have been seen to offer. As he wrote at approximately the same time as his retirement from his Cambridge chair: 'Before 1871 when Jevons' very important *Theory of Political Economy* appeared, I had worked out the whole skeleton of my present system in mathematics though not in English. My mathematical note XXI concentrated my notions.'[183] Such a statement is fully in keeping with Marshall's view, frequently reiterated, that he was merely standing on the shoulders of giants – and that Jevons was not one of them. Marshall's most flattering reference to Jevons is in an unpublished note probably written in the late 1890s where he says 'I reverence him now as among the very greatest of economists';[184] Marshall's least flattering reference to Jevons is in a letter to Edgeworth dated 18 April 1892 where he says 'Jevons' talk about utility & disutility struck the popular mind merely because it put out in broad clear light a very elementary fact, which could be explained even to children';[185] but Marshall's most characteristic reference to Jevons occurs where, coming directly to the point, he contrasts the elementary nature of Jevons' mathematical analytics with the polished professionalism of the real economists. There he writes:

> I think that the central argument of his *Theory* stands on a lower plane than the work of Cournot and von Thünen. They handled their mathematics gracefully: he seemed like David in Saul's armour. They held a mirror up to the manifold interactions of nature's forces: and, though none could do that better than Jevons when writing on money or statistics or on practical issues, he was so encumbered by his mathematics in his central argument, that he tried to draw nature's actions out into a long queue. . . . On many aspects of economics I have learnt more from Jevons than from any one else. But the obligations which I had to acknowledge in the preface to my *Principles* were to Cournot and von Thünen and not to Jevons.[186]

Marshall's position seems to have been that Jevons' *Theory* was not a bad book, but that no one who knew his Cournot and had read his von Thünen would want to describe it as a major breakthrough in science. Marshall, who generously described Jevons' notion of 'final degree of utility' as 'one of the most important of recent contributions to Economics',[187] discretely abstained from extending his list of previous contributors to embrace the books not only of Cournot and von Thünen but of Condillac (1776), Say (1803), Malthus (1820), A. Walras (1831), Whately (1833), Longfield (1833), Senior (1836) and Jennings (1855) as well: the subjectivist Eldorado was hardly an unvisited enclave in 1871, presumably because, to cite Schumpeter's wise words on a totally different topic, 'so brilliant a light will attract moths'.[188] Marshall himself, indeed, had been to the subjectivist Eldorado, and had carried away a good selection of nuggets such as those that he had stored for future use in his fragmentary 'Essay on Value' – partial equilibrium, the stages approach to adjustment, the assumption (if not the derivation from utility theory) of a downward-sloping demand curve, the forward-falling supply curve. Marshall's early Essay reveals that his intellectual system was far from complete when he made his notes, but it indicates as well just how sophisticated had become some of his core ideas in advance of his reading Jevons' *Theory*: 'I can't fix the date', Marshall wrote to Neville Keynes in 1883 in connection with the unpublished Essay, 'but I believe it was 1870. I know for certain it was before 1874.'[189] Memory can play strange tricks in cases such as this, where as little as one year can make so great a difference and where the great man himself is prepared to accept that the date in question might have been anything up to 1874. History is unlikely ever to reveal precisely how far Marshall had proceeded by 1871, inspired by the great strides made by Mill, Ricardo and Smith, by Cournot and von Thünen, in the direction of the *Principles* that were to immortalise his name two decades on. What is clear is that in the *annus mirabilis* of 1871 this most careful of craftsmen was laboriously engaged in the development of a marginalist economics and that the publication of the hare's *Theory* must have been a great disappointment to the tortoise. Maynard Keynes is particularly eloquent in contrasting the incompleteness of the hare who had seen something and rushed into print with the 'patient, persistent toil and scientific genius' of the tortoise who had perhaps seen as much but wanted to see still more before he committed himself in public: 'Jevons saw the kettle boil and cried out with the delighted voice of a child; Marshall too had seen the kettle boil and sat down silently to build an engine.'[190] A century and more after the events, of course, there is no disputing the fact that the engine and the tortoise have become the meat and potatoes while the kettle and the hare have been relegated to the sideboard of left-overs and hang-overs. Alfred Marshall could not have known in 1871, however, that his offerings were destined for the second-year core course and not merely for the final-year option. What he did know is that Jevons was for all intents and purposes the great British economist of the 1870s – and that he, Marshall, was not.

Marshall's first appearance in print was in connection with Jevons' work. It was no more than a review of Jevons' *Theory* which appeared in *The Academy* in 1872. It was evidently not merely because he felt he could have written the book that Marshall felt reluctant to write the review. As he stated in 1900 (inexplicably neglecting the existence of his second review, a piece on Edgeworth's *Mathematical Psychics* published, also in *The Academy*, in 1881): 'It has always been against my rule to write reviews. I have only written one in my life: that was of Jevons' *Theory* when it first appeared, and then I wrote only because there was no one else who had been working systematically on the subject of that book in England.'[191] The tone of the review does not suggest the jealous resentment that one would have expected from an author who had been 'working systematically' on a subject only to have seen the glory for the achievement in the eyes of the wider public go to another. For all that, the review is cool rather than welcoming, and its author capable of a surprisingly strong line in damning with faint praise. Marshall on the novelty of Jevons' contribution is one illustration of this tendency:

> The main value of the book . . . does not lie in its more prominent theories, but in its original treatment of a number of minor points, its suggestive remarks and careful analyses. We continually meet with old friends in new dresses; the treatment is occasionally cumbrous, but the style is always vigorous, and there are few books on the subject which are less open to the charge of being tedious.[192]

Marshall on Jevons' propensity to over-use the mathematical notation is a second: 'It is not intelligible to all readers. The book before us would be improved if the mathematics were omitted, but the diagrams retained.'[193] Marshall on Jevons' evident looseness in the use of ordinary English is a third: 'His lucidity serves to render darkness visible; to make us conscious of the absence of a specialised economic vocabulary, perhaps, on the whole, the severest penalty that the science has paid for its popularity.'[194] Marshall on Jevons' partial rather than general analysis is a fourth, and most of all in the context of the on-going competition in value theory between cost of production and final degree of utility: 'It is difficult to remember a prominent Ricardian writer who has not attained brevity at the expense of accuracy by employing the former of these expressions. Professor Jevons' use of the latter will have done good service if it calls attention to the danger of such parsimony.'[195] The general message of Marshall's review seems to be that Jevons did right to spell out in more detail the 'neglected truth'[196] with respect to utility to which the elliptical Ricardo only alluded in loose and unsystematic fashion; but that he would have made a far more constructive contribution if he had not set to one side the important insights with respect to supply to which the great classical theorists of labour cost had devoted so much of their attention. The reader rises from Marshall's review with the impression that Jevons' book, despite the fact that it states the known on marginal utility and next to nothing on the factors of production, is probably worth the odd few hours nonetheless, particularly if Mill is out on loan, Ricardo stolen despite the new security system, and Smith still at the binders. That was also the impression that Alfred Marshall almost certainly sought to convey. If he was disappointed that his first appearance in print should be a review of a book saying things which he himself could earlier have said, he was too much the gentleman to let his feelings show. Damning with faint praise is, however, a whole different cricket match.

Marshall consistently maintained that he had arrived at his theories by an independent route and that Jevons was not in the event one of the giants on whose shoulders he had elected to stand. Jevons himself said as much in 1879 in a letter to Foxwell: 'As regards Marshall's originality, I never called it in question in the slightest degree having neither the wish nor the grounds.'[197] Yet Jevons' theory is in truth somewhat older than Jevons' *Theory*; and one cannot help but speculate on the influence of the 1862 paper even if not the 1871 book. The 1862 meeting of the British Association was, after all, held in Cambridge, and in October. There is no evidence that Marshall (then a second-year undergraduate) actually attended the meetings, but Henry Fawcett must have done so, partly because he was Section Secretary, partly because of the political patronage of the Section President, Edwin Chadwick: as Marshall subsequently came into close contact with Fawcett once he had begun to lecture on economics, the possibility cannot be ignored that Marshall's route to mathematical Benthamism did indeed lead off from Jevons' paper, but indirectly, via the Cambridge oral tradition. Another possibility is that Marshall at some stage saw the summary of the paper which appeared in 1863 in the published report on the Cambridge proceedings (the abstract of the 'Notice' there consisting, however, of no more than one page of small type, without mathematics and without graphs); or read, for that matter, the paper itself when it appeared in 1866 in the *Journal of the Statistical Society of London* (the Society had almost 400 members at the time, and it is hard to imagine that none of them were involved in social science teaching in Cambridge). Commenting both on the significance of the 1862 paper and on Marshall himself, Jevons later wrote: 'The essential points of my theory were fully indicated as far back as 1862 at the Cambridge Meeting of the British Association. I have no reason to suppose that Marshall saw any printed report of my first brief paper.'[198] Nor did he have any reason to suppose that Marshall did not; but that inference Jevons wisely left for the reader himself to draw.

With respect to the *Theory* itself, Marshall was adamant that, having publicly lectured on marginal utility in Cambridge *before* the appearance of Jevons' book he could hardly be said to have discovered this important concept only in 1871. Memory can play strange tricks in cases such as this, however. Marshall recalled that he was in those early Cambridge days referring not to 'final utility' but to 'terminal-value-in-use',[199] but not that Jevons too had spoken of 'terminal value' – or that he himself, by the *Economics of Industry* and the *Pure Theory of Domestic Values* of 1879, had conspicuously

converted to 'final utility' in any case. Marshall later sought, moreover, to give the impression that he had in those early days absorbed
the significance as well as the nomenclature of the marginal revolution. Here too, however, as Professor Howey has explained, his
recall may have been less than perfect:

> Perhaps at this time it is helpful to note that Marshall wrote
> nothing at all prior to 1871; and that he touched on utility only
> three times in all his writing up to 1890: in the review of Jevons'
> *Theory*, in his *Economics of Industry*, and in his *Pure Theory of
> Domestic Values*. On none of these occasions did he use utility in
> any way that would lead a reader to think that he even held the
> idea highly, let alone that he had a paternal interest in it. It is clear,
> too, that no one has ever said that he had heard Marshall lecture
> on marginal utility or any topic resembling it during the years
> before 1871.[200]

Howey points out that Marshall's Inaugural Lecture on 'The Present
Position of Economics' contains only an oblique reference to Jevons
(mainly to do with the unfinished business of constructing a useful
economic science: 'Jevons might have done a great part of it, if his
life had not been cut short')[201] and no mention whatsoever of the
word 'utility'. All of this leads Howey to conclude that the derivation
of demand curves from marginal utility was, until something like a
decade and a half *after* the appearance of Jevons' *Theory*, a matter of
not much more than marginal concern for Alfred Marshall: 'In the
years from 1871 up to the time he went to Cambridge in 1885 the idea
of marginal utility played an inconsequential role in his work or
thinking on economic problems. Only in the *Principles* published in
1890 did marginal utility come forth as an important and integral part
of his economic analysis.'[202] Whatever Marshall knew (or did not
know) about marginal utility in 1871, Howey suggests, what is abun-
dantly clear is that Marshall did not fully appreciate the significance
of his knowledge until much later.

One would not, of course, have expected a confirmed ascetic to be
as interested in pleasure as he was in cost, nor an avowed Ricardian
to be as strong on demand as he was on supply; and the fact is that
even in 1890 Marshall, attuned though he may have been to the
importance of utility, stubbornly remained quintessentially himself
by ensuring that both blades of the scissors, both definitively present,
were not both precisely equal. Book III (which deals with passive
absorption) is as short as 45 pages and highly simplified. Book V (of

which the subject is active creation) is 149 pages in length and much more difficult. Shackle says that in 'books which propose a novelty' there is often to be detected 'a focal chapter or part, an "engine room" which contains the power of the whole argument. In Marshall's *Principles* we have book v.'[203] Shackle's conjecture as to the peculiar centrality of Marshall's Book V is persuasive, and also fully in line with Marshall's own recollections concerning the trajectory along which his treatise had evolved. One account plays down the importance of III relative to V: 'The purely analytical work in Book V of my Principles, with a part of Book III, were the kernel from which my volume expanded backwards and forwards to its present shape.'[204] Another account does not trouble to mention Book III at all: 'Thus was written the kernel of the fifth book of [the] "Principles". From that kernel the present volume was extended gradually backwards and forwards, till it reached the form in which it was published in 1890.'[205] Jevons' work might conceivably have exerted some influence on Marshall's thinking when he came to formulate the utility-based theory of the demand curve which is the centrepiece of Book III. Whether Jevons' shadow can be detected as well in Marshall's Book V is far more controversial and far less likely.

Marshall delayed publication of his major theoretical work until he was 48: 'I was in no hurry to publish because I wished to work out my doctrines on their practical side.'[206] Jevons, on the other hand, published his *Theory* when he was 36 (he was dead just over a decade later) – and when Marshall, not much younger, was all of 29. Almost twenty years may have separated their great books, but the two distinguished marginalists, it must not be forgotten, were virtual contemporaries nonetheless. That being the case, of course, one is tempted to speculate on the extent to which Pantaleoni was on the right track when he stated boldly, in a letter to Walras, that 'Jevons . . . . s'était déjà servi d'une partie des leçons de Marshall.'[207] The two distinguished marginalists were virtual contemporaries, and the main thrust of Pantaleoni's remark is that date of publication is, at least in this unique case, a misleading proxy for direction and force of influence. The fact that Marshall did not publish his theories until after 1871 does not, after all, mean that he kept them to himself. On the contrary, and it is perhaps because Jevons was himself on the fringes of the oral tradition that knows all secrets but copyrights none that the tone of his letter to Foxwell dated 14 November 1879 is positively defensive: 'I do not know what Marshall gave in his lectures in 1869, as I neither attended them nor [have] seen notes unless indeed the answers of some candidates. . . . In my book of 1871 (*Theory of Political Economy*) I could not possibly have borrowed anything from Marshall.'[208] Jevons was replying to a suggestion contained in a letter from Foxwell dated only two days earlier to the effect that it was all in Marshall and had been for some time: 'Marshall always spoke in the highest terms of your book from its first appearance. . . . As to priority, I think most of Marshall's work was about contemporaneously with yours: his lectures being delivered from 1869–1876 here.'[209] Elsewhere, in his famous essay of 1887 on 'The Economic Movement in England', Foxwell pays tribute to Jevons' *Theory* (which he describes as 'original and masterly') but cautions the reader not to neglect the 'personal and indirect influence' that had been exercised even before 1871 by the lectures of the much-unpublished Cambridge don: 'To the influence of this book, and of the teaching of Professor Marshall, who had *previously* revived and extended the analysis of Cournot, English economics owes a stimulus the full effects of which can scarcely be measured.'[210] Foxwell had personally attended Marshall's lectures in the years immediately preceding the *Theory* (sadly, he appears not to have written up and preserved his notes): he was therefore ideally placed to speak with authority on what Marshall had actually told his young charges.

Marshall is not mentioned in the first edition of the *Theory*. In the Preface to the second he is, and in the following words: 'At Cambridge (England) the mathematical treatment of economics is becoming gradually recognized owing to the former influence of Mr. Alfred Marshall, now the Principal of University College, Bristol, whose ingenious mathematico-economic problems, expounded *more geometrico*, have just been privately printed at Cambridge.'[211] The reference is to the *Pure Theory* papers of 1879 (Sidgwick had done his job well in selecting the *best* sections for publication), which so impressed Jevons that he wrote to Marshall to say that he was studying them carefully in connection with his own proposed revisions. Jevons made clear that he was not finding the papers easy ('Your problems are rather stiff', he stated candidly, 'and I have hardly succeeded in mastering them')[212] but that he regarded them nonetheless as being of considerable value to the mathematical subjectivist. Later in 1879 (almost certainly after the revisions in question had been made) he read the *Economics of Industry*. Edgeworth records how, at more or less the same time as the second edition of the *Theory* appeared, he made the arduous journey from 5

Mount Vernon, Hampstead, to 2 The Chestnuts, East Heath Drive, where his friend Jevons 'highly praised the then recently published *Economics of Industry*':[213] it was the young polymath's first exposure to Marshall's economics and also shows just how far his distinguished friend had come to appreciate Marshall's work. It was not always thus, and Jevons as late as 1875 (commenting on an account rendered by the ubiquitous Foxwell of the current state of oral economics in Cambridge) was quite capable of saying: 'I was not aware that Marshall had so long entertained notions of a quantitative theory of political economy, and think it is a pity he has so long delayed publishing something on the subject.'[214] Jevons' surprise is itself surprising in view of the fact that, as external examiner in the mid-1870s for Marshall's Cambridge candidates in political economy, he if anyone ought to have had an early idea of Marshall's notions. Apparently, however, he did not, but only discovered the meaning of Marshall in 1879 when it was already too late for him to enrich his own marginalism with a sprinkling of the ideas of his distinguished contemporary. Always assuming, of course, that he would have wished to do so – since it was also in 1879 that Jevons, taxed on the similarities between his work and that of Marshall, dismissed the whole issue of causality as fundamentally misguided: 'These questions are really of little or no importance now we have found such earlier books as those of Gossen, Cournot, Dupuit, etc.'[215] It being highly unlikely that Jevons had read Dupuit before 1877 and Gossen before 1878, the strong inference is that Marshall was by no means the only distinguished marginalist who had in the late 1860s made Cournot's *Recherches* his university. If, therefore, there are similarities between Jevons' work and that of Marshall, the causal influence might not be of the one upon the other at all (and neither said it was) but because of the influence exercised by Cournot's important if much-unread book upon both. And by many other important books, much-read or much-unread, as well: *natura non facit saltum*, Marshall was wont to insist, and neither did the manifold complexities of formal economic theory.

Whether Marshall built on Jevons, or Jevons built on Marshall, or both Marshall *and* Jevons built on third parties, British and foreign, one thing is clear, that there are indeed a remarkable number of similarities between the *Theory* which nipped in smartly and the *Principles* which lumbered on slowly behind. The *Theory*, for one thing, adopting the standard Benthamite posture of utility-maximisation/disutility-minimisation, posits that satisfaction is not an

intrinsic property of a given commodity but rather relative to changing circumstances and inversely variant (time-intervals being assumed 'infinitely short')[216] with quantity consumed: 'The very same
articles vary in utility according as we already possess more or less of
the same article.'[217] From perceived diminution in intensity of feeling
then follows logically the crucial distinction between total utility and
final degree of utility: 'The degree of utility varies with the quantity
of commodity, and ultimately decreases as that quantity increases.
No commodity can be named which we continue to desire with the
same force, whatever be the quantity already in use or possession.'[218]
As with the continuous downward-sloping utility curve, moreover, so
with the upward-sloping disutility function; and thus it was that
Jevons, applying the concept of marginal disutility to the supply of
inputs, was able to derive the theoretical prediction 'that no increment of labour would be expended unless there was sufficient
recompense in the produce, but that labour would be expended up to
the point at which the increment of utility exactly equals the increment of pain incurred in acquiring it.'[219] Such a *de facto* integration of distributional considerations with the more general theory
of utility and marginal utility is bound to have appealed strongly to
Marshall, who likewise broke with the classical dichotomy between
the theory of distribution and that of value.

  Jevons was so satisfied with his theory of incremental pleasure that
he even applied it (as Bernouilli had done and as Marshall was to do)
to the putative utility of money income itself: thus Jevons wrote that,
as compared with a family experiencing absolute deprivation, 'to a
family possessing one thousand pounds a year, the utility of a penny
. . . will be much less, because their want of any given commodity
will be satiated or satisfied to a much greater extent, so that the
urgency of need for a pennyworth more of any article is much
reduced'.[220] Strictly speaking, of course, Jevons had no right to make
such an interpersonal comparison of cardinal utility, having previously disqualified himself from doing so by denying the existence of
standard units of measurement: 'Every mind is . . . inscrutable to
every other mind, and no common denominator of feeling seems to
be possible.'[221] Jevons says that, precisely because the aggregation of
subjectivities simply cannot be performed, there is 'never', in his
Theory, 'in any single instance, an attempt made to compare the
amount of feeling in one mind with that in another. I see no means by
which such comparison can be accomplished.'[222] Jevons is not, however, in his 'never' and his 'any', being entirely fair to his own

practice. Jevons the purist may have believed that comparisons of utility were impossible, but Jevons the pragmatist correctly saw that without them economic science was unlikely to be of much use with respect to real-world problems. That is why it is Jevons' practice either to fall back upon the tried-and-tested standby of common sense (as where he says that a penny – twenty years later Marshall made it a shilling – means more to a poor man than it does to a rich one) or to employ the statistical demand curve for a commodity as a proxy for the assorted utility-functions of the individual consumers (a second-best methodology which proceeds along the arguably taut-ologous lines of measuring utility by exchange value on the grounds that theory postulates utility to be the cause of exchange value). The following is a case in point:

> We cannot really tell the effect of any change in trade or manufac-ture until we can with some approach to truth express the laws of the variation of utility numerically. To do this we need accurate statistics of the quantities of commodities purchased by the whole population at various prices. The price of a commodity is the only test we have of the utility of the commodity to the purchaser.[223]

Neither the substitution of common sense for factual information nor the employment of induction as a proxy for deduction is an ideal technique for quantifying the unquantifiable. They are, however, more likely than not the best techniques that can be found in an imperfect world by an economist who, despite the difficulties, is anxious for his results to be of use. Jevons was such an economist and so was Alfred Marshall. Both men used the same techniques for quantifying the unquantifiable. Compared with their actual practice, the fact that Jevons was on theoretical grounds opposed to interper-sonal comparison while Marshall was, however grudgingly, prepared to lend it some measure of theoretical respectability, does tend to appear less important than the similarities between their systems.

Both Jevons and Marshall were acutely aware of the economist's lack of the psychological data which is so important if economic theories are genuinely to have real-world relevance. Both were prepared, however, to treat revealed preference as a workable alter-native and to make use for operational purposes of the monetary measure of marginal desiredness of which Jevons writes: 'I never attempt to estimate the whole pleasure gained by purchasing a commodity; the theory merely expresses that, when a man has purchased enough, he would derive equal pleasure form the possession of a small quantity more as he would from the money price of it.'[224] Such a purchase-and-sale paradigm reminds the reader most forcibly of the centrality of interpersonal swaps (Smith's deer for Smith's beaver, not Robinson Crusoe long before Friday) to the theories of economising that were developed both by Marshall and by Jevons. Jevons' views on the catallactic perspective are particularly incisive (the result, perhaps, of having had the benefit of an economically-minded mother who took the trouble to read him Richard Whatley's *Easy Lessons on Money Matters* at the impressionable age of nine):

> Exchange is so important a process in the maximizing of utility and the saving of labour, that some economists have regarded their science as treating of this operation alone. Utility arises from commodities being brought in suitable quantities and at the proper times into the possession of persons needing them; and it is by exchange, more than any other means, that this is effected.[225]

Economics becomes, in such a perspective, a science of exchange ratios, not of isolated values. It is a perspective which is as characteristic of the work of Marshall as it is of that of Jevons.

The numbers collected via the inspection of real-world exchange ratios are subject, admittedly, to a wide range of impurities. Being *ex post* observations, for example, they are only likely to be perfectly congruent with *ex ante* intentions in a stationary state in which perfect information ensures that no expectations will be frustrated – and yet Jevons, like Marshall, made no secret of his belief that the normal state of the economic life was the dynamic: 'The real condition of industry is one of perpetual motion and change. Commodities are being continually manufactured and exchanged and consumed.'[226] Besides that, the equilibrium condition that to Jevons is that 'the ratio of exchange of any two commodities will be the reciprocal of the ratio of the final degrees of utility of the quantities of commodity available for consumption after the exchange is completed'[227] and that to Marshall is that incremental utility will be proportional to incremental cost is genuinely inertial not in the partial but only in the general case – and yet Jevons, like Marshall, saw that income allocated 'in such a way as to equalize the utility of the final increments of all commodities consumed'[228] was, while clearly the theoretical precondition for zero further shifting of expenditure in pursuit of the gains from trade, also a state of affairs never likely to obtain in the real world that surrounds the economic textbook. The meaning is clear, that the numbers collected via the inspection of real-world exchange ratios are not collected in those ideal economic conditions that would most closely resemble the perfect vacuum in physics – and yet that Jevons and Marshall alike were prepared to treat revelation of preference as something more robust than random.

Jevons was a strong advocate of good economic theories who welcomed in particular the use of diagrams and graphs, calculus and geometry, in the interests of precision: 'It is clear that economics, if it is to be a science at all, must be a mathematical science.'[229] Like Cournot before him and Marshall afterwards, Jevons made the point that economics as a science is concerned with the phenomena of infinitesimally small changes and continuous incremental doses, and that, whether words are used or other symbols, these phenomena by their very nature are mathematical: 'Economists cannot alter their nature by denying them the name; they might as well try to alter red light by calling it blue.'[230] No doubt there is much truth in Jevons' assertion, but so too is there much truth in his admission (as if in response to an invisible businessman, say, with an indivisible stock, who cries out that his own function happens to be step) that, in mathematical economics, 'every solution involves hypotheses which are not really true'.[231] Jevons was a strong advocate of good economic theories, but he was hardly prepared to settle for abstract formulations which were no more than first approximations; and thus it was that he, as Alfred Marshall was later to do, called for an alliance of the deductive with the inductive, the *a priori* with the *a postiori*. In Jevons' words: 'The deductive science of economics must be verified and rendered useful by the purely empirical science of statistics. Theory must be invested with the reality and life of fact.'[232] The *Theory* was not, it must be conceded, invested with much of the fact that its author evidently regarded as being of such great importance; but neither, to be fair, was the *Principles*. Schumpeter perceptively points out, comparing A. Smith with A. Marshall, that the former author sought to pack his suppositions and his tests into a single book while the latter was prepared to see them separated both in space and by a lapse of years (29 years, as it turned out). Thus Schumpeter, reflecting on the *Wealth of Nations*, observes that in it 'we find an approximately equal distribution of weights as between "theory" and "facts", although Marshall's superior art succeeded in banishing mere narration from the pages of the *Principles* – so that to readers who neglect *Industry and Trade*, his treatment looks more "purely theoretical" than it is and much more so than does A.

Smith's.'[233] The *Theory* stands to the body of Jevons' work in the same relationship as the *Principles* stands to Marshall's. It is hard to believe that the author of the *Investigations in Currency and Finance* and the *Coal Question* would not have produced his own *Industry and Trade* had the sea off Sussex not claimed him so young. Facts are facts, however, and the truth is that Jevons on value and distribution is a man of theoretical economics, not of applied.

Jevons, like Marshall, wanted to see an alliance between deduction and induction; but he made no secret of his belief that 'the difficulties of this union are immensely great'.[234] Jevons, like Marshall, was particularly concerned about the mutability of matter and the statistical problems associated with the *paribus* which perversely refuses to remain *ceteris*:

> Entirely to prove the good effects of Free Trade in England, for example, we ought to have the nation unaltered in every circumstance except the abolition of burdens and restrictions on trade. But it is obvious that while Free Trade was being introduced into England, many other causes of prosperity were also coming into action – the progress of invention, the construction of railways, the profuse consumption of coal, the extension of the colonies, etc., etc.[235]

Given such simultaneous variation, Jevons concluded, the economist has no alternative but to turn away from the tests and demonstrations that he would find of undeniable value in the resolution of simpler problems, and to rely instead on the validity of the logical deduction.

Such mutability, such variation, such change is yet another instance of Marshall's broader proposition that 'the element of Time. . . . is the centre of the chief difficulty of almost every economic problem'[236] that, in Jevons' *Theory*, is expressed in the following words: 'Time enters into all economic questions. We live in time, and think and act in time; we are in fact altogether the creatures of time. Accordingly it is rate of supply, rate of production, rate of consumption, per unit of time that we shall be really treating.'[237] Jevons leaves the reader in no doubt that he regards economics to be the study of the continuous flow, not the frozen stock; and makes clear that in the standard diagrammatic presentation of supply and demand a third dimension is always and everywhere implicit – that of time itself, alongside price and quantity. Time is also at the heart of Jevons' elliptical analysis of the relationship between cost of production and value of output. What Jevons says is that the former has no causal impact upon the latter: 'Labour once spent has no influence on the future value of any article: it is gone and lost for ever. In commerce, by-gones are for ever by-gones; and we are always starting clear at each moment, judging the values of things with a view to future utility. Industry is essentially prospective, not retrospective.'[238] What Jevons means is something significantly more restrictive, that cost has no influence on value once the commodity, produced and in the shops, has acquired the behavioural flexibility of land in the sense of Ricardo, a passive price-taker able to command no other reward but a quasi-rent in the sense of Marshall. That such conditions can and do exist is not at issue; and Jevons is entirely right (even if not to call it a 'somewhat novel opinion') to express the view that such is indeed a case in which 'value depends entirely upon utility'.[239] Simply, no one would want to argue that the demand-determined case is the *only* case, and least of all Jevons, whose declaration that 'industry is essentially prospective' is a clear indication to the reader that there is indeed economic life in the sense of Jevons above and beyond the market period in the sense of Marshall. The capitalist entrepreneur in the sense of Jevons cannot rewrite past history in the sense of Shackle, but he does retain the right to rethink his options should his expected values diverge too greatly from his actuals, his realised from his prospective. The discrete time-periods, the distinction between choosing and chosen, the profit that once earned turns out to be quasi-rent – all of this is explained in great detail in Marshall's *Principles*.[240] It is not explained in great detail in Jevons' *Theory*. That, however, does not mean that it is not there.

Jevons on cost may be largely elliptical, oblique and implicit, but not so Jevons on the 'Law of Indifference'. Here at least the author of the *Theory* takes proper care to ensure that what he says is what he means, and specifically that, given perfect information, 'in the same open market, at any one moment, there cannot be two prices for the same kind of article'.[241] Jevons is insistent that perfect information is the precondition for perfect competition: 'A market, then, is theoretically perfect only when all traders have perfect knowledge of the conditions of supply and demand, and the consequent ratio of exchange; and in such a market . . . there can only be one ratio of exchange of one uniform commodity at any moment.'[242] Jevons' reasoning is clear, that if competitors and customers are not up to date with current market conditions and differentiated alternatives, then even *minimus inter pares* acquires by virtue of their ignorance the monopolist's power to exploit. A convinced advocate of the market mode who believed that 'perfect freedom to exchange must be to the advantage of all',[243] an epistemological sceptic condemned to rely exclusively on the images of strength and direction of individuals' desires that were thrown up via revealed preferences in exchange situations, Jevons took the view that publicity 'tends almost always to the advantage of everybody except perhaps a few speculators and financiers' and was so persuaded as to its benefits that he was even prepared to recommend (as would be the case with laws specifying that prices should be posted publicly) that it be 'enforced on markets by public authority'.[244] Jevons' compulsory posting of prices is analogous to Marshall's governmentally-supplied tabular standard of values, while Jevons' hint that ignorance is power foreshadows the monopolistic competition that dwells in Marshall's 'special market'. Marshall also states that 'perfect competition requires a perfect knowledge of the state of the market'.[245] Such a statement is unlikely to provoke any great surprise on the part of the careful reader of the *Theory*.

There are evidently a certain number of parallels to be drawn between Marshall's economics and that of Jevons. Inevitably, however, there are the differences as well. Marshall, for one thing, believed that activities swell in importance relative to wants as a society evolves whereas Jevons (taking as typical the casual empiricism that 'the richer a man becomes, the less does he devote himself to business')[246] clung unsentimentally to the traditional view that work is the veil of tears: 'Consumption is the end and purpose. Labour is the painful exertion which we undergo to ward off pains of greater amount, or to procure pleasures which leave a balance in our favour.'[247] Marshall, again, was able to take a broader and more institutionally-informed approach to motives and goals than was Jevons, whose *Theory*, imbued as it is with the hedonics of Benthamite utilitarianism, is 'entirely based on a calculus of pleasure and pain; and the object of economics is to maximize happiness by purchasing pleasure, as it were, at the lowest cost of pain'.[248] Marshall believed that morality was of relevance to economics. Jevons, in contrast, formulated his theories as if for the exclusive use of the economic man: 'In economics we regard only commercial transactions, and no equalization of wealth from charitable motives is considered.'[249] Not only is such an approach more abstract than is that of Marshall, but it also lacks the developmental dimension of the later author's evolutionary economics. Marshall had a dynamics as well as a statics, Jevons (while recognising the need for a dual body of theory) only a statics. His reason for so limiting the scope of his

analysis appears to have been an amalgam of the logician's preference for first things first with the mathematician's tendency to rank
elegance above descriptiveness: 'It would surely be absurd to attempt
the more difficult question when the more easy one is yet so imper-
fectly within our power. . . . It is much more easy to determine the
point at which a pendulum will come to rest than to calculate the
velocity at which it will move when displaced from that point of
rest.'[250] Jevons may be faulted for the lameness of his excuse and for
failing to shunt the car of economic theory on to the dynamic lines
which had been occupied by economic phenomena for so long; and in
this respect his economics is not only different from that of Alfred
Marshall but inferior to it as well. Even so, the metaphor of the
pendulum, like a catchy tune, somehow engages the imagination. It
recurs in Marshall's *Principles*.[251] Nor is it the only construct which is
shared, in whole or in part, by the two great giants of English
post-classical economics.

Marshall, to the extent at least that his public statements are
indicative of his private thoughts, did not regard his own work as
having been much influenced by that of Jevons. His dismissal of
Jevons on marginal utility in the *The Academy* review of 1872 with a
statement which implies that even he, Marshall, had met it already is
typical of his attitude: 'It is a familiar truth that the total utility of any
commodity is not proportional to "its final degree of utility".'[252] His
attitude to the Austrians, interestingly enough, is more or less the
same:

> The Austrian School is on lines somewhat similar to a part of my
> own. But I knew nothing of Carl Menger till my own ideas were
> nearly in full shape: and Böhm Bawerk and Wieser were at that
> time at school, or students at the University. . . . The Austrians,
> and especially Böhm Bawerk, annoy me (though there is much in
> their work which I admire) by pretending to have revolutionized
> the bases of economics; whereas nearly all their doctrines appear
> to me to have been latent in the writings of the 'classical'
> economists.[253]

The image of the Austrian economists jostling against Jevons as all
bravely fought their way through Ricardo on the labour theory in
search of incremental pleasure is, frankly, more than a little bit
incongruous: apart form the fact that the interpretation of Ricardo as
a secret subjectivist is eminently controversial, the authors cited by
Menger himself, the founder of the Austrian school, as having

anticipated the modern theory of utility and value are the standard Continental ones (Turgot, Bastiat, Genovesi, Condillac, Galliani and Auguste Walras), accompanied by only three card-carrying classicals (one French, Say; two English, Senior and Lauderdale), all three conspicuously *non*-card-carrying when on their unorthodox off-days they formulated their explicitly utility-based theories of demand. Elsewhere Marshall, once again complimenting the Austrians for having formulated systems broadly similar to his own, mentions another great name, and one of only slightly less than Ricardian stature in his own canon: 'At about the same time as Jevons' *Theory* appeared, Carl Menger gave a great impetus to the subtle and interesting studies of wants and utilities by the Austrian school of economists: they had already been initiated by von Thünen.'[254] Initiation is, of course, no proof of adoption; and what Marshall says is fully in keeping with the concept of simultaneous but independent discovery that figures so prominently in discussions of why it was, for example, that Jevons and Menger published strikingly similar accounts in the same *annus mirabilis* of 1871. Marshall is wise not to assert causality; for there is little evidence to suggest that Menger had been influenced by von Thünen (just as there is, in Menger's work, little visible trace of Cournot). Marshall's references to the classical economists and to von Thünen in connection with the Austrian school are best interpreted, one suspects, not as the shrewd and pregnant suggestions of an intellectual historian who believes he has identified the founding fathers of a subsequent movement, but rather as indicative of the self-satisfied self-confidence of the advanced scholar who puts down a new book with the observation that the content is often acceptable but the matter for all that all too familiar. Just as Marshall took pains to play down the extent to which he had learned anything of significance from Jevons, so he consistently made clear that his debt to the Austrians was minimal. Thus, writing to Cannan in 1898 (some time, therefore, after the two volumes of *Kapital und Kapitalzins* had appeared in 1884 and 1889 respectively), he observed simply that he had been using the same definition of capital 'ever since about 1869, when I used to think in Mathematics more easily than in English';[255] while in a letter to Clark a decade later he audaciously cited the late date of 1874 ('By this time I had practically completed the whole of the substance of my Mathematical Appendix', with notable exceptions such as elasticity) and then observed, referring specifically to distribution, that 'I worked that out for the greater part while still teaching mathematics; and while still regarding myself as a mere pupil in the hands of great masters, especially Cournot, von Thünen and Ricardo, and while still extremely ignorant of economic realities. Between 1870 and 1874 I developed the details of my theoretical position; and I am not conscious of any perceptible change since the time when Böhm Bawerk and Wieser were still lads at school or College.'[256] Marshall, in short, did not regard his own work as having been much influenced by that of the Austrians.

Marshall was aware of the contribution of Carl Menger (1840–1921), and that in itself was no small accomplishment at a time when there were in Britain no specialist journals in economics: Jevons' *Theory* attracted popular interest (the review in the *Manchester Daily Examiner and Times* was half a page in length), but not so in Britain the *Habilitationsschrift* of an unknown foreigner. Few English economists could have appreciated that Menger was breaking both with the German orthodoxy of Roscher's Historical School and the English orthodoxy of the Ricardian labour theory, or recognised the extent to which he was seeking, in his *Grundsätze der Volkswirtschaftslehre* of 1871, to establish a new Austrian approach, theoretical and subjectivist in nature. Marshall, however, with his knowledge of languages and of Continental economics, was in a strong position to see the importance of Menger's new departure. He was also, if Hayek is to be believed, strongly influenced by it.[257] Influence is notoriously difficult to prove, and particularly so in the case of Marshall, whose acknowledgements to others (despite his well-known protestations to the contrary) are in truth erratic and whose insistence on Ricardo, Cournot and von Thünen to the detriment of Jevons, Menger and Walras is so strident as to be obsessive. That having been said, there are undoubted similarities as between the *Grundsätze* and the *Principles*. There are also some differences.

The most conspicuous similarity lies in the subjectivist interpretation of value as representing 'nothing inherent in goods, no property of them',[258] but as residing instead in the relationship between 'requirements for and available quantities of goods'.[259] Need-satisfaction is all; 'value does not exist outside the consciousness of men';[260] and thus it is that the economist must have (as did Alfred Marshall) something of the psychologist's openness to cognitive states in him. The proper study of economics being preferences revealed through exchanges, the economist is, of course, ideally placed to develop such an awareness of perceptions: they and nothing else are the substance for which price is the proxy.

Menger, like Jevons, attacked and rejected the cost of production theory of value: 'Among the most egregious of the fundamental errors that have had the most far-reaching consequences in the previous development of our science is the argument that goods attain value for us because goods were employed in their production that had value to us.'[261] Menger, again like Jevons, did so on the basis of the logically irrefutable observation that decisions made in past time cease to be choice-options in the present with respect to the future: 'Comparison of the value of a good with the value of the means of production employed in its production does, of course, show whether and to what extent its production, an act of *past* human activity, was appropriate or economic. But the quantities of goods employed in the production of a good have neither a necessary nor a directly determining influence on its value.'[262] Menger's use of the word 'appropriate', like Jevons' use of the word 'prospective', is, however, a reminder that the author, aware of the distinction between *ex post* and *ex ante* and clear in his own mind that all producing in advance of contracting is by definition a speculative enterprise, was prepared nonetheless to concede some active role to supplying based upon expectations. Menger and Jevons were in that sense fully in line with the dynamic approach to supply which is the centrepiece of Alfred Marshall's time-bound system. Marshall, the student of fresh fish, must have read Menger on the quintessential passivity of the supplier of a non-storable commodity in the market period with some appreciation: 'All perishable goods are, by their very nature, restricted in their marketability to a narrow time period.'[263] It is likely that he read Menger on the division of operational time into five discrete periods (the lags in adaptation being caused by the imperfect planning that is always and everywhere the concomitant of imperfect information) with greater appreciation still.[264]

Neither Menger nor Jevons was oblivious to the considerations of cost that were later to be spelled out in greater detail in Marshall's *Principles*; but both were, it cannot be denied, interested first and foremost in demand-side variables. Jevons wrote of 'utility', Menger of 'satisfaction', and both made much of the tendency for the marginal value to fall even as the total continues to rise. In Menger's words: 'The satisfaction of any one specific need has, up to a certain degree of completeness, relatively the highest importance, and . . . further satisfaction has a progressively smaller importance, until eventually a stage is reached at which a more complete satisfaction of that particular need is a matter of indifference.'[265] Menger was clearly searching for some technical term that could express the incremental concept succinctly and precisely. The term eventually adopted by the Austrians originated not in his own writings, however, but in the *Über den Ursprung und die Hauptgesetze des Wirtschaftlichen Wertes* of 1884 of his student and disciple, Friedrich von Wieser (1851–1926). It was *Grenznutzen*, a construction modelled on Jevons' 'final degree of utility' but with the difference that 'Grenze' (margin) took the place of Jevons' more terminal 'final'. Wicksteed, in his *Alphabet of Political Economy*, introduced the term into English in 1888, translating it as 'marginal utility': apart from knowing the book, Marshall also knew its author, having been an occasional member with him of the Economic Circle in London (other members were Foxwell, Edgeworth and Shaw). Marshall in his *Principles* acknowledges his debt both to von Wieser and Wicksteed for the use of the valuable technical term.[266] Needless to say, he did not ascribe to them the paternity of the notion as well. Marshall said that he had first met marginal utility (the notion if not the technical term) in the work of Ricardo, Cournot and von Thünen. And von Wieser said he had met it in Menger – as indeed he had.

Menger, unlike Jevons, was prone to ranking more than additional increments of one and the same consumable. He was also inclined, very much like Marshall, to rank the commodities themselves: 'The maintenance of our lives depends on the satisfaction of our need for food, and also, in our climate, on clothing our bodies and having shelter at our disposal. But merely a higher degree of well-being depends on our having a coach, a chessboard, etc. Thus we observe that men fear the lack of food, clothing, and shelter much more than the lack of a coach, chessboard, etc.'[267] Menger, in other words, developed a dual theory of need-satisfaction, a theory within the framework of which due weight was to be assigned to the nature of the thing to be consumed as well as to the intensity of the desire that was to be satisfied by the last unit purchased. It was, indeed, precisely because of his sensitivity to the nature of the commodity itself that Menger insisted on the utility of disaggregation within the broad product-categories, lest the economist fail to pick up variations in quality that can be so great as to represent products entirely differentiated save by name alone. Menger contrasts good foods with 'unpalatable foods', healthy accommodation with 'dark and wet rooms', proper medical care with 'the services of mediocre physicians'.[268] His appreciation of such differences is reminiscent of nothing so much as of Marshall's 'particular demand curve',[269] a theoretical construct which in itself is strongly reminiscent of the theories of monopolistic competition that were subsequently to be developed by Joan Robinson and E. H. Chamberlin.

Menger, like Marshall, was not so committed to the tolerant ethics of consumer sovereignty as to be unable to apply his own perception of ordinal utility to the nature of the consumables themselves: neither author saw it as problematic that food should in some absolute sense be of greater importance than tobacco, tea than alcohol, water than diamonds. Nor was Menger, again like Marshall, so seduced by the partial analysis into which liberal individualism can all too easily slide that he failed to see that, while only persons can make choices, nonetheless the truth is the whole: it was not Walras alone who was aware of inter-dependence and keen on complementarity, but virtually all economists, and not least Menger and Marshall, who had any developed understanding of the manner in which the market coordinates the complex even as it allocates the scarce. At each stage of production, Menger observes, each businessman makes implicit assumptions about the patterns of conduct which he expects his clients and his suppliers to adopt: given that, say, 'manufacturers of opera glasses very seldom produce the glass lenses, the ivory or tortoise-shell cases, and the bronze parts, used in assembling the opera glasses',[270] the businessman is condemned by the very logic of the division of labour to make those assumptions lest he make losses instead. *Ex ante* only individuals can make decisions. *Ex post*, however, the truth is not the unit act but the matrix of all flows; and thus it is that methodological individualism and the input–output table reveal themselves to be not incompatibles but complements.

This interdependence effect Menger fully appreciated. Not so, in Marshall's view, his famous student, Eugen von Böhm-Bawerk (1851–1914), whose work on savings and investment Marshall found to be deplorably close to that expository tradition in economics which assigns 'such disproportionate stress to some elements of the problem as to throw others into the background': 'Perhaps part of the air of paradox with which he invests his own theory of capital may be the result of a similar disproportionate emphasis, and an unwillingness to recognize that the various elements of the problem *mutually* govern one another.'[271] Nor was this the only flaw which Marshall was able to find in Böhm-Bawerk's theory of capital. Böhm-Bawerk, Marshall said, was wrong to adopt the narrow definition of capital which limits it in essence to man-made artefacts such as facilitate and abridge labour precisely because so narrow a definition has such limited explanatory power: 'Though he excludes houses and hotels, and indeed everything that is not strictly speaking an intermediate good, from his definition of capital, yet the demand for the use of goods, that are not intermediate, acts as directly on the rate of interest, as does that for capital as defined by him.'[272] Besides that, Marshall complained, Böhm-Bawerk tended to reason more like the technologically-determined engineer than the cost-conscious economist when he postulated, as if guided by a natural law, that the capital-intensive is inescapably the efficient:

> There are however innumerable processes which take a long time and are roundabout; but are not productive and therefore are not used; and in fact he seems to have inverted cause and effect. The true doctrine appears to be that, because interest has to be paid for, and can be gained by the use of capital; therefore those long and roundabout methods, which involve much locking up of capital, are avoided unless they are more productive than others.[273]

The ordinary businessman, Marshall observed pointedly, cannot afford the luxury of assuming without proof the existence of some 'universal rule that the use of roundabout methods of production is more efficient than direct methods',[274] but does not for all his scepticism deny that the machine-intensive, time-intensive technology might in his own specific conditions be the more economical: 'He never assumes that roundabout methods will be remunerative in the long run. But he is always on the look out for roundabout methods that promise to be more effective in proportion to their cost than direct methods: and he adopts the best of them, if it lies within his means.'[275] Böhm-Bawerk assumes the existence of a universal rule, the ordinary businessman compares extra cost with extra benefit, and it is clear enough where the cautious Marshall's sympathies lay.

One of the central tenets of Böhm-Bawerk's subjectivist theory of capital is the psychological *a priori* that saver-consumers are always and everywhere prone to value future satisfactions less highly than they do present ones. This psychological *a priori* is virtually the only aspect of his Austrian approach to capital-formation which Böhm-Bawerk took directly from the *Grundsätze*, where Menger had written as follows: 'Men are especially prone to let themselves be misled into overestimating the importance of satisfactions that give intense momentary pleasure but contribute only fleeting to their well-being, and so into underestimating the importance of satisfactions on which a less intensive but longer enduring well-being depends.'[276]

Böhm-Bawerk and Menger took the view that men are more naturally attracted by present pleasure than they are by deferred gratification. Marshall took a different view – a less abstract and deductive, a more anthropological and evolutionary view – that much depends on the men and on the social conditions that shape their attitudes. Savages and primitives, he conceded, do tend to put the *now* before the *later*, and in that way in some measure to render themselves the architects of their own underdevelopment: 'Children and nations in an early stage of civilisation are almost incapable of realising a distant advantage; the future is eclipsed by the present.'[277] Nonetheless, he was quick to add, matter is in motion; and 'when the child or the race grows up to maturity, it learns to exert itself for the sake of the future, as well as for the sake of the present'.[278] Thus it was that Marshall parted company with Menger and the Austrians who had built upon his psychological *a priori*: the backward underestimate the future and fail to make provision for it, Marshall accepted, but the more advanced demonstrably develop telescopic faculties and a capacity for self-denial which are all but impossible to reconcile with the Austrian view of man. It is ironical, therefore, that it is Marshall's view rather than Menger's which is of the two the more conducive to roundaboutness in the sense of Böhm-Bawerk: increasing prospectiveness means increasing frugality, increased prudence leads to a falling rate of interest, cheaper capital encourages the employment of capital. One is tempted to say that Böhm-Bawerk would in the circumstances have done well to switch mentors in mid-stream, so much more is Marshall's contingent evolutionism in line with his predictions concerning accumulation of capital than is Menger's postulation of an ever-constant human nature.

Marshall and Menger differed with respect to conduct and character. They also differed in their respective attitudes to mathematical economics. Marshall was fond of translating his theory of marginal utility into the terse language of the differential calculus. Menger, on the other hand, was content with simple numerical examples and fearful of any methodology that, by assuming continuity in the functional relationships, rendered itself incapable of incorporating indivisibilities in the commodities traded. Besides that, Menger reasoned, mathematics is a discipline of precision and certainty, whereas a great deal of economic action indeed takes place behind a thick veil of doubt in an arena where strategic interaction is of paramount importance and equilibrium values in advance of bargaining and contracting are theoretically indeterminate. Such a theoretical indeterminacy may be said to obtain, for instance, where one trading partner knows he is willing to accept as little as 10 bushels of grain for his horse, the other knows he is so desperate for a horse that he is willing to sacrifice up to 80 bushels of grain to acquire one, and both parties wish to exchange: clearly, 'the price of the horse can be formed between the wide limits of 10 and 80 bushels of grain and can approach either of the two extremes without causing the economic character of the exchange to disappear'.[279] An even more dramatic indeterminacy can be generated by making the second commodity as indivisible as the first (by making it not bushels of grain but, say, a cow).[280] Marshall was himself aware of the indeterminacy case, making it the centrepiece of his influential Appendix F on barter: there two parties, each a monopsonist with respect to one commodity and a monopolist with respect to the other, trade apples and nuts up to the point, theoretically unspecifiable in advance, where they cease to do so. Marshall, committed as he was to the calculus, banished this untidy result to an appendix. Menger, on the other hand, treated it as the typical swap in a deeply uncertain world where deer and beaver exchange on the basis of nothing so precise as Adam Smith's hours embodied; and opted to underline his uncertainty through conspicious abstention from the preciseness of mathematical economics.

There is much in Marshall, despite the differences, that is reminiscent of Menger, just as there is much in Marshall that is reminiscent of Jevons. Léon Walras (1834–1910) is, however, a more problematic case. Marshall's personal copy of the *Eléments de l'économie politique pure* (of which the first part appeared in 1874, the second in 1877) is only annotated up to page 65 (where Marshall comments of Walras on the demand function: 'a slovenly attempt. . . . it seems to have no use. . . . pass over this page')[281] and Walras' authority is only infrequently invoked in Marshall's numerous writings. There was some desultory and rather distant correspondence between the two economists in the years between 1883 and 1889 (Walras took the initiative, having been given Marshall's name by Foxwell in 1882), but it was neither especially cordial in tone nor especially rich in insight. Memory plays strange tricks, and in Marshall's case it appears to have caused him to place the correspondence with Walras somewhat earlier in his development than was the case. Thus, in a letter to Hewins in 1899, explaining that he did not wish his work to be judged 'hasty', Marshall wrote: 'As early as 1873 (I think that was the year) Walras pressed me to publish something about it; and I declined with emphasis.'[282] Elsewhere, in a memorandum written somewhat later (and in the third person) Marshall employed almost identical wording in explaining why he had put off the publication of his diagrams for so long: 'Though urged by the late Professor Walras about 1873 to publish these, he had declined to do so; because he feared that if separated from all concrete study of actual conditions, they might seem to claim a more direct bearing on real problems than they in fact had.'[283] Memory plays strange tricks, however; and the fact is that there is no record either of any such approach on Walras' part or of any known contact between the two economists before March 1883. Nor does it appear likely that Marshall so much as knew of Léon Walras' existence in the mid-1870s: the *Eléments* was not reviewed in England in 1874, and so minimal were the links with the Continent at that stage that Jevons died in 1882 without ever learning how closely Menger's book of 1871 resembled his own.

It was none other than Walras himself who was to be the first (in his *Théorie de la Monnaie* of 1886) publicly to link the three great names of the marginal revolution. In the second edition of his *Eléments* (published in 1889) Walras returned to the books of Jevons and Menger, calling them works 'antedating my own' in which 'the foundations of the new theory of exchange were laid in an independent and original manner'[284] (and quickly adding the disclaimer, so reminiscent of Jevons on Gossen, that in 1874 he 'had absolutely no knowledge of their existence').[285] Walras was the first publicly to link the three great names of the 1870s, Wicksteed (in the *Alphabet* of 1888) was the second – and Marshall, in his *Principles*, was the third.[286]

Marshall's *Principles* was itself a contribution very much in the 1870s mould, but its author was for all that hardly very friendly towards his immediate predecessors. Least of all, it would appear, was he friendly towards Walras. The fact is surprising in view of the evident similarities between the contributions of the two great economists. Walras employed the general rather than the partial framework; he used mathematics freely (saying that the opponents of the approach among economists 'can never prevent the theory of the determination of prices under free competition from becoming a mathematical theory');[287] he concluded that 'value. . . . comes from scarcity' and not from inputs – embodied save in so far as they too are scarce ('If labour has value and is exchangeable, it is because it is both useful and limited in quantity, that is to say because it is scarce');[288] he went beyond simple *rareté* in the sense of the *De la nature de la richesse et de l'origine de la valeur* of 1831 of his illustrious economist-father, Auguste Walras, and developed theories of the 'intensity of the last want satisfied' such as brought into sharp relief the concepts of utility and of the margin; he was alert to the role of the entrepreneur or 'organiser' and in sympathy with the cooperative mode of production; he formulated an approach to distribution and factor-pricing which is encapsulated in the observation concerning the wages of labour and the interest to capital that 'in a state of equilibrium, when cost of production and selling price are equal, the prices of the services are proportional to their marginal productivities, i.e. to the partial derivatives of the production function'.[289] In these and other ways Lausanne is remarkably close to Cambridge, Walras to Marshall. Yet Walras was in the last analysis the pure logician, the abstract theoretician, whereas Marshall's mode of attack was that of the social realist with one foot in the inductivist camp; Walras ignored the richness of historical and comparative evidence whereas Marshall positively revelled in the cultural and the institutional; Walras' analysis is convoluted whereas Marshall's (perhaps because the ordinary businessman to his discredit knows little of the *tâtonnement* and less of the *numéraire*) is less complicated; Walras' mathematics is as flashy as one would expect from a man who failed to win admission to the Ecole Polytechnique, Marshall's as subtle and as concealed as one would expect from a Cambridge First with no need to put his prowess on display; Walras' system is static, timeless and mechanical, Marshall's a set of developmental processes extending ever-upwards through replicated disequilibria in the direction of organic improvement. Differences these undoubtedly are; but it is unlikely if they can be said to cancel out the remarkable similarities between the two theorists in terms of interdependence and simultaneous determination, marginal utility and mathematical presentation.

So impressed was Lionel Robbins by the parallels, indeed, that he was able to write as follows on the subject of the disparities:

If one looks deep enough, the differences tend to disapper. Or perhaps it would be better said that the fundamental analytical techniques will be seen to be essentially the same in both systems. Demand for ultimate products as a function of price based upon comparisons of marginal utilities; cost functions involving the use of more than one scarce type of productive service; demand for services as a function of estimates of marginal contributions to the value of the final product; accumulation governed by investment opportunities and ability and willingness to sacrifice present enjoyments for future; the interconnectedness of all elements in the universe of discourse: all these architectonic conceptions are fundamental to both systems. . . . In regard to what Sir John Hicks has described as the statical foundations, the systems were to all intents and purposes the same. The differences were a matter of the shop-window.[290]

Even those who would not go so far in playing down the differences cannot help but be struck by the similarities – and by Marshall's conspicuous reticence with respect to the important contributions of his distinguished predecessor. His reticence is less in the case of Menger and Jevons, less still in the case of von Thünen and Cournot, least of all in the case of Smith, Ricardo and Mill. Whatever the reasons for the imbalance of acknowledgement, these authors at any rate would appear to have been the principal influences on Marshall's *Principles* in the very long gestation period which preceded the appearance of the book in the summer of 1890.

Keynes said that Marshall's 'characteristic doctrines were far developed by 1875; and by 1883 they were taking their final form'.[291] The publication of the ideas that were ultimately expressed in the *Principles* had evidently been considerably delayed by a cautious author who was anxious to do good but also afraid of being criticised. That being the case, of course, and 'having regard to the maturity of Marshall's thought when he first published his *Principles*', it is, in Guillebaud's words, 'scarcely surprising if there were no changes of major importance in his theory in the thirty years which elapsed between the appearance of the First Edition in 1890 and that of the Eighth and last Edition in 1920'.[292] Claude Guillebaud, Marshall's nephew and, like his uncle, a Fellow of St John's, was in an exceptionally strong position to say that Marshall's major insights had reached their final form by 1890 and that, as far as content is concerned, the text of the eighth edition is 'identical' with that of the first: it was he, after all, who prepared (over the 27 years subsequent to a suggestion made by Keynes in 1934) the *Variorum* ('ninth') edition, an undertaking with respect to which he later observed that 'the collating of the different editions does not appear to me to support the thesis that there was any real evolution or development of his ideas between 1890 and 1920'.[293] Youngson, ranging more widely, reaches much the same conclusion about Marshall's intellectual growth in those later years of his life: 'The views expressed in

Money Credit and Commerce, published in 1923, do not differ markedly from those to be found in the *Principles* or in the evidence given before the Gold and Silver Commission in 1887.'[294] The Marshall of 1890 was the Marshall he was to remain – and the *Principles* itself was built to last.

Built to last though it may have been, Marshall continued nonetheless to revise his book and new editions appeared in 1891, 1895, 1898, 1907, 1910, 1916 and 1920. It is curious that an author who had been honing and refining his insights since 1867 (and who only released them to the wider public at so late a date that they by then 'lacked the novelty and path-breaking powers which would have been acclaimed in them a generation earlier')[295] should have celebrated the appearance of his first edition by setting to work on the second edition that was to be only one year its junior. Nor is it clear why Marshall produced the last three editions (investing his own scarce time in their preparation and imposing a financial cost on the book-buying public such as a man with no known interest in royalty-maximisation cannot but have regretted), seeing as he at that stage was making so few changes that page-numbering from 1907 onwards could be left unaltered. A minor mystery concerning the final edition of the *Principles* is why a book published in 1920 contains a reference (complete with page-number) to an article by Taussig that only appeared in May 1921.[296] A far greater mystery concerning the final edition is why, given that two complementary volumes were then about to appear, the author saw the need for a new edition in 1920 at all. The least sympathetic explanation for Marshall's succession of new editions without new ideas is that Marshall was never satisfied but never discovered why he was never satisfied. A more sympathetic explanation would make much of Marshall's acute awareness that matter was in motion, together with Marshall's deep-seated desire to be properly understood.

With respect to the mutation of matter, Marshall was concerned lest the evolution of phenomena render out of date the uncorrected abstractions of high theory. The frequent alterations are in that sense indicative of the anxieties experienced by the nervous thinker when contemplating the march of events, and to which Marshall pointed in the preface to the fifth edition of 1907 in seeking to justify his repeated revisions: 'I had laid my plan on too large a scale; and its scope widened, especially on the realistic side, with every pulse of the Industrial Revolution of the present generation, which has far outdone the changes of a century ago, in both rapidity and breadth of movement.'[297] That the revisions before 1907 were modest may perhaps be accounted for by some perception that, however great the increase in rapidity and breadth, nonetheless *natura non facit saltum*; while the fact that the 1907 edition witnessed the last major redrafting of the work might even mean that the author was becoming more and more disillusioned with the theoretical framework of his *Principles* and was turning more and more to the applied economics that was to be his *Industry and Trade*. Marshall evidently had doubts about the longevity of the latter book, and expressed them in no uncertain terms in 1919 in a letter to Sir Frederick Macmillan: 'I have put so much more work into it than I put into my *Principles*, but I think it may run to a second edition – though, being more largely concerned with details that change from decade to decade, it may become superannuated ere long more completely than is likely to be the case with discussions of general "principles".'[298] Marshall, interestingly enough, entertained doubts about the longevity of the former book as well, and expressed them in not dissimilar terms in 1915 in a letter to C. R. Fay. There, writing of the march of events, he confessed: 'It drives me wild to think of it. I believe it will make my poor *Principles*, with a lot of poor comrades, into waste paper. The more I think of it, the less I can guess what the world will be like fifty years hence.'[299] Marshall, painfully aware that contingency is ubiquitous and today's news tomorrow's history, would in the circumstances have been saddened but not surprised by Professor Shackle's association of peaceful, orderly economic theory with a rational and a complacent economic world, a world of the 'Pax Britannica and the tranquil generation-and-a-half which had favoured and fostered a belief in a self-regulating, inherently and naturally self-optimizing, stable and coherent economic system':[300] 'Perfect competition was indispensable to that triumphant theory of value which prevailed from the 1890s to the Great Depression of the 1930s.'[301] Given the Victorian origins, it is remarkable not how little but how much Marshall actually finds to say about uncertainty (as opposed to science), disequilibrium (as opposed to stability) and imperfect markets (as opposed to economic powerlessness). Even so, Marshall was painfully aware that matter is in motion, that human attitudes are themselves subject to mutation and that it is, all things considered, no easy task to produce a classic in an environment of flux. It is for that reason all the more remarkable that Marshall strove for as long as he did to keep his big books up to date, eschewing the easy target which might have the greater short-run impact but then be lost to posterity and of which Keynes observes: 'Economists must leave to Adam Smith alone the glory of the Quarto, must pluck the day, fling pamphlets into the wind, write always *sub specie temporis*, and achieve immortality by accident, if at all.'[302] No one would wish to deny the living message of Adam Smith. Some, however, would want to maintain that Alfred Marshall, despite his own very real fears about the impact of changes on ideas, was himself in the event for far more seasons than merely his own. Thus Edgeworth, writing about *Money Credit and Commerce* in 1923, observed that the book does not become so bogged down in contemporary controversies as to show the threatening signs of premature dating, but rather presents economic theories that are of relevance in a variety of conditions and circumstances: 'If much of it might have been written in the 'eighties of last century, much of it will be read in the 'eighties of this century. It is, as far as what relates to human affairs can be, *in specie eternitatis*.'[303] Much the same could be said, one feels sure, about the *Principles*. The fact remains that the anxious Marshall continued to revise his book, and one reason was to prevent it from being left behind by the moving tide of matter.

The other reason for the frequent revisions was Marshall's deep-seated desire to be properly understood. Most of what took place in the second and later editions was, in Guillebaud's words, 'essentially a process of elucidation and attempted clarification rather than of the introduction of new ideas and the modification of old ones', the motive being (and this the editor had straight from the horse's mouth) that Marshall 'felt that his strength did not lie in exposition, and he was driven by the controversies and misunderstandings which his book evoked to seek incessantly to find new words in which to clothe his ideas in the hope of making clear his real meaning'.[304] One illustration of such repackaging and rearrangement has to do with the treatment of quasi-rent, of which Guillebaud writes:

> There was . . . no part of the *Principles* which underwent more incessant change during the final five editions than the chapters devoted to the exposition of quasi-rent. At the same time it does not appear that there was any real alteration in the content of the doctrine from first to last – it was simply a matter of successive attempts to meet criticism and to put a difficult and novel conception in as clear a form as possible.[305]

An alternative illustration of cosmetic representation without significant rethinking is the transfer of the long historical chapter on 'The Growth of Free Trade and Enterprise' from its original position as the opening section of the book to the lowly status of the Appendix A: the shift took place in 1907 (and was thus hardly a direct response to

Cunningham's criticisms in 1892 such as will be considered in the next chapter), and was perhaps indicative of Marshall's loss of interest in economic history (he never published the large-scale historical work for which he at one stage collected a great deal of material, and which he in later life dismissed as 'The White Elephant'),[306] but the fact remains that the substance remained essentially the same. Then there are the concepts which are present in earlier editions but only spelled out in detail in the later ones (the Representative Firm from 1891, the elasticity of supply from 1907), just as there are the concepts which are renamed but not fundamentally reworked: thus the term 'Consumers' Rent' (with its clearly distinguishable classical overtones) was superseded in 1898 by the more neutral 'consumer's surplus', while the utilitarian phraseology of 'pleasure' and 'pain' was increasingly deleted from the 1895 edition onwards in favour of more colourless expressions ('satisfaction', 'benefit', 'gratification') such as would not automatically trigger the reflex hostility of critics who were pro-Marshallian but anti-Benthamite. Some of the improvements which Marshall made in the explanatory power of his argument affected the Appendixes alone, which grew steadily longer and more technical: a good illustration of this process is provided by Guillebaud when he points, speaking of the third edition, to 'the expansion of Note XIV of the Mathematical Appendix from a meagre two paragraphs in the earlier editions to about six pages, containing what is perhaps the kernel of Marshall's theory of value'.[307]

It reflects well on Marshall's willingness to accept and reflect on criticism that he was patient enough to expand and explain in this way (although one cannot help but add that he could have spared himself the labour by being more rigorous and lucid, less prone to 'let the context explain his meaning',[308] in the first place). A good case gains nothing from exaggeration, of course, and the impression must not be given that the evolution of the *Principles* in the thirty years that separated the first edition from the last bore witness to not a single amendment of substance: the well-known alteration in 1910 to the line following the 'trees of the forest' simile proves the opposite, Marshall having become so concerned about the drift towards size that he altered his text from 'as with the growth of trees, so *it is* with the growth of businesses' to 'so *was it* with the growth of businesses as a general rule before the great recent development of vast joint-stock companies, which often stagnate, but do not readily die'.[309] The alteration is, arguably, an alteration of substance. As such, it serves as nothing so much as an eloquent reminder of just how few of Marshall's other alterations actually attained the radical status of this well-known exception. The anormals and the unrepresentatives apart, the typical change was the tinkering amelioration, and the final verdict, quite rightly, that of Claude Guillebaud:

> In conclusion, it may be said that a careful survey and comparison of the different editions of Marshall's *Principles* does not reveal any substantial development of his ideas, or even of his technique. It is a matter for regret that he should have devoted so many valuable years (he himself estimated that each edition involved fully a year's work) to bring out successive editions of the *Principles* – years which could have been more usefully spent in completing the great work which unfortunately at the end of his life he left unfinished. *Money Credit and Commerce* was a very different book from the one he could have written twenty years earlier; while the projected volume on 'the ideal and the practicable in social and economic structure, with some account of taxation and administration', which would have summed up the conclusion of a lifetime of observation and thought, never came into being at all.[310]

The evolution of the *Principles* in the thirty years following its birth, it is clear, involved costs as well as benefits. The opportunity costs undoubtedly being so much greater than the small benefits accruing to the small changes, what must remain something of a mystery is why a modern missionary who was anxious to do good chose to waste so much of his scarce time on the successive revisions of a work which, truth to tell, was basically the same book in 1920 as it had been in 1890.

The *Principles* of 1920 was in its essentials the *Principles* of 1890. Perhaps it was in its essentials the *Principles* of 1870 or 1875 as well: Marshall frequently spoke of the antiquity of his system and of its early evolution under the good guidance of the two Continentals and the three classicals, but his delay in publishing his principal insights makes it impossible to say whether his thinking of the early 1870s was characterised by the wisdom of maturity or, alternatively, the impetuosity of youth. The reconstruction of Marshall's intellectual evolution before 1890 is made that much more difficult by the fact that such unpublished material as has not been lost (some sets of lecture-notes, for example, or some uncompleted book-manuscripts) is grouped in the Marshall Library, Cambridge, by subject and not by date. Admittedly some of the items do bear dates that were added subsequently (either by the older Marshall himself or by Mary Paley

Marshall), and others can be dated within limits by the handwriting; but the problem of period is a real one nonetheless. Some of the essays and fragments that were prepared for publication in 1975 by Professor Whitaker do give a certain impression of the state of Marshall's system as it was before 1890: uncompleted and sketchy, however, they are hints rather than conclusions. Further impressions and hints can be culled from Marshall's published works in the 1870s and the 1880s. They are better than nothing (and the *Economics of Industry* is better than most), but they nonetheless do not touch on more than a minority of the topics that are synthesized so meticulously into the *Principles* of 1890 that was Marshall's lifelong obsession. Just as it is impossible to say anything of any particular interest about the evolution of Marshall's book in the thirty years following the publication of the first edition, so it is impossible, it would appear, to trace out the individual stages by which the embryo developed into the organism in the two decades that culminated in 1890. The most that can be said is that the young mathematician who wanted in some way to assist his society through economics was driven by his ambitions to study the classicals, the Continentals and the marginalists; and that he in 1890 published a long and comprehensive analytical account of the troubled discipline which, widely regarded as epoch-making at the time, has been the basis of textbook microeconomics ever since.

And yet there is more to the *Principles* than the short Book III on the demand-curve, let alone the long Book V on market equilibration of which Marshall thought so highly that he was able (in 1891) to write of it in the following manner: 'To myself personally the chief interest of the Volume centres in Book V. . . . It contains more of my life's work than any other part: and it is there, more than anywhere else, that I have tried to deal with unsettled questions of the science.'[311] No one would wish to minimise the importance of Book V, let alone of Book III; but the fact remains that there is more to Marshall than that which has been the basis of textbook economics ever since the first appearance of the *Principles* in 1890. Every undergraduate is today expected to be fully conversant with marginal utility and elasticity of demand, cost curves and supply curves, consumer's surplus and substitution at the margin. Most undergraduates would, however, transfer in horror to mechanical engineering for advanced mathematicians or business administration for aspiring entrepreneurs if asked to prove their aptitude for the vocation of economist by means of a disputation not on partial derivatives and general equilibrium but rather on notions that are of no less significance in the ambitious system that is Marshall's *Principles* – notions such as that 'the Mecca of the economist lies in economic biology',[312] or that 'time, which is the centre of the chief difficulty of almost every economic problem, is itself absolutely continuous',[313] or that 'the two great forming agencies of the world's history have been the religious and the economic'.[314] Marshall the Missionary wrote his *Principles* because he believed that his book had the potential to do good. Insofar as improved allocation leads to accelerated growth, insofar as accelerated growth leads to material improvement and more betterment, his elucidation of market processes is likely to have done such good. Insofar as collective progress presupposes a vanguard of economist-*virtuosi* and not merely of economist-technocrats, however, the impact of his *magnum opus* is likely to have been very much less. More than fifty years separates the first tentative steps in the direction of Mill from the final revisions when the author was eighty years of age. Half a century in the evolving, his book has nonetheless come down to posterity as a work of *how to* and *is* rather than a contribution to the *why* and the *ought-to-be* that the high-minded Marshall rightly regarded as the more important of his concerns.

7 Beyond the *Principles*

In 1892 Marshall, ever the educator, published another book, the *Elements of Economics of Industry*. In a letter dated 2 May 1910 to a Japanese correspondent, he said it was 'made rapidly chiefly by scissors and paste out of my *Principles*',[1] and elsewhere he character-ised it as an attempt to abridge the longer book in such a way as to adapt it 'to the needs of junior students'.[2] A new chapter on trades unions was provided but otherwise the nature of the simplification was excision, Marshall taking the view that 'the difficulty of an argument would be increased rather than diminished by curtailing it and leaving out some of its steps.'[3] The title was poorly chosen as it positively invites confusion with the very different book that is the *Economics of Industry* of 1879 (a confusion that much more likely by virtue of the fact that both books carry the same title – *Economics of Industry* – on their spines). Regardless of the title, the popularisation was a commercial success, running to three further editions (1896, 1899, 1913) and selling a total of 81 000 copies in all: degrees were being started in the burgeoning discipline, educated laymen were less and less regarding industry and trade as unacademic and dismal, and the time was clearly right not merely for the *Principles* but for an introduction to the *Principles* as well. Marshall, self-critical as usual, was not entirely satisfied with his *Elements*, and was writing to Foxwell as early as 1897 about the book that he evidently envisaged as being its successor: 'If ever I get my VM II finished, I have a notion of preparing carefully some semi-popular lectures; getting them taken down by shorthand; and thus working them up into a sort of Tourists' Guide to Marshall.'[4] Marshall may have had reservations about the utility of his *Elements*, but not so the critics and the press. Thus the *Westminster Review* welcomed the arrival of the book in 1892 with the normal clapping of hands to which Marshall must by then have become accustomed: 'Interesting, scientific and practical, the volume is destined to be read by the statesman as well as by the student, and might fairly appeal to a thoughtful public. It displays throughout the care and hard work which has been bestowed on its perfection.' The *Manchester Guardian* was if anything even more complimentary: 'So far as it goes, this is out and away the best manual on economics for a plain man to buy.'[5] No doubt it was, seeing as the only reasonable alternative would have been the *Principles* itself.

The two remaining books were left until extreme old age (although many of the insights had already reached students and colleagues via lectures and other manifestations of the Cambridge oral tradition). Precisely when they were written is less clear than their actual date of publication. *Industry and Trade* first appeared in August 1919 (with further editions in December of the same year, in 1920, 1921 and 1923) but part of it was delivered to the publisher and set up in type as early as 1904: the lag of fifteen years (an eventful fifteen years, moreover, which embraced such events as the First World War and the Russian Revolution) is the reason, no doubt, why some of Marshall's arguments have a slightly antiquated air about them, even by the standards of 1919. Similarly, *Money Credit and Commerce* was published in 1923 but draws heavily not only on evidence to Royal Commissions but also on Marshall's published and unpublished work on money and trade (both among his earliest concerns) dating back to the 1870s. Here as elsewhere, it is clear, Marshall's propensity to delay and to recycle makes it exceptionally difficult to trace out the precise stages (if such there were) in the development of his thought.

Industry and Trade is basically a study in applied economics, an empirical investigation into 'the technical evolution of industry, and its influences on the conditions of man's life and work'.[6] Marshall said he saw the more descriptive and factual book as a direct 'continuation' of the more abstract and theoretical predecessor which had supplied the 'foundations';[7] and there are indeed good grounds for regarding the evidence of the later book and the logic of the earlier one as standing to one another in the same relationship as tea and sugar, toast and jam. Nor is there any reason to think that Marshall came to factual knowledge only after he had exhausted the possibilities of abstract generalisation: regardless of the temporal order in which he chose to release his findings, Marshall took pains as early as the early 1870s to visit 'one or more representative works in each chief industry' in order in that way to 'understand the resources and the mode of operation of all elementary plant in general use', to 'study the relations between technique and the conditions of employment for men and for women'.[8] What he learned in the heat of the furnace is visible even in the rarefied atmosphere of the earlier synthesis; and the reader misses much in the *Principles* who misses the inter-country comparisons ('In India, and to a less extent in Ireland. . . .'),[9] the statistical tables (on the growth of population, for example),[10] the institutional data (the impact of the 'Common Rule' on wage-rates and observed differentials being a particularly interesting illustration in view of Marshall's own early interest when visiting factories in discovering the causes of variations in pay).[11] An attempt is clearly made even in the *Principles* to put the flesh of fact on to the skeleton of speculation; and for that reason it would be wrong to exaggerate the very real differences between that book of 1890 and the much later *Industry and Trade*. Both books in truth make use both of induction and of deduction, the proportions varying but the ingredients remaining the same. Interestingly, it was none other than W. J. A. Ashley (so much the historical economist on other occasions as to joke about the need for Marshall the high theoretician to employ a food-taster as soon as possible) who praised *Industry and Trade* as the best book on applied economics ever to have appeared in England (and its author as 'the greatest English writer'[12] in the field) not least because it managed so successfully to mix its methodologies. Thus Ashley, speaking of *Industry and Trade*, could hardly have been more complimentary about the book, calling it 'a masterly and informing survey of a large part of the field and a reconciliation of the abstract and the concrete – a reconciliation of which each side is equally in need.'[13] Edgeworth, more in sympathy with the logico-deductive method than was Ashley (and less confident about the extent to which empiricisms and observations can ever be relied upon to speak for themselves), shared with Ashley that recognition that the two approaches were regarded by Marshall as complements and not as substitutes: 'With Dr. Marshall facts and theory have been ever kept in close co-ordination; united as body and soul.'[14] Inductivists and deductivists alike, it is clear, should have taken Alfred Marshall at his word when he declared, as he so often did, that he was not a scholar who was easily to be categorised: 'You know I am always a little sceptical about the possibility of putting the work of a big man inside a pigeon hole. I suspect one is tempted to prune him severely when there is a difficulty about crowding him in.'[15] *Industry and Trade* may be the more inductive book, the *Principles of Economics* the more deductive one; but there is for all that the evidence of both important approaches in both of these influential volumes.

Industry and Trade is the more accessible to the general reader. By the same token it is the less satisfying to the economic specialist. The facts and figures are selective and unrepresentative: because Marshall's illustrations are typically drawn from capital-intensive industries and trades (coal, steel, tin-plate, railways, shipping, ship-building, banking), it is no surprise, for example, that the book is so much stronger on market imperfections such as trusts, cartels and combinations than it is on more intensive competition. Key issues are left unresolved – not merely the ongoing problem of why a forward-falling supply curve should ever cease to fall forward (a question to which Marshall at the end of his professional life as at the beginning was unable to find a satisfactory answer) but also issues rooted in institutions such as the extent to which Marshall believed wage- and price-fixing in Germany and America to be the product of national character relative to the extent to which these customs and conventions might be said to be the outcome principally of tariff protection. Marshall collected information from a variety of sources (some of them as unreliable as newspaper reports and insider gossip) but made few original calculations of his own: he proffered numerous policy recommendations on matters such as international trade where statistical evidence on reaction functions would seem to be a *sine qua non* if the 'Ricardian Vice' is indeed to be avoided, but he nonetheless never saw the need even to quantify the elasticity of demand. The fact that he was an obsessive collector of data introduced costs and delays into his work – not least because it must frequently have undermined his confidence in his anterior generalisations and thus stimulated him to collect still more data. The fact that data is mutable and prone to date means that theories directly induced from it are particularly likely to become as obsolete as the historical events upon which they are contingent: such an awareness of the present as history, however much it may have appealed to Ashley, not only undermines the reader's confidence in some at least of Marshall's propositions and predictions but also stimulates the reader to ask why then Marshall, once again concealing his specifically historical sections in an Appendix, states so explicitly that *Industry and Trade* 'has no claim whatever to be', is not in any sense 'a contribution to',[16] the burgeoning sub-discipline of economic history. All in all, therefore, there are a number of reasons why the economic specialist might find Marshall's book of 1919 unsatisfying in certain areas. On the other hand, it made a valuable contribution by demonstrating the symbiotic integration of fact and theory, and it also pioneered the use of comparative material in the study of industrial organisation. Nor should it be forgotten how many of its apparent shortcomings are the result of the intractability of the subject-matter itself: the economy is a difficult task-master, and the founder of modern textbook economics never sought in his more candid moments to conceal its ineluctable complexities.

Money Credit and Commerce, Marshall's final book, appeared in 1923, four years after the long-delayed *Industry and Trade*. Marshall was by then 81 years of age and not in a position to make the important contribution to macroeconomics that would have been possible only a few decades earlier. The book does not in the circumstances provide any fresh insights, but merely brings together a range of views that Marshall had already expressed elsewhere – in the fragmentary 'Essay on Money' ('written about 1871'),[17] in the two 'Pure Theory' papers (work on both, it would appear, 'considerably advanced'[18] by the early part of the decade) that Sidgwick arranged to have printed for private circulation in 1879, in the *Economics of Industry* of the same year, in the *Principles* itself, in testimony given to the Royal Commissions on the Depression of Trade and Industry (1886) and Gold and Silver (1887), in evidence presented to the Indian Currency Committee of 1899. The content of *Money Credit and Commerce* was not, in short, new. The topics treated in the book range from the specification of spendable assets (which Marshall, following Henry Thornton, saw as embracing near-money as well as money strictly defined), velocity (hardly constant and definitely interest-sensitive), economic fluctuations and purchasing power parity, the tabular standard of indexed values and the case for and against bimetallic convertibility. It is sad for the history of the quantity theory that Marshall's thoughtful, subjectivist, behavioural, motivational contribution to monetary economics appeared after and not before the mechanistic mindlessness of $MV = PQ$ of Fisher's *Purchasing Power of Money* in 1911 – and that Marshall in the event never provided the intellectual leadership to teachers and researchers in the macro-monetary areas that he was able to supply in the area of market equilibration.

Marshall after the *Principles* continued to turn out important papers. Of these, 'The Old Generation of Economists and the New' (1897) and 'Social Possibilities of Economic Chivalry' (1907) are, arguably, the most interesting, both stressing the evolutionary framework and the relationship between economic activity and social improvement that was to be the subject of a final book (regrettably, never completed, although the working manuscript does survive) on

Progress: its Economic Conditions. Marshall in this period was a member of the Royal Commission on Labour (1891–4), and Keynes reports that 'he played a big part in the drafting of the Final Report. The parts dealing with Trade Unions, Minimum Wage, and Irregularity of Employment were especially his work.'[19] Marshall greatly enjoyed his membership (which brought him into contact with unionists, co-operators and other economic actors with whom a cloistered academic simultaneously involved in revising as abstract a work as the *Principles* would undeniably have otherwise had less opportunity to mix) and recalled later that he had learned a great deal from the experience: 'I received from working men and other witnesses, and from members of the Commission, the most valuable education of my life.'[20] He also gave evidence to the Royal Commissions on the Aged Poor (1893) and on Imperial and Local Taxes (1897). With respect to taxation, Marshall's sophisticated analysis touched upon a wide range of issues including incidence and shifting, levies on income versus levies on capital, the optimal balance between local and national modes of public finance. With respect to poverty, Marshall welcomed the relief of distress, but recommended that this be provided by means of a dual system encompassing the private charities of the voluntary sector alongside the bureaucrats and the Poor Law Guardians of the 1834 system: not only would such a dual system increase the scope for the concerned citizen to become directly involved in the life of his community (a good thing in its own right in the view of a theorist of duty obviously much in sympathy with the ideals of T. H. Green) but it would in addition permit the careful investigation of each pauper's individual circumstances (so as not to inflict harsh treatment and the stigma of shame on the 'deserving poor' who had genuinely done all they could to avoid the state of dependency in which they nonetheless happened to find themselves).

Marshall told the Royal Commission on the Aged Poor that he had extensive personal knowledge of the conditions and attitudes of the working classes when fallen upon hard times: 'I speak from personal observation ranging over many years, and a study of almost everything of importance that has been written on the subject.'[21] Marshall himself had no practical exposure to the operation of the Poor Law *per se*; but then, he stressed,

I have had a good deal of indirect experience of the working of Charity Organisation Societies. I have been a member of them for a great many years, and at Oxford and Cambridge my wife has

been an active member of the committee. We make it an invariable
rule to discuss the questions in detail, if they have any difficulty, at
the next meal after she comes back.[22]

Few witnesses can have been as knowledgeable (his answers reveal
not only statistical data but also the impressions of working men with
whom the Cambridge professor had evidently taken the trouble to
discuss the problem of poverty); and few, it must be added, can have
been as patient (the questions return to the same topics two and even
three times, but the answers remain logical, clear, erudite and calm,
the witness modest enough to confess to lack of information when the
real fault lies in the vagueness and generality of the query itself).

Because the Royal Commission was expressly concerned with the
relief of poverty rather than its ultimate suppression, it is only to be
expected that Marshall's detailed testimony was confined to questions of social rather than economic policy. Central to his approach to
poverty was, however, his strong conviction that economic growth
and occupational upgrading – and not the stop-gap palliatives of
charity and welfare – were in themselves the principal antidotes to
the poison of absolute deprivation. This view, expressed clearly
enough in the *Principles* (if not in the *Industry and Trade* and the
Money Credit and Commerce which followed it) would almost certainly have been developed still further in Marshall's fourth and last
great monograph. Thus, referring only two years before his death to
the 'causes which govern the richness of the reward of work', he said:
'Those causes are the deepest concern to the student of the conditions of social well-being: and they are designed to have a prominent
place in the final volume of the present series.'[23] By then his strength
was failing (the complaint in 1916 of the inveterate complainer must
be taken seriously for once, that he was suffering from an 'inability to
work or talk for more than an hour at a time'),[24] but not his guarded
optimism concerning the completion of his Volume IV: 'Although
old age presses on me, I am not without hopes that some of the
notions, which I have formed as to the possibilities of social advance,
may yet be published.'[25] Those hopes were in the event unfounded:
postponement ultimately meant that *Progress: its Economic Conditions*, like so many other proposed projects, never actually saw the
light of day. Great though the benefits accruing to Marshall's many
activities may have been – and not least to his participation in the
work of the Royal Commissions – it would clearly be a mistake to
ignore the costs which these activities imposed by retarding the
progress of his academic work.

Marshall frequently complained (as in the following, from a letter to Ashley in 1901) about the pressure on his time: 'I can't get on with my big dish, because I am always being called off to cook little ones or to help others to cook theirs.'[26] Given the costs, Marshall would appear to have been remarkably generous with the benefits. Marshall, writing of Darwin, noted that 'it was by husbanding every atom of his small physical strength that Darwin was enabled to do so much of . . . that kind of work which influences the course of thought in future generations'.[27] Though writing explicitly of Darwin, Marshall was almost certainly referring implicitly to himself, knowing full well as he did how easily diversion can come to reduce the quality of thought. Yet he had made a decision early on in his life that he wanted to be something more than a 'mere thinker'; and he clearly saw some at least of the many temptations that came his way not as doors closing but as doors opening, not as time-wasting nuisances but as valuable opportunities directly related to what he perceived as being his mission. Marshall scrupulously avoided the lucrative outside outlets for his talents such as constantly tempt the established to neglect the important, preferring instead to live modestly on the stipend he received for his teaching and the royalties he received for his books. He was far from being the ivory-tower academic, however, whose every moment is devoted to his scholarship. Marshall was anxious to do good; and, just as he felt that his teaching and research were of some use to his community, so he felt that other activities too were worth pursuing for the same reasons. Four areas of activity in particular are of significance for an understanding of the way in which Marshall moulded his own life in accordance with his ideals and beliefs. These areas involve, respectively, the foundation of a British Economic Association, the creation in Cambridge of a specialist Tripos, the adoption of the Marshallian paradigm as the neoclassical orthodoxy, and the protection of the British economy from the expected ravages of reintroduced tariffs. These four areas are by no means unconnected – Marshall's life, like Marshall's thought, is better typified by interdependence than it is by atomism – but it will nonetheless be helpful to consider each in turn.

1 The British Economic Association

On 10 April 1890, while (and as) President of Section F for the 1890 (Leeds) meeting, Marshall circulated a paper to the members of the

Section proposing a discussion on the establishment in Britain of a professional organisation comparable to the Verein für Sozialpolitik (founded 1872) in Germany and the American Economic Association (founded 1885) in the United States. His circular letter of 24 October 1890 convening a meeting at University College, London, for 20 November of that year was the result. It was sent not merely to all university teachers of economics in Britain but also to the Section F Committee, the members of the Political Economy Club in London, and the council-members of the Statistical Societies in London, Manchester and Dublin. The very fact that so many of the individuals whom Marshall invited to the meeting were selected precisely because of their participation in existing associations underlines the obvious question of why he felt there was a need for something new. Even if the Club had degenerated since the glorious days of Ricardo and Malthus into not much more than a free trade pressure group, the same could hardly be said either of the Section or the Societies. Marshall was the President of the Section in the very year that saw the publication of his *Principles*, a Fellow of the London Statistical Society from 1880 until his death, and a member of its Council from 1884: what is striking is not that he invited delegates from existing associations to the meeting he convened to found a new one, but rather that he saw the need for a new body at all.

The British Association for the Advancement of Science was founded in York (under the sponsorship of the Yorkshire Philosophical Society) in 1831. The model was the Deutscher Naturforscher Versammlung, which had first met in 1822 in Leipzig. Quételet attended the 1833 meeting of the British Association as a representative of the Belgian Government; while in Cambridge for the conference he showed some papers on statistics to acquaintances including T. R. Malthus, Richard Jones and Charles Babbage; all deplored the fact that such papers had no natural home in any of the existing Sections; and thus was Section F born. The first Section President, in 1834, was Sir Charles Lemon (he was to serve a second term of office in 1836 and a third in 1843), but the second was in some ways the more interesting: Babbage himself, the Lucasian Professor of Mathematics at Cambridge, the inventor of an automatic calculating machine, the author of *Reflexions on the Decline of Science in England* (1830) and *On the Economy of Machinery and Manufacturers* (1832), an FRS, a polymath. Babbage had represented British science at the 1828 (Berlin) meeting of the Versammlung (when the President was none other than Alexander von Humboldt) and had been instrumental both in setting up the equivalent body in Britain and in convincing the officers of the Association that social science was in some way respectable. Adam Sedgwick, President for 1833, had been, like many other natural scientists of the time, deeply suspicious of hypothesis-testing in economics, and fearful as well lest its speculations inflame the passions and lead to discord. The welcome was accordingly cool which he accorded the new Statistics Section (the name was only changed to Economic Science and Statistics from 1856, to Economics from 1948), Sedgwick indicating in effect that he believed the topics to be treated by F would be compatible with the objectives of the BA 'so far as they have to do with matters of fact, with mere abstractions, and with numerical results. Considered in that light they give what may be called the raw material to political economy and political philosophy; and by their help the lasting foundations of these sciences may be perhaps ultimately laid'.[28] Cool though the welcome may have been, it would have been cooler still, and perhaps even non-existent, if the Section had not possessed so influential an ambassador in Babbage: a Fellow of the Royal Society who through his involvement in the British Association was translating into practice his opinion that the Society had done little to diffuse science to the wider world, a distinguished mathematician who clearly believed experiment and observation concerning business and markets to be academically respectable, Babbage was exceptionally well-situated to serve as a bridge between the older sciences and the new.

At first the usual pattern was for a politician, a public figure or a senior civil servant to be made President of the Section: distinguished economists can indeed be cited, including Thomas Tooke (1854), Nassau Senior (1860), William Newmarch (1861), Thorold Rogers (1866) and W. S. Jevons (1870), but the more normal choice would seem to have been an Edwin Chadwick (1862) or a W. E. Forster (1873). By the 1870s and the 1880s, however – by the time, say, of Henry Sidgwick's presidency in 1885 – the situation was clearly changing and the influence of the academics and the professionals (due in part to the simultaneous expansion in their numbers) was clearly increasing. The Section set up committees to conduct research and enlisted the services of scholars of the calibre of Edgeworth, Palgrave, Foxwell, Giffen and Alfred Marshall himself. It published reports on the adoption of the metric system of weights and measures (1872), on the reform of the law of patent (1879), on the employment of the precious metals as monetary assets (1888). It was used by

Leone Levi in the 1880s as a platform for his investigation of sliding scales, wage-rates and industrial disputes; and in 1900 (at the instigation of Mrs Ramsay MacDonald) it made a study of its own of the effects of legislation upon women's participation in the labour-market. Section F was increasingly active in providing a forum in the United Kingdom for distinguished economists from abroad – Léon Walras in 1887, Clément Juglar in 1896, Gustav Cassel in 1901, Knut Wicksell in 1906. It was broadminded enough to sanction the presentation (even if not by the author himself, who loathed public speaking) of as deductive and as mathematical a paper as Jevons' 'Notice' in 1862, while not afraid to elect as its President distinguished inductivists such as Clapham (1920), Ashley (1907), and Ingram (1879): Ingram's call to merge economics with sociology was not, however, answered until 1959, when F invited sociologists to join with it in a joint Section (they refused and formed Section N). By the time of Marshall, in short, Section F was coming to play a more and more important role in British economics (both theoretical and empirical). It was not an also-ran and an intellectual backwater. Rather, it was the cutting-edge and the coalface. Yet its President in 1890 saw the need for a new body.

One problem with the Section had always been the non-specialist nature of its audience: the Association encouraging multi-disciplinarity, a lecture by Giffen on England's economic decline was likely to pull in not only economists of the stature of Edgeworth (who, as Recorder in the year of Giffen's presidency, had to attend in any case) but also engineers who had holidayed in Germany and physicists who attributed all of England's ills to the use of a paper currency. Besides that, the membership was amorphous and shifting, due not least to the fact that the Association met only once a year, and then in different places: Whewell's description of it as 'an ambulatory body, composed partly of men of reputation and partly of a miscellaneous crowd'[29] does convey, perhaps all too well, the sensation of a travelling circus with an open-ended list of participants and no ongoing identity as an invisible college or community of scholars. Nor should the continuing mistrust of economics on the part of the older sciences be neglected. It is far easier for a later generation to laugh off the accusation that public discussion of current events is in some sense 'inflammatory' than it was for the men of Marshall's generation, and the same may be said of the charge that economics wastes resources that might otherwise have been devoted to science (a charge which John Jewkes stood on its head in his

Presidential Address of 1959 when he observed that perhaps science wastes resources that might otherwise have been devoted to economics). What is most alarming about Francis Galton's attack on the Section in 1877 is not his awareness of any real crisis in the discipline that tended to discredit it, but rather his obvious failure to grasp what, precisely, it is that economists actually do: no one will win either prizes for clarity or friends among economists who criticises Section F for neglecting the mathematical theory of statistics, who adds that the proper place for any such paper in the Association is in any case in Section A (Mathematics), and who concludes that, the transfer once made, there remains no further need for a separate F. Galton's attack on the Section may not have been entirely rational, but it is clear that he was not alone in conveying to the economists the impression that they were not entirely welcome.

Francis Galton, in requesting the Council 'seriously to consider whether the time has not now arrived when the Section might cease to form a part of the British Association', not only indicated to his colleagues that the BA ought in his view to confine itself to the discussion of 'purely scientific' subjects but also suggested to them that F was simply not needed owing to 'the fact that a society has been specially formed for the discussion of social and economical questions'.[30] While one is tempted to reply that the Royal Society (founded in 1662, it will be recalled, by Petty as well as Boyle) had, once the reforms of 1847 had excluded all but natural scientists, itself become precisely such a specialist organisation with respect to the pure sciences, one is forced also to concede that the human science society to which Galton referred had indeed been formed: the London Statistical Society was established in 1834 (one year after its counterpart in Manchester), with the objective of collecting and presenting factual information while not expressing party-political opinions or entering into current controversies on policy-related issues such as factory legislation or the Poor Laws on which it strove nonetheless to shed some light. The parentage of the Society was impeccable, the fully-employed Babbage having once again been instrumental. It had a more permanent existence than Section F (even if not the monthly meeting for which some members repeatedly agitated). From 1837 it published its own journal, which was to be edited by persons of the eminence of Sir Robert Giffen, Chief Statistician at the Board of Trade: Giffen edited the Society's *Journal* from 1876 to 1891, and served in addition as its Vice-President for 1880–81 and its President for 1882–4. The London Statistical Society, going from strength to strength, became the Royal Statistical Society in 1887 – only three years before Alfred Marshall sent out his circular letter of 24 October 1890 entitled 'Proposal to Form an English Economic Association'.

Marshall was on the Council of the Statistical Society (although residence in Cambridge effectively precluded any very active participation in the Society's administration). The *Journal* at his death published an obituary notice which is particularly important in view of its *de facto* status as the number-crunchers' final tribute to the economic theoretician: 'His place will be fixed by posterity. If some fringes drop, his robe of honour will be still ample enough to preserve his fame. No economist since Mill has had higher homage, or kept it so nearly unabated over a long life.'[31] Given Marshall's presence on the Society's Council, and given the not inconsiderable respect which he clearly commanded from inductivists and deductivists alike, one would have expected him not to propose the formation of a new Association but to favour instead the transformation of the existing Statistical Society into a more broadly-based Society for Economic Science and Statistics. Marshall in the mid-1880s did apparently believe such a transformation to be possible: many economists had joined the Society, both Foxwell and Palgrave sat with him on the Council, and the Society had even expressed some interest in continuity and clarity by declaring its intention to reprint scarce works of economic significance (including, presumably, foreign works in translation) that had gone out of print. Just as Marshall in the mid-1880s apparently believed that an expansion of the existing structure would prove possible, so he, however, soon came to recognise, together with his fellow economists, just how strong was the opposition of the statisticians to the incursion of generalisation. Few papers on economic issues with theoretical content were read at meetings of the Society, the Council showed no interest in the publication of a (monthly) economic review, let alone Palgrave's proposed dictionary, and the Statistical Society (rather like the British Association) seems in addition to have been labouring under the misapprehension that economics was in some way disreputably ideological in nature. The lack of love on the part of the statisticians was returned with interest by the economists, if the views expressed by Foxwell in a letter to Palgrave dated 25 November 1885 are anything like typical: 'The Society is filled with mere men of figures, a large number of whom . . . use their membership simply as a trade advertisement. . . . It is very cliquey, and too full of business men: I

mean mere men of business of course, for a business man may be as
educated as anyone else. It is extremely difficult to obtain a hearing
for anything new. . . . and the Society seems likely to perish from
sheer dulness.'[32] The statisticians did not much like the economists,
the economists did not much like the statisticians, and by 1887 it was
clear that the perceived need among economists for a professional
body would not be satisfied by means of a straightforward extension
of the Statistical Society: an entirely new association would have to
be created.

Marshall was among the last to recognise that divorce was inevitable (even after the Economic Association had been founded, he
continued to advocate an amalgamation with the Statistical Society).
Besides that, he was in the late 1880s so absorbed in the completion
of his *Principles* that he was simply not in a position to provide the
requisite leadership or take the appropriate initiatives. No doubt,
too, he had doubts about the new journal which he believed to be
indispensable for the success of the enterprise: he was too much the
scholar to edit the journal himself, Neville Keynes did not want the
job, and no other candidate appears to have been entirely to his
liking. Whatever the reasons for the procrastination, Marshall hesitated, his co-workers hesitated, the Oxford Branch of the Christian
Social Union did not hesitate, and the outcome was the publication at
Oxford in January 1891 (two months before the appearance of the
Economic Journal) of the first issue of the *Economic Review*. The
editor was the Rev. L. R. Phelps.

The new journal (which survived for 25 years) was inspired by the
High Church Christianity of the *Lux Mundi* group – of a group, in
other words, which sought explicitly 'to claim for the Christian Law
the ultimate authority to rule social practice'; 'to study in common
how to apply the moral truths and principles of Christianity to the
social and economic difficulties of the present time'; and 'to present
Christ in practical life as the living master and king, the enemy of
wrong and selfishness, the power of righteousness and love'.[33] Given
such objectives, it is no surprise to find that the new *Economic
Review* tended to favour articles which recognised the ethical and
religious side to economic life; or which (inspired by the reforming
zeal of radical Christians who wanted a tax on unearned rent and
State provision of dwellings for the poor) refused to separate inquiry
from intervention because of a strong sense of duty. Inevitably, being
Oxford-based (only two Cambridge economists, both clergymen,
were involved in its establishment: the Rev. A. Lyttleton and

William Cunningham), the new journal had a further bias in favour of the historical school and the historical method: although officially an organ for all approaches, the evidence reveals the proportion of technical, analytical, theoretical and mathematical papers actually published to have been exceptionally small. The new *Economic Review*, it is clear, was somewhat different from the new *Economic Journal* (even from the *Economic Journal* of 1891, which was far more tolerant towards alternatives to high theory than it later became); and for that reason it would be wrong to regard the two as close substitutes. At the same time, it would undoubtedly be equally wrong to play down the extent to which Marshall and his associates were disagreeably surprised by the appearance of the rival review. Thus Cunningham (by then a College lecturer at Trinity and therefore safe from the professor's wrath) wrote as follows in June 1890 to John Carter: 'I know that Marshall will be much disappointed at finding his scheme frustrated, and I know he does not think there is room for *both* ventures.'[34] Marshall had hoped to unite all strands of economic opinion in a single movement, and must have regarded the existence of the differentiated product as fundamentally divisive. Also, while not himself a practising Christian, he was so much in sympathy with the ameliorationist objectives of the Oxford Branch that he had at one stage proposed to his associates that their own new venture be called the *Journal of Social Reform*: he cannot in the circumstances have been very pleased to see himself shunted in the popular perception out of the tribe of sages and prophets and into the camp of the social eunuchs. At a purely technical level, there was the danger that the two reasonably similar titles would be confused. At a more fundamental level, no one likes to get a new idea and then see it adopted first by a rival who is that much quicker off the mark; and Marshall in this respect was no different from anyone else.

Professionalism was in the air even as Marshall completed his *Principles*; and he always made clear that his involvement in the events of 1890 was due to not much more than the 'accident'[35] that he (and not, say, Foxwell or Palgrave) happened to be President of F in the year in which something long ripening at last matured. Be it accident or be it design, the fact remains that it was not Foxwell or Palgrave but rather Marshall, in the right place at the right time as usual, who had the honour of convening the meeting at University College, London, which called into being the British Economic Association (known since 1902 as the Royal Economic Society) and the *Economic Journal*. If Marshall had not convened the meeting someone else, no doubt, would have done so. As things were, however, there is much truth in Maloney's *dictum* that Marshall succeeded in 1890 precisely because he was 'the unpopular apostle of an ambition which few economists could resist'.[36]

The new Association was intended to unify a divided profession; and Marshall, fearful of reopening the rivalries and animosities which had plagued British economics once the Ricardian orthodoxy had lost its monolithic dominance, took the opportunity of his address to the delegates at the University College meeting to warn against 'that waste of effort in bitter and ungenerous controversy which had long impeded progress'.[37] What he wanted, Marshall made clear, was professional self-consciousness and academic excellence without, however, the stifling reliance upon a single paradigm or a single criterion of professional expertise such as would inevitably condemn the science to sterility. The report of the meeting describes him as dismissing out of hand the idea that any one school of brother-economists was obviously 'right', any other school obviously 'wrong': 'Economics was a science, and an "orthodox science" was a contradiction in terms. Science could be true or false, but it could not be orthodox; and the best way to find out what was true was to welcome the criticism of all people who knew what they were talking about. In that way indeed he did hope they would exercise a wholesome influence on the character of economic discussion.'[38] As with the Association, so with its journal. In his circular letter of 24 October Marshall had stressed the need for tolerant impartiality and had advised that the full range of scholarly approaches be properly represented: 'Latterly the feeling has been growing that some security should be afforded that the journal should always represent all shades of economic opinion, and be the organ not of one school of English economists, but of all schools.'[39] In his speech on 20 November he returned to the theme of intellectual pluralism and made clear to the delegates that they must not expect from their journal a single standard of intellectual rigour:

The one influence which he hoped they would exercise would be that they would start from an absolutely catholic basis, and include every school of economists which was doing genuine work. He trusted that those who should control this journal would insist that all who wrote on criticism of others should take the writings of those others in the best possible sense, and in that way all schools might work amicably together, interpreting each other in the fairest and most generous manner; acting on that principle they would make sound progress.[40]

Marshall's references to 'genuine work' and 'people who knew what they were talking about' do suggest that he had at the back of his mind a more restricted range of doctrine and methodology than the tolerant pluralism of his explicit invocation would seem to indicate. If Marshall did entertain notions of such limits, however, he carefully kept them to himself, mindful no doubt of what the 1870s and early 1880s had cost British economics in terms of human relations and public support. Unification without conflict, he must have believed, was infinitely preferable to the *bellum* of the earlier period, even if the price of the conciliatory stance was the renunciation of common ground and theoretical consensus. Perhaps Marshall also believed that, given time, his own paradigm would edge out the also-rans and evolve into the charter of the Association and its journal; but that it could hardly expect to hold such sway unless and until the Association and its journal had in fact come into being. Irrespective of what Marshall himself may have believed, there is no disputing what actually occurred, that by the time of Marshall's death the Society and the *Journal* had been well and truly Marshallianised.

Marshall emphasised to the delegates at University College the need for tolerant impartiality and intellectual pluralism. Whether deeply sincere or merely skin-deep, his apparent agnosticism as to the central core of economic science inevitably led him to favour a relatively unrestricted membership. Not all economists agreed with him on the principle of open house, some saying that there was an obvious threat to professional standards where just anyone, irrespective of training and expertise, was allowed to join. Henry Higgs, for example, was somewhat sceptical about Marshall's advice 'that we should *not* be careful about exclusions', and expressed his misgivings in the following words in a letter to Foxwell: 'Get all the people you can, he argues, and those who are keen and interested in economics will alone remain. It seems to me that we were better without members who would waste the time and spoil the tone of the Club.'[41] Higgs, it is clear, would have preferred an association with restrictive requirements such as the stringent criteria that were imposed by the British Psychological Society when that body was established in 1901: prospective members had to prove either that they were 'recognized teachers in some branch of the subject' or that they had 'published work of recognized value'.[42] Yet there were not many academic posts in economics in the United Kingdom in 1890; not every businessman or civil servant had the time or the inclination to express himself by means of the lengthy monograph; in the absence of a specialist journal the outlets for periodical publication were either non-technical (such as the *Bankers' Magazine*) or non-economic (such as the *Journal of the Statistical Society*); and British economics continued in 1890 to be so divided as to make any single test of distinction manifestly unjust to at least one alternative approach. Besides that, there was the financing of the new journal to consider: the British Psychological Society applied a strict standard and commenced operations with 10 members, the British Economic Association employed a wide definition and by the end of 1891 had 710 members, and it is clear which society had the greater pool of internally-generated funds out of which to support its operations.

An open society was, admittedly, open to subversion from within. Interestingly, however, Marshall made the point in 1890 in a letter to James Bonar that he believed the threat to professional standards to be even greater where the membership was restricted: 'I am sorry you won't be present at the meeting; firstly because I think you might be converted to an open Society. No one, to whom I have spoken, except Foxwell, Edgeworth and yourself thinks a close society would be safe and the general opinion of those with whom I have conferred is that a close society would be inundated with Quacks, who could not be kept out, unless the society was so small as to be little more than a private club: but that Quacks would not care to come into a society which was open to all: and would not do much harm there, if they did come in.'[43] Whatever one may think of this argument, the fact remains that the Association was ultimately formed more or less as Marshall wished it to be, with a relatively open (as opposed to a 'learned') membership: the prospective member was to be asked merely to state that he was in sympathy with the objectives of the group, to win the approval of its Council, and to pay the small subscription of £1.1.0. The precedent of both the London Statistical Society and the American Economic Association was invoked in support of this compromise solution of little hurdles but not insurmountable ones. Marshall had his way. An important reason was the fact that there was virtually no significant opposition to his proposals. Here as usual, fate smiled on Marshall's mission.

An Association was to be formed, but Marshall insisted that it should not hold regular meetings or specialist conferences, at least in its initial stages. Given the open membership and the divided profession, it was probably his fear that colloquia would spell controversy and put on public display all the nastiness and mistrust which he had sought so scrupulously to sweep under the carpet of conciliation. Such a conjecture at any rate makes more sense than the excuse which Marshall himself gives, that 'discussions, unless conducted by a very strong Association, might do harm: they might be attended chiefly by people whose time was not very valuable'.[44] While some conference-attenders are without doubt inveterate timewasters, it does seem rather uncharitable of Marshall to throw out the idea of academic meetings altogether on the grounds that such gatherings are prone to attract undesirables. Nor was it entirely consistent of him to do so, seeing as he also maintained that the Political Economy Club, Section F and the Statistical Society already provided ample opportunity for discussion: most of the 200 delegates present at the University College meeting were probably involved in at least one of the existing bodies, their own experience had shown them that discussion need not degenerate into riot, and they had turned out in force precisely because they believed there to be unexplored ground which the existing associations had tended to neglect. But Marshall said discussion was invidious, and the delegates were honourable men. Only in 1906 was the proposal approved for the Society to hold an annual conference. That was also the year in which Marshall refused the presidency, saying that he was 'too unpractical & too little experienced' and thus not really in a position to offer much in the way of 'good guidance' at a time when there was 'really critical work to be done'.[45] Seldom has an economist exerted greater influence while seemingly doing his best to alienate his supporters.

Marshall was not in favour of communication among economists by means of regular meetings, but an economic journal was an altogether different matter. America had the *Quarterly Journal of Economics* (founded 1887). France had the *Compte-rendu des séances et travaux de l'académie des sciences morales et politiques* (1840), the *Journal des économistes* (1842) and the *Revue de l'économie politique* (1887). Germany had the *Zeitschrift für die gesamte Staatswissenschaft* (1844), the *Jahrbücher für Nationalökonomie und Statistik* (1863) and the *Jahrbuch für Gesetzgebung, Verwaltung und Volkswirtschaft* (later called *Schmollers Jahrbuch*) (1871). Britain had no economic journal at all, and it was in a very real sense more urgently needed even than the British Economic Association itself. Be that as it may, Marshall and his colleagues in 1890 saw to it that the foundation of the latter was coupled with the establishment of the former. The first issue of the *Economic Journal* appeared in March 1891. The first page of the first issue carries the following manifesto in defence of the tolerance of pluralism within the broad framework of a common identity: 'It will be the task of the Editor and his coadjustors, unbiased by their personal convictions, to select the ablest representatives of each important interest. The Association is not to be only 'British' in its love of fair play and free speech, but also 'Economic' in the character which the term suggests of special knowledge and scientific accuracy.'[46] Such a *plaidoyer* for *the one in the many, the many in the one* could well have been penned by Alfred Marshall, so closely did the views of the first editor of the *Economic Journal* resemble those of the President of F who somehow found himself at the head of a parade which others had formed. The first editor of the *Economic Journal* was Edgeworth, of whom Walras wrote in 1889: 'Je le crois un peu inféodé à Marshall.'[47] *Un peu* is *trop peu*: Keynes describes Edgeworth as a lifelong personal friend of Alfred Marshall, 'for whom his respect was unmeasured'.[48] Edgeworth retained responsibility for the *Economic Journal* from 1891 until his death in 1926. Ever deferential to the master, he cut short the acrimonious controversy concerning the historical sections in the *Principles* by refusing in 1892 to publish further attacks by William Cunningham (the pieces in question probably did greater harm to Marshall's reputation, of course, when they appeared instead in more popular journals like *The Academy* and the *Pall Mall Gazette*) and he rejected a review of Wicksteed by Barone lest it offend Marshall.[49] The tone of the *Journal* under Edgeworth's editorship was exactly as Marshall had intended it to be, incisive but not divisive, conciliatory and not confrontational. Here once again, it would appear, Marshall had landed on his feet.

Francis Ysidro Edgeworth (1845–1926) – the success of Alfred Marshall's mission was due in no small measure to him. And not merely because of the shared commitment to the Society and the *Journal*. Edgeworth also had the great advantage of being, in Schumpeter's memorable epithet, 'unleaderly':

Edgeworth lacked the force that produces impressive treatises and assembles adherents; amiable and generous, he never asserted himself in any claims of his own, he was over-sensitive on the one hand, overmodest on the other; he was content to take a backseat behind Marshall whom he exalted into Achilles; hesitating in conversation, absent-minded to a pathological degree, the worst speaker and lecturer imaginable, he was personally ineffective – unleaderly is, I think, the word.[50]

Keynes eloquently reinforces Schumpeter's impression of Edgeworth as a man with his head defiantly in the clouds: 'It is narrated that in his boyhood at Edgeworthstown he would read Homer seated aloft in a heron's nest. So, as it were, he dwelt always, not too much concerned with the earth.'[51] Marshall may have been strange but Edgeworth was stranger still, a man whose 'difficult nature . . . cut him off from a full intimacy in any direction' and caused him, in Keynes' analysis, even to abstain from marriage, and 'not for want of susceptibility': 'He liked to have the fewest possible material cares; he did not want to be loaded with any sort of domestic responsibility; and he was content without private comfort.'[52] Marshall may have been cautious but Edgeworth was positively indecisive, a man so hesitant and so tentative that L. L. Price is reported as having complained that 'he could hardly ever obtain from his "balancing friend" a definite conclusion on any matter, "except occasionally the damnation of an outrageous fallacy"'.[53] Marshall may have been moody but Edgeworth was little short of volatile, a man whose father being Irish and whose mother being Spanish, prompted one of Alfred Marshall's few known witticisms: 'Francis is a charming fellow, but you must be careful with Ysidro.'[54] The Fellow of St John's wrote a large-scale treatise intended to synthesise the principal insights of economic theory; the Fellow of All Souls wrote occasional and wrote discrete. The Cambridge BA of 1865 in mathematics wrote to be understood by non-specialist readers such as businessmen; the Oxford BA of 1873 in languages and philosophy wrote without concession to human frailty ('Quotations from the Greek tread on the heels of the differential calculus'),[55] to such an extent, indeed, that even the professional economist is likely to have much sympathy with Keynes' characterisation of him as 'illuminating the obscure by the more obscure'.[56] Above all, the shy Cambridge professor was able to force himself to take a lead when he saw that there was no honourable way of evading the initiative; whereas the self-deprecating Oxford professor was far too introverted and too reticent to do much more than put on public display 'his ostensible reverence for authority and disinclination to say anything definite on his own responsibility'.[57] The authority which Edgeworth most reverenced, needless to say, was that of none other than Alfred Marshall; and that is why it comes as no surprise to learn from John Creedy that, on his appointment to the Drummond Chair, Edgeworth received a letter from Marshall which began 'Hurrah! Hurrah!! Hurrah!!!'.[58] It must have suited Marshall well for the 'unleaderly' incumbent of the Oxford professorship to be a *de facto* disciple of his Cambridge counterpart. Besides which, of course, Edgeworth's shortcomings and eccentricities inevitably boosted Marshall's relative standing by default.

Marshall was exceptionally lucky that a Drummond Professor took up his office in 1891 who was entirely happy to make his home in the shadow of the *Principles*. L. R. Phelps (the editor-designate of the *Economic Review*) and W. J. Ashley (at the time Professor of Economic History in the University of Toronto) had also applied for the Chair, as had H. Llewellyn Smith and R. Inglis Palgrave – all four of them historical relativists, all four of them capable of leading Oxford economics down a very different route from that of the Cambridge orthodoxy. The choice in 1891 was in that sense a choice between alternative methodologies as well as a choice between competing individuals. Ashley at least entertained no unrealistic hopes about his own chances: 'I imagine they will elect Edgeworth', he wrote gloomily to Seligman on 13 December 1890, 'and Oxford will be doomed for its sins to unlimited psycho-mathematical economics.'[59] His prediction proved correct. Edgeworth was supported by a testimonial from Marshall and it is known that Jowett also contacted Marshall directly for specific advice on the ranking of the five candidates. It may reasonably be assumed that Jowett backed Edgeworth on the strength of the advice he received. Besides that, G. E. Goschen was on the appointing committee in his capacity as Chancellor of the Exchequer: he was also President of the British Economic Association (he had taken the Chair at the University College meeting) and as such a close collaborator with Edgeworth, the editor of its *Journal*. Goschen the moral thinker (his own Presidential Address was entitled 'Ethics and Economics') must have seen something of a bird of like feather in Edgeworth, whose reluctance to delete the *ought-to-be* from the economist's *explicanda* rather tends to situate him in the high-minded Victorian tradition of Mill and Sidgwick; Goschen the practical politician (ever-sensitive to the accusation of partisanship) must have regarded the reserved Edgeworth's conspicuous lack of interest in influencing public opinion as a refreshingly apolitical alternative to the social reforming of the social engineers (and not least the candidates close to the Christian Social

Union, who were popularly regarded as being somewhat socialistic); Goschen the committed economist (aware as he was of the deep divisions that still survived within British economics) must have felt that an orthodox figure such as Edgeworth would be eminently suitable to lead dissenting Oxford back into the fold.

Edgeworth had good publications, he had served in 1889 as President of the respected F (he was to enjoy a second term in 1922, the year of his retirement), and he was more or less the right age for the professorship – 46. He also had a morbid fear of being touched; he was fond of non-colloquial English ('was it very caliginous in the Metropolis?', he once asked T. E. Lawrence, just returned from a visit to London);[60] he believed that a difficult subject could not be explained simply and therefore multiplied mathematical demonstrations and 'increased repellent difficulty'[61] to such an extent that on one occasion only one student turned up to hear him;[62] and he appears to have experienced no personal sense of social duty with respect either to the selection of socially-relevant issues or to their treatment in a socially-responsible manner (even when his subject is as up-to-the-minute as is distributive justice, he manages to translate his utilitarian ethics and utilitarian psychology into a forest of abstractions and symbols so thick that the content is all but totally obscured). Looking backward at what he clearly regarded as the wasted decades of enigma and distance, L. L. Price was later to write as follows about the Drummond Chair in the age of Edgeworth: 'Economics at Oxford looked like slumbering quietly or in effect at least must languish comparatively as it rested, so to say, inert in Edgeworth's keeping. There was no active stir of a resonant hive of busy students gathering honey under his helping regime.'[63] Looking forward, the appointing committee must have known what Edgeworth was and what he was likely to remain – a scholarly eccentric, not a head and not a leader. Yet it was Edgeworth who assumed the Drummond Professorship in 1891, not Phelps or Ashley, Llewellyn Smith or Inglis Palgrave. Marshall had done what he could to help Edgeworth, but even he was not all-powerful: in the election of 1888, following the death of Bonamy Price, Marshall apparently favoured his former student L. L. Price, no doubt supported the candidatures of Keynes and Edgeworth, would probably have welcomed the opportunity to rid himself of the Cambridge historicals Cunningham and Foxwell, is not known to have regarded the Reverend Phelps as anything worse than silly – and yet it was Thorold Rogers who at the end of the day emerged the victor. Marshall was in the circumstances genuinely very lucky with respect to the outcome of an election which could have led, in the same year that the *Economic Journal* commenced operations, to the editor of the *Economic Review* taking up his office as the Drummond Professor at Oxford: Alfred Marshall's mission would hardly have been helped along by the conflict between dark blue and light which would then have rendered the 1890s strikingly similar to the 1870s in the bitterness of confrontation. As it was, the election of Edgeworth, sound but silent, meant that dark blue failed to emerge as an intellectual alternative, leaving the road open for light blue to race ahead. Oxford's loss was Cambridge's gain, and Koot's summing up of the situation a good indication of what in practice that meant:

> Price described economics at Oxford under Edgeworth as 'slumbering quietly'. He attracted few students to his 'recondite education' and, as an *ex officio* member, did not regularly attend meetings of the board of the Faculty of Modern History. Edgeworth's tenure prevented the flowering of promising developments in·historical economics at Oxford. Moreover, his unassertive personality, his work in obscure mathematical economics, and his deference to Marshall also prevented the creation of a theoretical school of economics at Oxford. First under Bonamy Price, then under Rogers, and finally under Edgeworth, economics at Oxford floundered without the direction of a strong leader such as contemporary Cambridge enjoyed under Marshall.[64]

Dark blue's loss was light blue's gain and fate once again conferred an unexpected welfare-surplus upon the Cambridge professor who was anxious to do good.

Edgeworth was an admirer but he was also an embarrassment. Thus, writing to Neville Keynes about the need to defend theoretical against historical economics, Marshall expressed his regret that his army was so small and then added pointedly: 'I don't count Edgeworth, because he is so extreme.'[65] Similarly, in a letter to Bowley, Marshall made no secret of his belief that Edgeworth had squandered a not-inconsiderable potential on spurious analytics that were merely a waste of time in the science of economics: 'Edgeworth might have done something great at it: but he has crushed his instincts between the cog wheels of his mathematical machinery.'[66] Twenty years before those letters, moreover, the well-trained Wrangler who could afford to hide the instrument that had done the work was writing in almost identical terms, in his review in *The Academy* of 1881 of the *Mathematical Psychics* of the same year, about the self-taught mathematician who seemed determined to put the polish of his symbols on public display: 'His readers may sometimes wish that he had kept his work by him a little longer till he had worked it out more fully, and obtained that simplicity which comes only through long labour.'[67] An economist who devoted years to the translation of economics into mathematics and back again can hardly have had much sympathy with an impatient colleague who awkwardly rushed prematurely into print; and Marshall also observed, with tactful understatement, that 'there is a certain air of unreality'[68] about some of the arguments in the book. The review is not always enthusiastic, but no one could say it is unfriendly – certainly not with the opening line that 'the book shows clear signs of genius, and is a promise of great things to come'[69] and a general conclusion as follows: 'Taking it at what it claims to be, "a tentative study", we can only admire its brilliancy, force, and originality.'[70] In view of such praise, and in view of Edgeworth's debt to Jevons (an influence to which Marshall returns in the course of his review), the reader is inevitably put in mind of Marshall's earlier review in *The Academy*, where the tone which he adopted towards Jevons was decidedly cooler. Time evidently heals at least some wounds.

Edgeworth's debt in *Mathematical Psychics* is to Jevons' *Theory*, most notably so in the realm of economic psychology (i.e. 'the conception of man as a pleasure machine')[71] and in the theory of bargained exchange (Edgeworth's discussion of the contract curve, the indifference curve, the box diagrams, and the trades and swaps made between Crusoe and Friday are particularly interesting in the light of the fact that Marshall praised the book but subsequently ignored the constructs). Edgeworth's debt, even in 1881, is, however, to Marshall as well, both for the exemplary use of mathematical reasoning in the two *Pure Theory* papers of 1879 and for the careful exploration of key issues of subjectivist theory in the *Economics of Industry*, also of 1879. Of these issues, one of the most important is the possibility of indeterminacy in wage-bargaining, together with the implications of such indeterminacy for the strategies of combinations: the theme of equilibrium a range rather than equilibrium a point is one to which Edgeworth warmed, despite the fact that uncertainty as a concept lends itself less readily to quantitative pyrotechnics than does the postulation of perfect knowledge. Marshall returned to the subject of indeterminacy in the *Principles*,[72] and there is also a useful

manuscript note on the topic in the Marshall Library. Dated 2
September 1905 and headed 'Problem of monopolies mutually dependent on one another's cooperation', the unpublished fragment
reminds the reader that, while Marshall knew about indeterminacy at
a time when the late-developing Edgeworth was still flirting with a
career as a barrister, yet the soil was hardly virgin even in the 1870s:
'The abstract side of the problem of two monopolists neither of
whom can dispense with the cooperation of the other was initiated in
Cournot's monumental *Recherches* . . . with all his customary force
& suggestiveness but with less than his usual precision.'[73] Marshall
sought to do what he could to supply that precision and so, later, did
Edgeworth. Marshall in 1919, interestingly, singles out three intellectual influences on his own theory of monopoly for particular praise:
Cournot, Pigou – and that of Edgeworth himself.[74]

Edgeworth appears not to have read Jevons' *Theory* until the
second edition appeared in 1879. It was also in 1879 that he first read
the *Pure Theory* papers and the *Economics of Industry*. Jevons was
his Hampstead neighbour and it is likely that the two utilitarians had
many opportunities for serious discussions in 1879 and 1880 on
various aspects of mathematical Benthamism. Edgeworth in the same
period was corresponding with Alfred Marshall in Cambridge about
economic and philosophical questions. The *Mathematical Psychics* of
1881 shows the influence of both of these father-figures, to say
nothing of Gossen, Walras and, of course, Cournot (whom Edgeworth calls 'the father of Mathematical Economics').[75] Marshall must
have been pleased with many aspects of Edgeworth's economics,
including his willingness to make interpersonal comparisons (as in the
following: 'Any just perceivable pleasure-increment experienced by
any sentient at any time has the same value'),[76] and, naturally
enough, his recognition of altruism as a significant force in economics. Marshall and Edgeworth first met after the publication of the
Mathematical Psychics. Acquaintance was to become friendship,
insofar as either man was capable of friendship. Edgeworth's admiration for Marshall was unbounded. Edgeworth was from 1890 the
editor of the British Economic Association's new *Economic Journal*,
from 1891 the incumbent of the prestigious Drummond Chair at
Oxford, for three decades a champion of the *Principles*. Always an
ally and never a competitor, Edgeworth was Marshall's friend in high
places at a time when Marshall needed all the support he could
muster.

2 The Cambridge Tripos

Prior to 1903 economics at Cambridge was taught as a subsidiary subject in the Moral Sciences Tripos and the History Tripos. Marshall was by no means happy with its subsidiary status. Professionalisation means specialisation, he argued; and specialisation means not a shared School (analogous to the Statistical Society) but rather a separate curriculum (analogous to the Economic Association). He accordingly set himself the objective of upgrading the standing of his discipline within his university. The benefit was indeed secured, but it had its cost. As Coats observes: 'The task of putting Cambridge economics on a sound footing must have been exhausting and time consuming. . . . Had he been working in an academic environment more conducive to specialized teaching and research, Marshall might well have completed the additional volumes of the *Principles* which his contemporaries so eagerly awaited.'[77] The volumes were not completed. The new degree-course was, however, established. Institutions as well as ideas being so important a part of Alfred Marshall's mission, one suspects that the loss of the research that might have been in fact represented somewhat less of subjective sacrifice to him than it would have done to the pure bookworm who lives for his scholarship: 'he saw in the development of original economic study', Pigou recalls, 'a means to the advancement of economic science, which itself was a means to the betterment of social life'.[78] That the establishment of the new Tripos imposed some subjective sacrifice on the Cambridge professor, committed as he was to new ideas as well as to new institutions, cannot, however, be denied.

As early as his return to Cambridge in 1885 Marshall was commenting adversely on the deterrent effect of the subsidiary status on the academic calibre of the economics intake. Thus, speaking of the Moral Sciences Tripos, he complained that not every born economist can be expected also to be a born philosopher: 'Many of those who are fitted for the highest and hardest economic work are not attracted by the metaphysical studies that lie at the threshold of that Tripos.'[79] Many, Marshall said, 'have not the taste or the time for the whole of the Moral Sciences, but. . . . have the trained scientific minds which Economics is so urgently craving';[80] and such a scarce and valuable commodity ought therefore to be properly channelled and carefully husbanded. Cambridge had a tradition of rationalism and empiricism and was ahead of Oxford in the physical sciences. With respect to the human sciences, however, it had tended to adopt a casual and gentlemanly approach that Marshall deeply deplored: 'The great scientific strength of Cambridge is not indeed indifferent to social problems; but is content to treat them in an amateur fashion, not with the same weighty seriousness that it gives to other studies.'[81] The subsidiary status of economics teaching was a case in point. It had, Marshall was convinced, significantly debased the quality of the economics intake in the Moral Sciences Tripos: 'The Mo. Sc. men, except the ablest, are mere parasites of textbooks: they know nothing & seem to care nothing about real life.'[82] The economics intake in the History Tripos was no more inspiring: 'They are Kittle-Kattle', Marshall said, 'intelligent, more or less earnest, but not very profound.'[83] All in all, Marshall sorrowfully reported to Neville Keynes in 1902, the Cambridge system had badly let him down: 'Put yourself in my position. I am an old man. For many reasons I could wish I were out of harness now. I have no time to wait. . . . Through causes for which no one is – in the main – responsible, the curriculum to which I am officially attached has not provided me with *one single* high class man devoting himself to economics during the sixteen years of my Professorship.'[84] This is a rather extreme assertion, particularly since men such as Clapham (BA, History), Flux (BA, Mathematics) and Pigou (BA, Moral Philosophy) cannot reasonably be regarded as low-class when compared with the Oxford names of Gonner, Harrison and Price whom Marshall nostalgically cites as having been superior students. Extreme though it may be, it is assertions such as this which provide the bedrock foundation for Marshall's campaign to raise standards by means of a specialist degree course.

The specialist Tripos was in a sense forced upon Marshall by developments outside Cambridge. For one thing, the expansion of higher education in the previous decade – and not least the foundation (under Hewins) of the London School of Economics in 1895 and the creation (under Ashley) of the Birmingham Faculty of Commerce in 1901 – had meant that good students had an ever-widening range of courses from which to select. As with undergraduate intake, moreover, so with business support in an era when the State had not yet become the principal source of funding: 'If our studies were made to give no room for what business men want, we must expect their money to go to new Universities; & we should continue money-starved.'[85] Then there was the international dimension, that of economic growth at home and abroad, dramatic improvements in transportation and communications, the emergence in the world economy of threatening rivals such as the protected producers of the United States and Germany: these and other pressures under-lined the fact that England could no longer act as if she were the workshop of the world. England's prosperity, Marshall wrote, could in an increasingly competitive environment simply not be taken for granted. Nor, indeed, could her defence; and that is why her very existence might ultimately 'depend on her keeping pace with the forward economic movement of nations against whom she may need to measure her force'.[86] The casual and gentlemanly approach to economics is in such circumstances not much of an asset; 'national security may have a higher claim than even cultured leisure';[87] and Britain needed her trained economists.

Precisely because Britain needed her trained economists, she could no longer afford the luxury of economics teaching that was inappro-priate to the needs of businessmen. Marshall believed that the non-analytical method of attack of the historical school fell into this category. There is for that reason a very real sense in which it would be true to say that his campaign to introduce a new Tripos in his subject was at one and the same time a campaign to wrest British economics free from the shackles of a specific intellectual alternative. The History Tripos had since 1873 included optional papers in political economy, but it was for all that mainly a degree in history (and one in which the first two years barely advanced beyond the medieval period). Marshall deplored the fact that Cambridge students had the opportunity of specialising in history without doing economics but not in economics without doing history, couching his proposals for the additional degree-course in the conciliatory language of pluralism, diversity and freedom of choice: 'Surely the University will not refuse our petition for a Tripos which opens a free path to true work. By a very little effort it can have two ideal Triposes, one historical, the other mainly economic, each helping the other.'[88]

The historical economists were not taken in by the plea for toler-ance. Aware as they must have been that the better economists would eschew the broad cultural base of the existing degree in favour of the narrow specialisation of the new one, convinced in addition that the new degree would have a strong bias towards theoretical speculation and away from the historical evidence, they sought to prevent Marshall from carrying out what they regarded as a *de facto* programme of backdoor proselytisation by means of early specialis-ation in doctrinaire dogmatism. Thus Cunningham, opposing the degree, called instead for a new Tripos in Economic History (neither pure economics nor pure history); and he was in the end supported by Foxwell, who had at first hoped to persuade Marshall to expand the coverage of historical subjects (including the history of economic thought, his own field of expertise). Cunningham and Foxwell correctly perceived what Marshall meant when he made innocent-sounding statements about the need for a curriculum to demonstrate flexibility and elasticity, and above all not to attempt too much: 'This trouble is at its worst when a curriculum is already full; and a study which claims a large share of thought and work is being compressed by the healthy and vigorous expansion of other studies to which it has no longer any close affinity; but which are rigidly bound in the same three years' curriculum with it. . . . That is the position of economics now.'[89] Whatever Marshall said, they correctly perceived, what Marshall meant was nothing other than the selective excision of the descriptive approach that was to them the hard core of their paradigm, and its replacement by the analytical alternative: half of the first two years of Marshall's new Tripos plus the bulk of the third was to be devoted to theory, there was to be little coverage of applied economics, and economic history (that almost exclusively of the nineteenth century) was to be relegated to the status of the intellectual footnote. Analytical potential was evidently to be the Cambridge *sine qua non*, and not the untinged photograph of external reality. It was the analytical turn of mind which in any case extended the greater appeal to Alfred Marshall, about whom (after studying the Cambridge professor's notes on the 200-odd pupils who attended his tutorials between 1895 and 1902) John Maloney has made the following observation: 'It is clear that he regarded the mathematicians so highly not because he had any great opinion of mathematical economics as such – his correspondence with Bowley makes it clear that he did not – but because he saw their analytical sophistication as symptomatic of a generalised intelligence which would triumph over more pedestrian rivals even in pedestrian fields.'[90] The new Tripos must evidently be seen not merely as Marshall's attempt to push in the new learning of which he felt British business to be more and more in need but also as an attempt to push out the old learning of the Cambridge fact-gatherers: they loaded the student's mind with inert details relating to commerce when what was really required was the inculcation of habits of rigorous thought, and they should for that reason, Marshall believed, be strongly advised to mind their own Tripos, while leaving to him the training of the practical economists.

Prior to 1903 economics at Cambridge was taught as a subsidiary subject in the Moral Sciences as well as in the History Tripos. Marshall wanted to liberate his discipline from the confines of the former degree course, just as he wished to rescue it from the latter. The need for liberation was, admittedly, not quite as pressing in view of the fact that there was no moral sciences school that required vanquishing in the same way as the historical school had represented a problem to be solved. Even so, the Moral Sciences Tripos had been a poor home for economic speculation. There was the 'practically prohibitive' pressure of time: 'No sound and realistic study of economics can be compressed into a three years' course together with mental science.'[91] There was the well-known difficulty that psychology is favourable to individually-orientated explanations whereas economics requires the socially-informed. There was an incompatibility between the economic and the philosophical mind-set which Marshall pointed up (but did not explain) in a letter of 1897 to Neville Keynes on the subject of one Jenkyn Jones, who was then applying for a post at Sheffield: 'An able man, tho' slow: but of course he knows economics as a branch of philosophy; i.e. he knows nothing about it.'[92] These shortcomings should not be neglected, but they did have their counterparts on the assets side. Logic, for one thing, was an important part of the Moral Sciences Tripos; and Marshall always took the view that higher education most sensitively fulfilled its social function not at the level of content ('I am intensely opposed to memory questions in a University',[93] he wrote to Foxwell at the height of the debate over the new degree) but rather insofar as it inculcated in its charges the appropriate mental discipline and taught them to think rigorously and thoroughly for themselves. Besides that, psychology and philosophy were valuable adjuncts to the development of the empathetic posture which Marshall regarded as so valuable a quality in business life: 'Economic studies call for and develop the faculty of sympathy, and especially that rare sympathy which enables people to put themselves in the place, not only of their comrades, but also of other classes.'[94] Also, Marshall's own mix of egotism and altruism would seem to presuppose a course of training not merely in the technicalities of elasticity and utility, price-theory and consumer's surplus, but also in the economic significance of the other-regarding orientation: thus Marshall was fond of giving advice that went against 'the maxim of orthodox Political Economists . . . that the world progresses on the whole best if each man looks after his own interests', both to employers (to overpay the half-starved worker) and to unions (to abstain from excessive pay-claims such as would reduce future employment-opportunities in a given skilled trade), and his rule in such cases was quite clearly that of the Kantian gentleman who sees clearly that it would be 'unreasonable for any persons to adopt a line of action, the general adoption of which by all others in their position will be injurious to the whole'.[95] Believing as he did so strongly that moral constraint is of relevance to economic activity (e.g. 'The beneficent pay high wages, & what is better give good surroundings'),[96] believing in addition that shared *ought-to-bes* often point not to market but to State (e.g. 'When a parasitic race of greedy money making men push down prices by destroying collective property in beautiful objects there is a prima facie ground for interfering'),[97] one would have expected Marshall positively to welcome the teaching of economic science in tandem with the moral and political philosophy of the Moral Sciences Tripos. Since, indeed, that Tripos was also actively involved in the inculcation of habits of mental discipline and the development of empathetic understanding, one would have expected Marshall to regard it as an excellent framework within which to develop his own special blend of economic studies. Be that as it may, the fact is that he did not, but opted instead to launch a campaign on behalf of an entirely new degree-course in economics.

The campaign was mounted by means of the pamphlet (*A Plea for the Creation of a Curriculum in Economics and Associated Branches of Political Science*, 1902) and the fly-sheet ('The Proposed New Tripos', 1903), both circulated to members of Senate, plus personal contacts, debates in Senate, and the occasional public lecture (such as 'Economic Teaching at the Universities in Relation to Public Well-being', read to a conference of the Committee on Social Education in 1902). As was so often the case in Marshall's charmed existence, the campaign was a success. The Moral Sciences, it turned out, were not particularly reluctant to hive off economics; while Cunningham and Foxwell (even supported by non-economic historians such as Gwatkin) simply lacked the influence to defend History against the new and more theoretical syllabus. Marshall's reiterated stress on tolerance and consensus, together with the long historical sections in his *Principles*, must have taken the wind out of the historicists' sails, conveying as they did the impression of a man of compromise: the proposed Tripos does not have one foot in each camp, but its introduction must have proceeded the more smoothly because that was widely believed to be the stance of its principal architect. Marshall's trusted lieutenant had been far more outspoken, having stated bluntly in his *Scope and Method of Political Economy* of 1891 that 'mere historical research cannot by itself suffice for the solution of theoretical problems':[98] 'Much that is said by the historical school consists of mere negative criticism; and on the positive side, there is often wanting an adequate discrimination between what really belongs to economic science, and what is no more than economic history pure and simple.'[99] However much Alfred Marshall may secretly have shared John Neville Keynes' reservations about statistical–empirical thinkers unwilling or unable to make constructive use of hypothetical–universal generalisations, it undoubtedly did his cause no harm that any such hostility on his part had remained unexpressed: what he said was that there was work for all, and this reassurance (taken all too easily as a defence of equal work for all) must have lulled the unwary into a false sense of security. Meanwhile, Marshall was able to rely on Keynes' support in the campaign for the Tripos, just as he had earlier relied on Keynes' evaluation of draft chapters of the *Principles*. That work, together with the *Scope and Method* of the following year, contains the essence of the paradigm that was further consolidated by the Tripos. The coincidence that the latter work was completed and the former was published in the very year that saw the foundation of the British Economic Association powerfully underscores the significance of Maynard Keynes' observation that 'the modern age of British economics can. . . . be dated from that year'.[100] The Tripos of 1903 was one of the first great events of that modern age, its successful introduction a tribute to the assiduity of Neville Keynes as it is to what Neville Keynes called the 'manoeuvring'[101] of Alfred Marshall.

The time was right for the introduction of the new degree. As early as 1894 the Section F Committee had been studying ways of expanding the pool of trained economists available to British industry; other institutions (Jevons' old Owens College being one) were increasingly seeking to supply that which was increasingly in demand; and the tariff reform controversy brought into sharp relief, also in 1903, the national security and the foreign trade arguments that favoured the Tripos (together, it must be said, with the need for careful economic reasoning and adequate factual evidence, both conspicuously underrepresented in much of the debate of that year). The time was right to propose a new degree that, cut loose from history and from metaphysical speculation, would at last provide the way-in to the real world that young businessmen more and more required. Looking backward from the perspective of 1905, Marshall was able to report that Cambridge had done her duty and been successful in so doing: 'Our new curriculum is gradually becoming known. More students, and especially more sons of leading business men who are preparing to follow in their fathers' business, have entered it this year than in either of its first two years.'[102] Looking forward from the perspective of 1902, of course, his task had been the difficult one of convincing his academic colleagues that an economics degree of interest to the commercially-minded would not degenerate into the routine *how-tos* of a business studies degree that the Cambridge Senate would almost certainly have blocked. Marshall's success in 1903 was evidently due in no small measure to his ability to steer his craft safely between the two extremes of the insufficiently practical on the one hand, the insufficiently learned on the other. Native shrewdness inevitably had its part to play, but it must not be forgotten that Marshall was first and foremost an academic economist, neither a businessman himself nor a scholar who was uninterested in exchange. Marshall himself, in short, had the great good fortune already to have situated his shop at precisely the spot where he was most likely to attract interested parties coming from both directions.

Thus it was that his proposed new Tripos dealt with topics such as price-discrimination, speculation, pure monopoly, payment by piece-work (topics, in other words, that were bound to appeal to business-men) but dispensed with practical instruction in *how-to* areas such as accountancy which would certainly have alienated the sympathies of traditional academics. His reason was no more manipulative than his conviction that a good mind can absorb for itself 'the more important parts of standard treatises on factory accounts, depreciation, etc.',[103] and that formal instruction in the detailed applications of commercial techniques would represent a waste of time and effort: 'For they fill the mind, without enlarging it and strengthening it. And the ablest business men tell us that it is faculty rather than knowledge which the business man of to-day needs. It is a powerful and capacious mind, rather than one already crammed with dead matter, that a University should send out to the work of the world.'[104] Neither the businessmen nor the traditional academics could really raise any objection to this defence of rigour and challenge in preference to commercial rel-evance, narrowly defined, seeing as it is the nub of Marshall's argument that the mind that has been trained is economically more valuable to the productive enterprise than is the mind that has merely been stuffed. Marshall's argument was for analytical economics, not for Latin and Greek, but it was for all that an argument that was far from new in the Cambridge of 1903.

So highly did Marshall the political economist rank the formation of appropriate attitudes and aptitudes above the inculcation of narrowly vocational skills that the reader is surprised less by his failure to incorporate accountancy into his new Tripos than by his omission of topics and courses such as might have promoted within the student the development of further attitudes and aptitudes still. The faculty of imagination, for example, such as Marshall believed to be the essential concomitant of entrepreneurial alertness: 'Every study exercises, in varying degrees, the three inseparable faculties, perception, imagination, and reason: the use of these three is the centre of the intellectual life of every University. . . . Imagination is the greatest of the three: it makes the great soldier as well as the great artist, the great business man, and the student who extends the boundaries of science.'[105] Economic activity being concerned with the remote, the unseen, the interdependent, the anticipated, the uncertain, imagination is the precondition for progress through the thicket of complexities; and it therefore comes as somewhat of a disappointment that the new Tripos, so strong on data-collection and statistical measurement, was simultaneously so weak on lessons of direct relevance to the *ex ante* conjecturing and postulating which is the sensitive decision-maker's unique contribution to allocation and growth. As with the faculty of imagination, moreover, so with the capacity to empathise: Marshall, speaking of the wage-bargain struck between a privileged but educated employer and his lower-class subordinates, observes of that employer that 'his economic studies at a University are pretty sure to enable him to enter into their point of view', but the actual courses that enter into his proposed new Tripos hardly add up to a training in *Verstehen* such as 'welds the nation into one'.[106] The historical subjects probably provided some of the requisite background knowledge, and Marshall's own observations (however unsupported by evidence) on the relationship between earnings, character, nature of expenditure and mode of employment must have fostered some kind of sociological perspective. Simply, they were not enough, and empathetic understanding in the new Tripos all too quickly gives way to abstract analysis – so quickly, indeed, that the genuinely anthropocentric economist who took Marshall on man at his word would have been well advised to make a thorough study of contemporary fiction instead, or to volunteer to spend a year at

Toynbee Hall, or to register for a social science course at the newly-founded London School of Economics.

The new Tripos could have done more to promote the faculty of imagination and the capacity to empathise, both of them, in Alfred Marshall's view, important attributes in practical economic life. It could also have done more to encourage the sense of teamwork which Marshall eulogised as an unexpected by-product for prospective businessmen of University sport: 'They see how, on the river and in the football field, the student learns to bear and to forbear, to obey and to command; and how constant discussion with his friends sharpens his wits, makes him ready and resourceful, helps him to enter into the points of view of others, and to explain his own.'[107] As with the sense of teamwork, moreover, so with the perception of duty: Marshall denied that businessmen inevitably become greedy and self-serving, and stressed that 'just and noble sentiments might be introduced into counting-house and factory and workshop'.[108] Marshall's hidden curriculum evidently extended to upgrading the tone of business life. His explicit curriculum did not: if the sense of teamwork was to be left to rowing and football, then the perception of duty was to be delegated to economic evolution to develop. Of course his new Tripos could have done more to make clear to businessmen that they had social obligations as well as individual opportunities. Had it done so, however, it might have been less readily acceptable to all sectors of the community. As it was, Marshall's new Tripos pleased many, offended few, and was adopted by Cambridge University without any great opposition being manifest.

Marshall was successful in 1903 on the important issue of the new Tripos. He had been, it must be noted, somewhat less successful in 1896 with respect to the very different issue of whether or not to open the Cambridge BA to the women students of Newnham and Girton. Women had been taking the degree examination on an unofficial basis since 1870, officially since 1881; and from 1895 they demanded to be awarded degrees as well. Marshall in the 1870s had lectured at Newnham and had married an educated woman without whose support, encouragement and constructive criticism his scholarly work would never had been completed: 'Mr. and Mrs. Marshall', the *Bristol Times and Mirror* once wrote, 'can hardly be considered apart from one another. Jowett always used to speak of them "in the dual or plural numbers".'[109] In the 1870s Marshall wrote enthusiastically to his mother about the liberated status of women in America, praised his women students at Bristol for being able so successfully to combine their studies with a healthy family life, and effectively answered in the affirmative the question raised by Mill and others of 'whether the quick insight of woman may not be trained so as to give material assistance to man in ordering *public* as well as private affairs'.[110] Marshall in the 1890s was a different man. Perhaps because by his mid-50s he had relapsed into type and adopted the patronising attitude towards women which his father had taken, perhaps because the organicist and the evolutionist came to value the upgrading and the educating that begins in the good home above the individual woman's freedom of choice, Marshall in the 1890s became very critical indeed of the attempts of 'aggressive womanhood' to 'resemble men':[111] only the violent and sometimes obstructive tactics of the 'new unionism' that radicalised the late-Victorian unskilled seems to have upset him so much as he grew older.

All universities in Britain except for Oxford and Cambridge had by 1895 agreed to admit women to degrees. Marshall was keen that Cambridge should do so as well, with the minor proviso that the degrees in question should be called not BA but EBA or ABA: 'Some such degrees as these should be granted to women without delay.'[112] Women should be granted the status of *Externata* or *Associata* without delay, but to make them full members of the University would be going too far: 'We moderates want them to manage their own affairs and allow men to manage theirs.'[113] In order to make his case against the admission of women to the BA, Marshall in 1896 circulated an eight-page fly-sheet ('On Cambridge Degrees for Women') to all members of the Cambridge University Senate. In it he reminded his fellow Senators that the very rigidity of the three-year course threw up a potential conflict of loyalties with which no young lady ought to have to wrestle: 'However severe the illness of those dear to her, however urgent the need for her presence at home, she must keep her terms under penalty of losing recognition for her work. If she decides to go her own way, and let her family shift for themselves, she gets her honours; but her true life is impoverished and not enriched by them.'[114] Cambridge degrees for women would thus favour the irresponsible woman while deterring from higher education her sister with the higher nature – precisely the opposite of the selective standard which a morally-minded community ought to apply. Besides which, not only could women not be spared from home for the full three years, but their admission to Cambridge degrees would prove demoralising to the male students compelled to sit the same papers. All examinations, after all, 'test receptivity and diligence in prescribed lines: and these are the strong points of women.'[115] What examinations do not pick up is 'constructive work' done in 'after years', and it is there that women, however gifted they might be in the undergraduate quiz, reveal themselves quite unambigously as the weaker sex: 'For reasons many of which are beyond their control, the Tripos is for most of them the end of all vigorous mental work.'[116] That being the case, it would be a misleading indicator of potential achievement to mix women and men for purposes of assessment: women may perform well on paper, but it is men who perform well in life.

Marshall was not opposed to higher education for women, only to the admission of women to the Cambridge BA. Women and men alike would benefit, he said, if women were taught and examined separately. Even the enlightened Americans, he pointed out, were already recognising the dangers inherent in co-education: 'No one thinks now that Harvard and Yale will become mixed Universities.'[117] Cambridge should not fall victim to a threat which the wise Americans had narrowly averted. At the level of teaching, of course, it did not: the colleges themselves remained resolutely single-sex. At the level of examining, however, Marshall's campaign was doomed to failure, and women were indeed admitted to the University's BA. Remarkably few other instances can be cited where Alfred Marshall's mission was not an unqualified success.

3 The Triumph of the Paradigm

Marshall's economics conquered England as rapidly as the Inquisition had conquered Spain and the Revolution was to conquer Russia: by the time of the latter-day Ricardo's retirement from his Cambridge Chair 18 years after the publication of his *Principles*, the intellectual system which he had refined and synthesised had already been adopted as the neo-classical orthodoxy by the vast majority of British economists. There was, to be frank, little real competition: traditional Ricardianism had run out of steam, Ruskinites and Marxians were never very numerous, Jevonian utilitarianism was too incomplete to attract disciples. Virtually the only real challenge to the Marshallian hegemony came in fact from the economists of the English historical school. Marshall's triumph was in a sense their defeat.

Early English historical economists were Richard Jones (1790–

1855), T. E. Cliffe Leslie (1827–82) and Arnold Toynbee (1852–83), late English historical economists scholars such as Edwin Cannan (1861–1935) and Sir John Clapham (1873–1946), and the principal English historical economists active in the critical years of the Marshallian ascendancy the following: J. E. Thorold Rogers (1823–90), William Cunningham (1849–1919), Sir William J. Ashley (1860–1927), W. A. S. Hewins (1865–1931) and H. S. Foxwell (1849–1936). The school having no clear leader and no unifying text, it is sometimes easier to point up the differences among the various authors than to point to the similarities which gave them a common identity. That having been said, most if not all of the English historical economists would probably have accepted that their shared paradigm incorporated most if not all of the following five characteristics.

First, historical relativism. The historical economists rejected the universals and the generalisations of the pure theoreticians, both classical (Koot describes Ricardo as 'the arch-enemy of English historical economics')[118] and neo-classical (Ashley omitting Marshallian concepts such as marginal utility from his Birmingham curriculum altogether on the grounds that they were 'not much more than a verbal description of the superficial facts at a particular point in time').[119] In place of principles they fell back on practice and devoted themselves to data-collection where more abstract thinkers would have been content with tendency laws. Some, no doubt, did believe that their empirical investigations and statistical evidence were in effect only confirming by inductive means the truth of the orthodox theories that had been spun out by the great deductivists; but most, it is clear, were persuaded that theories are specific to time and place and that different conditions render appropriate quite different generalisations. Their concern with the applied and the actual made them take an interest in developments in neighbouring social science disciplines such as sociology (as where they explained the absence of factor-price equalisation through reference to the inhibiting effect on competition and mobility of custom, habit and the sense of community) and politics (as where, writing about mercantilist regulations or the Elizabethan Poor Law, they made the point that State intervention might have been as appropriate to the material and intellectual environment of the sixteenth century as the *laissez-faire* bias of *Manchestertum* was normal in the optimistic competitiveness of the 1840s). Such interdisciplinarity led them in turn to an acknowledgement of the non-rational side to economic life (as in the case of the supra-individual forces of race, religion and patriotism), to an awareness of the affectual basis for corporatism (witness their defence of voluntary associations such as trades unions). It also led them to reject the use of the mathematical apparatus: the simplifications of symbolism obscured the underlying social realities and relationships, they argued, while a maximising framework predicated upon utility and interest takes for granted precisely that structure of motivation which, being historically contingent, is better determined *ex post facto*. More generally, their concern with historical relativism and historical contingency led them into the disequilibrium world of institutional dynamics, evolutionary economics, stages of economic development such as is far more easily described in the comparative language of carefully-collected facts than it is in the over-confident verities of mechanistic mathematics. It is no surprise that it was as a direct consequence of their scepticism about economic theorising that the new sub-discipline of economic history was to be created. Nor should it be a surprise that they had so great an interest in the history of economic thought: old facts according ill with new theories, it is only to be expected that the economists of the English historical school should have sought to discover how the past actually thought of itself rather than compressing antecedent experience into the straitjacket of the unique present's specific truths. The English historical economists tended to treat economic thought as complementary to economic history; and that tendency too is indicative of their commitment to historical relativism.

Second, moral commitment. The English historical economists were moralists with a deep sense of collective duty and social obligation who had little time for the economic man's asocial and amoral request to be left alone to maximise his own personal happiness. As Hubert Llewellyn Smith put it in a paper to the Oxford Economic Society in 1887:

> We deny the right of any man to do what he likes with his own, we demand that he shall so use it as to fulfil his duty to Society in which he is placed. And we do not despair of gradually forming a public opinion which shall regard not as an ornament but as a blot on society the man who uses his wealth be it great or small regardless of the interests of the Society in which he lives.[120]

William Cunningham made a similar point in his eulogy of 'the willingness to make habitual sacrifices of personal convenience and personal advantage for the public benefit':[121]

> It is misleading to take individual happiness as a unit from which the good of mankind can be built up. To insist that the national wealth consists of the aggregate of the wealth of individuals is plausible; but the welfare of the community is something more than the aggregate sum of the satisfaction enjoyed by separate individuals. Man is a social being, and it is very difficult to reckon up the satisfaction derived from doing a generous act; Dr. Marshall has pointed out that 'much of the best work of the world has no price, and evades altogether the economic calculus'. From the point of view of consumption it is always better to give than to receive; freedom for the individual to pursue his own private interests does not necessarily lead to the greatest welfare in the community. If, on the other hand, we start by trying to form a conception of the good of the community as a whole, the difficulty is set in a different light, and we can say that the individual finds his personal welfare by sharing in the life of a well-ordered community.[122]

The individual, Cunningham argued, always stands to gain from the pre-existence of a self-policing ethical constraint which bridles his desires and enforces his compliance – if only because the alternative is *anomie* and moral normlessness is social chaos: 'The claim of the undisciplined to have liberty to do as they like must result in mere anarchy. . . . The liberty of self-disciplined men is the goal to be aimed at, and those societies have most inherent vitality which are bearing this steadily in mind.'[123] Cunningham, it is clear, was simply not prepared to accept that the commercial spirit and the unregulated pursuit of pecuniary gain were in and of themselves adequate to ensure the viability of the decentralised market economy: interest and contract, utility and exchange, are of unquestionable importance for economic progress, Cunningham conceded, but only in combination with 'the sense of public spirit, and of duty to the public' that serve as 'the salt which helps to keep every form of civic life free from corruption'.[124] Cunningham was, of course, more than merely an academic (holding, initially, a University appointment, from 1884 to 1888, before withdrawing from Marshall's reach into the relative safety, from 1888 to 1906, of a College position at Trinity): he was also an ordained clergyman of the Church of England (and as such vicar of Great St Mary's, Cambridge, from 1887 to 1908, and Archdeacon of Ely, 1908–1919). A man whose whole life was informed by his profound religiosity (he appears never to have entertained any doubts about the self-imposed credo which he articulated as follows as early as 1866: 'I believe it to be incumbent on me to obey Christ's command, and that I should be culpable did I not do so'),[125] Cunningham was bound to associate moral commitment in general with *Christian* ethical constraint in particular: thus he wrote in 1910, praising Christian ideals (and contrasting them with the 'ruthless disregard for human life'[126] of modern market capitalism), that it was his view that 'Christianity goes far deeper than any social morality and brings more effective influence to bear upon the personal life'.[127] Cunningham's commitment to specifically *Christian* ethics was shared by Ingram and by Cliffe Leslie (both of them sons of Anglican clergymen); by Richard Jones, Thorold Rogers and L. R. Phelps (all three, like Cunningham, ordained Anglicans); by Hewins (whose twin obsessions with interventionist authority and revealed religion come together in his dictum that 'the modern State is the Christian Church in its workaday clothes');[128] by Ashley (whose childhood in Bermondsey was deeply informed by evangelical Christianity – his father, journeyman hatter and devout Baptist, prided himself on abstention from tobacco, alcohol and card games – and whose adult life was an ongoing search, as his daughter later made clear, for the opportunity both to understand God's ways and to serve God's purpose: 'Ashley when he was over sixty still described himself as an "evolutionary socialist". He might also have described himself as an evolutionary Christian').[129] Whether religious in inspiration or secular in nature, the crucial point about the moral commitment of the high-minded children of T. H. Green and Arnold Toynbee is that their economics was in effect inseparable from their ethics.

Third, social reform. The English historical economists, concerned as they were with the actualisation of their ideals, saw it as their duty to become involved in the elucidation and resolution of contemporary social problems. Activists rather than fatalists, their crusading zeal is well captured by Ashley in the following:

> I agree with Comte and St. Paul – with the former that prevision is possible, and that we can hasten and assist the transition, or in the words of the latter that we can be fellow-workers with God. And so I should not stand aside and say, "Well, perhaps it will be so, but I'm rather sorry" – but rather say "It must be, and therefore it must be good, and therefore I must help it".'[130]

Ashley was keen to do what he could to accelerate the process of improvement, and so too was Thorold Rogers, who went so far as to define the careful collection of primary data as in itself a moral activity, the historian of economic and social life being by dint of his very inductivism 'therefore engaged in seeking out past causes for present distresses'.[131] It is easy enough to object that the evidence gleaned from original sources such as College records and farm accounts and presented in Rogers' magisterial *History of Agriculture and Prices in England* (of which the first volume appeared in 1866, the sixth and final volume posthumously in 1902) in truth tells the reader everything about movements in wages and prices from 1259 to 1793 but nothing about England in Rogers' own time; and tempting in addition to point out that a strict interpretation of historical relativism would in effect render invalid the arguing from the specific to the general, the *a priori* theorising and the hypothesis-testing, which seem to be at the root of Rogers' claims for the social utility of economic science. What is particularly interesting in the circumstances is that Rogers himself did not draw these inferences, but argued instead that the historical economist was placed by virtue of his observations in the enviable position of being able 'to suggest remedies for the evils under which society is labouring'.[132] Unexpected and even inconsistent though so optimistic a conclusion may have been, it was also fully in keeping with the reforming spirit with which the ethics of the English historical school was imbued. Thus Foxwell, writing in the bad years of the 1880s, was happy to report that the old and 'unmoral' economics (the economics of individualistic self-seeking and greedy materialism) was rapidly giving way to an applied and a programmatic economics which, resolutely purposive and defiantly anti-deterministic in nature, held with great conviction that 'a man must act as honorably in his industrial capacity as he would in his private relations' and that no man should be allowed, 'by pleading "the state of the market", to excuse himself from the ordinary obligations of humanity': 'With the old school, the worst scandals were calmly referred to "demand and supply", as though such a reference were final. With the new school, if the conditions of the market are such as to lead to injustice or to swell the mass of social wreckage, these conditions must be overhauled, and as far as may be rectified.'[133] Foxwell's defence in the 1880s of the reforming spirit is echoed by that of Hewins, for whom the distress occasioned by the depression was the very catalyst that caused the privileged son of a

Midlands merchant to search out a more socially-relevant economics than that represented by the 'pseudo laws' of the classical analytics:

> My practical interest in economic questions began with the depression of trade in the late seventies and the early eighties. This involved great hardships and I wanted to know the reason. From that time until I went to Oxford I read many economic books, but they did not help me. I disliked their theoretical outlook, their materialism leavened with sentiment and their remoteness from real events as I saw them in South Staffordshire. The 'economic man' made no appeal to me. There was little correspondence between the industrial system of the economic text-books and the industry that was being carried on around me and the men and women actually engaged in it. I wished to make life worth living for all those people troubled with great anxieties owing to the breakdown of the industrial machine; to bring about an improved social order and direct our activities to an end great enough to give them a diginity and a meaning.[134]

Hewins, dissatisfied with the narrow abstractions of the theoretical economics with which he came into contact while a student (of mathematics), broadened his perspectives by contributing articles on distinguished economists to Palgrave's *Dictionary of Political Economy* and to the *Dictionary of National Biography*, an enterprise which, in his words, 'destroyed for ever in my mind the illusion that Adam Smith and his successors represented the only English economic tradition'.[135] Even more important for his intellectual development was, however, the period he spent working with Charles Booth as a trainee volunteer (Beatrice Potter served a similar apprenticeship) on the seventeeen-volume study that was to appear in 1902–3 under the title of *The Life and Labour of the People of London*: the subject of the investigation was not lords and ladies but (in the tradition of Toynbee and, later, of Toynbee's student from 1881, Ashley, on living standards in the Industrial Revolution) the common man, the conclusion reached that at least one-third of the population of London was condemned to the misery and degradation of absolute deprivation. Booth's facts and data (reinforced by the evidence collected by Seebohm Rowntree in York and the Royal Commission on the Poor Laws) demonstrated clearly that statistics has a service function to perform in the campaign for social reform; and validated in that way the social significance of a methodological perspective of which the point of departure was historical relativism but for which moral commitment above all else constituted the source of energy that powered the enterprise.

Fourth, State intervention. The English historical economists were not doctrinaire statists and planners but nor were they dogmatic advocates of *laissez-faire* and unrestricted freedom of trade. Their position was entirely pragmatic, that in some cases important social problems were best resolved through recourse to individualistic initiative and the market mechanism while in other cases the servant of the national interest had no choice but to make common cause with the socialist by recommending central direction and political leadership. The profound eclecticism of their mixed approach to policy and progress is well illustrated by the attitude of W. J. Ashley. Thus Ashley in the historic election-year of 1906 took the opportunity Crosland-like to advise the left to steward well the golden goose of money-making that had demonstrably delivered improvement in tandem with growth: 'It may seem an odd thing to say at the very time that a Labour Party has made its appearance in the House of Commons, but I believe it to be true, nevertheless, that the path to social reform will lie in future as much through the administrative expediencies of business as through humanitarian sentiment.'[136] Yet it was the same Ashley, convinced that property-rights are never so absolute as to override social duties, who also called for State controls to combat instabilities and irregularities of employment (a prime cause of poverty), to mediate between powerful groups in society (automaticity having so frequently bred not harmony but conflict) and, more generally, to ensure, in the words of his daughter, that

> truly social results were to be reaped from private enterprise. Industry itself was undergoing an inner revolution in the substitution of large and impersonal combinations for personally conducted businesses. . . . To Ashley it seemed to demand a new vigilance on the part of Governments, lest the industrial machine should get out of hand and endanger the human values, of which it ought to be the servant and not the master.[137]

Ashley, in short, was an advocate of interventionism where intervention was needed (with respect, say, to bimetallism, indexation and the tariff) but also of delegating to individuals those choices which individuals were seen to make best (including those choices of a

chivalrous nature for which Ashley believed an increasingly chivalrous community would increasingly wish to opt). Ashley's position on
the middle ground was that of Thorold Rogers and W. A. S. Hewins
as well – the former castigating the economic liberals for targeting
their hypothetical constructs on the maximisation of wealth rather
than the alleviation of poverty and insisting that the (historical)
economist is, 'as I have often alleged, only removed in a slight degree
from the practical politician',[138] the latter criticising the Ricardians
for having provided the inspiration to the labour theory socialists and
maintaining that, while welcoming some forms of State intervention
(support to education, for instance, or State regulation of wages in
preference to the bilateral nastiness of collective bargaining), yet he
was first and foremost a man more moderate even than the Fabians:
'I have always regarded Fabianism with contempt and have attached
no practical importance to it.'[139] As with Birmingham, Oxford and
the LSE, so with Marshall's Cambridge, where William Cunningham
penned the following defence of action based on ideals: 'Though Man
is an animal, he is not merely an animal, since he is rational; he is not
merely the plaything of blind forces, but he has powers of intelligence
and will, which enable him to modify these forces, and thus to
suspend the operation of the principles which seem to forebode
inevitable evil.'[140] One instance of man's mastery over matter is the
Malthusian theory of population, where conscious self-control can
suspend the increase in the number of mouths to feed, sustained
economic growth can mean improved division of labour and economies of scale in the industrial sector, and scientific advance can
retard diminishing returns even at the Ricardian margin of cultivation. A second instance of man's power to shape and form is voluntary service on the Toynbee Hall model: thus, just as Hewins had
been active in the Oxford University Extension in London, Lanca-
shire and Yorkshire, so Cunningham was involved in the work of its
Cambridge counterpart in Bradford, Leeds and Liverpool, and clearly
saw such involvement as indicative of the much-to-be-desired triumph
of man's 'intelligence and will' over the ever-present threat of the
tyranny of 'blind forces'. A further instance of the same triumph of
the man-made over the cheap and natural is the other-regarding
sense of social responsibility of the Christian capitalist, called upon
by the very logic of his status as an employer 'to give his thought and
care to ameliorate the conditions and raise the character of the lives
of those who are dependent on him – not out of any mere humanitarian sentiment of brotherhood but because this is the duty enjoined

by his Master on all who administer any part of His household'.[141] State intervention is thus only a fourth instance in Cunningham's work of action based on ideals. Hardly a doctrinaire statist or planner, Cunningham had a pragmatist's openness to political action guided by scholarly investigation where no better means could be found for transforming the collectivity and boosting its welfare. Such a pragmatism, such an openness, were intrinsic characteristics of the guarded welcome extended by the historical school to both sectors of the modern mixed economy: private sector or public sector, businessman or politician, there was good work to be done by all in rendering the Invisible Hand the humble servant of the public interest.

Fifth, economic nationalism. The English historical economists were fact-gatherers and students of concrete, clearly-delimited social situations. They were in the circumstances hostile to the asocial psychologism of that Robinson Crusoe analysis which relates its propositions exclusively to the isolated individual: cultural uniqueness and experiential heterogeneity are not, they reasoned, *obiter dictum* but rather *sine qua non*, and thus it is that the useful economist has no choice but to anchor his arguments quite explicitly in the firm soil of time and place. Their antipathy to reductionist individualism, their propensity to situate atomistic action in the context of social organism, eloquently demonstrate the extent of their indebtedness to theorists of non-rational conservatism and unintended outcomes such as Sir Henry Maine, whose *Ancient Law* of 1861 appears deeply to have impressed itself upon Cliffe Leslie when he wrote the following:

> The germ from which the existing economy of every nation has been evolved is not the individual, still less the personification of an abstraction, but the primitive community – a community one in blood, property, thought, moral responsibility, and manner of life; and. . . . individual interest itself, and the desires, aims, and pursuits of every man and woman in the nation have been moulded by, and received their direction and form from, the history of that community.[142]

Cliffe Leslie's tendency to employ the socio-cultural construct of community as if it were a synonym for the politico-legal concept of nationhood reminds the reader forcefully indeed of the manner in which the English historical economists tended to speak of the socialised individual as if the term were synonymous with the good citizen. Cunningham on the radical incompatibility of cosmopolitanism and patriotism is a case in point:

In the present day, and among the progressive peoples of the world, nationality is the heritage of human experience on which each citizen enters. The savage may excel the civilised man in the quickness of sense-perception, or the power of endurance; but he has no part in the skill and wisdom and strength of character which have been accumulated through all the ages. The citizen of every nation is the heir of a great past, and he proves himself worthy of his inheritance by handing on an improved tradition of a well-ordered social life to the future. But the anti-patriot prefers to be an isolated unit of humanity: he finds no inspiration in the national past, and has no aspirations for the national future.[143]

Cunningham went further, in the wake of the tariff controversy of 1903, by launching an attack on consumption-maximising free-traders who appeared to him to have lost all perception of the duty they owed to their kith and kin dwelling overseas in the bosom of a great Empire: 'It is humiliating to find that many of the present generation of citizens in the Mother Country are so supine that they desire to shirk these responsibilities, and are so ready to pour scorn on all who endeavour to take imperial responsibilities seriously.'[144] Just as Cunningham's mind moved logically from community to nationhood, from nationhood to Empire, so too did that of Hewins, who evidently invested in the campaign for imperial preference all the moral fervour of a crusade against social fragmentation: 'The Empire movement as it has come within my experience is not a reversion to protection, but a revolt against the individualist conception of society in this country.'[145] It was not India or West Africa, needless to say, but rather the white Dominions that Hewins had in mind when he noted of his family that 'we had relations in many parts of the British Empire',[146] or when he derived his sentimental imperialism from the multi-generational rootedness of his sound English forebears in the healthy English soil of the Vale of Evesham and the North Cotswolds:

> Members of our family had gone from there in every generation since the days of Elizabeth to all parts of the British Empire. I suppose the view from Willersley Hill or any of the high ground in that part of the Cotswolds over the Vale of Evesham is one of the most beautiful and possesses as many historic memories as can be found in England. It is the country of great Benedictine Abbeys, Evesham, Pershore, Winchcomb, Tewkesbury and many others a little farther away; the country where great causes have been fought from the beginning of our island story; the country from

which Shakespeare derived his inspiration; where Iberian, Briton, Angle, Dane, Norman and Breton have been made one enduring race, and where can be traced in history and tradition, in place names and language, the continuity of our country's history from the days of the Roman occupation. I cannot describe the impression all this made on me. We had lived for 350 years on the slope of Dovers Hill (where Shakespeare saw the 'Coursing on Cotsall') and before then at Bretforton hard by. We were part of it, linked up with the history of the abbeys for many generations, holding on to the same lands when these beautiful shrines were destroyed and the social system they represented was ruined. Who can measure the effect of direct influences of this kind on one's mind? They certainly gave me a lasting faith in the future of the British Empire.[147]

So emotive a defence of *Blut and Boden* cannot but recall the powerfully tribalistic underpinnings of List's exclusionist protectionism or of the marriage between economic and political unity which the *Zollverein* had been intended to promote. The German historical economists, like their English counterparts, took the nation rather than the individual as their unit of analysis; and it should in the circumstances be noted that the English authors must have approved of Roscher, Schmoller, Hildebrand and Knies not merely because the *Kathedersozialisten* were committed to *Sozialpolitik*, intervention and reform, not merely because the Continental historicists rejected the axiomatic abstraction of the naiver *Smithianismus* in favour of socially-contingent induction but also because the Germans took their *Volkswirtschaft* and their *Nationalökonomie* in the most literal sense possible. It is no mere accident that one of the very few instances of the German terminology being employed in the English language should be found in the final tribute paid by one historical economist to another, namely in that obituary notice in the *Economic Journal* of 1919 where Herbert Foxwell describes William Cunningham as 'a great National Economist, the modern representative of an old English tradition, unfortunately interrupted by the atomism and premature cosmopolitanism of the *laissez-faire* age.'[148] Foxwell thus saw Cunningham as Cunningham undeniably saw himself, as the spiritual heir to a Great Britainness extending backwards to the macrocosm of medievalism, the Elizabethan discovery of the nation-state, and the mercantilist economics of an integrated era in which good citizens were at least as concerned with national power as they

were with personal pelf. It was a not-dissimilar sense of national
consciousness which had animated Ashley upon his return to England
from Toronto and Harvard in 1900 to take up the newly-created
Chair of Commerce in Birmingham: convinced that lack of training in
accounts, languages, management, had been a significant reason why
English businessmen had fallen behind their German and American
rivals, it was clearly his nation that he had in mind as he searched for
ways 'of contributing to her prosperity and well-being by creating a
University department which might help to produce intelligent and
public-spirited "captains of industry".'[149] Ashley's academic mission,
like so much else in his life and work, was 'guided and restrained by
the thought of the social bond – the thought of society as an organism
or body of interconnected relations'.[150] The society being *his* society,
his *English* society, it is no surprise that he abandoned the Baptists
and moved to the Church of England (becoming active in the Church
Social Union and contributing regularly to the *Economic Review*
even after the *Economic Journal* had come on stream). His pilgrim-
age is paralleled (if not by Hewins who, attracted at an early age by the
corporatist orderliness of medieval Catholicism, went over to Rome)
by the conversion from the Calvinist Presbyterianism of his Edinburgh childhood to the national church of his fellow Caius undergraduates of William Cunningham, who evidently found in the social
Christianity of the Church of England more than a little of the
emphasis on citizenship rights and collective duties which a man so
strongly committed to social progress alongside individual gain and
personal salvation was bound most enthusiastically to applaud. Cunningham's economic history was, not surprisingly, not economic
history in general but the history of the homeland in particular. Much
the same must be said of the other English historical economists as
well. Of course exceptions can be cited (Cliffe Leslie's comparative
study of European land-tenure systems being one, the same author's
familiarity with the Continental critics of Ricardianism being
another), but they only serve to prove the rule, that even a knowledge of German is no barrier to insularity – and least of all so in the
case of a school which, committed to economic nationalism, took the
national whole and not the isolated individual as its fundamental unit.

The English historical economists couched their arguments in the
language of economic nationalism at a time of increasing pressure
from foreign competitors, in a period when the English orthodoxy
stubbornly backed Spencer despite the fact that the Kaiser increas-

ingly talked Hobbes: their ranking of national power and public plenty above economic efficiency and individual consumption should, given the circumstances, have made a significant contribution to the popularity of neo-mercantilists writing in defence of protection by means of tariffs and even of conscription. The English historical economists, moreover, advocated State intervention in the world of private property and market exchanges at the very time when pragmatic regulation and eclectic provision were becoming the order of the day: no one could have supposed that the Liberal Government elected in 1906 would obtain better advice from the abstractions of the *a priorists* than it would from the English cousins of the German eulogists of beneficent leadership (to say nothing of their American disciples who had in 1885 introduced a clause into the constitution of the newly-formed American Economic Association that, stressing the importance of *political* economy, read: 'We regard the State as an agency whose positive assistance is one of the indispensable conditions of human progress').[151] The English historical economists, again, called for social reform in a Britain neither as optimistic about automaticity as Manchester not as fatalistic about subsistence as Ricardo: due not least to the evidence on destitution and deprivation that had been collected by the historical school itself, State sector reforms were being adopted involving education, housing, poor relief, unemployment benefits, pensions, health insurance for low-income groups, the important role of altruistic businessmen and charitable associations was widely recognised, and corrective action seemed to be in the air such as the economic orthodoxy seemed incapable of integrating. The English historical economists, furthermore, made themselves the prophets of a moral commitment tinged with Christian ethics which must have had a considerable appeal to the responsible late-Victorians and the duty-bound Edwardians: the *Zeitgeist* had great reservations about unbridled self-interest, excessive competition and materialism without meaning, and cannot therefore but have found itself deeply in sympathy with the high moral tone of the idealistic heterodoxy. The English historical economists, finally, were strong exponents of historical relativism and factual specificity at a time when the opposition went in for the unsupported generalisations of high theory: quite apart from the not inconsiderable attractions of number, weight and measure to a wide readership better on common sense than on professional pyrotechnics, the very fact that the writings of the historical school were so accessible and so comprehensible must have stood them in good stead when seeking to reach the broader British public. For all of these reasons one would have expected the English historical economists to have scored an outstanding success, what Ashley called the 'hair-splitting analysis of abstract doctrine'[152] to have been relegated to the obscurity of footnotes and appendix. It was not to be so. The period from the *Principles* to the First World War was not the era of the English historicals but rather, in Schumpeter's words, 'emphatically the Marshallian Age. His success was as great as A. Smith's.'[153] Marshall's triumph was in a sense their defeat.

Few would wish to deny the excellence of Marshall's economics the pride of place which must be its due in any account of the triumph of his paradigm. Nor, however, can there be many who would wish to maintain that the historical school was itself entirely without blame for its early eclipse and ultimate dissolution. Had it been a stronger, healthy, more robust growth, it would not have been so easily shunted on to a dead-end siding by the undeniably chill wind that blew from Cambridge University in the East. As it was, Marshall's success was to some extent merely by default.

A major problem was that the English historical economists were united as much by what they opposed as by what they proposed: anti-Ricardian and anti-deductivist in their research programme, they combined forces to refute the classical hypotheses with respect to population expansion or diminishing returns but were conspicuously heterogeneous when it came not to finding errors in the work of others but to providing a concrete alternative of their own. The more ambitious German historical school was positive as well as negative in its shared aspirations (committed as its members were to common constructs such as stages of economic development and laws of social evolution). The English historical school, by way of contrast, was united by its negativity and otherwise characterised by its diversity. Thus some of the economists were favourable to the material constraints of the evolutionary approach whereas others made much of free will and moral choices in keeping with ideals; some were friendly to the unions and the socialists while others (never actually becoming complete free-marketeers, however) were very frightened indeed by the thought of a socialist revolution; some believed fact-gathering to be nothing more than the gathering of facts, others saw it as a way of generating testable hypotheses *ex post facto*, still others recognised that the very search for evidence itself presupposed some antecedent theory to govern the selection of evidence. Ingram was idiosyncratic in his adherence to Comtean positivism. Rogers was idiosyncratic in his advocacy of Cobdenite free trade and his insistence (based upon his study of the way in which the Statute of Artificers of 1563 had served to keep down the wages of labour) that it is market rather than State that most benefits the working man. Neither Ingram nor Rogers – nor, for that matter, anyone else – produced a great book like Mill's *Principles* or that of Marshall such as might have become the unifying manifesto that reduced the degree of division in the camp: while it is undeniable that the radical empiricist is not well-suited, precisely because of his unwillingness to generalise, to the task of formulating an ambitious theoretical statement of his methodology and objectives, it is no less undeniable that the sceptical outsider is right to maintain that in the absence of such a statement he fails to see exactly which theoretical tenets it is that give the school its unique identity. The school was, in short, too loosely articulated to be expected to provide a reasonable alternative to a more unified community that enjoyed the unifying guidance of an epoch-shaping text.

The English historical economists had no text comparable to Marshall's *Principles*. Nor did they have a leader comparable (with all his limitations) to Marshall himself. Thorold Rogers was, arguably, the nearest approximation: he was a scholar of unquestioned integrity (it apparently took him almost twenty years to collect and collate the data for his *History*), he was known to be friendly to labour (in favour of laws enforcing employers' liability and protecting friendly societies) but also to be an advocate of free markets and enterprise, he was not too academic to be drawn into controversy (far from it: there cannot be many university teachers who have also been Members of Parliament, as he was, for Southwark, as a Liberal, from 1880 to 1885 and for Bermondsey, 1885–6), and he was the occupant (twice, in fact, from 1863 to 1868 and again from 1888 to 1890) of the prestigious Drummond Chair at a time when Oxford University still welcomed the historical approach. Yet Thorold Rogers was an eccentric outsider whose difficult personality prevented him from ever actually becoming the focal figure that the English historicals unquestionably needed. For one thing, he was secretive, unapproachable and reclusive, as Kadish makes clear: 'Although as a lecturer he was said to be amusing and instructive, he was a poor teacher when it came to personal instruction. He had a tendency to keep most of his work to himself.'[154] Also, he grew embittered as he grew older: increasingly reluctant to engage in futile struggles, increasingly isolated and aware of his isolation, increasingly prone to warn younger men not to ruin their careers by tilting against established dogmas, the sad fact is that 'age and experience made him sceptical where younger men were enthusiastic.'[155] Not that the younger, more dynamic Thorold Rogers of the 1860s was much more of an asset to the historical school: a bombastic orator ('The Whigs were sneaks, the Unionists were liars, and the Tories were thieves',[156] he once pronounced, presumably not winning many friends in the process), a bluff, rude, loud man with a strong line in dirty stories and a propensity 'to impute evil motives'[157] (not least to Jews), a sworn enemy of academic sinecurists who attacked College lecturers for being 'perfunctory, irritating, repressive' and their Professorial colleagues for the 'lazy apathy' of the 'utterly unoccupied', a political radical who invited unpopularity by favouring the admission of women and who positively courted disaster by attacking what he called 'the barrenness of landlordism' in a university of which all the colleges (and many of the students) were dependent upon landed endowments, Rogers was probably innocent of the charge that he compromised himself as a scholar by indulging from the Oxford position in party-political controversies but for all that guilty of the no less serious charge that he brought historical economics into disrepute. Thorold Rogers was clearly not the intellectual leader that the historical school so urgently required, but nor was Bonamy Price, Rugby schoolmaster (under Arnold) and historical economist (albeit without serious claims to distinguished scholarship), who succeeded him in 1868 by a vote of 620 to 193 and who then occupied the Drummond Chair for a full twenty uneventful years. The historicals' loss was the Marshallians' gain, and a loss it undeniably was: Price, in Coats' words, was no more than 'a genial nonentity who denied that economics was a science and asserted that it was merely a practical, common-sense subject employing rule-of-thumb methods and enunciating familiar truisms'.[158] If under Rogers Oxford economics had seemed anti-conservative (witness Rogers' support for the Reform Bill of 1867, or his opposition to the idea of a hereditary House of Lords, or his attack on bribery and corruption in national politics) and anti-Establishment (witness Rogers' attempt to expand the teaching of political economy in the Oxford curriculum at the expense of classics despite the complaints of the clergymen that such a movement smacked of materialism), under Price it merely seemed dull (witness Price's reluctance to do anything in particular to advance the claims of his subject or his approach). Ashley might have exercised the requisite influence, but he was abroad for precisely the period when the *Principles* was sweeping across England (from 1888 to 1892 as Professor of Constitutional History and Political Economy in Toronto, from 1892 to 1900 as Professor of Economic History – the first such post in the English-speaking world – at Harvard). Ashley was absent, Price was a nonentity, Rogers was an eccentric; and then there was the remarkable abdication of professional responsibility on the part of Foxwell and Cunningham. Each had an independent power-base in London (Foxwell as Professor of Political Economy at University College from 1881 to 1922, Cunningham as Tooke Professor of Statistics at Kings College from 1891 to 1897), but both nonetheless continued to reside in Cambridge and to treat their Cambridge affiliation as if Cambrige were Britain's sole forum for academic debate. Each was in a position where he could easily have established a non-Marshallian government in exile capable of offering to the consumer of ideas a genuine choice of paradigms. Each remained fixated instead on a Cambridge-based battle which the analytical economists were almost certain to win. Neither Foxwell nor Cunningham was, professionally or temperamentally, a born leader. Nor, of course, was Alfred Marshall, whose mission was therefore advanced in no small measure by the conspicuous shortcomings of the opposition that a beneficent fate had somehow dealt him.

The English historical economists had no comparable text and no countervailing leadership. They also lacked an academic centre in which to rally. Cambridge in the age of Marshall (despite the involvement there of Foxwell and Cunningham) could hardly be regarded as their natural home. Neither could Oxford in the age of Edgeworth that followed the era of Rogers and Price: the *Economic Review* continued to be edited from that University, the Church Social Union remained strong there, but by the time of Marshall's retirement from Cambridge, only L. L. Price could be said to be actively engaged in Oxford in mounting a rearguard action against Edgeworth on the question of technical economics. Price in 1907 became Oxford's first lecturer in economic history (Reader from 1909 until his retirement in 1921), but his conversion to historical economics evidently came as late as the tariff controversy of 1903: Marshall's former student had earlier been orthodox enough even to serve on the council of the *Economic Journal* and as honorary secretary of the Economic Association, and it was as an orthodox Marshallian that he had made his name in the narrowness of an Oxford that was yet to come up with the idea of PPE. One Price does not in any case make an Oxford. Nor was it to Oxford that the distinguished Oxford historical Ashley went when in 1900 he at last returned home but to the Faculty of Commerce in Birmingham. Ashley could, of course, have taken advantage of his international reputation to transform Birmingham in the run-up to the War into that which Oxford had been in the 1870s and 1880s, namely a centre of academic excellence in the historical economics. To some extent he did attempt to do so, as is illustrated by the fact that economic history and applied economics were assigned considerable prominence in his new syllabus while the role of economic theory was kept minimal. Yet Ashley in 1900, in his ongoing drive to be useful, was increasingly persuaded of the value of vocationalism, and increasingly took the view that the promotion of pure scholarship was of less urgency (especially in an industrial and commercial centre such as Birmingham and in a Faculty which owed so much to the ever-practical Joseph Chamberlain) than was the inculcation of relevant skills. Oxford and Cambridge, he felt obliged to say, had not done their duty with respect to the education of the business classes: 'As an Oxford man, I say it with sorrow – the alienation of the business classes in England from the older Universities has gone so far that it is practically hopeless to expect to bring them now within their embrace.'[159] Depressed by the frequency with which the children of the business classes returned from the older universities totally unsuited for a career in the family firm, impressed in addition by the social utility of the close links between commerce and higher education which he had seen forged in North America, Ashley designed his new curriculum with the social responsibility primarily in mind of fostering innovation and enterprise in the United Kingdom. The concern of that curriculum with the practicalities of organisation and location of industry in preference to the learned erudition of the inductivist genuinely unwilling to predict, well illustrates the strength of his conviction, expressed in 1926, that 'in the large a University must be described as primarily the home of professional education'.[160] Perhaps it must; but the commitment to the commercially-relevant *how to* undeniably meant that the Birmingham Faculty under Ashley in effect disqualified itself for the no less ambitious task of serving as a rallying point for the professional heterodoxy. As with Birmingham under Ashley, moreover, so with the LSE under Hewins. The School had been founded by the Webbs and their fellow Fabians in 1895 (the model was the Ecole des Sciences Politiques in Paris), its ethos reflecting from the start the social engineer's conviction that a cadre of expert social scientists would have to be formed if major social problems were to be solved. Hewins, then 30 and fully aware that the University Extension was the best academic outlet he as a historical economist was likely to find in Edgeworth's Oxford, became its first Director. He was not a Fabian (accusing the Fabians in fact of having rescued orthodox deductivism from 'the limbo of forgotten fallacies' to which its own lack of economic justification would otherwise have consigned it: 'Bernard Shaw I should think would scarcely survive the death of the Ricardian theory of rent'),[161] but he was in sympathy with many of the social reforms that the Fabians proposed. His own contribution to the ethos of the School was a defence of the role that could be played by practical businessmen with respect to important policy-issues such as the alleviation of poverty; and with it an Ashley-like plea for an extension of commercial education. Fabians and Hewins alike, it is clear, regarded the School less as a centre of academic excellence than as a sort of intellectual's Toynbee Hall, a training-college for policy-shapers and wealth-creators for whose specialised needs the more prestigious institutions had evidently failed to cater. Thus it was not merely for reasons of methodological purity that the School came to emphasise the statistical, the relevant and the applied, and to play down the value of theoretical abstraction to the useful social scientist. Hostile to the remoteness and materialism of orthodox economic theory, Hewins invited Marshallians such as Edgeworth and Giffen to lecture but obviously felt more comfortable in the society of Cunningham and Foxwell, who were also invited. The School probably did have the potential in its early years to develop into a reasonable alternative to Marshall's Cambridge, despite the fact that it was newly-formed and had not yet acquired the patina of status by association. Yet the School did not immediately seize its opportunity; and when finally it did so it was as something quite different from the safe haven for English historicals that Hewins could have provided, had he so wished, at the very time when the alternative paradigm was most in need of a harbour. Here once again, it would appear, the fortunate Marshall landed on his feet.

The English historical economists failed because they had no text, no leader and no centre. They also failed because they tried to do so much. The last great historical to meet all five of the criteria which define the approach was the R. H. Tawney of *The Acquisitive Society* (1920), *Religion and the Rise of Capitalism* (1926) and *Equality*

(1931); and even as he wrote the unified paradigm was already beginning to crumble and fragment in response to repeated assaults from the pitiless process of division of labour. Thus the notion of nationhood was to be hived off to political scientists such as Wallas and citizenship-rights sociologists such as Hobhouse; intervention was to become the study of Cambridge economists such as Pigou and professional pragmatists such as Beveridge; social reform was to go to the voluntary bodies and the specialist poverty-watchers; moral commitment was to end up the concern of the philosophers and the bishops; and the end-result was that the English historical economists, stripped of all else, were left with nothing but their economic history to expound. Given the vast dimensions of their former empire, they can hardly have been pleased with the outcome of a march into specialisation which arrogated to them the study of past practices while taking from the concern with contemporary problems which in the early days had provided the primary source of legitimation for their investigations. Pleased or not pleased, they were in no doubt that historical economics was being compressed into economic history and that there was little they could do to arrest the steady diminution of their research programme. Powerlessly they looked on as the sub-discipline of applied-economics-in-the-past emerged before their very eyes, it status rendered that much more inferior to the theoretical alternative by virtue of the fact that the hypotheses it was asked to test were not its own but those of the orthodoxy it had once sought to vanquish. In 1904 the first full-time lectureship in economic history was created, in London, for Lillian Knowles. In 1909 the first Chair of Economic History was established, at Manchester, for George Unwin. In 1926 an independent professional body, the Economic History Society, was founded, its first President, Ashley, then in the last year of his life, clearly betraying some bitterness when ostensibly welcoming the separateness that the new departure represented: 'The theoretical economists are ready to keep us quiet by giving us a little garden plot of our own; and we humble historians are so thankful for a little undisputed territory that we are inclined to leave the economists to their own devices.'[162] In 1927 the new-old field of study acquired a specialist journal, the *Economic History Review* – the first editors were Tawney at the LSE and Lipson at Oxford. In 1928 Cambridge itself created a Chair of Economic History – the first incumbent was Clapham, who had the courage in his Inaugural to pay the following tribute to the great names of an ambitious paradigm that Cambridge would never have honoured with a Chair had the intellectual discipline in question not shrunk so significantly in scope:

> My single regret, when I think of its relatively late recognition in this University, is that the man who nursed it here, and who was known in all Universities as one of the two outstanding English economic historians of his time, William Cunningham, never received from Cambridge the professorial rank which he deserved. Nor, for that matter, did his rather younger colleague, Sir William Ashley, from Oxford.[163]

Perhaps Cunningham and not Clapham would have been the first incumbent of the Cambridge Chair if he, like Clapham, had acknowledged his limitations and been an economic historian first and foremost. Perhaps he would; but then he would not have been a historical economist. His success would have been purchased at the price of his aspirations. It was a price he would not have been willing to pay. It is in the circumstances sad and ironical that the unguided division of labour happened ultimately to bring about precisely that narrowing of interests which the stubborn man of principle would never have been prepared to countenance. In so doing, of course, the unguided division of labour made its own small contribution to the elimination of the competing paradigm that was the principal contemporary alternative to Marshall's own.

The English historical economists failed because the unguided division of labour cut down the territory of their paradigm. They also failed because of the curious phenomenon that their chief adversary was also in some measure an ally – because Marshall himself, in other words, was prepared to chide pure theorists for making irresponsible generalisations 'based on the circumstances of one time and place'[164] and for neglecting 'the wholesome influence of the criticisms of the historical school';[165] because even historical economists were forced to concede that the paradigm exposed in the *Principles* and in *Industry and Trade* demonstrated a considerable measure of overlap with their own (as where Clapham, referring in his Inaugural to Marshall's fascination with historical evidence, and appreciative, no doubt, of the instrumental role that Marshall himself had played in converting him from political to economic history and assisting him to secure his first professorship, in 1902, at Yorkshire College, Leeds, felt the need to state the obvious, that 'to him, as well as to Cunningham, the foundation of this chair is a memorial').[166] The *Times* obituary of Alfred Marshall probably went too far when it asserted that the master theoretician, in addition to the working out of the abstract propositions with which his Cambridge name is more commonly associated, also both covered essentially the same ground as his principal competitors and covered it better than they did: 'Marshall's own knowledge of economic facts was enormous, far greater than that of any members of the school who prided themselves on heaping up statistics. None of his old pupils can forget the mass of blue books among which he lived, and which, when he had mastered them himself, he would press on them in alarming quantities as absolutely essential to their education.'[167] The *Times* obituary probably went too far but there is no disputing the presence of historical economics within the broad church of Marshall's synthesis. Thus Marshall was capable of pointing to the significance of historical relativism and of warning extreme deductivists not to neglect contingent induction, extreme exponents of comparative statics not to lose sight of the developmental dimension. He was a man of strong moral commitment who believed in the functionality of altruism as well as interest and was convinced that evolutionary processes were favourable to ethical as well as material betterment. He was an advocate of social reform, prepared to accept that free competition might be unable to eliminate great social evils such as poverty and not afraid in such circumstances to call for the man-made instrument and the visible hand. He had a bias towards *laissez-faire* but also a pragmatist's acceptance of State intervention consensually legitimated – as in the case of the Factory Acts and the provision of schooling, 'things which most people think should be done by Government in its capacity of guardian for the less well to do, & the less educated classes, though in a highly developed democratic state they might probably best be left to private initiative'.[168] He had the classical liberal's propensity to take the unique individual as his fundamental unit of analysis but also the totalitarian corporatist's openness to the notion of economic nationalism – a duality between contract and status, between ownership and citizenship, which Marshall transcends with particular cleverness in the following discussion of the patriotic sentiments: 'In fact the spirit of nationality is akin to that which unites the members of a great private firm, who value its good name & fame even more than the income which it yields to them.'[169] All in all, one is forced to concede, there is no disputing the presence of historical economics within the broad church of Marshall's comprehensive synthesis. Since that synthesis offers so much else as well, it is perhaps only to be expected that quite a number of rational consumers would come to rank it above its less multi-faceted competitor. What is somewhat less to be expected is how quickly Marshall's broad church came to be regarded, by friend and foe alike, as little more than a narrow church of equilibrium positions, comparative statics and high analysis. The reason for the changeover is not clear. Perhaps it is no more than the well-known fact that so elaborate a paradigm is bound to attract simplifiers.

The overlap between Marshall's own paradigm and that of the English historical economists was a not-insignificant reason why the less ambitious approach ultimately lost out to its omnibus alternative. The same cannot be said of Marshall's personal involvement in academic politics, however. There were not many university posts in economics in Marshall's day, and schoolmastering without research was an all-too-common fate. It is in the circumstances much to Marshall's credit that he did not abuse his power and standing to convert such posts as there were into appointments for his disciples while simultaneously ensuring that proponents of alternative paradigms never secured a foothold on the academic ladder. Marshall's tolerance of diversity and sense of fair play were such that no member of the historical school was in a position seriously to maintain that political economy's senior professor had operated a government-and-opposition strategy within the profession. Marshall seems, if anything, to have bent over backwards to be non-discriminatory. As Coats explains:

> He was reluctant to speak ill of his fellow economists and was neither opinionated nor irresponsible. Had he wished, he could no doubt have ruined the chances of any candidate he strongly opposed, and certainly Ashley at Oxford in 1888 and William Smart at Glasgow in 1896 feared that Marshall would 'run' one of his own candidates. In the event, the elections went to Thorold Rogers and Smart, respectively, neither of whom could be regarded as a Marshallian; and when the Birmingham chair of commerce was filled in 1900, Ashley, the successful contender, was delighted by Marshall's testimonial, despite the fact that his chief rival was Foxwell, Marshall's (admittedly somewhat contentious) Cambridge colleague.[170]

Marshall could have used his influence to secure the appointment at Birmingham of a votary committed to his mission, or at the very least to rid himself of a local nuisance. Instead he used his influence to bring about the return to Britain of an acknowledged rival. Without Marshall's support there is a strong likelihood that the homesick Harvard man would have had to remain where he was, and here the contents of a letter from the Birmingham Principal to the Cambridge Professor are highly relevant: 'You will be interested to hear that we have to-day appointed W. J. Ashley as our first Professor in the Commercial Faculty, chiefly owing to the testimony of yourself on the economic side, and of Dr. Cunningham on the personal side.'[171] Marshall must have known that the price of his candour would be the acquisition by an acknowledged rival of a valuable power-base, but he told the truth nonetheless. As with Ashley, moreover, so with Cunningham, whose application in 1889 for the Tooke Professorship at King's College, London, Marshall strongly supported despite the fact that a historical's chair undeniably carried with it the threat of a historical's centre. Marshall in his testimonial referred to Cunningham's early work of 1882 on *The Growth of English Industry and Commerce* (the *magnum opus* in the event of a long-lived and exceptionally prolific author) and praised the book highly, saying that it 'will certainly obtain a permanent place in economic literature. It is based on a thorough and wide knowledge; it shows a powerful grasp and great breadth of philosophic thought, combined with much judgement and discretion, and not without strong signs of an aptitude for economic analysis'.[172] Marshall could have exploited the opportunity not to praise but to play down the value of Cunningham's inductions, not to highlight the Cambridge empiricist's 'aptitude' for theory but to warn that a scholar with no theoretical alternative of his own would be capable at best of dressing in borrowed clothing (as was to be the case somewhat later with Edwin Cannan at the LSE, who contrived both to attack the Marshallian orthodoxy and to use the content of the *Principles* as the analytical core for his lectures). It reflects well on Marshall that he resisted the temptation on this and similar occasions. Marshall's paradigm, being the standard by which applicants for academic positions in Britain rapidly came to be judged, clearly made a considerable contribution to homogeneity of opinion by helping conformists to identify undesirables in order the better to weed them out. It is far more difficult to blame Marshall in his personal capacity for the early eclipse and ultimate dissolution of the English historical school.

Marshall sought to live quietly but was on occasion compelled to become involved in controversy. The English historical economists in three separate instances were responsible for disturbing that tranquillity and provoking that action. There was the Tripos, where degree courses in economics were originated at the LSE and Birmingham in 1901 (two years before Marshall's own at Cambridge) and where the external challenge of Hewins and Ashley was compounded by the internal opposition of Foxwell and Cunningham. There was the Tariff, where the proponents of nationalism and opponents of dumping advanced the relativist's case that the freedom of trade defended by Marshallians in the tradition of Smith and Ricardo had in effect been rendered irrelevant by the march of events. And there was 'The Perversion of Economic History'.

William Cunningham had been a lecturer in political economy and economic history at Cambridge since 1884 and was one of the applicants for Fawcett's chair in 1885. He had hoped, his daughter writes, that 'Marshall would have been content to carry on the teaching of analytical economics at Oxford and that he would be left with room to develop a school of empirical political economy at Cambridge'.[173] Disappointed when Marshall instead bested him in the Cambridge election, there was subsequent friction when Marshall *de facto* downgraded the status of history by insisting that Cunningham devote two terms out of three to theory (basically, Mill): Cunningham resented this interference with his academic freedom (Fawcett had encouraged him to teach as he saw fit), and he also took the view that the theory he was so high-handedly asked to teach not only cut down on the time he had available for history but was a positive hindrance to a clear understanding of practical reality. Both Cunningham and Marshall were men of principle, with the result that relations between the assertive Scotsman and the shy Londoner were, as Audrey Cunningham describes them, strained to say the least: 'It is simple to recognize that personal feeling must be overcome, but when it seems that the interest of historic truth and sound learning are at stake, the position is far more difficult. If two men of opposite views both have this feeling, it is scarcely possible that their relations should be cordial.'[174] Little things in such circumstances became magnified out of all proportion, even sentence-structure and syntax: thus Cunningham was one of the few to notice in Marshall's Inaugural that induction is normally praised in the past tense, deduction defended in the present. After three years Cunningham had had enough of disparagement and moved in 1888 from a University appointment to the Trinity position where he remained until 1906. Even before 1890, in short, he was resentful of Marshall's centralising tendencies and fearful lest abstract laws should displace concrete facts in economic science. The situation was volatile even before 1890. The lengthy section on historical development which opened the first edition of the *Principles* was the spark which ignited the inevitable conflagration. Had it not been that spark, it would have been another: Cunningham was a difficult man who enjoyed controversy, and even before 1890 he was beginning to show all the signs of occupational bitterness and frustration at work. Be that as it may, the fact is that it happened to be the two opening chapters of the first Book I which constituted the red flag before the bull that caused him to charge into print.

Cunningham's paper, 'The Perversion of Economic History', appeared in the *Economic Journal* of 1892. Its theme is that economic history is a difficult subject and that analytical economists are therefore wrong to treat it superficially: 'With the equipment of some two or three badly chosen books', Cunningham complained, those economists are quite happy to 'decide the most difficult problems off hand, or sketch you the history of the world with easy confidence.'[175] A *little* knowledge is a dangerous thing, Cunningham warned. Then he supported his assertion with a case in point: 'Professor Marshall is never content to be commonplace; his views are always fresh; his statements have the piquancy that belongs to what is unexpected, while they seem the more convincing since they are put forth with an easy confidence which appears at first sight to arise from fulness of knowledge.'[176] Seldom can an accusation of rubbish-talking and downright ignorance have been phrased with greater delicacy. Yet such an accusation it undoubtedly was, and Cunningham had made it his business assiduously to ferret out chapter and verse. Marshall on Greece and Rome, for instance: 'The real difficulty about Professor Marshall's sketch is not that particular facts are mis-stated, but that the whole description is so much in the air that it scarcely touches the facts at all.'[177] Or Marshall on the medieval towns: 'Professor Marshall seems to think that because the town was free as a town, the inhabitants enjoyed personal economic freedom in the modern sense; but it is hard to conceive any statement that should be more utterly contrary to the facts.'[178] Or Marshall on the relationship between early industrialisation and the enclosure-movement of Tudor times: 'The factory system came after the period of depopulation and sheep-farming, as it came after the building of Solomon's Temple and the Siege of Troy; but neither the one nor the other had anything to do with helping to introduce the factory system.'[179] Or Marshall on the removal of industries from towns in the thirteenth century:

'Professor Marshall rarely gives any accurate reference for his historical statements. Professor Marshall's statement in this case is seen to
be a mere conjecture which more thorough knowledge would have
shown to be inadmissable.'[180] A *little* knowledge is a dangerous thing,
Cunningham warned. He also sought to demonstrate that, with
respect to factual evidence relating to real-world phenomena, a *little*
knowledge was all the knowledge that Marshall had.

Nor was that little knowledge that Marshall did have a random
cross-section, in Cunningham's view, of all the knowledge that he
ought to have had. Far from it, Cunningham maintained, since it was
his depressing diagnosis that Marshall belonged to that deplorably
unscientific school of analysts who select their observations of external reality on the basis of whether or not those observations can
easily be squared with the tyranny of the universal generalisation.
Such an approach is inevitably biased and therefore represents nothing
less than a disastrous misuse of historical evidence: 'Economists will
not leave it alone; they do not pursue it seriously, but try to incorporate some if its results into that curious amalgam, the main body of
economic tradition; and the result is the perversion of Economic
History.'[181] Ordinary economists, Cunningham insisted, ought to
allow each specific set of data the freedom to spell out its own unique
pattern – whereas instead they rush to squeeze all that is or ever was
into the standard size of free competition and the laws of supply and
demand. Such a neglect of actual facts, impartially interrogated, is
deeply to be regretted, seeing as it 'prevents the economist from
finding out the narrow limits within which his generalisations are
even approximately true.'[182] Herbert Spencer is one economist who
never managed to reconcile his theoretical truths with mundane
evidence relating to the world of reality: 'If the facts illustrate his
doctrine, he is willing to allude to them; if they do not illustrate it,
they merely obscure the great truths he has already formulated in
so-called Economic Laws.'[183] Alfred Marshall is another economist
whose use of the same analytical framework irrespective of the
special circumstances of time and place was bound to generate
inaccuracies such as are well illustrated by those that result from
excessive reliance on the Ricardian theory of rent: 'The attempt to
interpret mediaeval rents in the light of this theory is an anachronism,
and shows a misunderstanding of the whole conditions of rural
life.'[184] As with the theory of rent, so with the self-interest axiom and
the solid *a priori* 'that the same motives have been at work in all ages,
and have produced similar results':[185] such an attempt to explain past

phenomena in terms of current doctrine on the 'economic' motives simply cannot succeed, and in Marshall's *Principles*, Cunningham stated, it demonstrably did not. Thence the verdict of the Council-member of the Royal Historical Society on the high theorist who only found in the historical record those observations which could easily be squared with the tyranny of the universal generalisation: 'It is well to draw attention to the risks which even a very able man runs in attempting to construct history from general principles, instead of submitting to build it up bit by bit from definite data of fact.'[186]

Cunningham criticised Marshall for assuming the same body of theory to be of universal applicability. He also accused Marshall of adopting a naive approach to historical dynamics. Relativist though he was, Cunningham was too much the Christian and the Hegelian to treat change over time as entirely random: his daughter recalled clearly that 'the ideas of creation as a continuous process and of development in the revelation of truth seemed to Cunningham reason-able'.[187] Cunningham was prepared in some measure to infer progress from Scripture and science, even if, admittedly, less prepared to do so than were those distinguished of members of the historical school who, genuinely evolutionary economists, had a real sympathy which Cunningham did not share with List or Comte on stages of social development. What he was not prepared to do was to accept the validity of the specific historical schema put forward by Marshall, which seemed to identify human progress with some inevitable pro-gression from family and tribe to unit individual, social convention to selfish interest, mercantilist direction to freedom of trade, national-ism to cosmopolitanism. Not only is such a putative progression totally unsupported by any scientific evidence more convincing than the isolated anecdote, Cunningham said, but it would not even if supported be indicative of anything that could unambiguously be regarded as betterment or improvement. Marshall the rational liberal may have had few reservations about individual and interest, but not so Cunningham the cautious conservative, who stressed the centrality of corporation and class, continuity and custom. Marshall the calcu-lating maximiser, moreover, may have welcomed market freedom and the moral victory of man over Leviathan, but not so Cunningham the patriotic interventionist: Cunningham opposed progression in income taxation and the socialisation of industry, but he did advocate subsidisation of labour-intensive industries (to expand employment opportunities), incentive-schemes for domestic investment (to keep British capital at home), the protective tariff (to defend nation and

Empire from economic aggression), and in these and other ways showed himself to be more nearly the regulator in the sense of Mun than the anti-statist in the sense of Mill. Cunningham's image of the 'good society' being so very different from that of Marshall, it is only to be expected that the two economists who were also philosophers should have disagreed so strongly on the historical evidence – and on the lessons for human development that might reasonably be drawn from it.

Marshall was fond of reiterating that he saw the academic, in Pigou's words, as 'a servant of society', as a social actor whose purpose and function it is 'to follow with constant mind the flying feet of truth'[188] – and not to be deflected from that lofty objective by the transitory temptations of current controversies. Stung by Cunningham's criticisms, Marshall felt he had no choice but to make an exception: it was, after all, his reputation as a careful and an impartial scholar that had been impugned by no less an authority than a Cambridge colleague who had been his pupil. Uncorrected, the arguments and assertions in Cunningham's paper might erroneously have been taken by readers (both British and foreign) not personally acquainted with Marshall's work as an accurate assessment of Marshall's contribution, and that Marshall simply could not allow: 'For these reasons I have broken through my rule of not replying to criticisms.'[189] The 'Reply' followed hard on the heels of the 'Perversion' in the pages of the *Economic Journal*: Edgeworth was, quite rightly, keen to ensure that both sides were properly represented.

Cunningham had phrased his accusation of rubbish-talking and downright ignorance with exemplary delicacy. Marshall was only too pleased to follow suit in his assessment of Cunningham: 'His endeavours to interpret me to other people are almost as conspicuous for their industry as for their incorrectness.'[190] Cunningham, Marshall said, had obviously studied the *Principles* with care, and the only objection that could reasonably be raised was that he had evidently failed to understand what he had read: 'His criticisms proceed on assumptions that I hold opinions which in fact I do not hold, and which I believe I have not expressed; while in several cases I think I have definitely expressed opposite opinions.'[191] Cunningham on Marshall on the Middle Ages, for instance: 'As regards mediaeval free cities, I do not hold the opinions Dr. Cunningham attributes to me, and I cannot guess why he supposes I do.'[192] Or Cunningham on Marshall on the facts:

Dr. Cunningham's suggestions as to the way in which the earlier chapters of my *Principles* were written, are not well founded. . . . These two chapters are a mere introduction; they have no claim to be history; but they were not written without due consideration of those simple and well-known 'actual facts' which Dr. Cunningham supposes me to have neglected.[193]

Or Cunningham on Marshall on constancy of motivation and uniformity of laws: 'The whole volume is indeed occupied mainly in showing how similar causes acting on people under dissimilar conditions produce more or less divergent effects. The leading motive of its argument is the opposite of that which Dr. Cunningham ascribes to it.'[194] Cunningham, Marshall concluded, was not so much disagreeing with his ideas as failing to grasp what, precisely, it was that he was trying to say. He himself, he indicated, was not so much disagreeing with Cunningham as attempting to put the record straight.

The *Principles* being a synthesis that reconciles a number of schools and approaches, it is no surprise that Cunningham had found in it the abstract ahistoricity towards which his criticisms were directed first and foremost. No relativist with respect to mind and matter could, for example, be expected to accept the permanence and the generality of Marshall's dogmatic declaration concerning value that 'the foundations of the theory as they were left by Ricardo remain intact',[195] let alone Marshall's broader statement that economics and physics are, methodologically speaking, qualitatively of the same ilk: 'The laws of human action are not indeed as simple, as definite or as clearly ascertainable as the law of gravitation; but many of them may rank with the laws of those natural sciences which deal with complex subject-matter.'[196] Nor could a historian and an inductivist be expected to share the love of logic and formal demonstration that is explicitly the essence of the Mathematical Appendix and implicitly at the heart of the whole theoretical enterprise. Yet there is far more to the *Principles* than the abstract systematisation alone, and Cunningham could easily have taken some comfort from the numerous passages such as the following in which Marshall states clearly how frequently it is the case that economic laws are in practice situation-specific: 'Though economic analysis and general reasoning are of wide application, yet every age and every country has its own problems; and every change in social conditions is likely to require a new development of economic doctrines.'[197] Cunningham ought, indeed, to have been sensitised to Marshall on contingency by the repeated warnings not only in the *Principles* but in the Inaugural as well that the attitudes and drives of the traditional Hindu simply cannot be modelled on those of the City man: 'The study of economic history has done good service . . . in proving that habits and institutions which had been assumed to be inherent in human nature are comparatively of modern growth.'[198] Cunningham shows a singular lack of imagination in assuming that Marshall's theory of rent was a theory of land-rent alone: the discussion makes clear that rent is 'the income derived from almost every variety of Differential Advantage for production',[199] and the theory therefore legitimately applicable to a wide range of times and places irrespective of the discrete conventions that govern the tenure of land. Cunningham shows a singular lack of charity in setting to one side virtually all the important issues on which he and Marshall thought as one – academic research as civic duty orientated towards the production of practical results; the moral dimension of *oughtness*, always superior to empirical investigation for its own sake; pragmatic interventionism and the potentially constructive role of the State; the need for an interdisciplinary economics if the results relating to wealth-gathering are to be more than merely 'hypothetically valid'. All in all, one is compelled to observe, the dessicated and dehydrated Marshall of the 'Perversion' is only a shadow of the fuller and richer Marshall of the *Principles*, and that is why it is the 'Reply' in the last analysis that must carry the day: Marshall there states that he had been misinterpreted, and few students of his work would wish to disagree.

Yet there is one issue in the two opening chapters of the first *Principles* with respect to which the differences between Cunningham and Marshall were real enough, and that concerned custom. Cunningham the cultural conservative made much of stability and habit. Marshall the liberal economist, on the other hand, saw calculative rationality, self-interest and supply and demand wherever he looked. Even in the pre-commercial societies, Marshall said, a careful study of the matching of means to ends beneath the still surface of the long-done thing reveals that 'there may be running many keen little pursuits of private gain', many 'sly devices for getting the best of one's neighbours': 'The very quiet affords time and opportunity for elaborate manoeuvring in small matters.'[200] That elaborate manoeuvring, Marshall asserted, had a tendency to undermine the stability of even the most traditionalised society and in effect to substitute the customs appropriate to achievement for the customs associated with ascription. In emphasising the mutability of convention, in declaring that 'in fact custom is more or less plastic',[201] Marshall was only identifying himself with those economists such as Thorold Rogers who accepted that there was an inevitable movement from status to contract. Cunningham was less happy about the inevitability of the movement or about the significance of contractual elements within the overall framework of the status-based society. In 1907 Marshall transferred his historical sections from the opening chapters to the Appendix. Perhaps this was because Cunningham's observations on custom had at last got through to him, or perhaps the reason was that Marshall in the intervening fifteen years had come into contact with new evidence which led him independently to question the validity of his schema. What is clear is simply this, that there was nothing else of substance in the 'Perversion' that could have caused him to revise his views. Nor was there anything of substance, either in the 'Perversion' or in the numerous other writings of the English historical economists, that was able ultimately to impede the triumph of Marshall's paradigm – or to save their own from defeat and oblivion.

4 The Tariff and the Succession

Britain was the home of Ricardo and Mill on comparative advantage, of Cobden and Bright on freedom of trade. She knew what it had meant to be the workshop of the world even as she ruled the waves. By the late 1890s she was having to come to grips with the fact that the world was no longer her own special market, the waves no longer synonymous with the *Mare Nostrum* on which the sun never set. By the late 1890s she was learning to her cost the implications for the open British economy of the long production-runs and technological innovation that were facilitated in the American manufacturing sector by the availability of a huge domestic market that was also protected by tariffs from foreign competition. She was coming in addition to appreciate the fundamental irony that she was increasingly purchasing commodities labelled 'Made in Germany' even as the Kaiser was increasingly emerging as a political and a military threat. Unease was in the air, and it was not merely for himself but for a very large number of his fellow countrymen that Alfred Marshall was speaking when in 1901 he voiced his concern that Britain might not forever be Great: 'Our real danger is that we shall be undersold in the product of high class industries, and have to turn more and more to low class industries. There is no fear of our going backwards absolutely, but only relatively. . . . This might be tolerable if peace were assured; but I fear it is not. Here I am very sad and anxious.'[202]

Unease was in the air, but so was intervention. In 1894 Sir William Harcourt had brought in an estate duty with a graduated scale while in 1909 Lloyd George was to impose surtax on higher incomes. The old age non-contributory pension (a much-welcomed alternative to dependence upon relatives or the discomfort and stigma of the workhouse) was introduced in 1908, part of a mould-breaking period of reform under Asquith and the Liberals. It was followed in 1911 by a system of national insurance for lower-income recipients against the contingencies of sickness and (in some industries) unemployment: Bismarck had introduced similar reforms a quarter of a century earlier and no one could say they had impaired the German economic performance. In 1902 the Education Act cheapened and broadened access to local authority secondary schools. In 1907 the School Medical Service had been set up to inspect and treat pupils whose academic performance was being affected by their health defects. The years of Marshall's late maturity, it is clear, were years of pragmatic interventionism, just as the years of his youth had been the years in which *laissez-faire* thinking was at its zenith.

Joseph Chamberlain, Mayor of Birmingham from 1873 to 1876 (thereafter Member of Parliament for Birmingham – John Bright's colleague – from 1876 to 1906), had been an early convert to pragmatic interventionism. Convinced that misery and poverty (and with them the neighbourhood effects of criminality and disease) were caused in no small measure by inadequate education and lack of decent housing, he embarked as Mayor on an ambitious programme of municipal socialism (the domestic equivalent of the White Man's Burden abroad) that he successfully persuaded the community to finance by means of high local rates. Town planning to reduce congestion is not unlike tariff reform to protect jobs; and it is no surprise that it was the very same pragmatic interventionist who, translated from Birmingham to Westminster, in 1903 resigned the post of Colonial Secretary that he had held since 1895 in order to launch a major campaign for imperial preference and a tariff wall.

The fact that Britain only adopted Empire free trade and the general tariff in 1932 must not be allowed to conceal just how great was the support for Joseph Chamberlain's crusade at a time when unease was in the air and the cosmopolitan orthodoxy appeared unable to allay popular fears: as early as 1906, for example, there were only eleven Conservative Members of Parliament who were still opposed to the reintroduction of protection.

Chamberlain was a persuasive orator but he was no economist. As he wrote to Hewins: 'I do not pretend to be an economic expert. I once read Mill and tried to read Marshall. You must supply the economic arguments.'[203] Hewins agreed to do this and became (despite the fact that all the two had in common apart from a commitment to imperial integration was a shared acknowledgement of the practical politician's ignorance in matters of economic policy) Joseph Chamberlain's chief adviser. Nor was he the only historical economist to rally to the cause. An openness to historical relativism is bound to provoke speculation on the extent to which the theories of the 1840s are relevant in changed circumstances, a patriot's interest in economic nationalism to breed and form neo-mercantilist strategies orientated not to world welfare but to zero-sum trade diversion. The urgings of moral commitment led, similarly, to concern with social reform and with State intervention (including tariff policy) such as contributes to social reform. All things considered, it is only to be expected that Chamberlain's campaign would prove attractive to the English historical mind (just as protective measures had long proved palatable to its German equivalent): liberal individualism had had its day, a new and more national phase in history was about to begin, and it was the job of the thinker to move with the times.

Thus Cunningham, speaking as a Christian as well as an economist, made a conservative's appeal for the welfare of the ongoing community to be ranked above the self-interest of the isolated utility-maximiser: 'The indulgence of the personal desire for immediate enjoyment is apt to distract from a consideration of the well-being of the community. As individual lives are shorter than the life of the community the aggregate of personal interest, at any one time, can never be identical with that of the community as a whole.'[204] Cunningham's point was in effect this, that it little benefits a nation if it gains in cinemas and motor-cars but loses its cultural identity and social cohesion in the process. Thence a good argument for the moral protection afforded national differentiation by the tariff: 'The world is likely to be poorer if all are reduced to a similar level.'[205] Even within the Empire, Cunningham said, the British, while acknowledging the responsibility of an older nation 'for bringing a civilising influence to bear on territories which are occupied by primitive peoples',[206] had wisely sought to protect local *mores* from corruption by cosmopolitanism: 'Considerable care has been taken to recognise racial distinctions, and assimilation and amalgamation have never been regarded as an ideal to be aimed at.'[207] That tolerance which the Englishman demonstrates for the established way of life of the Hottentot, Cunningham believed (he did not cite evidence to support his generalisation), the Englishman ought to show for his own traditions and conventions; and a tariff restraining the free play of economic forces, even if it did in the event reduce the level of consumer welfare, could hardly be regarded as too high a price to pay for the privilege of purity. Nor, Cunningham insisted, did the historical record lend any particular support to the orthodox expectation that consumer welfare would in fact be put in jeopardy by a return to protection. The rapid economic advance of Germany and the United States would seem if anything to suggest that it might have been List and Carey, not Ricardo and Mill, who had best grasped the nature of the relationship between trade and growth: 'Since other countries are progressing more rapidly under Protection than Great Britain is doing under Free Trade, we may hesitate about accepting the assurance that the introduction of Free Trade was an important element in contributing to our rapid progress in the latter half of last century.'[208] Protected trade and rapid growth need not prove incompatible, Cunningham argued. He also said that, were protection and advance in fact to be alternatives, it must then be the former rather than the latter for which the rational community opts: an industrial England cannot afford in an insecure environment to depend upon the rest of the world for her food and raw materials, she cannot rely on foreigners bent upon their own industrialisation forever to admit her manufactures duty-free, and the inference is that the well-known Tudor programme for plenty accompanied by power must in such circumstances rapidly be reassessed in the light of the wise *dictum* of the celebrated Georgian that 'defence. . . . is of much more importance than opulence'.[209] As Joseph Chamberlain put it: 'Success breeds envy; jealous eyes watch our progress, measure our strength or weakness, and seek out the joints of our armour.'[210] It was Cunningham's message that there was much good sense in Chamberlain's politics of fear, and that Englishmen would therefore be well advised to swap their Senior for their Child lest their homeland become their *Piccadillyplatz*.

Just as Cunningham was a willing convert to Chamberlain's crusade, so too was Ashley. Based in Birmingham, Ashley was able to witness at first hand the not-inconsiderable harm that unrestricted importation was inflicting upon the British staples: confronted on the one hand with the spectacle of foreign trusts dumping their surplus products in an unprotected market, on the other with British workers genuinely concerned about employment prospects, Ashley argued strongly that the Ricardian ideal of world free trade, international division of labour, perfect factor mobility, competition without frontiers, was in effect inappropriate to the less-than-utopian conditions of a beleaguered and vulnerable Britain, which should in her concrete circumstances reject classical trade theory and close the door. Much of poverty could already be attributed to the vagaries and irregularities of fluctuating markets, Ashley said, indicating that the tariff would at least provide some stability of employment for British labour. Even more poverty was likely to result, Ashley added, were the erosion of the manufacturing base not rapidly to be arrested by means of protection: invisibles such as shipping services were themselves under pressure from foreign competition, the *entrepôt* trade was bound one day to decline, the tertiary sector is in any case no great creator of new jobs (even free traders such as A. L. Bowley had treated this controversial assertion as a proven fact), and the conclusion Ashley was forced to draw was that the traditional industries such as textiles, shipbuilding, iron and steel would simply have to be saved. Ashley's experience in America had convinced him that large corporations and even trusts need not mean activity seriously detrimental to the welfare of the community: low pay and frequent layoffs being more common in the competitive conditions of the London sweated trades than in the highly concentrated market structures of the American monoliths, the great evil of class conflict being more a concern in the country that had opted for comparative advantage than in the nation which had fearlessly faced up to protection and power, the historical relativist felt obliged to admit that it might in truth be no bad thing if the corporate society with strong intermediate institutions and nationalistic economic policies did turn out to be the next stage of economic evolution in the old world as it had been in the new. Ashley's experience in Canada (a country which was itself to adopt a preferential tariff in 1908) had reinforced in him a commitment to Empire in general, the overseas Englishness of the White

Dominions in particular: apart from the cultural case for an Empire tariff (a case much strengthened, no doubt, by the demonstrated solidarity with Britain of her overseas dependencies at the time of the Boer War, in the face of a generally hostile world public opinion), Ashley was aware that the domestic market was too small to allow even a protected Britain to reap maximal economies of scale and that Empire free trade could become *de facto* the *Zollverein* that, boosting her average productivity, made her manufactures that much more attractive in an increasingly competitive world. Protection in Germany, Ashley said, illustrated clearly the manner in which tariffs could promote economic growth – economic growth which in that country had been translated into public finance for Bismarck's welfare state as well as across-the-board improvements in living standards (both of them reasons why the Social Democrats had abandoned their call for revolution in favour of a revisionist stance that the non-Ricardian non-Marxist could not but find infinitely more congenial). Protection in Germany, Ashley believed, provided a useful illustration of how a nation governed by sensible pragmatists could intervene in trade policy with the same degree of success that had been her just reward in the field of technological and commercial education. The fact that she had been so active without at the same time widely being called corrupt suggested to Ashley that the debate about *dirigisme* had moved on significantly since the time when Adam Smith issued his warnings: the Reform Acts of 1867 and 1884, the adoption of the secret ballot, the civil service reforms, the improvements in education, these and many other advances in the direction of democracy must have indicated to Ashley that the time had come even in the homeland of classical liberalism finally to trust the State. All things considered, therefore, it is no great surprise that Ashley, based by pure coincidence in the birthplace of municipal socialism, proved a willing convert to Chamberlain's crusade: Ashley, abroad, had already inspected the future at first hand and had satisfied himself that it indeed could be said to work.

Ashley, like Hewins and Cunningham, proved a willing convert to Chamberlain's crusade. Alfred Marshall, on the other hand, did not, but continued to defend the old orthodoxies even in the altered circumstances that so depressingly differentiated the harried England of his old age from the Merrie England of his childhood:

> Sixty years ago it was different. Then open ports were merely an important aid: they were not a necessity as now. . . . Many of our

exports were such as foreigners could get only from us, at all events at a reasonable price; and our manufacturers wanted very few foreign products. . . . In fact, there never had been, and never can be again a monopoly of so great a share of the best business of the world as we then had.[211]

Free trade was a luxury in the England of Cobden and Bright, Marshall argued – whereas subsequently it had become the *sine qua non* for the sustained prosperity of an advanced industrial nation such as his own: 'I . . . have gradually settled down to the conclusion that the changes of the last two generations have much increased the harm which would be done to England by even a moderate protective policy, and that free trade is of more vital necessity to England now than when it was first adopted.'[212] Long a supporter of free-trade policies, Marshall was forced carefully to evaluate his logic when he was asked in 1903 by C. T. Ritchie, the new Chancellor of the Exchequer in Balfour's Cabinet, to prepare the report on tariffs and protection that was later revised and published as the 'Memorandum on Fiscal Policy of Foreign Trade' (1908). Part of the text was, tragically, lost in the post from Italy, where Marshall was spending the summer of that eventful year; but the sections that survive leave no doubt that Marshall believed that the problem of rivalry was still to be solved via efficiency and not via protection, even in a period of rapid industrial advance abroad and mounting political tensions such as might one day lead to war. Presumably Marshall felt that his new Economics Tripos (his other major concern in 1903) would make its own small contribution to the generation of the expertise that was so desperately required if the British economy was to remain competitive as well as open.

Marshall was, as it happens, less than satisfied with the 'Memorandum', evidently regarding the simplifications and abridgements he had had to introduce for the benefit of his Whitehall readership as serious shortcomings in the work of an academic economist. Thus, speaking of the 'Memorandum', he conceded publicly that 'it offends against my rule to avoid controversial matters; and, instead of endeavouring to probe to the causes of causes, as a student's work should, it is concerned mainly with proximate causes and their effects.'[213] Aware as he was that he had himself made policy-recommendations without falling back on the cautious diffidence that was his standard support, he ought not to have been surprised when Bonar Law attacked his report as 'frankly partisan'. Yet surprised he was, and hurt, and he wrote to *The Times* to make it known that he had throughout his labours consciously been 'preserving a non-partisan attitude': 'This Memorandum is written from the point of view of a student of economics rather than an advocate of any particular policy'.[214] It was misunderstandings of precisely this nature that Marshall had consistently sought to avoid by means of his repeated refusals to be drawn into controversies pyramided upon half-truths and inadequate information. The statement of the 'humdrum economist' to the Industrial Remuneration Conference of 1885 is a case in point: 'I imagine that the object of our meeting is not to argue with one another; that cannot be done properly except in books.'[215] Marshall must have known as he saw the storm clouds gathering that he would one day be asked for his yes/no verdict on the tariff question; and he must have dreaded the prospect of having at that time to discard his conditioning-clauses in order to speak out decisively. As late as 1901 he was still capable of writing to Ashley that, able to see both sides of the argument, he was hesitant, tentative, 'sitting on the fence', and afraid most of all of economic dogmatists who jumped straight to conclusions:

> As in the Factory Act days the 'Economists' known to the people were not real economists, but sordid people who claimed economic authority for their own ends, and so brought discredit on economics, so now there are signs that economics will be discredited by the claim of economic authority for Free Trade doctrines in their popular and incorrect form.[216]

Bonar Law's claim that the Marshall of the 'Memorandum' was indulging in effect in just such an act of partisan discrediting must inevitably have been exceptionally distressing to him.

As a careful scholar, Marshall could see the case against free trade as well as in its favour. In Germany in 1868 (in Dresden) and 1870 (in Berlin), in the United States in 1875, he had seen at first hand competitor-economies that were flourishing despite (even if not because of) protective tariffs; and he had also come into contact with the ideas of List, Carey and the economists who championed their insights. He was entirely prepared to accept the relativist's case that the relevance of theory is constrained by time and place – so much so, in fact, that he made the following (admittedly loosely-worded) manuscript note to himself only one year after the dramatic events of 1903: 'Protection is reasonable (not necessarily expedient) for Canada. . . . For American dumping is so strong in Canada as to throttle newest industries. . . . they must have help, perhaps; & if so protection is the simplest though probably not the best method.'[217] Marshall could see, in short, that the arguments of the protectionists and the imperialists were not simply to be dismissed out of hand as nonsensical; but there are for all that few if any indications that he himself ever seriously contemplated a breach with the old ortho- doxies and the competitive mode of business regulation. Unlike Ashley, he was sceptical that the large organisations fostered by a protective order would in fact prove the dynamic vanguard of cre- ative destruction, arguing in effect that the cosseted are more likely to target a quiet life: 'If you are Trusted, you will become sleepy in time.'[218] Like Smith, he was convinced that competition is the gate- way to efficiency, that 'risk taking strengthens character'[219] – and that the imaginativeness of the entrepreneur is of far more value to '*National* Industry and Trade'[220] than is the restrictiveness of the bureaucrat: 'Industrial leadership is the doing today what other people will be doing tomorrow, & wishing they had done today.'[221] Such leadership can to some extent be stimulated by State interven- tion in the form most of all of technical education. It can never be stimulated by the repression of challenge such as would be the free gift of the new mercantilism.

Yet both Germany and America had sheltered their domestic producers; and the result (the very reason for Chamberlain's crusade in 1903) was that Britain had come to lag behind in world trade in manufactures. Marshall appears never to have come to grips with the paradox that protection abroad had demonstrably succeeded where open ports at home had revealed themselves to be a second-best. That he acknowledged and admired the economic achievements of protected nations is, however, beyond doubt. Thus, referring to America, he wrote as follows: 'The quantity of industrial energy & trained ability and of mobile capital available for new enterprises in the United States alone are greater than in the United Kingdom, or even in the British Empire.'[222] Given such achievements, it is only natural that he should in 1900 have made a note to himself to the effect that an alliance with the North Americans and other peoples of British descent, while not necessarily a desirable thing in itself, was unambiguously preferable to closer links within the Empire: 'Indus- trial supremacy. . . . may come to the anglosaxon race & remain with them. It cannot come to the British Empire; because. . . . even though that may become a political unity, it never can become an economic unity.'[223] Nor was Marshall in 1900 oblivious to the military

benefits that would accrue to the British defence effort from closer
collaboration with the budding superpower that was already coming
to rule the waves in the Pacific. Economic growth, Marshall reflected,
was itself of strategic importance: 'The military responsibilities of
England require that she should not only remain prosperous but
should also maintain a strong economic position relating to other
nations. . . . War is becoming ever more a commercial enterprise &
the most expensive of all enterprises.'[224] International aggression was
a serious concern with Alfred Marshall, who not only anticipated the
Kaiser's War as early as the turn of the century but, writing to
Maynard Keynes in 1915 about the Germans' obsession with 'unham-
pered expansion', accurately predicted the inevitability of Hitler's
War as well: 'I shall not live to see our next war with Germany; but
you will, I expect. . . . I think of the next war almost as much as of
the present; and the two together oppress me.'[225] Defence was of
more importance than opulence, opulence generated wealth to fund
defence; and both arguments, the military and the economic, could
easily have led Marshall to assert that Britain's national interests
were best served neither by imperial protection nor by world free
trade but rather by a third expedient – a North Atlantic community
or 'federated Anglo-Saxondom' that would couple the first industrial
nation with the great power of the future. Marshall never went so far
as to make so strong an assertion. What is more than likely, however,
is that he believed that imperialism and protectionism would weaken
Britain's special relationship with the United States; and that he was
opposed to those measures at least in part because of the threat they
embodied to that relationship.

The tariff controversy provided economists with an unusual opportunity to become involved in current affairs. Edgeworth seized the
initiative and drafted a letter which, published in *The Times* of 15
August 1903 (and reprinted for good measure in the *Economic
Journal* in September of that year), roundly attacked Chamberlain's
schemes on the grounds that economic theory spoke with one voice in
favour of freedom of trade. The letter was signed by fourteen
distinguished British economists; and Marshall, despite his fear of
misrepresentation and his congenital caution, was one of them. Coats
writes that 'Marshall subsequently regretted having signed the "manifesto"' and gives as the reason the fact that 'he was accused of
addressing the layman in condescending terms':[226] in view of the
sheer dogmatism of Edgeworth's text and its exceptional narrowness
with respect to alternative points of view, it is not difficult to see why
Marshall might have been ashamed at having put his cachet to a

perspective which even the layman knew to be only one among several. Another reason for Marshall's regret must have been the diminution in the prestige of the profession which he believed the events of 1903 to have caused by involving economists in practical politics (where they had no right to be) and by putting divisions on public show (which was bound to erode trust): the animosities of 1903 were not on the scale of the 1870s but they were great nonetheless, probably accounting, for instance, for the fact that Ashley was never elected President of the Royal Economic Society (he did, of course, become President of Section F in 1907, and remains unique among the great economists in having had the honour of a funeral service in Canterbury Cathedral – the result of having been appointed Diocesan Lay Reader by the Archbishop of Canterbury in 1925). Besides that, Marshall (whose writings show that he held strong views on unemployment, poverty, the unions, the income tax and virtually all the other principal issues of his time) had consistently managed to keep himself above party politics, and the normally reticent professor cannot but have been annoyed with himself that in signing the letter he had also broken his rule.

Herbert Foxwell did not sign Edgeworth's letter but instead wrote one of his own attacking the high theoreticians for failing to address practical realities. Foxwell's letter appeared in *The Times* of 20 August 1903. It by no means endeared him to his Cambridge colleague. Foxwell later said that it had been James Bonar who 'induced Marshall, against M.'s better judgement, and after M. had twice refused, to sign the Professors' Manifesto. It was just because he felt that his signature was a blunder that he was so angry with me for attacking it.'[227] Be that as it may, the greater blunder could well have been Foxwell's own. As Coats explains:

> There is reason to believe that the events of 1903 may have directly influenced the choice of Pigou as successor to Marshall at Cambridge in 1908, a decision that ensured the pre-eminence of economic theory at the leading academic centre of British economics. The evidence is, inevitably, only circumstantial and indirect; but Foxwell, the chief Cambridge contender and the most bitterly disappointed candidate, always believed that his rejection of the free trade doctrine had counted decisively against him. Marshall was said to have actively canvassed on Pigou's behalf, and there is abundant evidence that he strongly disagreed with the views of those economists who actively supported Chamberlain.[228]

Coase, however, denies the existence of so close a causal link be-

Alfred Marshall's Mission

tween the Tariff Reform Campaign of 1903 and the choice of Pigou in 1908: 'The decision to appoint Pigou would, I believe, have been the same had the tariff controversy of 1903 never occurred.'[229] Coase is not saying that Marshall was pleased with Foxwell's involvement in the 1903 campaign. What he is saying is that 1903 did no more in effect than to reinforce Marshall's already-formed resolution that Foxwell ought not to succeed him in the Cambridge chair. The distinguished Coase is on this occasion more persuasive than the erudite Coats, if only because Marshall had sedulously transformed the Cambridge Faculty into a principal centre of excellence in analytical economics and could not possibly have wished to hand on the torch to an inductivist candidate likely to extinguish the flame that he had lit: 'Marshall did not share Foxwell's antipathy to theory or his enthusiasm for the historical approach in economics',[230] and Marshall was not one to allow the opposition the opportunity to reverse the success of his mission.

Foxwell disagreed with Marshall on a number of issues, and not least among these was the status of Ricardian economics. Marshall greatly revered the classical thinker's rigorous logic. Foxwell, on the other hand, was hostile to what he evidently regarded as a methodology that was as insidious as it was abstract. Thus Foxwell, as was recorded in Chapter 6, attacked 'Deductive Playthings' like Ricardo's *Principles*, saying of Ricardo's great work that its study was 'like giving a child a razor to play with' and complaining bitterly that it was 'the first edition of this disastrous book, which gave us Marxian Socialism and the Class War'. By contrast, as Koot points out, Foxwell noted on the flyleaf of his personal copy of the second edition of Malthus' *Essay on Population*, (now in the Kress), that 'this is a fine example of the historical method, the only possible method for the tolerable treatment of questions of practical economics.'[231] Marshall admittedly had the moderate's openness towards the eclectic employment of historical evidence in applied economics, but he could hardly be expected to welcome as his successor a historical economist who was so hostile to pure theory in general, his reverenced Ricardo in particular. Marshall also knew from personal experience that Foxwell was more likely to be dogmatic than conciliatory when actually drafting a syllabus that integrated theory and practice: their quarrel over the status of history in the new Tripos appears to have been just one more in a long series of disagreements on teaching and topics. Thus in 1900 Foxwell wrote to J. N. Keynes that 'we have had a good many differences on these

matters; culminating in his having engaged Pigou to deliver an elementary course – a man, of all I have heard, least qualified to deal with a
general class as he is such a prig.'[232] Foxwell and Marshall had evidently crossed swords on a number of occasions, and Marshall seems
to have formed much the same assessment of his belligerent colleagues's difficult character as did J. M. Keynes when Keynes wrote
of Foxwell that 'his open wilfulness was an essential part of him, but
it stood in his way in the attainment of his ends in English academic
circles which hate a row.'[233] Marshall, reflecting on Foxwell, once
observed that 'we differ in opinion a good deal, and in temperament
perhaps even more.'[234] It would clearly have been unthinkable for
Marshall in 1908 to have sought to pass on his mantle to so obstinate
and opinionated an anti-Ricardian: what Cambridge most required
was some mix of theory and tolerance, and it was in precisely that mix
of analysis and compromise that Foxwell was so conspicuously lacking.

Besides that, Marshall seems never to have had a very high opinion
of Foxwell's intellectual stature. The testimonial he wrote in 1875 for
Foxwell (who had in 1870 taken a First in moral sciences under his
tutelage at St John's) hardly suggests the admiration of one great
mind for another: 'He has given elementary lectures in Political
Economy at Leeds with great success, and great benefit to himself.
He has a clear and easy style, and is remarkably successful in
interesting beginners in their work.'[235] In his Presidential Address on
'Some Aspects of Competition' Marshall in his text makes not a
single reference to 'The Growth of Monopoly, and its Bearing on the
Functions of the State' which Foxwell (Section Secretary from 1882
to 1888) had read to F a mere two years earlier: only in a footnote
does Marshall 'specially refer' to Foxwell's ambitious paper, and
even there manages to sound patronising by grouping Jevons' successor to the University College Chair with the 'younger English
economists'.[236] At the time of the 1908 election Marshall not only
opposed the appointment of Foxwell to his own vacant professorship
but also opposed the creation of a second professorship specifically
for Foxwell. Marshall in 1908 was not in the least opposed to the
creation of a second (presumably historically-orientated) professorship for Clapham – who, appointed as intended when the Chair of
Economic History was finally established two decades later in 1928,
reminded his Cambridge colleagues that Marshall in fact 'was a
greater economic historian than he let the world know. He had
discarded as irrelevant to his main purposes more historical knowledge than many men acquire. . . . He was eager to get historical

work done. Long ago – I owe this personal reference to his memory – he pointed out to me tracts of economic history which needed someone's work. Then he pointed at me and said: "Thou art the man".'[237] Clapham was the man; and Marshall in 1908 was not in the least opposed to the creation of a second professorship provided that Clapham was the beneficiary. Foxwell was, however, another matter; and here Marshall evidently made it his business to ensure that there was to be no second chair for a long-serving associate who in his opinion was simply not of professorial calibre. Thus he wrote to J. N. Keynes in 1908 that, with respect to Foxwell, 'I have a fear of his judgements. On Finance in particular, one of the subjects proposed for him, I think his judgement is extraordinarily bad. He seems never to see more than one side of any complex question. . . . Even if Foxwell were still in his prime, I should hesitate to put him on the same intellectual line with Clapham.'[238] Writing to Foxwell to console him on his rejection in 1908, and obviously aware that the 'oldest' of his colleagues must have been bitterly disappointed at the election of one of the newest ('Please do not answer this just now: for you must be feeling sore'), Marshall tactfully adopted a more flattering tone: 'I have heard no one, not even among the most enthusiastic supporters of Pigou's claims, who is not deeply pained by the thought that it has not been possible to crown your long and trusty work by a high reward.'[239] Foxwell, so embittered by the events of 1908 that as late as 1927 he was still refusing to support Pigou for the Presidency of the Royal Economic Society, was not taken in by Marshall's superficial kindnesses, correctly conjecturing in 1912 that he believed Marshall to have 'in his inner feelings a very honest contempt; and at any rate, he has left me in no sort of doubt as to the value he sets on any service it is in my power to render'.[240] Things had clearly altered since the late 1870s and early 1880s when Foxwell was so eloquently extolling Marshall's merits to Jevons and Walras, all and sundry, that Cliffe Leslie had declared him lost to any other tradition: 'Marshall seems to be his real demigod.'[241] Sad as the embitterment and the disillusionment of the St Johns man must inevitably have been who had already served his College for thirty years (from 1875, after Extension work in deprived areas in the North of England, until 1905) as Lecturer and was at the time of Marshall's retirement in the early stages of a stint of similar length (from 1905 to 1936) as its Director of Economic Studies, Marshall's assessment of his intellectual stature cannot have come as a complete surprise: the *Social Aspect of Banking* (1886) or the *Papers on Current Finance* (1919) are worthy contributions but not for all that lasting ones, while the famous article of 1887 on 'The Economic Movement in England' is famous not so much for Foxwell's own opinions as for the factual evidence which he musters to support them. If, moreover, a lasting contribution warranting a personal chair was indeed made by a Cambridge historical of Foxwell's generation, then it was not in any case made by Foxwell at all, but rather by the distinguished author of the three-volume *Growth of English Industry and Commerce* (a book which, by the time it had passed through its sixth edition in 1912, had established its preeminence in the contemporary literature of histori-cal economics) and of more than thirty other books as well. In Maloney's words: 'It can be presumed that no one dared remind Marshall, on his retirement in 1908, that to date Cunningham had written more works of political economy than all other Cambridge dons, living and dead, put together.'[242] Clapham would not have stood a chance against Cunningham; and that, presumably, is an important reason why the plans for the second chair were dropped so abruptly in 1908. Foxwell, Marshall probably believed, would have been much less of a challenge.

Foxwell and Marshall were on opposite sides of the fence with respect to bimetallism. Foxwell attributed deflation and slow growth in the 1890s to an ill-advised demonetisation of silver at a time when world gold production was stagnating, and proposed international bimetallism at fixed ratios. Marshall, on the other hand, remained a monometallist and a gold standard man, an advocate of stable prices who took the view that experimentation would result in inflation. Foxwell complained that Marshall, 'knowing nothing of English bi-metallists. . . . is filled with suspicion of them. In fact he regards them as unmitigatedly soft money men, most unfairly of course.'[243] Marshall, one would guess, had more or less the same reservations about Foxwell's grasp of the monometallists' case. Then there was the question of State intervention. Foxwell believed that socialism could be prevented only by abandoning the commitment to *laissez-faire*; and he further championed public spending on the grounds that an expansion in civil service employment tended to boost stability in the economy as a whole. Marshall, less afraid of socialism and instability, more pragmatic on the public sector involvement, was, in contrast to Foxwell, more cautious and more conservative: he was prepared to countenance the diffusion of economic intelligence and the provision of State education but had serious reservations about public sector housing schemes, counter-cyclical public works and governmental regulation of natural monopolies. Here once again, it would appear, Foxwell and Marshall did not see eye to eye. To the list of distance factors must be added the status of intellectual history (given that, in Coase's assessment, 'Foxwell's speciality, the history of economic thought, was to Marshall a subject of secondary importance'),[244] the religious underpinnings (Foxwell was a Methodist, Marshall an agnostic), the ethical overlay (Foxwell found theories of self-interested individualism and greedy competitiveness morally offensive whereas Marshall concentrated on the manner in which private vices can successfully promote the wealth of nations). The list of distance factors is a long one; and that is why it is by no means obvious that the appointment of Pigou in 1908 in effect illustrates (as Foxwell believed it to have done) Marshall's 'savage revenge'[245] upon his Cambridge colleague for the letter of 1903. Perhaps it does; but what it is far more likely to illustrate is the accurate identification by a secular missionary anxious to do good of the candidate for the succession most likely to carry on the tradition. Foxwell was quite clearly not the man. Nor was Ashley, the second of the three applicants shortlisted for the chair (the last for which this busy form-filler in effect applied: the LSE could not risk a third tariff-reformer after Hewins and Mackinder, lest it become publicly associated with a single position; Ashley was not seriously considered for its vacant Directorship in 1908, and after the Cambridge fiasco the eminent inductivist evidently reconciled himself to the idea of Birmingham as a permanent base). That left Pigou.

Arthur Cecil Pigou (1877–1959) was Marshall's 'favourite pupil'[246] and his choice for the chair. Reflecting on the outcome immediately after the election Marshall stated: 'Pigou is in my opinion likely to be recognised ere long as a man of quite extraordinary genius: and I hoped that he would be elected to the Profesorship.'[247] The views of the outgoing incumbent on the future of economics in Cambridge must have carried considerable weight with the appointing committee. Nor did Marshall leave things entirely to chance. One of the electors, J. N. Keynes, records in his diary that Marshall had come to see him to discuss the professorship: 'He speaks in the highest terms of Pigou and is clearly most anxious that he should be elected.'[248] Another elector – Edgeworth – stayed at Balliol Croft the night before the interviews and presumably discussed the candidates with the senior theoretician whom he so greatly respected: Edgeworth had in any case praised Pigou highly in the *Economic Journal* as early as 1904[249] and was himself no historical inductivist but rather a mathematical economist with a strongly analytical bent (as well as sharing with Pigou, of course, a commitment to free trade). Pigou had a reasonable if not yet a distinguished list of publications and had demonstrated his administrative skills through his involvement with Marshall in the campaign for the new Tripos. Perhaps his age was in his favour: Foxwell at 58 was only seven years younger than Marshall himself, Ashley was already 48, but Pigou was a fresh face of only 30.

Had Foxwell or Ashley been appointed, somewhat less of British economics would no doubt have been devoted to careful exegesis of the *Principles of Economics* than proved the case when a disciple with what L. L. Price called an 'almost filial' respect for the 'utterances of Professor Marshall'[250] succeeded to the Cambridge chair. As E. A. G. Robinson states:

> It was primarily through Pigou that the Marshallian tradition was handed down and became the Cambridge school of economics. . . . To the end Pigou remained a devoted and almost uncritical pupil of Marshall's, indeed an almost idolatrous worshipper. It was Pigou, more than any other, who brought up a generation of Cambridge economists in the conviction that (in his often-repeated words) 'it's all in Marshall' and the belief that if they were in error, it was because they had misunderstood Marshall or had overlooked some esential passage in the holy writ.[251]

There is inevitably a price to be paid for filial piety in the form of the inflexible dogmatism which it has a tendency to breed and shape: it seems to have been because of Pigou's intellectual rigidity, for example, that Marshall himself had 'strong reservations'[252] about the conclusions concerning maximum satisfaction at which Pigou arrived in his *Wealth and Welfare* of 1912. The historicist alternative would unquestionably have been far less palatable to Marshall, however, than was even Pigou's most extreme use of oversimplified hypotheses and 'tendency laws' bereft of Mill's valuably realistic 'disturbing causes'[253] to derive concrete recommendations for practical policy; and for that reason alone Marshall was no doubt very relieved indeed that a Pigou was there when a Pigou was needed.

A Pigou was there when a Pigou was needed; but the truth is that the canny Marshall had had the great good sense not to leave the question of the discipleship entirely to chance. As early as 1899 he was writing to Neville Keynes of his wish to hire a 'young lecturer on economics, who has time and strength to do drill work for men of medium ability'.[254] He was evidently much impressed by the internal labour-market represented by the German '*privat docents*', supervised lecturers whose task it was 'to understudy the parts of the older teachers who were also learners, and to learn while teaching'.[255] The principle of learning on the job and of moving from the elementary to the more advanced work as the man matures appears to have appealed to the young Pigou as well, of whom Kadish writes: 'Economics was awarded by Pigou the status of a mystery. Either one learnt it the proper way by spending a sufficient number of years at the feet of a recognised master, or else one was not an economist.'[256] Pigou must in the circumstances have been delighted when the great Professor Marshall in 1901 used his authority to appoint the inexperienced young man to a teaching post *de facto* in Cambridge University. The fee (£100) came from Marshall's own pocket. The brief was to teach, on the professor's behalf, the 'high-class beginners' doing the general course, thereby leaving the great man free to concentrate his efforts on advanced economics. The relationship proved idyllic. As Kadish explains: 'Pigou seemed content to accept Marshall's work as his own point of departure and to proceed along lines largely determined by the master. Pigou was safe, loyal, and unquestionably competent. . . . Marshall had found his ideal *privat docent*.'[257] Marshall clearly decided at a very early stage that Pigou was destined for great things. In 1900 he wrote: 'Mr. Pigou shows in some respects exceptional genius.'[258] By 1902 this assessment had been upgraded to the declaration that 'Pigou will be one of the leading economists of the world in his generation.'[259] Marshall therefore went out of his way to recruit the young paragon almost from the moment that Pigou obtained his First at King's in 1899 (ironically enough for the future champion of the *a priori*, in the History Tripos). Pigou was then twenty-two. The age is significant, Marshall being (unlike, say, Ashley) a strong believer in early specialisation in preference to set-in-his-ways maturity: 'If a man has not learnt to be thorough before he is twenty-two, he will never learn it.'[260] Twenty-two is as twenty-two does. This much, however, is certain: if a Pigou was there when a Pigou was needed, the reason must be, at least in part, that the retiring captain had begun no later than the ultimate successor's twenty-second birthday to lay his snare.

Under Pigou's leadership, the heritage of the 'great father figure of English economics' who was himself so much imbued with 'the virtue of respect for one's elders and betters in the family of economists' was maintained remarkably intact: 'In fact', Hutchison observes, 'for some time, theoretical economics in England consisted very largely of the discussion and interpretation, often textual, of Marshall's *Principles*.'[261] Maloney, referring to basically the same period, reaches basically the same conclusion: 'If professionalisation consists, as Weber suggested, of the "routinisation of charisma", then at least the historian is never in a moment's doubt as to whose charisma stood to be routinised.'[262] Pigou was eminent enough in 1908 to be elected to the Cambridge chair but also young enough to be able to retain it for a full thirty-five years. His long stewardship, from 1908 to 1943, was followed by that of D. H. Robertson, who continued down to 1957 the reverential Cambridge tradition of passing on the *Principles* to posterity. Around the leaders gathered the followers, selected because they were sympathetic to the ideas not of Cunningham but of Marshall and self-selected because even when at their most critical, their language, their methodology and their mode of attack remained unmistakably that of the Marshallian orthodoxy: Sraffa, Guillebaud, Keynes, the Robinsons, the Hickses – despite their differences, all united by a common identity deriving from a common set of scriptures. And thus something happened which Marshall could not have foreseen any more than that he could have foreseen a loyal Robertson half a century later at the helm (and not a young Foxwell anxious to obliterate all traces of the *ancien régime*): without ever making much of an effect to do so, the economist on whom the sun never ceased to shine ended up *de facto* the prophet of a self-perpetuating cult. As Schumpeter says:

> Marshall created a genuine school, the members of which thought in terms of a well-defined scientific organon, and supplemented this bond by strong personal cohesion. Professor Pigou, his successor in the Cambridge chair; Professor Robertson, who succeeded Pigou; and Lord Keynes – to mention only a few of the most familiar names – were formed by his teaching and started from his teaching, however far they may have traveled beyond it. . . . Though some of them grew to dislike Marshall, not only his modes of thought but also his personal aura, his stamp is still upon them all.[263]

And upon us as well. Of course there was what Pigou (in later years somewhat less idolatrous than might have been predicted from the filial piety of three decades earlier) called the 'moral dictatorship' of the master's insights and of which he observed that 'this attitude cannot but have checked enterprise and initiative'.[264] There can be no doubt that Marshallian economics has over the years stifled much that was new lest it challenge the hegemony of the old; and that the textbook tradition erected upon it has done much harm by shunting questioning young minds on to the wrong line of over-confident formulation. Such stifling and such shunting are only to be expected in the case of an author whose ideas so decisively shape and form the thinking of his generation. Intolerance and atrophy are, however, singularly inappropriate in the case of Alfred Marshall, whose mission it was to unify, synthesise and reconcile, not to tyrannise, dogmatise or oppose. Marshall would, one suspects, have been deeply shocked by the rigidity and the selectivity which his followers contributed to his paradigm while studiously perpetuating what they believed to be its core. He did not live to see the process of institutional ossification. Alfred Marshall died on Sunday, 13 July 1924. He is buried in St Giles' Churchyard, Huntingdon Road, Cambridge. His books were left to the University, which also ultimately inherited the bulk of his estate and future royalties from his works in copyright. Mary Paley Marshall devoted most of the twenty years of her widowhood to assisting in the establishment and administration of the Marshall Library: 'So when Alfred passed beyond her care, to preserve this tradition and to keep *his* books still living in the hands of the succeeding generations of students became her dearest aim.'[265] Pigou was his literary executor.

8 Conclusion

Alfred Marshall was anxious to do good. He was also anxious to do good quite specifically through economics. Green and Jowett, Carlyle and Ruskin, looked over his shoulder even as he formalised the concepts of elasticity and quasi-rent; Toynbee Hall and the University Extension Movement, the Charity Organisation Societies and the union provident funds, put him on the alert even as he theorised about monopoly prices and equilibrium states; Darwin the evolutionist and Spencer the improver, Foxwell the Methodist and Ashley the Churchman, stared meaningfully back at him from the mirror even as he translated marginal utility and economies of size into the terse language of the differential calculus; and the result is a distinctive whole qualitatively different from the sum of the parts, an intellectual organism that is not the simple aggregate of its discrete cells. The mix is quite unlike anything that had been seen before or has been encountered since. It is in that mix that Alfred Marshall's mission is most clearly to be found.

Marshall unified the paradigm by stressing the complementarity of cost of production in the sense of the Ricardians with final degree of utility in the sense of the Jevonians, fact-gathering in the sense of the historicals with logico-deductivism in the sense of the neo-classicals. Marshall enriched the discipline through the refinement of technical tools (many of them owing much to distinguished forebears including Cournot and von Thünen) and synthesised the disparate elements into a single whole: scholars will differ about how much was new and how much merely borrowed but not about the parentage of the comprehensive intellectual structure within the framework of which the particular demand curve and the representative firm are so tidily reconciled with the four discrete time periods, the Giffen good with the normal value, the stationary state with the forward-falling supply curve, the diminishing marginal utility of money with the diminishing physical productivity of land. Marshall secured the institutionalisation of an analytically-informed but commercially-relevant programme of economics teaching at his own University by means of his involvement in the new Tripos; and he also made a major contribution to the professionalisation of economic investigation (broadly and tolerantly defined, thanks in no small measure to his own personal recommendation) through the role he played while President of F in the setting-up of the Economic Association.

Marshall was no Comtean but he was for all that convinced that the useful economist had to be as interdisciplinary in approach as was required to capture the multi-faceted nature of the phenomena to be studied. Thus he showed the psychologist's interest in subjective perceptions including real cost and non-hedonic motivation, combining it with the sociologist's awareness that approbation and self-approbation are relevant even in the economic marketplace (the reason why soulful capitalists resist price-cutting despite a recession, why sensitive workers eschew an abnormal increase in effort, why conspicuous consumers prefer the fashionable to the durable). Marshall was in addition a truly *political* economist, in that he saw it as part of his task to define the proper boundaries between individual interest (the textbook case of the Invisible Hand that directs the free and voluntary swap of apples for nuts), intermediate corporations (as where the sense of responsibility of all for each leads to the formation of self-help groups such as trades unions or producer cooperatives) and State intervention (as instanced by the collective provision of public goods ranging from improved intelligence via the tabular standard to accelerated growth via the subsidisation of the scale economy, the taxation of the rising cost). All of this unambiguously situated within the framework of a social organism condemned by the momentum inherent in matter to continuous change (and thus rather to disequilibrium and uncertainty than to *stasis* and foresight): given the initiative and the imagination of the inspired entrepreneur in the competitive market, even recognising that *natura non facit saltum*, the fact is that change is absolutely continuous and today's *status quo* therefore quintessentially contingent.

That, indeed, was precisely the point of Alfred Marshall's mission. Continuous change, Marshall believed, meant continuous progress – continuous improvement in tastes (from alcohol to tea, flaunting ostentation to quiet enjoyment), continuous betterment in character-traits (from deceitfulness to honesty, grasping greediness to concerned altruism). Without upgrading, Marshall said, change would be kaleidoscopic and meaningless, psychologically destabilising and socially divisive. Accompanied, however, by upgrading, Marshall preached, change then becomes purposive and legitimate, economic growth the source of moral growth as well as material. Looking at the Britain of his own times, Alfred Marshall was able even then to identify the Invisible Hand of a beneficent teleology in the world around him. Looking to the future, Marshall was able to conceive of a world still further improved, bettered beyond belief by evolution powered by economics. Alfred Marshall, anxious to do good, made it his mission to contribute what little he could to that improvement and that betterment which in his view tended to convert the dismal science of self-centred cost-accounting into the ethical science of hope through change.

Notes and References

1 Introduction

1. J. M. Keynes, 'Alfred Marshall, 1842–1924', in A. C. Pigou (ed.), *Memorials of Alfred Marshall* (1925) (New York: Augustus M. Kelley, 1966), p. 37.
2. A. Marshall, Speech at the Meeting of the British Economic Association, 14 June 1893, in *Economic Journal*, Vol. III, 1893, p. 389.
3. J. Viner, 'Marshall's Economics in Relation to the Man and to his Times' (1941), in J. C. Wood (ed.), *Alfred Marshall: Critical Assessments* (London: Croom Helm, 1982), Vol. I, p. 253.
4. Keynes, 'Alfred Marshall', in *Memorials*, p. 37.
5. Ibid, p. 11.
6. Cited in ibid, pp. 2–3.
7. C. W. Guillebaud, 'Some Personal Reminiscences of Alfred Marshall' (1971), in Wood, op.cit., Vol. I, p. 95.

2 Childhood and Cambridge

1. Keynes, 'Alfred Marshall', in *Memorials*, p. 3.
2. Ibid, p. 2.
3. Cited in A. Sidgwick and E. M. Sidgwick, *Henry Sidgwick: A Memoir* (London: Macmillan, 1906), p. 137.
4. Cited in ibid, p. 201.
5. Cited in ibid, p. 62.
6. Cited in ibid, p. 68. It was apparently Dakyns, whom Marshall had met at Clifton, who introduced him to Sidgwick. See Keynes, 'Alfred Marshall', in *Memorials*, p. 5.
7. Cited in ibid, p. 198.
8. Cited in N. G. Annan, *Leslie Stephen: His Thought and Character in Relation to his Time* (London: MacGibbon & Kee, 1951), p. 199.
9. A. Marshall, Speech at the Meeting for a Sidgwick Memorial, 16 November 1900. Cited in Keynes, 'Alfred Marshall', in *Memorials*, p. 7.
10. Letter from A. Marshall to J. N. Keynes dated 4 September 1900, in Marshall Library (University of Cambridge), Keynes Letters 1 (118).
11. Keynes, 'Alfred Marshall', in *Memorials*, p. 7.
12. Ibid, pp. 7–8.

13. A. Marshall, Farewell Address on leaving Bristol, 29 September 1881. Cited in ibid, p. 16.
14. A. Marshall, 'The Future of the Working Classes' (1873), in *Memorials*, p. 104.
15. A. Marshall and Mary Paley Marshall, *The Economics of Industry*, 2nd ed. (London: Macmillan 1881), p. 45.
16. A. Marshall, *Principles of Economics* (*PE*), 8th ed. (1920) (London: Macmillan, 1949), p. 5.
17. A. Marshall, 'Social Possibilities of Economic Chivalry' (1907), in *Memorials*, p. 327.
18. *PE*, pp. 202–3.
19. Mary Paley Marshall, *What I Remember* (Cambridge: Cambridge University Press, 1947), p. 20.
20. Cited in J. K. Whitaker, *The Early Economic Writings of Alfred Marshall, 1867–1890* (London: Macmillan, 1975), Vol. I, pp. 6–7.
21. A. Marshall, 'The Present Position of Economics' (1885), in *Memorials*, p. 155.
22. *PE*, p. 116.
23. A. Marshall, undated fragment. Cited in Keynes, 'Alfred Marshall', in *Memorials*, p. 10.
24. Ibid, p. 11n.
25. A. Marshall, Letter to *The Times* of 22 August 1914, p. 7.
26. Idem.
27. A. Marshall, undated fragment. Cited in Keynes, 'Alfred Marshall', in *Memorials*, pp. 10–11.
28. A. Marshall, undated fragment, in *Memorials*, p. 360.
29. Letter from A. Marshall to James Ward dated 23 September 1900, in *Memorials*, p. 418.
30. A. Marshall, unpublished fragment, (n.d.). Cited in Whitaker, *The Early Economic Writings of Alfred Marshall*, Vol. I, p. 6.
31. Marshall, Farewell Address on leaving Bristol. Cited in Keynes, 'Alfred Marshall', in *Memorials*, p. 16.
32. Letter from A. Marshall to James Ward dated 23 September 1900, in *Memorials*, pp. 418–19.
33. Annan, *Leslie Stephen*, p. 243.
34. Keynes, 'Alfred Marshall', in *Memorials*, p. 10.
35. *PE*, p. 1. Emphasis added.
36. A. Marshall, undated fragment. Cited in Keynes, 'Alfred Marshall', in *Memorials*, p. 37–8.
37. A. Marshall, Preliminary Statement and Evidence before the Royal Commission on the Aged Poor (1893), in J. M. Keynes (ed.), *Official Papers by Alfred Marshall* (London: Macmillan, 1926), p. 205.
38. R. McWilliams-Tullberg, 'Marshall's "Tendency to Socialism"' (1975), in Wood, op.cit., Vol. I, p. 391.
39. T. W. Hutchison, 'Economists and Economic Policy in Britain After 1870', *History of Political Economy*, Vol. I, 1969, p. 255.
40. Marshall, Statement to the Royal Commission on the Aged Poor, in *Official Papers*, p. 223.

41. Ibid, p. 209.
42. Marshall, Farewell Address on leaving Bristol. Cited in Keynes, 'Alfred Marshall', in *Memorials*, p. 16.
43. H. Spencer, *Social Statics* (London: John Chapman, 1851) p. 323.
44. A. Marshall, *The New Cambridge Curriculum in Economics and Associated Branches of Political Science: Its Purpose and Plan* (London: Macmillan, 1903), p. 8.
45. Marshall, undated fragment. Cited in Keynes, 'Alfred Marshall', in *Memorials*, p. 10.
46. A. C. Pigou, 'In Memoriam: Alfred Marshall' (1924), in *Memorials*, p. 83.
47. *PE*, p. 631.
48. Marshall, 'The Future of the Working Classes', in *Memorials*, p. 118.
49. A. Marshall, 'Where to House the London Poor' (1884), in *Memorials*, p. 148.
50. Letter from A. Marshall to Mrs Bosanquet dated 2 October 1902, in *Memorials*, p. 445.
51. A. Marshall, 'Co-operation' (1889), in *Memorials*, pp. 228–9.
52. Letter from A. Marshall to Mrs Bosanquet dated 2 October 1902, in *Memorials*, p. 445.
53. *PE*, p. 470.
54. A. Marshall, 'The Old Generation of Economists and the New' (1897), in *Memorials*, p. 305.
55. R. H. Tawney, *The Acquisitive Society* (1921) (London: Collins, 1961), p. 39.
56. Letter from A. Marshall to Bishop Westcott dated 24 January 1900, in *Memorials*, p. 386.
57. Cited in R. Terrill, *R. H. Tawney and His Times* (Cambridge, Mass.: Harvard University Press, 1973), p. 66.
58. Cited in ibid, p. 36.
59. J. M. Winter and D. M. Joslin (eds), *R. H. Tawney's Commonplace Book* (1912–14) (Cambridge: Cambridge University Press, 1972), p. 46.
60. Ibid, p. 76.
61. Ibid, p. 72. Tawney became more friendly to Marshall after the appearance of *Industry and Trade*, however. See his review in the *Daily News* of 13 October 1919, where he states: 'Dr. Marshall's knowledge of the facts of industrial organisation is immense, and no reader can fail to derive both information and stimulus from his elaborate study of it.'
62. A. Marshall, 'Some Aspects of Competition' (1890), in *Memorials*, p. 282.
63. Cited in A. W. Coats, 'Sociological Aspects of British Economic Thought *circa* 1880–1930', *Journal of Political Economy*, Vol. 75, 1967, p. 718n.
64. Cited in A. W. Coats, 'Alfred Marshall and the Early Development of the London School of Economics: Some Unpublished Letters' (1967), in Wood, op.cit., Vol. IV, p. 139.
65. B. Webb, *My Apprenticeship* (London: Longmans, Green and Co., 1926), p. 442.

66. A. Marshall, Discussion of A. L. Bowley's paper 'Changes in Average Wages (Nominal and Real) 1860–1891'. *Statistical Journal*, Vol. 58, 1895, p. 280.
67. Webb, *My Apprenticeship*, p. 179.
68. Ibid, p. 180.
69. Annan, *Leslie Stephen*, p. 199.
70. J. K. Galbraith, 'Take a leading Roll', *Sunday Times*, 21 July 1985.
71. J. K. Galbraith, 'A Different Journey' (1977), in his *A View From the Stands* (London: Hamish Hamilton, 1987), p. 290.
72. See in particular his *Citizenship and Social Class and Other Essays* (Cambridge: Cambridge University Press, 1950) and D. A. Reisman, 'T. H. Marshall on the Middle Ground', in K. E. Boulding (ed.), *The Economics of Human Betterment* (London: Macmillan, 1984).
73. Marshall, 'The Future of the Working Classes', in *Memorials*, p. 102.
74. Marshall, 'Some Aspects of Competition', in *Memorials*, p. 260.
75. A. Marshall, 'Memorandum on the Fiscal Policy of International Trade' (1903), in *Official Papers*, p. 393.
76. A. Marshall, *Money Credit and Commerce* (1923) (New York: Augustus M. Kelley, 1965), p. 219.
77. A. Marshall, 'Some Features of American Industry' (1875), in Whitaker, *The Early Economic Writings of Alfred Marshall*, Vol. II, p. 364.

3 Cambridge and Bristol

1. M. Marshall, *What I Remember*, p. 11.
2. Keynes, 'Alfred Marshall', in *Memorials*, p. 15.
3. J. M. Keynes, 'Mary Paley Marshall' (1944), in his *Essays in Biography* (1951). Republished as Vol. X (London: Macmillan, 1972) of *The Collected Writings of John Maynard Keynes*, p. 233.
4. M. Marshall, *What I Remember*, p. 7.
5. Ibid, p. 3.
6. Ibid, p. 8.
7. Keynes, 'Mary Paley Marshall', in *Essays in Biography*, p. 234.
8. M. Marshall, *What I Remember*, p. 10.
9. Keynes, 'Mary Paley Marshall', in *Essays in Biography*, p. 235.
10. M. Marshall, *What I Remember*, p. 14.
11. Ibid, p. 13.
12. Ibid.
13. Letter from W. S. Jevons to his wife dated 9 December 1875. In R. D. C. Black (ed.), *Papers and Correspondence of William Stanley Jevons*, Vol. IV (London: Macmillan, 1977), p. 148.
14. M. Marshall, *What I Remember*, p. 22.
15. Ibid.
16. Letter from A. Marshall to E. R. A. Seligman dated 23 April 1900. In J. Dorfman (ed.), 'The Seligman Correspondence III', *Political Science Quarterly*, Vol. 56, 1941, p. 409.
17. Eckstein (pseud.), 'Alfred Marshall. Professor of Political Economy,

Cambridge' (1972), in Wood, op.cit., Vol. I, p. 150.
18. Letter from A. Marshall to C. Colson (*circa* 1907), in 'Alfred Marshall, the Mathematician, as Seen by Himself', *Econometrica* Vol. I, 1933, p. 222.
19. Letter from A. Marshall dated 2 May 1910. Cited in R. McWilliams-Tullberg. 'Economics of Indusrty' (1972), in Wood, op.cit., Vol. IV, p. 246.
20. H. S. Foxwell, 'The Economic Movement in England', *Quarterly Journal of Economics*, Vol. II, 1887, p. 92.
21. Review in *The Academy* of 8 November 1879. Reprinted in T. E. Cliffe Leslie, *Essays in Political Economy* (London: Longmans, Green, & Co., 1888), pp. 73–4.
22. Ibid, p. 74.
23. Ibid, p. 81.
24. Ibid, p. 82.
25. Ibid, p. 81.
26. Cited in A. Kadish, *Apostle Arnold: The Life and Death of Arnold Toynbee 1852–1883* (Durham, NC: Duke University Press, 1986), p. 86.
27. Keynes, 'Mary Paley Marshall', in *Essays in Biography*, pp. 232, 241.
28. M. Marshall, *What I Remember*, pp. 25–6.
29. Ibid, p. 19.
30. Webb, *My Apprenticeship*, pp. 350–51.
31. Ibid, p. 373.
32. Letter from A. Marshall to Louis Dumur dated 2 July 1909, in *Memorials*, pp. 459–60.
33. A. Marshall, fragment dated 19 March 1923, in *Memorials*, p. 368.
34. Keynes, 'Mary Paley Marshall', in *Essays in Biography*, p. 242.
35. Webb, op.cit., p. 352.
36. A. Marshall, 'The Province of Political Economy' (1874), in R. Harrison, 'Two Early Articles by Alfred Marshall' (1963), in Wood, op.cit., Vol. IV, p. 127.
37. Letter from A. Marshall to his mother dated 18 July 1875. In Marshall Papers (in Marshall Library, Cambridge), Letters 3(72).
38. Letter from A. Marshall to his mother dated 5 July 1875. In Marshall Papers, Letters 3(70).
39. H. M. Robertson, 'Alfred Marshall' (1976), in Wood, op.cit., Vol. I, p. 443.
40. Keynes, 'Mary Paley Marshall', in *Essays in Biography*, p. 241.
41. Cited in Sidgwick and Sidgwick, *Henry Sidgwick*, pp. 72–3.
42. S. Rothblatt, *The Revolution of the Dons: Cambridge and Society in Victorian England* (London: Faber & Faber, 1968), p. 243.
43. Letter from W. S. Jevons to J. D'Aulnis dated 7 July 1874, in Black, *Papers and Correspondence of William Stanley Jevons*, Vol. IV, p. 62.
44. Letter from W. S. Jevons to A. Marshall dated 23 June 1877, in ibid, p. 205.
45. Letter from W. S. Jevons to J. Robson dated 5 October 1875, in ibid, p. 134.
46. E. Abbott and L. Campbell, *The Life and Letters of Benjamin Jowett* (London: John Murray, 1897), Vol. II, p. 61.

47. A. Kadish, *The Oxford Economists in the Late Nineteenth Century* (Oxford: Clarendon Press, 1982), pp. 95–6.
48. Ibid, p. 87.
49. Pigou, 'In Memoriam: Alfred Marshall', in *Memorials*, p. 87.
50. Letter from Benjamin Jowett to Mary Paley Marshall dated 11 April 1887. In Marshall Papers, Letters 1 (127).
51. *PE*, p. 570.
52. Ibid, p. 165.
53. Marshall, 'The Future of the Working Classes', in *Memorials*, p. 101.
54. Cited in Keynes, 'Alfred Marshall', in *Memorials*, p. 55.
55. Letter from A. Marshall, *Western Daily Press*, 25 January 1887. Cited in J. K. Whitaker, 'Alfred Marshall: The Years 1877 to 1885' (1972), in Wood, op.cit., Vol. I, p. 121n.
56. Summary of Marshall's Lecture 'Some Aspects of Modern Industrial Life' (1877). Cited in ibid, p. 146.
57. Ibid.
58. Summary of Marshall's Lecture 'The Aims and Methods of Economic Study' (1877). Cited in ibid, p. 138.
59. Summary of Marshall's Lecture 'Some Aspects of Modern Industrial Life' (1877). Cited in ibid, p. 144.
60. Letter from A. Marshall, *Pall Mall Gazette*, 1 December 1883. Cited in A. Kadish, 'Marshall on Necessaries and Travel', *History of Economic Thought Newsletter*, No. 26, 1981, p. 17.
61. Marshall, 'Social Possibilities of Economic Chivalry', in *Memorials*, p. 324–5.
62. *PE*, p. 75.
63. M. Marshall, *What I Remember*, p. 19.
64. *PE*, p. 6.
65. Letter from A. Marshall to W. A. S. Hewins dated 12 October 1899. Cited in Coats, 'Alfred Marshall and the Early Development of the London School of Economics', in Wood, op.cit., Vol. IV, p. 135.
66. E. Cannan, 'Alfred Marshall, 1842–1924' (1924), in Wood, op.cit., Vol. I, p. 66.
67. Letter from A. Marshall to C. Colson (*circa* 1907). Cited in 'Alfred Marshall, the Mathematician, Seen by Himself', loc.cit., p. 222.
68. Keynes, 'Alfred Marshall', in *Memorials*, p. 17.
69. Eckstein, 'Alfred Marshall', in Wood, op.cit., Vol. I, p. 150.
70. Letter from A. Marshall to Bishop Westcott dated 23 January 1901, in *Memorials*, p. 397.
71. Letter from A. Marshall to A. L. Bowley dated 3 March 1901, in *Memorials*, p. 421.
72. Letter from A. Marshall to B. Mukherjee dated 22 October 1910, in *Memorials*, p. 471.
73. Letter from A. Marshall to L. Fry dated 7 November 1914, in *Memorials*, p. 484.
74. Letter from A. Marshall to F. W. Taussig dated March 1915, in *Memorials*, p. 490.
75. Letter from A. Marshall to Lord Reay dated 12 November 1909, in *Memorials*, p. 465.

76. A. Marshall, *Industry and Trade* (*IT*) (London: Macmillan, 1919), p. vi.
77. Letter from A. Marshall to H. H. Cunynghame dated 7 April 1904, in *Memorials*, p. 450.
78. Cited in Whitaker, 'Alfred Marshall: The Years 1877 to 1885', in Wood, op.cit., Vol. I, p. 103.
79. Keynes, 'Mary Paley Marshall', in *Essays in Biography*, p. 240.
80. Cited in Keynes, 'Alfred Marshall', in *Memorials*, p. 39n.
81. Ibid, p. 45n.
82. Letter from A. Marshall to J. B. Clark dated 24 March 1908, in *Memorials*, p. 417.
83. Eckstein, 'Alfred Marshall', in Wood, op.cit., Vol. I, p. 150.
84. Ibid.

4 Oxford and Cambridge

1. Letter from H. S. Foxwell to L. Walras dated 30 December 1882, in W. Jaffé (ed.), *Correspondence of Léon Walras and Related Papers* (Amsterdam: North-Holland Publishing Company, 1965), Vol. I, p. 738.
2. H. S. Foxwell, Introduction to W. S. Jevons, *Investigations in Currency and Finance* (London: Macmillan, 1884), p. xliii.
3. Foxwell, 'The Economic Movement in England', loc.cit., p. 92.
4. M. Marshall, *What I Remember*, p. 39.
5. Cited in Kadish, *The Oxford Economists in the Late Nineteenth Century*, p. 76.
6. Cited in Whitaker, *The Early Economic Writings of Alfred Marshall*, Vol. I, p. 28.
7. Cited in Kadish, *The Oxford Economists in the Late Nineteenth Century*, p. 199.
8. A. Marshall, 'Benjamin Jowett' (1893), in *Memorials*, pp. 292, 293–4.
9. M. Marshall, *What I Remember*, p. 39.
10. Annan, *Leslie Stephen*, p. 123.
11. Ibid, pp. 198, 221.
12. G. Faber, *Jowett: A Portrait with Background* (London: Faber & Faber, 1957), p. 35.
13. Keynes, 'Alfred Marshall', in *Memorials*, p. 65.
14. Ibid, p. 64.
15. Faber, *Jowett*, p. 180.
16. Letter from A. Marshall to J. N. Keynes dated 30 April 1883. Cited in Whitaker, *The Early Economic Writings of Alfred Marshall*, Vol. I, p. 22.
17. Foxwell, 'The Economic Movement in England', loc.cit., p. 93.
18. B. Jowett, 'Memoir', in A. Toynbee, *Lectures on the Industrial Revolution in England* (London: Rivingtons, 1884), p. x.
19. A. Marshall, Preface to L. L. F. R. Price, *Industrial Peace* (London: Macmillan, 1887), p. viii.
20. Cited in ibid.
21. Ibid.

22. Jowett, 'Memoir', loc.cit., p. xviii.
23. Cited in ibid, p. xxi.
24. Kadish, *Apostle Arnold*, pp. ix, x.
25. Jowett, 'Memoir', loc.cit., p. xvii.
26. A. Toynbee *'Progress and Poverty': A Criticism of Mr. Henry George* (London: Kegan Paul, Trench & Co., 1883), pp. 53–4. The original lecture was delivered *extempore* by Toynbee on 18 January 1883. The pamphlet is based on the shorthand writer's record of what was said by Toynbee only weeks before his death.
27. Toynbee, *Lectures*, p. 35.
28. Ibid, pp. 86, 87.
29. Ibid, p. 93.
30. Marshall, 'Social Possibilities of Economic Chivalry', in *Memorials*, p. 336.
31. Letter from A. Marshall to Edward Caird dated 22 October 1897, in *Memorials*, p. 398.
32. *PE*, p. 9.
33. Marshall, Preface to *Industrial Peace*, p. viii. And elsewhere he observes, no less tactfully, of Toynbee that 'economic study bears its fruit late in life; & that it may be difficult for any one to convince those who did not know him how great his promise was'. Letter from A. Marshall to H. S. Foxwell dated 30 March 1883, in Marshall Papers, Letters 3(13).
34. Toynbee, *Lectures*, p. 31.
35. Ibid, p. 121.
36. Ibid, p. 120–21.
37. Ibid, p. 144.
38. Ibid, p. 21.
39. Ibid, p. 83.
40. Ibid, p. 17.
41. Ibid.
42. Ibid, p. 145.
43. Ibid, p. 26.
44. *PE*, p. 14.
45. Cited in Kadish, *Apostle Arnold*, p. 94.
46. Cited in ibid, p. 80.
47. Toynbee, *Lectures*, p. 147.
48. *PE*, pp. 441, 75n.
49. M. Richter, *The Politics of Conscience: T. H. Green and His Age* (London: Weidenfeld & Nicolson, 1964), p. 19.
50. Ibid, p. 13.
51. Jevons, *Investigations*, p. 356.
52. Richter, *The Politics of Conscience*, p. 13.
53. The paper is reprinted in Whitaker, *The Early Economic Writings of Alfred Marshall*, Vol. II, pp. 387–393.
54. A. Marshall, lecture on 19 February 1883, as reported in the *Daily Bristol Times and Mirror* of 20 February 1883. Reprinted in G. J. Stigler. 'Alfred Marshall's Lectures on Progress and Poverty' (1969), in Wood, op.cit., Vol. IV, p. 150.
55. Cliffe Leslie, Review in *The Academy*, loc.cit., p. 73.

56. Foxwell, 'The Economic Movement in England', loc.cit., p. 92.
57. Cited in Sidgwick and Sidgwick, *Henry Sidgwick*, p. 394.
58. J. Maloney, *Marshall, Orthodoxy and the Professionalisation of Economics* (Cambridge: Cambridge University Press, 1985), pp. 1–2.
59. Letter from A. Marshall to J. N. Keynes dated 28 October (no year but the context indicates 1888), in Marshall Library, Keynes Letters 1(71). The story of Marshall's 'mini-campaign' in 1885 to persuade Keynes to apply for the vacancy at Balliol is told in detail in A. Kadish, *Historians, Economists, and Economic History* (London: Routledge, 1989), pp. 149–50. The letter of 1888 reminds the reader yet again just how tenacious Marshall could be – and how manipulative.
60. M. Marshall, *What I Remember*, p. 42.
61. Cited in ibid.
62. Keynes, 'Mary Paley Marshall', in *Essays in Biography*, p. 245.
63. M. Marshall, *What I Remember*, p. 41.
64. Ibid.
65. Ibid, p. 50.
66. W. A. S. Hewins, *The Apologia of an Imperialist* (London: Constable, 1929), Vol. I, p. 27.
67. Cited in T. Gårdlund, *The Life of Knut Wicksell* (Stockholm: Almqvist & Wiksell, 1958), p. 343.
68. Letter from A. Marshall to E. C. K. Gonner dated 9 May 1894, in *Memorials*, p. 381.
69. Ibid, p. 382.
70. A. L. Bowley, review of A. C. Pigou (ed.), *Memorials of Alfred Marshall*, *Clare Market Review*, Lent Term, 1926.
71. Keynes, 'Alfred Marshall', in *Memorials*, p. 38.
72. Ibid, p. 60n.
73. Ibid, p. 60.
74. Ibid, p. 58.
75. C. J. Hamilton, review of A. C. Pigou (ed.), *Memorials of Alfred Marshall*, *The Servant of India* (n.d.). This item, together with the review by Bowley mentioned above, may be found in Marshall's Scrapbook, in the Marshall Library, Cambridge.
76. Cited in Kadish, *The Oxford Economists in the Late Nineteenth Century*, p. 32.
77. A. Cunningham, *William Cunningham: Teacher and Priest* (London: SPCK, 1950), p. 19.
78. Cited in Kadish, 'Marshall on Necessaries and Travel', loc.cit., p. 16.
79. E. A. Benians, 'Reminiscences', in *Memorials*, p. 80.
80. Ibid, p. 78.
81. Letter from A. Marshall to E. C. K. Gonner dated 9 May 1894, in *Memorials* p. 380.
82. A. C. Pigou, *Alfred Marshall and Current Thought* (London: Macmillan, 1953), p. 4.
83. D. H. MacGregor, 'Marshall and His Book' (1942), in Wood, op.cit., Vol. II, p. 114.
84. Ibid.
85. Cited in Keynes, 'Alfred Marshall', in *Memorials*, p. 51.

86. *IT*, pp. 356–7n.
87. Letter from A. Marshall to E. C. K. Gonner dated 9 May 1894, in *Memorials*, p. 381.
88. L. L. Price, review of Marshall's *Elements of Economics of Industry* (1892), in Wood, op.cit., Vol. IV, p. 13.
89. Keynes, 'Alfred Marshall', in *Memorials*, p. 51.
90. Benians, 'Reminiscences', in *Memorials*, p. 78.
91. Letter from A. Marshall to E. C. K. Gonner dated 9 May 1894, in *Memorials*, p. 381.
92. MacGregor, 'Marshall and His Book', in Wood, op.cit., Vol. II, p. 115.
93. L. Robbins, *The Evolution of Modern Economic Theory* (London: Macmillan, 1970), p. 250.
94. Webb, *My Apprenticeship*, p. 352.
95. Ibid, p. 368.
96. Cited in Robertson, 'Alfred Marshall', in Wood, op.cit., Vol. I, p. 443.
97. Keynes, 'Alfred Marshall', in *Memorials*, p. 57.
98. Cited in R. F. Harrod, *The Life of John Maynard Keynes* (London: Macmillan, 1951), p. 117n.
99. Cited in R. H. Coase, 'Marshall on Method' (1975), in Wood, op.cit., Vol. I, p. 409.
100. Maloney, *Marshall, Orthodoxy and the Professionalisation of Economics*, pp. 64–5.

5 Economics and *Principles*

1. *The Times*, 30 May 1885, p. 10.
2. See 'Proceedings of the Forty-Third Anniversary Meeting of the Statistical Society, September 1877', *Journal of the Statistical Society*, Vol. XL, 1877, pp. 342–3 and 468–74.
3. J. K. Ingham, 'The Present Position and Prospects of Political Economy' (1878), in S. H. Patterson (ed.), *Readings in the History of Economic Thought* (New York: McGraw-Hill, 1932), p. 483.
4. Ibid, p. 481.
5. Ibid, p. 504.
6. W. Bagehot, 'The Postulates of English Political Economy' (1876), in his *Economic Studies* (London: Longmans, Green, and Co., 1880), p. 1.
7. Ibid, p. 3.
8. Ibid.
9. W. Cunningham, 'Political Economy as a Moral Science', *Mind*, Vol. III, 1878, p. 369.
10. Maloney, *Marshall, Orthodoxy and the Professionalisation of Economics*, p. 9.
11. B. Price, *Chapters on Practical Political Economy* (London: C. Kegan Paul & Co., 1878), p. 16.
12. Ibid, p. 7.
13. Ibid, pp. 15, 16.
14. Ibid, p. 6.
15. J. E. Cairnes, *Some Leading Principles of Political Economy Newly*

Expounded (London: Macmillan, 1874), p. 13.
16. Ibid, p. 47.
17. W. S. Jevons, *The Theory of Political Economy*, 2nd. ed. (1879), ed. by R. D. C. Black (Harmondsworth: Penguin Books, 1970), p. 187.
18. Ibid, p. 72.
19. W. S. Jevons, 'The Future of Political Economy', *Fortnightly Review*, Vol. XX, 1876, p. 619.
20. Ibid, p. 620.
21. H. S. Foxwell, Introduction to A. Menger, *The Right to the Whole Produce of Labour* (1886) (London: Macmillan, 1899), p. lxxviii.
22. J. S. Mill, *Principles of Political Economy* (1848), in J. M. Robson (ed.), *The Collected Works of John Stuart Mill* (Toronto: University of Toronto Press, 1965), Vol. II, p. 338.
23. A. W. Coats, 'The Historicist Reaction in English Political Economy, 1870–90', *Economica*, Vol. 21, 1954, p. 144.
24. Jevons, 'The Future of Political Economy', loc.cit., pp. 630–31.
25. Ibid, p. 627.
26. H. Spencer, *Principles of Sociology*, Vol. I (Williams & Norgate, 1876), pp. 505–6.
27. Ibid, pp. 508–9.
28. Spencer, *Social Statics*, p. 434.
29. C. Darwin, *The Origin of Species* (London: John Murray, 1859), p. 5.
30. Ibid, p. 61.
31. Ibid, p. 133.
32. Ibid, p. 460.
33. H. Spencer, *The Man Versus the State* (London: Williams & Norgate, 1884), p. 78.
34. Spencer, *Principles of Sociology*, Vol. III (London: Williams & Norgate, 1896), p. 598.
35. Spencer, *Social Statics*, p. 411.
36. C. Darwin, *The Descent of Man* (London: John Murray, 1871), Vol. I, p. 81.
37. Ibid, p. 166.
38. Ibid, p. 162.
39. Ibid, p. 163.
40. Jevons, 'The Future of Political Economy', loc.cit., p. 619.
41. T. Carlyle, *Past and Present* (London: Chapman and Hall, 1843), p. 24.
42. J. Ruskin, *'Unto This Last': Four Essays on the First Principles of Political Economy* (London: Smith, Elder and Co., 1862), p. 4.
43. Ibid, pp. 7–8.
44. Carlyle, *Past and Present*, p. 394.
45. Ruskin, *'Unto this Last'*, p. 32.
46. Ibid, pp. 1, 4.
47. Ibid, p. 119.
48. Ibid, p. 122.
49. Carlyle, *Past and Present*, pp. 6–7.
50. Ibid, p. 7.
51. Ibid, p. 6.
52. Ibid.
53. Ibid, p. 7.

54. Ibid, pp. 260–61.
55. Ibid, p. 261.
56. Ruskin, *'Unto this Last'*, p. xiii.
57. Carlyle, *Past and Present*, p. 7.
58. Ruskin, *'Unto this Last'*, pp. 173, 103.
59. Carlyle, *Past and Present*, p. 270.
60. Political Economy Club, *Revised Report of the Proceedings at the Dinner of 31st May, 1876* (London: Longmans, Green, Reader & Dyer, 1876), p. 8.
61. Ibid, p. 32.
62. Ibid, pp. 20–21.
63. Ibid, p. 26.
64. Marshall, 'The Present Position of Economics', in *Memorials*, p. 152.
65. Ibid, p. 163.
66. Ibid, p. 158.
67. Ibid, p. 164.
68. Ibid, p. 171.
69. Ibid, p. 165.
70. Ibid, p. 166.
71. Ibid, p. 168.
72. Ibid, p. 165.
73. Ibid, p. 168.
74. Ibid, p. 154.
75. *PE*, p. xii.
76. Marshall, 'The Present Position of Economics', in *Memorials*, p. 154.
77. *IT*. pp. 697–9.
78. Marshall, 'The Present Position of Economics', in *Memorials*, p. 153.
79. Ibid, p. 156.
80. Ibid.
81. Ibid, p. 158.
82. Ibid, pp. 156–7.
83. Ibid, p. 160.
84. Ibid, p. 165.
85. Ibid, p. 162.
86. Ibid, p. 135.
87. *PE*, p. 290.
88. Marshall, 'The Present Position of Economics', in *Memorials*, p. 156.
89. *PE*, p. 417.
90. Marshall, 'The Present Position of Economics', in *Memorials*, p. 163.
91. Ibid, p. 174.
92. A fuller account of this evolutionary process is provided in D. A. Reisman, *Alfred Marshall: Progress and Politics* (London: Macmillan, 1987), esp. Chapter 2.
93. *PE*, p. 6.
94. *IT*, p. vii. See also *Alfred Marshall: Progress and Politics*, Chapter 4.1.
95. F. Y. Edgeworth, 'Reminiscences', in *Memorials*, pp. 70, 71.
96. A. Marshall, Paper to the Industrial Remuneration Conference (1885), in *Industrial Remuneration Conference: The Report of the Proceedings and Papers* (London: Cassell, 1885), p. 173.
97. Unpublished note dated 7 May 1919, in Marshall Papers, Red Box 1

(3), envelope entitled 'Progress and Ideals'.

98. Ibid.

99. Unpublished note dated 4 November 1920, *locus* as above.

100. Letter from A. Marshall to Lord Reay dated 12 November 1909, in *Memorials*, p. 462.

101. Ibid, p. 464.

102. F. W. Taussig, 'Alfred Marshall' (1924), in Wood, op.cit., Vol. I, p. 74.

103. Cited in E. T. Grether, 'Alfred Marshall's Role in Price Maintenance in Great Britain' (1934), in Wood, op.cit., Vol. II, p. 58.

104. Letter from A. Marshall to Messrs Macmillan & Co. dated 12 April 1887. Cited in C. W. Guillebaud, 'The Marshall–Macmillan Correspondence over the Net Book System' (1965), in ibid, p. 253.

105. Ibid, pp. 253–4.

106. Letter from A. Marshall to F. Macmillan dated 17 September 1898. Cited in ibid, p. 269.

107. Letter from A. Marshall to F. Macmillan dated 5 March 1898. Cited in ibid, p. 264.

108. Letter from A. Marshall to F. Macmillan, n.d. (probably October 1898). Cited in ibid, p. 269.

109. Letter from A. Marshall to F. Macmillan dated 17 September 1898. Cited in ibid, p. 268.

110. Letter from A. Marshall to Bishop Westcott dated 26 October 1899, in *Memorials*, p. 385.

111. A. Marshall, note dated 1 October 1887. Cited in Whitaker, *The Early Economic Writings of Alfred Marshall*, Vol. I, p. 89.

112. Letter from A. Marshall to J. N. Keynes dated 2 December 1889, in Marshall Library, Keynes Letters 1 (93).

113. C. W. Guillebaud, 'The Evolution of Marshall's *Principles of Economics*' (1942), in Wood, op.cit., Vol. II, p. 166.

114. J. A. Schumpeter, *History of Economic Analysis* (London: George Allen & Unwin, 1954), p. 833.

115. Cited in Webb, *My Apprenticeship*, p. 410.

116. All the reviews mentioned in this section may be found in Marshall's Scrapbook, in the Marshall Library.

117. Cited in Maloney, *Marshall, Orthodoxy and the Professionalisation of Economics*, p. 80.

118. Schumpeter, *History of Economic Analysis*, p. 836.

119. Cited in Sidgwick and Sidgwick, *Henry Sidgwick*, p. 100.

120. Letter from A. Marshall to H. S. Foxwell dated 22 July 1883. Cited in Stigler, 'Alfred Marshall's Lectures on Progress and Poverty', in Wood, op.cit., Vol. IV, p. 191n.

121. A. Marshall, 'A Reply', *Economic Journal*, Vol. II, 1892, p. 518.

122. Letter from A. Marshall, *The Times*, 23 November 1903, p. 10.

123. Letter from A. Marshall to A. C. Pigou dated 17 June 1902, in *Memorials*, p. 432.

124. Cited in Gårdlund, *The Life of Knut Wicksell*, p. 343.

125. Letter from A. Marshall to F. Y. Edgeworth dated 27 April 1909, in *Memorials*, p. 442.

126. *IT*, p. ix.

127. Maloney, *Marshall, Orthodoxy and the Professionalisation of Economics*, p. 52.
128. Letter from A. Marshall to J. B. Clark dated 24 March 1908, in *Memorials*, p. 418.
129. Edgeworth, 'Reminiscences', in *Memorials*, p. 67.
130. Keynes, 'Alfred Marshall', in *Memorials*, p. 48.
131. Ibid, pp. 32, 33n.
132. Ibid, p. 37.
133. Letter from A. Marshall, *The Times*, 25 January 1889, p. 13.
134. Letter from A. Marshall, *The Times*, 19 August 1910, p. 4.
135. Letter from A. Marshall, *The Times*, 22 August 1914, p. 7.
136. Letter from T. E. Page, *The Times*, 25 August 1914, p. 7.
137. Letter from 'Union Jack', *The Times*, 25 August 1914, p. 7.
138. Letter from A. Marshall, *The Times*, 26 August 1914, p. 9.
139. Ibid.
140. Letter from A. Marshall, *The Times*, 29 December 1915, p. 9.
141. See the letter from A. Marshall to E. Cannan dated 7 January 1898, in *Memorials*, pp. 404–6.
142. See on this Guillebaud, 'The Evolution of Marshall's *Principles of Economics*', in Wood, op.cit., Vol. II, pp. 179–80.
143. See Chapter 7 of the present book.
144. Letter from A. Marshall to H. H. Cunynghame dated 28 June 1904, in *Memorials*, p. 451.
145. Letter from A. Marshall to A. W. Flux dated 19 March 1904, in *Memorials*, p. 408.
146. Letter from A. Marshall to J. Bonar dated 4 February 1891, in *Memorials*, p. 374.
147. Letter from A. Marshall to E. C. K. Gonner dated 9 May 1894, in *Memorials*, p. 382.
148. Ibid, p. 383.
149. Pigou, 'In Memoriam: Alfred Marshall', in *Memorials*, p. 85.
150. H. S. Jevons, review of Marshall's *Industry and Trade* (1920), in Wood, op.cit., Vol. IV, p. 21.
151. Maloney, *Marshall, Orthodoxy and the Professionalisation of Economics*, p. 62.
152. Pigou, 'In Memoriam: Alfred Marshall', in *Memorials*, p. 85.
153. A. Marshall, 'Mr. Mill's Theory of Value' (1876), in *Memorials*, p. 121.
154. Pigou, 'In Memoriam: Alfred Marshall', in *Memorials*, p. 86.
155. Keynes, 'Alfred Marshall', in *Memorials*, pp. 46, 48.
156. Pigou, 'In Memoriam: Alfred Marshall', in *Memorials*, p. 85.
157. D. H. Robertson, *Economic Commentaries* (London: Staples Press, 1956), p. 17.
158. Cited in Coats, 'Sociological Aspects', loc.cit., p. 722.
159. W. A. Weisskopf, *The Psychology of Economics* (London: Routledge & Kegan Paul, 1955), p. 163n.
160. Ibid, p. 168.
161. Letter from A. Marshall to Lord Reay dated 12 November 1909, in *Memorials*, p. 461.
162. Letter from A. Marshall to Beatrice Potter dated 11 July 1891, in

Marshall Library, Letters 3 (91).
163. Edgeworth, 'Reminiscences', in *Memorials*, p. 73.
164. Keynes, 'Alfred Marshall', in *Memorials*, p. 47.
165. T. W. Hutchison, *A Review of Economic Doctrines 1870–1929* (Oxford: Clarendon Press, 1953), p. 62.
166. Robbins, *The Evolution of Modern Economic Theory*, p. 215n.
167. L. Robbins, *Autobiography of an Economist* (London: Macmillan, 1971), pp. 105–6.
168. *PE*, p. vii.
169. Ibid, p. 339n.
170. Ibid, p. viii.
171. Ibid, p. 224.
172. G. J. Stigler, *Production and Distribution Theories* (1941) (New York: Agathon Press, 1968), p. 63.
173. *PE*, p. 56n.
174. Stigler, *Production and Distribution Theories*, p. 63.
175. Ibid, p. 61.
176. Keynes, 'Alfred Marshall', in *Memorials*, pp. 45, 47.
177. Letter from L. Walras to V. Pareto dated 12 March 1892, in Jaffé, *Correspondence of Léon Walras*, Vol. II, pp. 486–7.
178. Cannan, 'Alfred Marshall 1842–1924', in Wood, op.cit., Vol. I, p. 70.
179. A. W. Coats, 'The Rule of Authority in the Development of British Economics', *Journal of Law and Economics*, Vol. 7, 1964, p. 96.
180. Schumpeter, *History of Economic Analysis*, pp. 838–9.
181. Ibid, p. 924.
182. Ibid, p. 839.
183. Ibid.
184. Letter from A. Marshall to J. B. Clark dated 24 March 1908, in *Memorials*, p. 416.
185. Marshall, 'Mr. Mill's Theory of Value', in *Memorials*, p. 119.
186. Robbins, *The Evolution of Modern Economic Theory*, p. 64.
187. *PE*, p. v.

6 The Evolution of the *Principles*

1. Letter from A. Marshall to C. Colson (*circa* 1907), in 'Alfred Marshall, the Mathematician, as Seen by Himself', loc.cit., p. 221.
2. A. Marshall, undated note (*circa* 1904). Cited in Whitaker, *The Early Economic Writings of Alfred Marshall*, Vol. I, p. 50n.
3. Letter from A. Marshall to J. B. Clark dated 24 March 1908, in *Memorials*, p. 416.
4. Schumpeter, *History of Economic Analysis*, p. 838.
5. R. S. Howey, *The Rise of the Marginal Utility School 1870–1889* (Lawrence: University of Kansas Press, 1960), p. 88.
6. Hewins, *The Apologia of An Imperialist*, Vol. I, p. 27.
7. The paper may be found in Whitaker, *The Early Economic Writings of Alfred Marshall*, Vol. I, pp. 119–159.
8. Mill, *Principles of Political Economy*, Vol. II, p. 242.

9. Ibid, Vol. III, p. 475.
10. Ibid, p. 930.
11. Ibid, pp. 947–8.
12. Ibid, p. 942.
13. Ibid, p. 705.
14. Ibid, p. 754.
15. Book IV, Chapter 7, in ibid, pp. 758–96.
16. Marshall, 'The Future of the Working Classes', in *Memorials*, pp. 101–18.
17. Letter from A. Marshall to H. S. Foxwell dated 14 April 1897, in Marshall Library, Letters 3 (32).
18. A. Marshall, 'Lecture notes on Mill Book IV' (probably early 1870s), in Marshall Library, Papers, Box 5 (2).
19. A. Marshall, undated note (*circa* 1904). Cited in Whitaker, *The Early Economic Writings of Alfred Marshall*, Vol. I, p. 50n.
20. *PE*, p. 416.
21. Jevons, *Theory of Political Economy*, p. 72.
22. *PE*, p. 671.
23. Ibid, p. 672.
24. Ibid, p. 417.
25. Ibid, p. 671.
26. Ibid, p. 670.
27. Ibid, p. 79n.
28. D. Ricardo, *On the Principles of Political Economy and Taxation*, (1817), ed. by P. Sraffa and M. H. Dobb, in *The Works And Correspondence of David Ricardo* (Cambridge: Cambridge University Press, 1951), Vol. I, p. 11.
29. Ibid, p. 20.
30. Ibid, p. 12.
31. Ibid.
32. *PE*, p. 671.
33. Ricardo, *Principles* p. 382.
34. Jevons, *Theory of Political Economy*, p. 217.
35. G. F. Shove, 'The Place of Marshall's *Principles* in the Development of Economic Theory' (1942), in Wood, op.cit., Vol. II, p. 133.
36. See D. A. Reisman, *The Economics of Alfred Marshall* (London: Macmillan, 1986), pp. 59–64.
37. Ibid, pp. 176–184.
38. Ibid, pp. 181–2.
39. Robbins, *The Evolution of Modern Economic Theory*, p. 204n.
40. Reisman, *The Economics of Alfred Marshall*, pp. 45–50.
41. Schumpeter, *History of Economic Analysis*, p. 837.
42. Marshall, 'Mr. Mill's Theory of Value', in *Memorials*, p. 121.
43. Whitaker, *The Early Economic Writings of Alfred Marshall*, Vol. I, p. 50.
44. Cited in Cannan, 'Alfred Marshall', in Wood, op.cit., Vol. I, p. 67.
45. *PE*, p. 626.
46. Schumpeter, *History of Economic Analysis*, p. 835. See also MacGregor, 'Marshall and His Book', in Wood, op.cit., Vol. II, p. 126.

47. *PE*, p. 626.
48. See, for instance, ibid, p. 628n.
49. Ibid, p. 449.
50. Letter from A. Marshall to A. L. Bowley dated 21 February 1901, in *Memorials*, p. 420.
51. Undated fragment, in *Memorials*, p. 358.
52. *PE*, pp. 626–7.
53. Ibid, p. 484n.
54. Schumpeter, *History of Economic Analysis*, p. 835.
55. Unpublished note dated 17 October 1902, in Marshall Papers, Red Box 1 (3).
56. A. Smith, *The Wealth of Nations* (1776), ed. by E. Cannan (London: Methuen, 1961), Vol. I, p. 127.
57. *PE*, p. 75n.
58. Smith, *The Wealth of Nations*, Vol. II, p. 308.
59. Letter from A. Marshall to Louis Dumur dated 2 July 1909, in *Memorials*, p. 459.
60. *PE*, p. 624.
61. Ibid.
62. Ibid, p. 629.
63. Smith, *The Wealth of Nations*, Vol. I, pp. 63–4.
64. Ibid, Vol. II, p. 30.
65. Ibid, Vol. I, p. 186.
66. Ibid, Vol. I, p. 62.
67. Ibid, Vol. I, p. 65.
68. A. Smith, *Lectures on Justice, Police, Revenue and Arms* (1762–3), ed. by E. Cannan (Oxford: Clarendon Press, 1896), pp. 176–7.
69. S. von Pufendorf, *Of the Law of Nature and Nations* (1672) (London: J. Walthoe *et al.*, 1729), p. 466.
70. F. Hutcheson, *A System of Moral Philosophy* (Glasgow: R. and A. Foulis, 1755), Vol. II, p. 54.
71. Smith, *The Wealth of Nations*, Vol. I, p. 192.
72. A. Marshall, lecture on 5 March 1883, as reported in the *Daily Bristol Times and Mirror* of 6 March 1883. Reprinted in Stigler, 'Alfred Marshall's Lectures on Progress and Poverty', in Wood, op.cit., Vol. IV, p. 173.
73. Smith, *The Wealth of Nations*, Vol. I, pp. 297, 368.
74. *PE*, p. 240.
75. A. Marshall, 'The Pure Theory of Foreign Trade' (*circa* 1876), in Whitaker, *The Early Economic Writings of Alfred Marshall*, Vol. II, p. 49.
76. *PE*, p. 178.
77. Cited in Maloney, *Marshall, Orthodoxy and the Professionalisation of Economics*, p. 206.
78. A. Marshall, letter dated 20 October 1889, correspondent not known. Cited in Whitaker, *The Early Economic Writings of Alfred Marshall*, Vol. I, p. 52.
79. A. Marshall, lecture on 19 February 1883, as reported in the *Daily Bristol Times and Mirror* of 20 February 1883. Reprinted in Stigler,

'Alfred Marshall's Lectures on Progress and Poverty', in Wood, op.cit., Vol. IV, p. 149.
80. Lectures on Socialism and the Functions of Government (1886), Marshall Papers, Box 5, 1E.
81. *PE*, p. 488.
82. Ibid.
83. Ibid.
84. Ibid, p. 487.
85. Letter from A. Marshall to H. S. Foxwell dated 12 February 1906, in Marshall Papers, Letters 3 (49).
86. Maloney, *Marshall, Orthodoxy and the Professionalisation of Economics*, p. 209.
87. Ibid, p. 208.
88. Schumpeter, *History of Economic Analysis*, p. 834.
89. Letter from A. Marshall to E. R. A. Seligman dated 6 April 1896, in Dorfman, 'The Seligman Correspondence', loc.cit., p. 407.
90. *PE*, p. ix.
91. Letter from A. Marshall to C. Colson (*circa* 1907), in 'Alfred Marshall, the Mathematician, as Seen by Himself', loc.cit., p. 222.
92. Letter from A. Marshall to J. B. Clark dated 2 July 1900, in *Memorials*, p. 413.
93. Letter from A. Marshall to L. Walras dated 1 November 1883, in Jaffé, *Correspondence of Léon Walras*, Vol. I, p. 794.
94. *PE*, pp. viii–ix.
95. A. A. Cournot, *Researches into the Mathematical Principles of the Theory of Wealth* (1838), tr. by N. T. Bacon, with an Essay on Cournot and Mathematical Economics by I. Fisher (New York: Macmillan, 1927), p. 50.
96. Ibid, p. 149.
97. Ibid, p. 68.
98. Ibid, p. 11.
99. Ibid, p. 140.
100. Ibid, p. 141.
101. Ibid, p. 127.
102. A. Marshall, undated fragment, in *Memorials*, p. 359.
103. *PE*, p. 453.
104. Cournot, *Researches*, p. 4.
105. Ibid.
106. Ibid, p. 2.
107. Ibid, p. 5.
108. A. Marshall, manuscript note *circa* 1882. Cited in Whitaker, *The Early Economic Writings of Alfred Marshall*, Vol. I, p. 85.
109. See *IT*, p. 399n.
110. *PE*, p. viii.
111. L. Walras, *Elements of Pure Economics* 2nd. ed. (1889), tr. by W. Jaffé (London: George Allen & Unwin Ltd., 1954), p. 483.
112. Letter from A. Marshall to A. W. Flux dated 7 March 1898, in *Memorials*, pp. 406–7.
113. Ibid.

114. A. Marshall, 'Distribution and Exchange' (1898), in *Principles of Economics*, 9th (variorum) ed., edited by C. W. Guillebaud (London: Macmillan, 1961), Vol. II: Notes, p. 69n.
115. Letter from A. Marshall to J. B. Clark dated 2 July 1900, in *Memorials*, p. 413.
116. A. Marshall, undated fragment, in *Memorials*, pp. 359–60.
117. Letter from A. Marshall to J. B. Clark dated 2 July 1900, in *Memorials*, p. 412.
118. A. Marshall, manuscript note dated 11 December 1919. Cited in Whitaker (ed.), *The Early Economic Writings of Alfred Marshall*, Vol. II, p. 249n.
119. A. Marshall, undated fragment, in *Memorials*, p. 360.
120. J. H. von Thünen, *The Isolated State*, Part II (1850), in B. W. Dempsey, *The Frontier Wage* (Chicago: Loyola University Press, 1960), p. 193.
121. Marshall, 'Distribution and Exchange', in *Principles*, Vol. II, p. 232.
122. Stigler, *Production and Distribution Theories*, p. 344.
123. Letter from A. Marshall to J. B. Clark dated 2 July 1900, in *Memorials*, pp. 412–13.
124. Marshall, 'Distribution and Exchange', in *Principles*, Vol. II, pp. 232–3.
125. Von Thünen, *The Isolated State*, p. 307.
126. Letter from A. Marshall to J. N. Keynes. Cited in Coase, 'Marshall on Method', in Wood, op.cit., Vol. I, p. 413.
127. Von Thünen, *The Isolated State*, p. 203.
128. *PE*, p. 433n.
129. Von Thünen, *The Isolated State*, p. 255.
130. *PE*, p. 433.
131. Ibid, p. 332n.
132. Ibid, p. 120n.
133. Ibid, p. 366n.
134. Von Thünen, *The Isolated State*, p. 312.
135. Ibid.
136. *PE*, p. 429.
137. Ibid, p. 336.
138. Von Thünen, *The Isolated State*, p. 272.
139. Ibid, p. 306.
140. *PE*, p. iv.
141. A. Marshall, undated fragment, in *Memorials*, p. 360.
142. A. Marshall, notes on von Thünen (*circa* 1868–81), in Whitaker, *The Early Economic Writings of Alfred Marshall*, Vol. II, p. 251.
143. *PE*, p. 433n.
144. Von Thünen, *The Isolated State*, p. 265.
145. Ibid.
146. Ibid, p. 267.
147. Ibid, p. 266.
148. Ibid, p. 233.
149. Ibid, p. 313.
150. Ibid, p. 219.

151. Ibid, p. 316.
152. Ibid, p. 340.
153. A. Marshall, undated fragment, in *Memorials*, p. 360.
154. Von Thünen, *The Isolated State*, p. 222.
155. Ibid, p. 316.
156. Ibid, p. 315.
157. Ibid, p. 325.
158. Ibid, p. 340.
159. Ibid, p. 337.
160. Ibid.
161. Ibid, pp. 336–7.
162. Ibid, p. 340.
163. Ibid.
164. Ibid.
165. Ibid.
166. Ibid, p. 208.
167. Ibid, p. 329.
168. Marshall, 'Social Possibilities of Economic Chivalry', in *Memorials*, p. 331.
169. *PE*, p. 621.
170. Ibid, p. 470.
171. Von Thünen, *The Isolated State*, p. 313.
172. Ibid.
173. Ibid, p. 356n.
174. Ibid, p. 328.
175. Letter from A. Marshall to E. R. A. Seligman dated 21 October 1896, in Dorfman, 'The Seligman Correspondence', loc.cit., p. 408.
176. See Whitaker, *The Early Economic Writings of Alfred Marshall*, Vol. I, p. 49n.
177. Letter from A. Marshall to E. R. A. Seligman dated 21 October 1896, in Dorfman, 'The Seligman Correspondence', loc.cit., p. 408.
178. Letter from A. Marshall to J. B. Clark dated 11 November 1902, in *Memorials*, p. 414.
179. *Principles*, Vol. II, p. 263. The passage was deleted from the 4th edition onwards.
180. *PE*, p. 85n.
181. Ibid.
182. Hutchison, *A Review of Economic Doctrines*, p. 64.
183. Letter from A. Marshall to C. Colson (*circa* 1907), in 'Alfred Marshall, the Mathematician, as Seen by Himself', loc.cit., p. 221.
184. A. Marshall, undated fragment, in *Memorials*, p. 99.
185. Letter from A. Marshall to F. Y. Edgeworth dated 28 April 1892, in Marshall Papers, Letters 3 (61).
186. A. Marshall, undated fragment, in *Memorials*, pp. 99, 100.
187. Marshall, 'Mr. Mill's Theory of Value', in *Memorials*, p. 128n.
188. Schumpeter, *History of Economic Analysis*, p. 475.
189. Letter from A. Marshall to J. N. Keynes dated 8 December 1888, in Marshall Library, Keynes Letters 1 (85).
190. Keynes, 'Alfred Marshall', in *Memorials*, p. 23.

191. Letter from A. Marshall to E. R. A. Seligman dated 13 May 1900, in Dorfman, 'The Seligman Correspondence', loc.cit., p. 710.
192. A. Marshall, 'Mr. Jevons' Theory of Political Economy' (1872), in *Memorials*, p. 95.
193. Ibid, p. 99.
194. Ibid, p. 96.
195. Ibid, p. 95.
196. Ibid, p. 93.
197. Letter from W. S. Jevons to H. S. Foxwell dated 14 November 1879, in Black, *Papers and Correspondence of William Stanley Jevons*, Vol. V, p. 80.
198. Ibid.
199. Letter from A. Marshall to L. Walras dated 1 November 1883, in Jaffé, *Correspondence of Léon Walras*, Vol. I, p. 794.
200. Howey, *The Rise of the Marginal Utility School*, p. 87.
201. Marshall, 'The Present Position of Economics', in *Memorials*, p. 163.
202. Howey, *The Rise of the Marginal Utility School*, p. 80.
203. G. L. S. Shackle, *The Years of High Theory* (Cambridge: Cambridge University Press, 1967), p. 124.
204. Letter from A. Marshall to C. Colson (*circa* 1907), in 'Alfred Marshall, the Mathematician, as Seen by Himself', loc.cit., p. 222.
205. Eckstein, 'Alfred Marshall', in Wood, op.cit., Vol. I, p. 150.
206. Letter from A. Marshall to L. Walras dated 1 November 1883, in Jaffé, *Correspondence of Léon Walras*, Vol. I, p. 794.
207. Letter from M. Pantaleoni to L. Walras dated 8 August 1889, in ibid, Vol. III, p. 341.
208. Letter from W. S. Jevons to H. S. Foxwell dated 14 November 1875, in Black, *Papers and Correspondence of William Stanley Jevons*, Vol. V, p. 80.
209. Letter from H. S. Foxwell to W. S. Jevons dated 12 November 1879, in ibid, p. 78.
210. Foxwell, 'The Economic Movement in England', loc.cit., pp. 88, 92. Emphasis added.
211. Jevons, *Theory of Political Economy*, p. 65.
212. Letter from W. S. Jevons to A. Marshall dated 12 May 1879, in Black, *Papers and Correspondence of William Stanley Jevons*, Vol. V, p. 63.
213. Edgeworth, 'Reminiscences', in *Memorials*, p. 66.
214. Letter from W. S. Jevons to H. S. Foxwell dated 7 February 1875, in Black, *Papers and Correspondence of William Stanley Jevons*, Vol. IV, p. 101.
215. Letter from W. S. Jevons to H. S. Foxwell dated 14 November 1879, in ibid, Vol. V, p. 80.
216. Jevons, *Theory of Political Economy*, p. 96.
217. Ibid, p. 106.
218. Ibid, p. 111.
219. Ibid, p. 221.
220. Ibid, p. 170.
221. Ibid, p. 85.
222. Ibid.

223. Ibid, p. 174.
224. Ibid, p. 85.
225. Ibid, p. 126.
226. Ibid, p. 138.
227. Ibid, p. 139.
228. Ibid, p. 170.
229. Ibid, p. 78.
230. Ibid.
231. Ibid, p. 80.
232. Ibid, p. 90.
233. Schumpeter, *History of Economic Analysis*, p. 835.
234. Jevons, *Theory of Political Economy*, p. 90.
235. Ibid, p. 88.
236. *PE*, p. vii.
237. Jevons, *Theory of Political Economy*, p. 119.
238. Ibid, p. 186.
239. Ibid, p. 77.
240. See Reisman, *The Economics of Alfred Marshall*, esp. Chapter 3.2 and 11.2.
241. Jevons, *Theory of Political Economy*, p. 137.
242. Ibid, p. 134.
243. Ibid, p. 171.
244. Ibid, p. 134.
245. *PE*, p. 488.
246. Jevons, *Theory of Political Economy*, p. 197.
247. Ibid, p. 188.
248. Ibid, p. 91.
249. Ibid, pp. 170–71.
250. Ibid, p. 138.
251. *PE*, p. 287.
252. Marshall, 'Mr. Jevons' Theory of Political Economy', in *Memorials*, p. 95.
253. Letter from A. Marshall to C. Colson (*circa* 1907), in 'Alfred Marshall, the Mathematician, as Seen by Himself', loc.cit., p. 222.
254. *PE*, p. 77n.
255. Letter from A. Marshall to E. Cannan dated 7 January 1898, in *Memorials*, pp. 404–5.
256. Letter from A. Marshall to J. B. Clark dated 24 March 1908, in *Memorials*, pp. 416, 417.
257. See F. A. von Hayek, 'Introduction' to C. Menger, *Principles of Economics* (1871), tr. by J. Dingwall and B. F. Hoselitz (New York: New York University Press, 1976), p. 26.
258. Menger, *Principles*, p. 116.
259. Ibid, p. 115.
260. Ibid, p. 121.
261. Ibid, p. 149.
262. Ibid, p. 147.
263. Ibid, p. 246.
264. Ibid, p. 88.

265. Ibid, p. 125.
266. *PE*, p. 79n.
267. Menger, *Principles*, p. 123.
268. Ibid, p. 142.
269. *PE*, p. 379n.
270. Menger, *Principles*, p. 86.
271. *PE*, p. 484n.
272. Ibid.
273. Ibid, p. 485n.
274. Ibid, p. 69n.
275. Ibid, p. 299.
276. Menger, *Principles*, p. 148.
277. Marshall and Marshall, *The Economics of Industry*, p. 37.
278. Ibid.
279. Menger, *Principles*, p. 199.
280. Ibid, p. 186.
281. See L. Walras, *Eléments d'économie politique pure* (Lausanne: Corbaz, 1874), p. 65. Marshall's personal copy of this book is kept in the Marshall Library, Cambridge. Professor Whitaker was the first to draw attention to its existence: he also suggests that the copy might be the one which Walras sent Marshall in October 1883. There is no complete catalogue of the books in Marshall's possession at the time of his death.
282. Letter from A. Marshall to W. A. S. Hewins dated 12 October 1899. Cited in Coats, 'Alfred Marshall and the Early Development of the London School of Economics', in Wood, op.cit., Vol. IV, p. 133. Coats' conclusion, that there is no evidence of such contact in 1873, is supported by other authors. See in particular J. K. Whitaker and K. O. Kymn, 'Did Walras communicate with Marshall in 1873?', *Revista Internazionale di Scienze Economiche e Commerciali*, Vol. XXIII, 1976, pp. 385–9. The consensus seems to be that the correspondence only began in 1883, petering out some six years later. The absence of letters from Walras to Marshall in the Marshall Papers suggests that Marshall did not regard the exchange of views as particularly rewarding: he appears to have kept all letters that he felt to have contained something of interest.
283. Eckstein, 'Alfred Marshall', in Wood, op.cit., Vol. I, p. 150.
284. Walras, *Elements*, p. 206.
285. Ibid, p. 207n.
286. *PE*, p. 676.
287. Walras, *Elements*, p. 47.
288. Ibid, p. 202.
289. Ibid, p. 385.
290. Robbins, *The Evolution of Modern Economic Theory*, p. 25.
291. Keynes, 'Alfred Marshall', in *Memorials*, p. 18.
292. Guillebaud, 'The Evolution of Marshall's *Principles of Economics*', in Wood, op.cit., Vol. II, p. 166.
293. C. W. Guillebaud, 'The Variorum Edition of Alfred Marshall's *Principles of Economics*' (1961), in ibid, Vol. II, p. 210.
294. A. J. Youngson, 'Marshall on Economic Growth' (1956), in ibid, Vol. IV, p. 95.

295. Keynes, 'Alfred Marshall', in *Memorials*, p. 18.
296. *PE*, p. 84n.
297. *Principles*, Vol. II, p. 45. Also in *PE*, p. xi.
298. Letter from A. Marshall to F. Macmillan dated 31 May 1919, in Marshall Papers, Letters 7 (65).
299. Letter from A. Marshall to C. R. Fay dated 23 February 1915, in *Memorials*, p. 490.
300. Shackle, *The Years of High Theory*, p. 5.
301. Ibid, p. v.
302. Keynes, 'Alfred Marshall', in *Memorials*, p. 36.
303. F. Y. Edgeworth, review of *Money Credit and Commerce* (1923), in Wood, op.cit., Vol. IV, p. 27.
304. Guillebaud, 'The Evolution of Marshall's *Principles of Economics*', in ibid, Vol. II, p. 167.
305. Ibid, p. 181.
306. Ibid, p. 184n.
307. Ibid, p. 170.
308. Ibid, p. 168.
309. *Principles*, Vol. II, p. 343 and *PE*, p. 263. Emphasis added.
310. Guillebaud, 'The Evolution of Marshall's *Principles of Economics*', in Wood, op.cit., Vol. II, p. 184.
311. *Principles*, Vol. II, p. 40.
312. *PE*, p. xii.
313. *PE*, p. vii.
314. *PE*, p. 1.

7 Beyond the *Principles*

1. Letter from A. Marshall dated 2 May 1910. Cited in McWilliams-Tullberg, 'Economics of Industry', in Wood, op.cit., Vol. IV, p. 246.
2. A. Marshall, *Elements of Economics of Industry* (London: Macmillan, 1892), p. v.
3. Ibid.
4. Letter from A. Marshall to H. S. Foxwell dated 14 April 1897, in Marshall Papers, Letters 3 (32).
5. Both reviews may be found in Marshall's Scrapbook, in the Marshall Library.
6. *IT*, p. v.
7. *PE*, p. xi.
8. *IT*, p. vii.
9. *PE*, p. 187.
10. Ibid, p. 157n.
11. Ibid, p. 586.
12. Cited in Maloney, *Marshall, Orthodoxy and the Professionalisation of Economics*, p. 72.
13. Cited in Anne Ashley, *William James Ashley: A Life* (London: P. S. King & Son, 1932), p. 103n.
14. Edgeworth, review of *Money Credit and Commerce*, in Wood, op.cit., Vol. IV, p. 22.

15. Letter from A. Marshall to E. R. A. Seligman dated 29 March 1899, in Dorfman, 'The Seligman Correspondence', loc.cit., p. 408.
16. *IT*, p. vi.
17. Keynes, 'Alfred Marshall', in *Memorials*, p. 28.
18. Ibid, p. 21. In *MCC* (p. 330) Marshall mentions 1869–73 as the date of composition of much of 'The Pure Theory of Foreign Trade'.
19. Ibid, p. 52.
20. *IT*, p. vii.
21. Marshall, Statement to the Royal Commission on the Aged Poor, in *Official Papers*, p. 99.
22. Ibid, p. 217.
23. *MCC*, p. 234.
24. Letter from A. Marshall to W. H. Dawson dated 5 June 1916, in Marshall Papers, Letters 3 (4).
25. *MCC*, p. vi.
26. Cited in Ashley, *William James Ashley*, p. 137.
27. *PE*, p. 210n.
28. Cited in R. L. Smyth, 'The History of Section F of the British Association 1835–1970', in N. Kaldor (ed.), *Conflicts in Policy Objectives* (Oxford: Basil Blackwell, 1971), p. 156.
29. Cited in O. J. R. Howarth, *The British Association for the Advancement of Science: A Retrospect 1831–1921* (London: British Association, 1922), p. 87.
30. Cited in 'Proceedings of the Forty-Third Anniversary Meeting of the Statistical Society, September 1877', loc.cit., pp. 342–3.
31. Royal Statistical Society, *Annals of the Royal Statistical Society 1834–1934* (London: Royal Statistical Society, 1934), p. 234.
32. Cited in A. W. Coats, 'The Origins and Early Development of the Royal Economic Society', *Economic Journal*, Vol. 78, 1968, p. 352.
33. Cited in Kadish, *The Oxford Economists in the Late Nineteenth Century*, p. 184.
34. Cited in ibid, p. 186.
35. Cited in Smyth, 'The History of Section F', loc.cit., p. 168.
36. Maloney, *Marshall, Orthodoxy and the Professionalisation of Economics*, p. 65.
37. 'The British Economic Association', *Economic Journal*, Vol. I, 1891, p. 5.
38. Ibid, pp. 4–5.
39. Cited in J. M. Keynes, 'The Society's Jubilee 1890–1940', *Economic Journal* Vol. 50, 1940, p. 403.
40. 'The British Economic Association', loc.cit., p. 5.
41. Letter from H. Higgs to H. S. Foxwell dated 20 June 1890. Cited in the Supplementary Note by Clara Collett to the Obituary of Henry Higgs, *Economic Journal*, Vol. 50, 1940, pp. 359–60.
42. Cited in Coats, 'The Origins and Early Development of the Royal Economic Society', loc.cit., p. 359.
43. Letter from A. Marshall to J. Bonar dated 25 July 1890, in Keynes, 'The Society's Jubilee', loc.cit., p. 404.
44. 'The British Economic Association', loc.cit., p. 8.
45. Letter from A. Marshall to T. H. Elliott dated 25 May 1906, in Marshall Papers, Letters 1 (13).

46. Editorial Note, *Economic Journal*, Vol. I, 1890, pp. 1–2.
47. Letter from Léon Walras to Luigi Perozzo dated 13 October 1889, in Jaffé, *Correspondence of Léon Walras*, Vol. II, p. 359.
48. J. M. Keynes, 'Francis Ysidro Edgeworth' (1926), in *Essay in Biography*, p. 255.
49. See Robbins, *The Evolution of Modern Economic Theory*, p. 196.
50. Schumpeter, *History of Economic Analysis*, p. 831.
51. Keynes, 'Francis Ysidro Edgeworth', in *Essays in Biography*, p. 266.
52. Ibid.
53. Cited in J. Creedy, *Edgeworth and the Development of Neoclassical Economics* (Oxford: Basil Blackwell, 1986), p. 19.
54. Cited in Keynes, 'Francis Ysidro Edgeworth', in *Essays in Biography*, p. 265.
55. Ibid, p. 257.
56. Ibid, p. 264.
57. Ibid, p. 265.
58. Creedy, *Edgeworth*, p. 10.
59. Cited in Kadish, *The Oxford Economists in the Late Nineteenth Century*, p. 197.
60. Cited in Creedy, *Edgeworth*, p. 11.
61. L. L. Price, cited in ibid.
62. See Kadish, *The Oxford Economists in the Late Nineteenth Century*, p. 202.
63. Cited in Creedy, *Edgeworth*, p. 11.
64. G. M. Koot, *English Historical Economics, 1870–1926* (Cambridge: Cambridge University Press, 1987), p. 92.
65. Letter from A. Marshall to J. N. Keynes dated 30 January 1902, in Marshall Library, Keynes Letters 1 (125).
66. Letter from A. Marshall to A. L. Bowley dated March 1901. Cited in Creedy, *Edgeworth*, p. 16.
67. A. Marshall, review of *Mathematical Psychics* (1891), in Whitaker, *The Early Economic Writings of Alfred Marshall*, Vol. II, p. 267.
68. Ibid, p. 265.
69. Ibid.
70. Ibid, p. 267.
71. F. Y. Edgeworth, *Mathematical Psychics* (London: C. Kegan Paul & Co., 1881), p. 15.
72. *PE*, p. 521.
73. Unpublished note, in Marshall Papers, Miscellaneous Open Box 2.
74. *IT*, p. 399n.
75. Edgeworth, *Mathematical Psychics*, p. 82.
76. Ibid, p. 101.
77. Coats, 'Sociological Aspects', loc.cit., p. 713.
78. Pigou, 'In Memoriam: Alfred Marshall', in *Memorials*, p. 89.
79. Marshall, 'The Present Position of Economics', in *Memorials*, p. 171.
80. Ibid, p. 172.
81. Ibid, p. 173.
82. Letter from A. Marshall to H. S. Foxwell dated 14 February 1902, in Marshall Papers, Letters 3 (44).
83. Letter from A. Marshall to J. N. Keynes dated 27 May 1889, in

Marshall Library, Keynes Letters 1 (90).

84. Letter from A. Marshall to J. N. Keynes dated 30 January 1902, in Marshall Library, Keynes Letters 1 (125).

85. Letter from A. Marshall to H. S. Foxwell dated 8 May 1901, in Marshall Papers, Letters 3 (41).

86. Marshall, *Plea*, in *Principles*, Vol. II, p. 165.

87. Marshall, *The New Cambridge Curriculum in Economics*, pp. 7–8.

88. A. Marshall, 'The Proposed New Tripos' (Cambridge flysheet, 1903), p. 4.

89. Marshall, *Plea*, in *Principles*, Vol. II, p. 161.

90. Maloney, *Marshall, Orthodoxy and the Professionalisation of Economics*, pp. 233–4. This is presumably the reasoning behind Marshall's declaration to J. N. Keynes in his letter dated 16 August 1897 that, until a specialist degree be started, 'mathematical casuals will remain almost the only men worth teaching economics in Cambridge'.

91. Marshall, *Plea*, in *Principles*, Vol. II, p. 162.

92. Letter from A. Marshall to J. N. Keynes dated 16 August 1897, in Marshall Library, Keynes Letters 1 (111). The letter continues in the same vein: 'I could not heartily recommend him for the post: but I have written him a testimonial praising his earnestness & general ability; & hinting that he might some day get to know something about economics if he tried.'

93. Letter from A. Marshall to H. S. Foxwell dated 14 February 1902, in Marshall Papers, Letters 3 (44).

94. Marshall, *Plea*, in *Principles* II, p. 180.

95. A. Marshall, note dated 30 April 1921, in Marshall papers, Miscellaneous Open Box 2, envelope labelled 'Trade Unions/Unemployment'.

96. A. Marshall, note dated 28 October 1905, in Marshall Papers, Miscellaneous Open Box 2, Various Notes (1).

97. A. Marshall, note dated 20 February (no year, but could be *circa* 1920–21), in Marshall Papers, Red Box 1 (3).

98. J. N. Keynes, *The Scope and Method of Political Economy* (London: Macmillan, 1891), p. 252.

99. Ibid, p. 300.

100. Keynes, 'The Society's Jubilee', loc.cit., p. 409.

101. Cited in Maloney, *Marshall, Orthodoxy and the Professionalisation of Economics*, p. 64.

102. Letter from A. Marshall, *The Times*, 23 November 1905, p. 4.

103. Letter from A. Marshall, *The Times*, 18 December 1905, p. 13.

104. Letter from A. Marshall, *The Times*, 29 December 1905, p. 5.

105. Marshall, *The New Cambridge Curriculum in Economics*, p. 9.

106. Ibid, p. 19.

107. Ibid, p. 17 On the Tripos see also Kadish, *Historians, Economists, and Economic History*, esp. Ch. 6.

108. Marshall, 'The Present Position of Economics', in *Memorials*, p. 173.

109. *Bristol Times and Mirror*, 9 June 1925.

110. Marshall, 'The Future of the Working Classes', in *Memorials*, p. 101. Emphasis added.

111. Letters from A. Marshall to H. Plunkett dated 17 May 1910 and to L. Dumur dated 2 July 1909, in *Memorials*, pp. 468, 459.
112. A. Marshall, 'On Cambridge Degrees for Women' (Cambridge Flysheet, 1896), p. 1.
113. Letter from A. Marshall to E. R. A. Seligman dated 19 March 1896, in Dorfman, 'The Seligman Correspondence', loc.cit., p. 406n.
114. Marshall, 'On Cambridge Degrees for Women', p. 5.
115. Ibid, p. 6.
116. Ibid, p. 7.
117. Ibid.
118. G. M. Koot, 'English Historical Economics and the Emergence of Economic History in England', *History of Political Economy*, Vol. 12, 1980, p. 188.
119. Cited in Koot, *English Historical Economics*, p. 112.
120. Cited in Kadish, *The Oxford Economists in the Late Nineteenth Century*, p. 72.
121. W. Cunningham, *Christianity and Social Questions* (London: Duckworth, 1910), p. 54.
122. W. Cunningham, *Christianity and Economic Science* (London: John Murray, 1914), pp. 92–3.
123. Cunningham, *Christianity and Social Questions*, pp. 12–13.
124. Ibid, p. 50.
125. Cited in A. Cunningham, *William Cunningham*, p. 11.
126. Cunningham, *Christianity and Economic Science*, p. 70.
127. Cunningham, *Christianity and Social Questions*, p. 183.
128. Cited in Koot, *English Historical Economics*, p. 177.
129. Cited in A. Ashley, *William James Ashley*, p. 36.
130. Cited in ibid.
131. J. E. T. Rogers, *The Economic Interpretation of History* (New York: G. Putnam's Sons, 1888), p. 165.
132. J. E. T. Rogers, *Six Centuries of Work and Wages* (1884) (London: Allen & Unwin, 1949), p. 8.
133. Foxwell, 'The Economic Movement in England', loc.cit., p. 102.
134. Hewins, *Apologia of an Imperialist*, Vol. I, pp. 14–15.
135. Ibid, pp. 22–3.
136. Cited in A. Ashley, *William James Ashley*, p. 97.
137. Ibid, p. 110.
138. J. E. T. Rogers, *The Industrial and Commercial History of England* (London: T. Fisher Unwin, 1892), p. 457.
139. Cited in Koot, *English Historical Economics*, p. 172.
140. Cunningham, *Christianity and Social Questions*, p. 5.
141. Ibid, p. 189.
142. T. E. Cliffe Leslie, *Essays in Political and Moral Philosophy* (London: Longmans, Green & Co., 1879) p. 230.
143. W. Cunningham, *The Case Against Free Trade* (London: John Murray, 1911) p. 16.
144. Ibid, p. 11.
145. Hewins, *Apologia of an Imperialist*, Vol. I, p. 3.
146. Ibid, p. 14.

147. Ibid, pp. 21–2.
148. H. Foxwell, Obituary of William Cunningham, *Economic Journal*, Vol. 29, 1919, pp. 384–5.
149. A. Ashley, *William James Ashley*, p. 88.
150. Cited in ibid, p. 106.
151. Cited in Schumpeter, *History of Economic Analysis*, p. 756n.
152. Cited in A. Ashley, *William James Ashley*, p. 35.
153. Cited in Schumpeter, *History of Economic Analysis*, p. 830.
154. Kadish, *The Oxford Economists in the Late Nineteenth Century*, p. 181.
155. Ibid.
156. Cited in ibid, p. 177.
157. N. B. de Marchi, 'On the Early Dangers of Being Too Political an Economist: Thorold Rogers and the 1868 Election to the Drummond Professorship', *Oxford Economic Papers*, Vol. 28, 1976, p. 372.
158. Coats, 'Sociological Aspects', loc.cit., p. 714.
159. Cited in Koot, *English Historical Economics*, p. 111.
160. Cited in A. Ashley, *William James Ashley*, p. 95.
161. Hewins, *Apologia of an Imperialist*, Vol. I, pp. 31–2.
162. W. J. Ashley, 'The Place of Economic History in University Studies', *Economic History Review*, Vol. I, 1927, p. 4.
163. J. H. Clapham, *The Study of Economic History: An Inaugural Lecture* (Cambridge: Cambridge University Press, 1929), p. 7.
164. *PE*, p. 464.
165. Ibid, p. 641.
166. Clapham, *The Study of Economic History*, p. 9.
167. Obituary of Alfred Marshall, *The Times*, 14 July 1924, p. 16.
168. Alfred Marshall, unpublished note dated 18 May 1908, in Marshall Papers, Miscellaneous Open Box 2, Various Notes (1). The evolutionary dimension is underlined by the fact that 'highly developed' replaces 'truly', which has been struck out.
169. Alfred Marshall, unpublished note, no date, in Marshall Papers, Miscellaneous Open Box 2, Various Notes (1).
170. Coats, 'Sociological Aspects', loc.cit., p. 722.
171. Letter from Professor Oliver Lodge to A. Marshall dated 31 July 1901. Cited in A. Ashley, *William James Ashley*, p. 94n.
172. Cited in A. Cunningham, *William Cunningham*, p. 69.
173. Ibid, p. 64.
174. Ibid, p. 65.
175. W. Cunningham, 'The Perversion of Economic History', *Economic Journal*, Vol. II, 1892, p. 492.
176. Ibid, p. 498.
177. Ibid, p. 495.
178. Ibid, p. 496.
179. Ibid.
180. Ibid, p. 497.
181. Ibid, p. 491.
182. Ibid, p. 495.
183. Ibid, p. 494.
184. Ibid.

185. Ibid, p. 493.
186. Ibid, p. 498.
187. A. Cunningham, *William Cunningham*, p. 11.
188. Pigou, 'In Memoriam: Alfred Marshall', in *Memorials*, p. 90.
189. Marshall, 'A Reply', loc.cit., p. 518.
190. Ibid.
191. Ibid, p. 517.
192. Ibid, p. 515.
193. Ibid, p. 507.
194. Ibid, p. 508.
195. *PE*, p. 417.
196. Ibid, p. 32.
197. Ibid, p. 30–31.
198. Marshall, 'The Present Position of Economics', in *Memorials* p. 169.
199. Marshall, 'A Reply', loc.cit., p. 512.
200. Ibid, p. 510.
201. Ibid.
202. Letter from A. Marshall to Bishop Westcott dated 20 January 1901, in *Memorials*, p. 393.
203. Cited in Hewins, *Apologia of an Imperialist*, Vol. I, p. 68.
204. Cunningham, *Christianity and Social Questions*, p. 53.
205. Ibid, p. 38.
206. Cunningham, *Christianity and Economic Science*, p. 55.
207. Cunningham, *Christianity and Social Questions*, p. 36.
208. Cunningham, *The Case Against Free Trade*, p. 34.
209. Smith, *The Wealth of Nations*, Vol. I, p. 487.
210. J. Chamberlain, Introduction to Cunningham, *The Case Against Free Trade*, p. vii.
211. Discussion on F. Schuster's paper 'Foreign Trade and the Money Market', Institute of Bankers, 16 December 1903. In *Journal of the Institute of Bankers*, Vol. XXV, 1904, p. 95.
212. Letter from A. Marshall to the Secretary of the Unionist Free Trade League. Reprinted in *The Times*, 23 November 1903, p. 10.
213. A. Marshall, Memorandum on Fiscal Policy of International Trade (1908), in *Official Papers*, p. 368.
214. Letter from A. Marshall, *The Times*, 23 November 1908, p. 15.
215. Statement to Industrial Remuneration Conference, in *Report*, p. 173.
216. Letter from A. Marshall to W. J. A. Ashley dated 1901. Cited in A. Ashley, *William James Ashley*, p. 137.
217. A. Marshall, manuscript note dated 25 June 1904, in Marshall Papers, Miscellaneous Open Box 2, envelope headed 'Export prices & dumping'.
218. A. Marshall, manuscript note dated 14 August 1905, in *supra*.
219. A. Marshall, manuscript note dated 14 July 1904, in *supra*.
220. Emphasis added. Letter from A. Marshall to *The Times*, 23 November 1908, p. 15. This was apparently the working title of the book that later appeared as *Industry and Trade*.
221. A. Marshall, manuscript note dated 18 August 1900, in Marshall Papers, Miscellaneous Open Box 2, Various Notes (1).
222. Ibid.

223. Ibid.
224. A. Marshall, manuscript note, n.d., in Marshall Papers, Miscellaneous Open Box 2, Various Notes (2).
225. Letter from A. Marshall to J. M. Keynes dated 21 February 1915, in *Memorials*, p. 482.
226. A. W. Coats, 'Political Economy and the Tariff Reform Campaign of 1903', *Journal of Law and Economics*, Vol. 11, 1968, p. 213.
227. Cited in ibid, p. 221.
228. Ibid, pp. 225–6.
229. R. H. Coase, 'The Appointment of Pigou as Marshall's Successor: Comment' (1972), in Wood, op.cit., Vol. IV, p. 222.
230. Ibid, p. 226.
231. Cited in Koot, *English Historical Economics*, p. 128.
232. Cited in ibid, p. 132.
233. J. M. Keynes, 'Herbert Somerton Foxwell' (1936), in *Essays in Biography*, p. 283.
234. Letter from A. Marshall to H. S. Foxwell dated 31 May 1908, in Marshall Papers, Letters 3 (56).
235. Testimonial from A. Marshall, 1875. Cited in Black, *Papers and Correspondence of William Stanley Jevons*, Vol. IV, p. 145.
236. Marshall, 'Some Aspects of Competition', in *Memorials*, p. 276.
237. Clapham, *The Study of Economic History*, p. 8.
238. Letter from A. Marshall to J. N. Keynes dated 13 December 1908, in Marshall Library, Keynes Letters 1 (137).
239. Letter from A. Marshall to H. S. Foxwell dated 31 May 1908, in Marshall Papers, Letters 3 (56).
240. Cited in Koot, *English Historical Economics*, p. 242n.
241. Cited in ibid, p. 46.
242. Maloney, *Marshall, Orthodoxy and the Professionalisation of Economics*, p. 92.
243. Cited in Koot, *English Historical Economics*, p. 241n.
244. Coase, 'The Appointment of Pigou as Marshall's Successor', in Wood, op.cit., Vol. IV, p. 226.
245. Cited in A. W. Coats, 'The Appointment of Pigou as Marshall's Successor: Comment' (1972), in ibid, Vol. IV, p. 240.
246. Keynes, 'Alfred Marshall', in *Memorials*, p. 44.
247. Letter from A. Marshall to H. S. Foxwell dated 31 May 1908, in Marshall Papers, Letters 3 (56).
248. Cited in Coase, 'The Appointment of Pigou as Marshall's Successor', in Wood, op.cit., Vol. IV, p. 226.
249. See F. Y. Edgeworth, review of A. C. Pigou, *The Riddle of the Tariff* (1904). Cited in ibid, p. 234n.
250. L. L. Price, review of A. C. Pigou, *The Riddle of the Tariff* (1904). Cited in Koot, *English Historical Economics*, p. 101.
251. E. A. G. Robinson, 'Arthur Cecil Pigou', in D. L. Sills (ed.), *International Encyclopedia of the Social Sciences* (New York: Macmillan and Free Press, 1968), Vol. 12, p. 91.
252. K. Bharadwaj, 'Marshall on Pigou's *Wealth and Welfare*' (1972), in Wood, op.cit., Vol. IV, p. 206.

253. J. S. Mill, *Essays on Some Unsettled Questions of Political Economy* (1844), in *Collected Works*, Vol. IV (1967), p. 330.
254. Letter from A. Marshall to J. N. Keynes dated 23 February 1899. Cited in Kadish, *Historians, Economists, and Economic History*, p. 191.
255. Cited in ibid, p. 177.
256. Ibid, pp. 213–14.
257. Ibid, p. 193.
258. Cited in ibid, p. 192.
259. Cited in ibid, p. 195.
260. Cited in ibid, p. 211.
261. Hutchison, *A Review of Economic Doctrines*, p. 62.
262. Maloney, *Marshall, Orthodoxy and the Professionalisation of Economics*, p. 24.
263. Schumpeter, *History of Economic Analysis*, p. 833.
264. A. C. Pigou, Presidential Address to the Royal Economic Society, *Economic Journal*, Vol. 49, 1939, pp. 219–20.
265. Keynes, 'Mary Paley Marshall', in *Essays in Biography*, p. 248.

Index

elasticity of demand 67, 124, 177
  price 118
elasticity of supply 170
Ely, Richard T. 98
Emerson, Ralph Waldo 17
empathy 208
Empire free trade 247
employers 204
equilibrium 103, 150, 263
  long-run 118
  market 172
  short-run 111
equilibrium values, theoretical
  indeterminacy 162–3
estate duty 244
ethics 8, 9
  economics and 116, 117
  see also moral; morality
Evangelical Christianity 3, 6, 40,
  215
evolution 41
exchange
  bargained 198
  conditions of 76
  history of 164
exchange ratios 150–1

Faber, Geoffrey 40
Fabians 15, 219, 229, 230
factor incomes 129
Factory Acts 233, 250
factory system 237
Faculty of Commerce, Birmingham
  University 201, 229
Fawcett, Henry 51, 143, 236
Fay, C. R. 168
Fellows, resignation on
  marriage 28–9
First World War 8, 93
Fisher, Irving 123, 178
Flux, A. W. 127, 201
food staples 125
foreign competition 243
Forster, W. E. 13, 183
Fortnightly Review 29, 78
Foxwell, H. S. 22, 30, 38, 41–2,
  51, 89, 109, 120, 122, 143, 145,
  146, 147, 159, 163, 174, 183,
  186, 188, 190, 191, 196, 203,

  204, 205, 212, 216, 222–3, 228,
  230, 234, 236, 261, 263
  relations with Marshall 253–8,
  259
free enterprise 68, 226
  unguided 116
free trade 17, 45, 64, 71, 82, 112,
  221, 226, 244, 246, 247, 258
freedom 134–5
  see also liberty

Galbraith, J. K. 16
Galton, Francis 60, 68, 185
general equilibrium theory 103
Genovesi, A. 156
George, Henry 50–1, 89
Germany 8, 93, 202, 222, 243,
  246, 248, 250, 251
Giffen, Sir Robert 183, 184, 185,
  230
Girton College 209
Gladstone, W. E. 71
gold standard 257
Gonner, E. C. K. 54, 94, 201
goods, perishable 158
Goschen, G. E. 50, 195–6
Gossen, H. H. 138–9, 147, 164,
  199
Great Depression 168
Green, T. H. 41, 42, 47–8, 49, 50,
  52, 179, 215, 263
Grote Club 3–5, 6
Guillebaud, Claude 2, 58, 166,
  169, 171, 261
Gwatkin, H. M. 205

Hamilton, C. J. 55
Harcourt, Sir William 244
Harrison, F. 201
Harrod, Sir Roy 58
Harvard 211, 228
Hayek, F. A. von 157
Hegel, G. W. F. 7, 41, 48, 88,
  120, 134
Hewins, W. A. S. 15, 16, 35, 53,
  107, 163, 201, 212, 215,
  216–17, 219, 221–2, 223,
  229–30, 236, 245, 248, 258
Hicks, J. R. 166, 261

*For Product Safety Concerns and Information please contact
our EU representative GPSR@taylorandfrancis.com Taylor & Francis
Verlag GmbH, Kaufingerstraße 24, 80331 München, Germany*

T - #0029 - 230425 - C0 - 216/138/17 [19] - CB - 9780415668507 - Gloss Lamination